P9-CFA-167

SOCIAL WORK SKILLS

A PRACTICE HANDBOOK

Second Edition

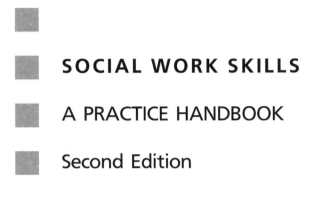

SOCIAL WORK SKILLS

A PRACTICE HANDBOOK

Second Edition

Pamela Trevithick

Open University Press

Open University Press
McGraw-Hill Education
McGraw-Hill House
Shoppenhangers Road
Maidenhead
Berkshire
England
SL6 2QL

email: enquiries@openup.co.uk
world wide web@ www.openup.co.uk

and Two Penn Plaza, New York, NY 10121-2289, USA

First published 2005

Copyright © Pamela Trevithick

All rights reserved. Except for the quotation of short passages for the purposes of criticism and review, no part of this publication may be reproduced, stored in a retrieval system, or transmitted, in any form, or by any means, electronic, mechanical, photocopying, recording or otherwise, without the prior permission of the publisher or a licence from the Copyright Licensing Agency Limited. Details of such licences (for reprographic reproduction) may be obtained from the Copyright Licensing Agency Ltd of 90 Tottenham Court Road, London, W1T 4LP.

A catalogue record of this book is available from the British Library.

ISBN-13 978 0335 214990 (pb) 978 0335 215003 (hb)
ISBN-10 0335214 991 (pb) 0335 215 009
Library of Congress Cataloging-in-Publication Data
CIP data applied for

Typeset by BookEns Ltd., Royston, Herts.
Printed in the UK by Bell and Bain Ltd, Glasgow

CONTENTS

Acknowledgements   vii

Introduction   1

1   The knowledge base of social work: 22
    theoretical, factual and practice knowledge

2   Social work skills, interventions and practice   60
    effectiveness

3   Understanding human beings   90

4   Communication, listening and assessment skills   113

5   Basic interviewing skills   140

6   Providing help, direction and guidance   190

7   Empowerment, negotiation and partnership skills   218

8   Professional competence and accountability   242

Conclusion   255

Appendix 1: Behaviourist approaches   260
Appendix 2: Cognitive approaches   264
Appendix 3: Crisis intervention   267
Appendix 4: Person/client-centred approaches   271
Appendix 5: Psychosocial approaches   275
Appendix 6: Task-centred approaches   279
Appendix 7: Ecological perspectives in social work   282
Appendix 8: Feminist perspectives in social work   286
Appendix 9: Radical/progressive/activist perspectives   289
             in social work
Appendix 10: *Stages of Change* (or *Cycle of Change*)   292
Appendix 11: National Occupational Standards on the   296
             knowledge base of social work

References   299
Index   325

for
Charlie Beaton

ACKNOWLEDGEMENTS

Some themes in this second edition have been substantially revised, although I did not set out to do this. Instead I meant merely to amend certain sections so that practitioners and students had more up-to-date references and concepts to draw on. However, the more I read and wrote, the more confused and lost I became until I reached a point where I had to stop and to start again. I am fortunate that I had an editor who trusted my need to wander off in this way. The obstacle that hindered my progress was *knowledge* or the *knowledge base of social work*. This tantalizing subject seems so accessible and perhaps it is for others but not for me. I felt compelled to understand more about what constitutes social work's knowledge base. In this process, I have waded through Schön's *swampy lowlands* (1991: 43) and stumbled through a landscape of dense, unclear and inapplicable theories, some with their own concepts and language – or knack of saying the same thing but in a different way. I have also found some wonderfully illuminating pieces of writing publications that have been inspiring in their thoughtfulness and clarity. In some ways, I may have allowed myself to become lost and bewildered on purpose, perhaps thinking that if I can't find my way out of this jungle, how can practitioners or students manage this task? Of course, they may be more 'fit for purpose' or 'fit for practice' than me. Whichever way, at times it proved hard to find some of the paths or the markers that other authors have left behind.

I am indebted to the commissioning editor at Open University Press, Rachel Gear, whose encouragement and guidance has enabled me to explore new themes and to include these in this text. Rachel's editorial skills and expertise – and trust in my judgement – has made the writing of this text an enjoyable and memorable experience. I am also grateful for the thoughtfulness and professionalism demonstrated by other Open University staff. In particular, I would like to thank Amy Blower, James Bishop, Hannah Cooper, Kathleen Evesson, Lin Gillan, Sharon-Lee Lukas, Shona Mullen, and Nikki Tomlinson.

The generosity of a number of colleagues and friends has helped to make this second edition possible. In particular, I would like to thank Robert French for again adding his insightful comments on this edition,

Hilary Burgess for her astute comments on the Introduction to this text, Sally Richards for coming to my aid at an crucial moment and Dave Gordon for the encouragement and support he has given me over the past few years. I would also like to thank other members of the Research Centre for the Study of Poverty and Social Justice, particularly Bill Beaumont, Sarah Cemlyn, Michelle Kelly Irving and Elaine Allenby-Parker. In addition, I am grateful to Judy Carver, Chris Charters, Ali Chown, Mark Cox and the Faculty computer team (David Hurst, Paul Croft, Debra Jacobson, David Midwinter, Julie Steen, Scott Wishart), Amy Durbin, Mark Doel, Anna Harvey, Penny McLennan, Phillip Lewis, Joyce Lishman, Stuart Matthews, Rachel Mirrlees, Karen Postle, Michael Preston-Shoot, Gillian Ruch, Katherine Sugg and Liz Wilson. I would also like to thank the British Academy, whose grants have enabled me to attend international conferences and to broaden my knowledge base in key areas.

Writing a text of this kind can be demanding of others. My son, Tom, warrants a special mention for being so loving, patient and understanding, and I am again grateful to Bridget for her support and love, and for offering her help at an important point. I am also grateful to Charlie Beaton and Donald Branch for the commitment they have given to me, and my work, over the years. My greatest thanks is reserved for Charlotte Paterson, who has shared her scholarship and time with great generosity, and in ways that have been deeply sustaining throughout the writing of this text. However, all errors are mine.

As a social worker, I would like to thank the people that I have worked with over the years; people who have taught me so much. It is their stories, and their courage in situations of adversity, that still fuels my commitment to the principle of social injustice, and to the important role that social work can play to help remedy these injustices. I would also like to thank my tutees and the students I have taught over the past sixteen years. The teaching and learning we have shared has been a two-way process, and I feel grateful to have had the opportunity to learn so much.

INTRODUCTION

...there are no easy remedies in social work, especially when
we are confronted daily with oppression and deprivation ...
(Coulshed and Orme 1998: 3)

Social work has changed a great deal in recent years (Cree 2002). This is
true of the UK and other parts of the world. However, one fundamental
feature remains the same, namely that social work involves working with
some of the most complex problems and perplexing areas of human
experience and, for this reason, social work is – and has to be – a highly
skilled activity. The complexity of this task is highlighted in the definition
of social work agreed by the International Association of Schools of Social
Work (IASSW) and the International Federation of Social Workers (IFSW)
in 2001 – a definition that has been incorporated into the National
Occupational Standards for Social Work (TOPSS 2004: 12):

The social work profession promotes social change, problem-solving
in human relationships and the empowerment and liberation of
people to enhance well-being. Utilising theories of human behaviour
and social systems, social work intervenes at the points where people
interact with their environments. Principles of human rights and
social justice are fundamental to social work.

(IASSW/IFSW 2001)

The purpose of this text is to describe this skilled activity and to identify
how social work skills and interventions can be used in practice to
enhance our effectiveness and help bring about positive outcomes. It
focuses in particular on 50 generalist skills commonly used in social work.
A number of core skills underpin the effective use of these generalist skills,
namely the importance of communication and interviewing skills;
observation, listening and assessment skills; problem-solving and
decision-making skills; and organizational and administrative skills. The
book was written to bridge a gap because few texts have been written
specifically on the theme of social work skills. The fact that the first
edition of this text has been translated into Spanish and Korean, and will
shortly appear in Japanese and Chinese, indicates the extent of this gap.
The gap has also been noted in relation to social work education and is
evident in the limited coverage given to social work skills teaching on

some social work programmes. In fact, for some courses the picture has changed little since Marsh and Triseliotis (1996) published their research on social work training, which found that 51 per cent of the newly qualified social work and probation practitioners interviewed thought that there was too little coverage of social work skills training on their courses. In a list of recommendations, Marsh and Triseliotis emphasize the importance of using concrete practice situations in relation to skills teaching and 'better and more applied teaching of psychology' (1996: 219) – two themes that are covered in this text.

Four main perspectives inform this second edition. First, the view that in order to be effective, social work practitioners must work from a sound knowledge base, that is, one that is relevant and identifiable. A second perspective sees social work as essentially a 'capacity building' activity: a perspective that emphasizes the important role that social workers can play in terms of enhancing individual, family, group and environmental capacities. A third perspective recognizes that social work is very much about relating: about the benefits and limitations that people experience in their relationships with others. The importance of the capacity to relate can be seen in the way that people relate to themselves, others and to society. It is here that people sometimes turn to social work, and to other professions, for help to address the difficulties they are experiencing. The capacity to relate can be identified most visibly in the way people communicate, which leads to the fourth perspective on the importance of communication skills within social work. Although these perspectives are described under separate headings, they overlap and interweave in ways that are multifaceted and intricate but which together provide a basis for a more coherent practice framework.

The importance of a sound knowledge base

In order to acquire and to perfect a 'toolbox' or 'basket' of practice skills and interventions, we need to have a sound knowledge base from which to begin to understand people and their situations and to formulate plans of action appropriate to the circumstances encountered. This involves understanding how experiences are perceived, understood and communicated by people, and how this impacts on behaviour and life situations, both positive and negative. To some extent, this understanding will always be incomplete and uneven because, in the realm of human experience, life is unpredictable and some uncertainty is inevitable (Marris 1996a). This complexity is acknowledged by the General Social Care Council (GSCC) and the National Occupational Standards (NOS) and by other influential bodies within social work:

> Social work in its various forms addresses the multiple, complex transactions between people and their environments. Its mission is to

enable all people to develop their full potential, enrich their lives, and prevent dysfunction. Professional social work is focused on problem-solving and change. As such, social workers are change agents in society and in the lives of the individuals, families and communities they serve. Social work is an interrelated system of values, theory and practice.

(IASSW/IFSW 2001)

Central to this purpose is the development of skills and interventions that are capable of influencing 'people and their environments'. This can be a formidable task and an area where no profession or practice approach can claim complete success, a point emphasized in a discussion document from the Prime Minister's Strategy Unit at the Cabinet Office, entitled *Personal Responsibility and Changing Behaviour: The State of Knowledge and its Implications for Public Policy*:

> This paper has set out a body of theories, evidence and possible policy applications. The field remains relatively underdeveloped. Many more policy makers are familiar with economic principles or law than with psychology. There have been few attempts to pull together the knowledge base in a systematic way, and policies to influence behaviour are often ad hoc. . . . Looking to the future there is an evident need to strengthen our theoretical and empirical understanding of what drives behaviour and behavioural change. . . . Policy should not simply proclaim personal responsibility or blame, but needs to be shaped around the ways in which people actually think and feel, and the social and psychological forces that influence behaviour.

(Halpern and Bates 2004: 67)

We can continue to extend our knowledge through research but we still need to be able to 'pull together' and use what we know. It is interesting to note that this discussion document covers a wide range of social problems and includes several professional groups, such as teachers, nurses and doctors. However, social work and social workers are not mentioned and this is happening more and more in relation to documents of this kind. Yet perhaps more than any other profession, social work has a long history and a great deal of experience in the area of helping people with limited resources to change their lives, and has an extensive library on this subject. Social work's particular contribution in the field of social welfare and social change lies in the fact that practitioners work with people from some of the most deprived and disadvantaged sectors of the population and, as a result, we have developed specific knowledge, skills and understanding from the concentrated work we continue to perform in this area. A further contribution lies in the way that our values shape our work − a perspective that embraces the importance of social justice.

This values perspective is most evident in the way that we communicate with service users, carers and others, as well as in the 'attitudes, methods and practices of practitioners and their agencies' (Clark 2000: 360). According to the status that certain groups hold within society, the right to social justices can be threatened and lead to prejudice and discrimination. These injustices can be based on an individual's class, race, gender, age, disabilities, sexual orientation, religious/spiritual beliefs, culture, health and geographic location (such as the divisions that exist between the north and south of England), or simply on the fact that some people are poor and behave in ways that reveal their lack of life chances and social exclusion. Social work is not unique in its values perspective, but other professions may not have given this issue the same importance, although the picture is changing. For example, in recent years there has been considerable coverage on the impact of poverty and deprivation in relation to health in the *British Medical Journal* (Watt 2001: 175–6) and the *Lancet* (Horton 2002: 186).

For any knowledge to be valuable in social work, it has to be relevant and applicable to the issues regularly encountered in practice. On the other hand, practice also needs to inform knowledge – and in an ongoing way – through conceptualizing what we do in ways that revise existing theories where they are at odds with the experiences of practice. However, too often the knowledge generated from practice is not written up and published, which means it is not available for other practitioners, and other professionals, to use and to develop further. The view held by a number of practitioners and academics is that the world of theorizing and writing 'belongs' to the realm of academics. Although not intended, the introduction of an evidence based perspective in social work has had the effect of eroding some practitioners' confidence in relation to the knowledge and theory base of social work practice. This is a worrying development and one that needs to be addressed.

Social work as capacity building

The notion of 'capacity' is widely used within social welfare contexts yet is rarely defined. It is derived from the Latin *capax*, meaning 'able to take in'; 'the ability to receive or contain'; 'holding power' (*Oxford English Dictionary*). It is normally used to describe the personal resources or abilities that people have at their disposal (Sheldon 1995: 126). However, the term capacity is not only an account of *what is* (actual and present abilities) but also of *what can be* (potential and future abilities). It highlights the *potential* for greater capacities to be developed or learned (French 1999). On the other hand, existing capacities, skills or abilities can be lost through underuse or lack of practice, or through the impact of stress, fatigue, anxiety, low morale, trauma and so forth. The notion of capacity is central to the work of Winnicott, a paediatrician and psychoanalyst who was influential in social work in the 1950s and 1960s (1958, 1965). Hence, through our involvement with people and their environments, the capacities of both can change; they can be enhanced, maintained or can deteriorate. This may become evident in changes that occur in the way that people relate to themselves (self-esteem, self-worth), to others and to those structures and organizations that have an impact on their lives. This links the concept of capacity to the importance of relating (Trevithick *et al.* 2004); together, both are central to the framework for practice competence described in this text. Indeed, the perspective I am adopting sees social work as a *capacity building activity*.

For example, when attempting to assess what is present or not present, needed or not needed in a particular encounter or area of work, it can be helpful to conceptualize this in terms of human and environmental capacities and to do so from three perspectives. First, it is important to identify the capacities, strengths and limitations that we bring, as practitioners, to our work with others. Second, to acknowledge the capacities that service users and carers bring to the situation. Since the capacities that all parties bring are almost always influenced by the wider social and cultural environment within which we work and live, this leads to a third range of capacities that need to be identified, namely those relating to the capacities located in the wider social and cultural environment. This also includes other agencies and organizations: in effect, anyone or anything likely to influence, both positively and negatively, the direction and effectiveness of work undertaken. And just as our environment acts on us, so too do we – and other people – act in ways that influence our environment. Our work setting is particularly important in this context. This focus on capacities, and capacity building, enables us to combine an ecological perspective (see Appendix 7) with that of a strengths perspective (Saleebey 2003): two perspectives that are central to the requirements written into the National Occupational Standards (TOPSS 2002). It also enables us to link to other important concepts such as *social capital* (Pierson and Thomas 2002: 435) and *development*, including community development, human growth and development, professional development and research and development.

A commonly used term within social work is 'coping capacity': 'Social workers do not work with those people who have problems but with those who have difficulty coping with those problems' (England 1986: 13). The capacity to cope can grow as a result of positive experiences or it can decline or shrivel through the impact of negative experiences and neglect (Salzberger-Wittenberg 1970: 162). From this perspective, every encounter can have the potential to be a growth-enhancing and capacity building experience. It can also be an encounter that results in a greater defensiveness and further withdrawal from the challenges that are a part of life (Weick 1983) and a weakening of existing capacities.

For example, in situations where people are haunted by negative experiences, whether in the present or the past, precious emotional, physical and intellectual energy can be tied up trying to cope or survive the internal and external conflicts, demands and hurdles that life throws their way. When energy is tied up in this way, the capacity to change, that is, to embrace new experiences or ways of being, is reduced. This may call for us to explore initiatives and interventions that can ease the pressure being experienced, so that energy can be freed up and redirected to embrace change, growth and development. This may involve practical forms of help, such as providing assistance with household chores, childcare responsibilities or transport. In my experience, practical interventions of this kind are greatly valued by service users and carers (Ennis, E. 2000: 265) and, in certain circumstances, they can be more important than advanced, specialist or more costly interventions.

Similarly, the concept of capacities can help us to understand the resourcefulness – or lack of resourcefulness – that some practitioners bring to their work. As a positive attribute, it describes the ability to think about others in ways that are flexible, creative and that open up new possibilities (Gambrill 1997: 102); the capacity to work with conflict and contain others' anxiety; a sense of curiosity and interest to explore new ideas, new practice approaches or interventions; the courage to work from a clear value base and to be sensitive to the values that others hold; and so forth. Hopefully, we have all encountered professionals of this calibre and are moving in this direction ourselves. On the other hand, we have no doubt encountered professionals for whom this kind of resourcefulness is beyond their reach. Instead, we encounter a range of limitations such as people who are rigid and inflexible; who feel troubled if they are not in control; who feel seriously demeaned by people who question their decisions or authority; and who cannot take their gaze off themselves and their own needs, thereby failing truly to appreciate the plight of others.

It is not my intention to be critical: we come to be the people we are through a range of experiences, some of which are not sought and seem beyond our control. I mention these personal and professional capacities because they influence our work. Our work – and effectiveness – is also influenced by our working environment, hence the importance of looking at the whole picture rather than one aspect. As a general rule: 'A deskilled, demotivated, stressed, overworked workforce is not well placed to help other people' (Adams *et al.* 2002a: 294) or to make sound and effective decisions (O'Sullivan 2000: 86). The current organization of social work has been criticized in this regard (Jones *et al.* 2003).

A relationship perspective

A third perspective relates to the quality of the relationship we seek to build with service users and carers and with other professionals and involved individuals. In the past, the relationships we created were considered a central aspect of social work and essential to good practice, but in recent years the importance and value given to the relationship has become 'confused and ambivalent' (Howe 1998: 45). A perspective that uses the relationship as a central feature is sometimes called a relationship based perspective or a relational approach. Although a *relational* perspective can be found in other disciplines, such as teaching, health, management, group relations and organizational theory and change (French and Vince 1999), with regard to social work in recent years it has tended to be linked to client-centred or psychosocial approaches or to casework.

Concepts such as empathy, warmth and genuineness are often associated with the work of Carl Rogers (1951, 1961) and later followers, such as Truax and Carkhuff (1967). This perspective implies that all points of contact and connection can have a profound impact, although we may never know their full significance. However, Edwards and Richards (2002) remind us of the importance of a relational perspective in teaching and learning. Some practice approaches, such as those drawing on behaviourism, may give the relationship less importance than other approaches. However, some writers in this field acknowledge the importance of empathy, warmth and genuineness on the part of the worker but stress that: 'A good working relationship is a necessary but not sufficient condition for being an effective helper in this field' (Hudson and Sheldon 2000: 65). As practitioners struggling to balance different demands and tasks, it can be difficult to recognize how important we are to the people we work with. However, as with all practice approaches, the quality of the relationship that is created depends to a great extent on the knowledge, skills, values and qualities that we bring to the work and the culture within which the work is located.

The importance of this perspective is evident with regard to the new social work degree, where the relationship between social workers and service users and carers is mentioned in several places in the requirements laid down in the Quality Assurance Agency's Benchmark Statement (QAA 2000), National Occupational Standards and the General Social Care Council's *Rules and Requirements*, although not always using the same terminology. It is also important with regard to government policy and practice, where we find the relationship between people, organizations and other areas of life in concepts such as *joined up services* (connecting individual needs to the services provided or relating one resource to another), *joined up thinking* (how best to locate, select, critically analyse, adapt and creatively apply the different theories and practice approaches that abound within health and welfare contexts) and in concepts such as *partnership*, *empowerment* and *choice*. These policies describe a commitment to enhance the *quality of the relationship* between the services on offer, those who deliver services and the people who receive them. This is a point taken up by the Minister for State, Jacqui Smith:

> Service users and carers deserve the best service possible. They have the right to expect that the people providing their care and support are well trained, competent and confident and will work with other professionals to secure the best possible support package to meet their needs. Employers have an obligation to see that their staff are adequately trained to provide the services and can make a real difference to the quality of life of the people they are there to support.
>
> (Smith 2004)

I return to the role of service users and carers later in Chapter 4. One of the dangers of a relational perspective is that it can inadvertently interpret 'personal troubles' and their solutions in terms of the individual and not in terms of 'public issues' (Mills 1959: 130), thereby failing to acknowledge wider social or political causation. As a result, professional relationships can be co-opted and incorporated into policy and practice directives in ways that mean the relationship loses its essential qualities and instead runs the risk of being 'increasingly seen in procedural, legal and administrative terms' (Howe 1998: 45).

The importance of communication skills

This fourth perspective emphasizes the importance of communication and interviewing skills in social work. If we look at most of the 50 generalist skills described in this text, the majority involve communication in one form or another. As human beings we are, in fact, always communicating something, although this may not be intelligible to ourselves or to others. It may require some deciphering, which can be likened to learning a different language or, more precisely, a new dialect. As practitioners, to achieve an understanding about what is being communicated means using everything at our disposal in order to come alongside the experiences of the people with whom we work. From this perspective, I do not believe that it is possible to be an effective practitioner without being an effective communicator. This, in turn, implies that for effective communication to be possible we need to have an extensive knowledge base and the capacity to relate and to communicate with others. Central to this knowledge is the capacity to know ourselves (Dominelli 2002b: 9; Crisp *et al.* 2003: 32), that is, to know the boundary of our own thoughts, feelings and experiences. From this place, it is possible to understand others, but without becoming merged or adopting a stance that is too distant to enable us to empathize or understand what is happening to the other person (Thorne 2002: 179–80).

If, as I suggest, social work is about extending individual and environmental capacities, then to use our knowledge to help understand what is happening – and why – is essential for change to be possible, enduring and meaningful. Within this task, one of the most complex issues to unravel is the extent to which people are entitled to be *helped* without the expectation that they should also be required to *help themselves*. Recent UK government initiatives increasingly question the idea of people being dependent on state welfare provision and benefits 'as of right', stressing instead that 'rights' need to be linked to 'responsibilities' (Halpern and Bates 2004: 7). This shift emphasizes the importance of 'citizens' developing a greater sense of personal responsibility, seen in terms of self-sufficiency, self-management, self-help, self-motivation and self-efficacy. Despite government reassurances, there remains a concern that this shift can leave people who rely on state support increasingly marginalized and excluded, such as those who are sick and disabled or are unable to care for themselves for other reasons.

Ideological shifts of this kind can have a profound effect on social work because, like other professions, social work is influenced by the political context in which it is located. It can be hard to be *helpful*, or to feel comfortable in the role of *helper*, in a climate where the notion of *help* is not legitimated – a task made more complex by outside constraints that limit our capacity to be helpful (Macdonald 2002: 425). I consider the idea of helping others to be a central task of social work, yet we need to be critically reflective about what it means to help other people. Does helping others imply that as practitioners we are stuck in 'compulsive caregiving' (Braye and Preston-Shoot 1995: 129)? Does it imply a need to create unhealthy dependencies in order to feel superior, or a need to exercise power and control over others in order to feel important? Or are we being helpful in ways that provide stability, or that enable new opportunities to develop? How much we engage with others is an important issue and one that impacts on our practice in terms of how we conceptualize and embrace notions of empowerment, partnership and choice. These are complex practice issues (Thoburn *et al.* 1995) and more difficult to achieve than is sometimes suggested.

By developing relationships that take account of our importance to each other, and the reciprocal nature of our connection, we are attempting to avoid adding ourselves to the pile of disappointing experiences, failures and 'let downs' that many service users and carers have experienced. By remaining within clear professional boundaries, being true to our word, keeping to the commitments we have made, never promising more than we can deliver and responding as closely as possible within agency constraints to the needs identified by the individual, we are offering the possibility of a new and different experience. If all goes well, this can increase confidence and form a basis from which to explore other relationships and possibilities. Within the confines of inner city or rural neglect or decay, these possibilities may be few and hard to identify, but every experience, positive or negative, carries with it the possibility of influencing the next stage in a person's life (Salzberger-Wittenberg 1970: 162). The challenge here is a formidable one, namely how to sort out and work through the barriers that inhibit progress, so that these experiences can be turned into opportunities for growth and change.

Positive experiences engender hope and trust and convey a comforting sense of being understood and accepted. As human beings we have a deep-seated wish to be understood, to be accepted for who we are and for our lives to have meaning and purpose (Howe 1996: 94). This desire is as true for people who come from deprived sectors of the population, who form the vast majority of social work service users, as it is for people who come from other, more advantaged sectors. Although at times this desire for meaning and understanding may elude us, nevertheless most of us continue to yearn for someone who can bring this sense of understanding and meaning into our lives and with it the transformation that this possibility offers. Some find this through religion, while others turn to their families or friends to fulfil the need. Another, smaller cross-section are forced to look to professionals for this kind of understanding and meaning, perhaps because they have not had enough love or care, or enough positive experiences, to be able to trust others. Or perhaps the capacity to adapt – or to give and take, which is central to the task of relating – has broken down and needs to be addressed or *mended*.

On the other hand, negative experiences can reaffirm old suspicions and doubts, deepen mistrust, shatter hope and produce even greater despair. Too often service users are burdened by the load they are carrying and arrive into the situation with a bundle of negativity and with too little belief in the possibilities that change can offer. Try as we may, we cannot avoid the fact that some service users pose a threat to themselves (Huxley 2002: 64–5; Pritchard 2000b: 338–40) and/or to others (Hester *et al*. 1996), whether intentionally or not (Pritchard 2000a: 309–10). All forms of risk need to be acknowledged in any assessment or evaluation process (Kemshall and Pritchard 1999). As far as possible, all judgements, whether positive or negative, should be backed by evidence. If, as practitioners, we can involve ourselves in the experience of relating to another human being, we too can develop and learn from the encounter, about ourselves and about other people (Howe 1987: 113). That is our ultimate reward. To be invited to enter another person's world, if only for a brief time and in a limited way, can in itself be a mark of trust and hope and, from this place, so much can happen. The small gains that some service users achieve can feel to them, and to us, like major successes and act as a reminder that some people can travel a long way on a little, while others need much more in order to move their lives forward. That is not to idealize poverty and the sense of shame and social exclusion that can haunt the lives of poor people, but it is important to remember that, as human beings, we are complex and unique individuals and always more than our suffering (Angelou 1994).

The context of social work

Social work has been the focus of many changes over the past few years, some of which have had a positive impact whilst others have led to confusion, uncertainty (Lishman 2002: 97) and a sense of fragmentation (Orme 2001: 611-24). Underpinning these changes is a commitment to ensuring quality care for those who use social care services, leading to the establishment of national standards in relation to health and social services, and a framework for assessing performance and effectiveness (Huber 1999: 2). Some of the developments introduced since 2000 have radically changed the organization of social work and social work education in the UK. For this reason, it is important to include a brief account of the context for these changes and how they impact on the current organization and culture of social work. Without this understanding, it is not possible for us to see where social work is located in the overall picture or to influence its shape and future direction. Although this section is written with UK practitioners and students in mind, it provides useful comparative material for readers from other countries.

The 'modernization programme'

The reform of the welfare state was an important aspect of government policy under the leadership of Margaret Thatcher. This also became part of the modernizing programme of the Labour Government, which came to power in May 1997. The starting point for Labour's reforms was the White Paper, *Modernising Social Services* (Department of Health 1998b). Further proposals were set out in other White Papers, particularly *Modernising Government* (Cabinet Office 1999) and *A Quality Strategy for Social Care* (Department of Health 2000b). These encapsulate the government's commitment to improve the organization of social services and the quality of care provided in every sector, based on a 'what works is what counts' approach to service delivery (DoH 1998b: 93). However, concerns about the organization and quality of care were not confined to social care but also included the health service – concerns that would link reforms in social care to reforms in the health service (Means *et al.* 2003: 74). The changes introduced also saw much greater involvement on the part of the government in the design, delivery and monitoring of services, and the development of a more 'centralist' and 'managerialist' policy framework (Harris 2003). The complex and interlocking set of reforms that were set up are summarized in this section under two main headings:

improving the organization, delivery and monitoring of services, and improving the quality of care provided.

Improving the organization, delivery and monitoring of services

In terms of improving the organization, delivery and monitoring of services provided, the new requirements called on social services to meet a range of service objectives in order to address specific outcomes, performance targets and systems to manage and monitor performance. The principles underpinning these reforms were outlined in *Modernising Government*, and include:

- a focus on outcomes to enable working across organizational structures
- the promotion of partnership between different areas of government and with the voluntary and private sectors
- greater use of evidence and research
- consultation with service users
- the use of targets and performance monitoring to secure quality and continuous improvement in public services
- additional investment to be conditional on improved results
- a greater valuing of public services by developing skills and rewarding results

(Cabinet Office 1999)

These principles are the hallmarks of Labour's modernization pro-gramme. They can be seen in the requirements made of local authorities in initiatives such as the *Long Term Care Charter,* the *Fair Access to Care, Best Value* and the setting up of the National Care Standards Commission. Other requirements have focused on improving the services for specific groups, such as those described in the White Paper on learning disability, *Valuing People* (Department of Health 2001).

Whilst many principles outlined above are to be welcomed, according to Harris the introduction of 'business thinking' into the service provision agenda has demoralized social workers, and led to increased work pressures, greater scrutiny and being required to gatekeep and to ration services (Harris 2003: 36). The changes introduced have been summarized as follows:

The partial withdrawal of the state from direct welfare provision, and the delegation of responsibilities to private and voluntary organisa-tions, has been accompanied by a substantial growth in the mechanisms for regulation and control over an increasingly fragmented welfare sector. ... The implications of this are far-reaching with the move to regulation through contracting, monitoring and inspection seen as symptomatic of wider cultural changes and the development of an *audit society,* in which accountability is achieved through constant checking and verification. . . . Within the state itself there has been a shift in power towards the centre as successive governments have sought to restrict the autonomy of local government by increasing control over local expenditure and services.

(Means *et al.* 2003: 73)

In response to criticisms about the burden of inspection in social care, in 2004 the government introduced a single, comprehensive and independent inspectorate – the Commission for Social Care Inspection (CSCI) – in an attempt to rationalize the process of inspection. The CSCI incorporates the work formerly undertaken by three previous bodies: the Social Services Inspectorate (SSI), the Joint Review team of the SSI/Audit Commission, and the functions of the National Care Standards Commission (NCSC) in relation to social care. The CSCI's task is to regulate adult and children's services through a process of registration and inspection, such as local authority 'star ratings'. The CSCI works closely with its equivalent in health care, namely the Commission for Healthcare Audit and Inspection (CHAI) and it is suggested that these two organizations may be merged at some future date.

Whilst the introduction of a coherent framework for the provision of services is an important development, the failure to provide sufficient additional funding to meet the cost of inspection and regulation has resulted in resources and funding being diverted from the direct provision of services. Also, there remains considerable doubt as to whether the changes introduced will meet their objective, namely an improvement in service provision (Sinclair 2002: 435).

Improving the quality of care provided

In terms of the quality of social care provided by the workforce, serious problems were noted. For example, it is estimated that 1.2 million people are employed as social care workers but approximately 80 per cent of this workforce have no recognized qualification or training in social care (Barton 2000: 318). In addition, the absence of mechanisms to monitor and regulate the standard of practice and conduct, and the lack of confidence in some aspects of the education and training provided were also raised as causes for concern (Department of Health 1998a: 84–5). A third area of concern related to the limited research undertaken in the field of social care. To address these concerns, three organizations were given responsibility to meet specific requirements, namely those relating to practice standards and workforce regulation (GSCC), training (TOPSS) and research (SCIE). These bodies occupy a central place in the current organization of social work education and practice and for this reason their responsibilities are described in greater detail. Whilst equivalent organizations have been set up in Wales, Scotland and Northern Ireland, there are some differences in terms of the following account, which relates to England only.

GSCC

In England, the General Social Care Council (GSCC) became fully operational in October 2001. The composition of this Council is interesting. For example, Council members are appointed by the Secretary of State, with a lay person in the chair and all key interests represented. However, service users and lay people form a majority on the Council, which is seen by some as 'an indication of the government's concern to avoid any perception of the Council as a self-regulating professional body' (Means *et al*, 2003: 88). Its role is to ensure that work standards within the social care sector are of the highest quality, which involves three main areas of responsibility:

- setting conduct and practice standards for all social services staff, published as Codes of Practice. Staff will be required to conform to these standards as a condition of their employment
- where recognized training has been undertaken, the Council is responsible for registering social care workers, including social workers, on the Social Care Register. It also has the power to suspend or to deregister individuals who infringe the codes of conduct and practice
- the GSCC replaces the Central Council for Education and Training in Social Work (CCETSW) as the regulatory body for social work education and training

TOPSS

A different body, the Training Organisation for the Personal Social Services (TOPSS), was given responsibility for promoting and developing training within the social care sector. The functions of TOPSS are:

- to maintain the occupational standards underpinning the qualifications recognized by social care staff and employers
- to carry out workforce analysis
- to identify training needs and ensure they are met
(Department of Health 1998b: 94)

As the body with responsibility for developing the social care workforce, and formulating national occupational standards for each section of the workforce, TOPSS works in conjunction with both employers and the General Social Care Council. In relation to social work, an important function of TOPSS England has been the development of the National Occupational Standards for Social Work (TOPSS 2004).

Skills for Care

Plans are in place for TOPSS England to become part of the Skills for Care and Development, where it will have specific responsibilities for the adult social care workforce in England. The Skills for Care and Development will also include the care councils for Wales, Scotland and Northern Ireland and these will be joined in April 2005 by the emerging Children's Workforce Development Council for England. At this point, it is proposed that Topss England will be renamed as Skills for Care.

SCIE

To bridge the lack of reliable research evidence about 'what works' in social care, a third body was launched in October 2001, namely a Social Care Institute for Excellence (SCIE). This initiative came out of the White Paper, *A Quality Strategy for Social Care* (Department of Health 2000b), which described SCIE's main role:

- establishing and developing a rigorous knowledge base founded on the views and experiences of users, research evidence, Social Services Inspectorate and Audit Commission reports and the experiences of managers and practitioners
- producing authoritative and accessible guidelines on effective social care practice and service delivery
- ensuring dissemination through creative partnerships across the diverse range of organizations involved in the research, monitoring, regulation, commissioning and provision of social care.

(Department of Health 2000b)

The challenge faced by SCIE is formidable given the lack of clarity that exists about what constitutes the knowledge base of social care, as well as a shortage of research and lack of funding for social care research programmes at a national level. Of particular concern is the lack of research relevant to practice, and how to disseminate research findings in ways that make it accessible to practitioners. Given this situation, 'It is as yet uncertain to what extent SCIE will be able to address these problems and whether, as a not-for-profit company limited by guarantee, it will be able to preserve its independence from government' (Means *et al*. 2003: 90). Nevertheless, SCIE has produced a number of key publications, including knowledge reviews, position papers, practice guides, reports and resource guides – some of which are cited in this text, such as the knowledge reviews relating to assessment (Crisp *et al*. 2003) and communication skills (Trevithick *et al*. 2004) in social work education, and the use of knowledge (Pawson *et al*. 2003) and research in social care (Walter *et al*. 2004). SCIE also provides important website which provides information and access to publications free of charge (www.scie. org.uk).

Another important resource worthy of mention is the Social Policy and Social Work subject centre (SWAP), which is part of the Higher Education Academy in the UK. SWAP's work involves disseminating and developing good practice in learning, teaching and assessment in relation to social work and social policy. Further details of SWAP's work can be found on its website (http://www.swap.ac.uk).

Changes in social work education

The impetus to introduce changes in social work education was in keeping with the government's modernization agenda, and also influenced in part by the publicity surrounding the inquiries into the death of children known to social services (Blom-Cooper 1985; Gough 1993), the most recent being the tragic death of Victoria Climbié (Department of Health 2003; Laming 2003). These changes were published in the *Requirements for Social Work Training* (Department of Health 2002), and included the introduction of the new degree in social work. A feature of these changes also included tighter controls, such as the requirement that social work students should complete at least 200 days of assessed practice learning, in at least two practice settings, working with at least two user groups (DoH 2002: 3). In addition, the Deparment of Health also stipulated that students would be expected to have at least 200 days, or 1,200 hours 'structured academic learning under the direction of an eductor' (2002: 4). To achieve these aims, additional funding has been made available to support practice learning, plus a bursary scheme to address the shortage of people entering social work training.

Whilst many of these changes have been welcomed by academics and students, some difficulties remain. For example, the availability and quality of practice placements remains a problem. Also, the requirement to provide 200 days 'structured academic learning' places a considerable burden on academics, who have to meet other university administrative and research requirements. (A useful summary on the regulation of social work education can be found on the SWAP website).

Changes in the law

Since the late 1980s, there have been several major pieces of legislation affecting social work practice, such as powers and responsibilities assigned to social workers in relation to the Mental Health Act 1983, the Children Act 1989, the National Health Service and Community Care Act 1990, the Criminal Justice Act 1991 and Crime and Disorder Act (Brammer 2003: 1). Some areas of law have been superseded by subsequent legislation, making it difficult to keep abreast of these changes and to understand how they apply in practice (Brammer 2003: 9). For example, since the Criminal Justice Act 1991, six other acts have been passed. Or again, the guidance issued in relation to the Children Act runs into ten volumes with more guidance due. A similar situation exists in the area of community care legislation (Munby 2002: 443). Further changes are being implemented in the integration of children's services with education, and the development of Children's Trusts, which draw on proposals incorporated in the Green Paper, *Every Child Matters* (DfES

2003). The Children Act 2004 provides the legal framework for the reform of children's services, which are outlined in detail in *Every Child Matters: Change for Children,* published in December 2004 (DfES 2004). Similar changes are proposed in the reorganization and integration of adult services – outlined in the consultative Green Paper on *Adult Social Care* (DoH 2005).

Other legislative changes are also important, such as those relating to domestic violence under the Family Law Act 1996 (Harwin *et al.* 1999; Hague and Malos 2005); the Carers (Recognition and Services) Act 1995, the Disability Discrimination Act (1995) and new mental health legislation is on the horizon. The UK's membership of the European Union means that social work is subject to EU legislation (Munby 2002: 443) and the incorporation of the Human Rights into English law, which came into force in October 2000, opens up further protection of rights for the individual (Williams 2001). The rights of children are embodied in the United Nations Convention on the Rights of the Child, which the UK government has signed.

In support of legislation, the government draws up codes of practice and guidance. These are important because they state what the government expects and requires of local authorities in relation to good practice. For example, guidance issued under section 7(1) of the Local Authority Social Services Act 1970 means that, where local authorities fail to act in accordance with the guidance, a complaint can be made to the Ombudsman (Brammer 2003: 39) or it may count as evidence against them in legal proceedings. The difference between regulations, codes, guidance, duty and powers is as follows:

- **Codes** – convey the message *you ought/should* (Department of Health 1989: 2).
- **Duty** – 'a mandatory obligation to carry out a particular function, something which the authority shall do' (Brammer 2003: 479), or *must* do.
- **Guidance** – guidance that explains regulations reaffirms the message *you must.* However when guidance sets out good practice, it conveys the message that *it is highly desirable to . . .* or *unless there is good reason not to, you should . . .* rather than *you must* (Department of Health 1989: 2).
- **Regulations** – convey the message *you must/shall* (Department of Health 1989: 2).
- **Powers** – 'a discretion to act, often expressed as something which *may* be done' (Brammer 2003: 481).

The expectations that derive from legislation, and the language of official documents, are important because these regulate social work practice – often in the form of agency policy guidelines and requirements – a point that is emphasized by Roberts and Preston-Shoot:

Social work is empowered, guided and controlled by its legal mandate. This mandate is made up of three elements. The first is organizational, in that most social work in the UK is practised from within the structures of the statutory social services. The second is functional, in that the law determines the powers and duties with which social work is endowed. The third is procedural, in that the law largely determines the nature and extent of social work accountability, both to service users and to the community generally.

(Roberts and Preston-Shoot 2000: 183)

This subject is important from a different standpoint because a familiarity with the law and requirements of government may be an important lever from which to argue for services to be provided (Braye and Preston-Shoot 1995: 66). This is not only relevant to current UK legislation but also European legislation when implemented, but this is only possible where 'the law itself is pro-liberty' (Williams 2004: 48). For example, some commentators believe that the Human Rights Act, which came into force in October 2000, will have 'a profound effect on social work' (Croft and Bereford 2002: 391). However, others are more cautious: 'Despite the 1998 Human Rights Act, social workers may be denied the legal wherewithal to protect and promote the basic rights to which their clients are entitled' (Williams 2004: 50). It will be interesting to see how the picture unfolds over the next few years.

Outline of the text

In the first section of this second edition, two new chapters have been added, together with this revised Introduction. Another major change is that throughout the text greater emphasis has been given to sociological perspectives. Chapter 1 focuses on the knowledge base of social work and outlines the way that different types of knowledge – divided broadly into theoretical, factual and practical knowledge – are central to effective practice. The underpinning theme is that all actions, including the implementation of particular practice approaches, perspectives, generalist or specialist skills and interventions, are intellectual in character, making it important to describe in detail the knowledge base that informs social work. Chapter 2 identifies how we can apply knowledge in practice. In particular, it looks at what we mean by a range of different terms, such as competence, skill, intervention, perspective and practice, and argues that for these to be transferable they have to be linked to a sound knowledge base. In order to illustrate how these concepts can be used, ten practice choices are described and applied to a case example from practice. Chapter 3 gives an overview of a number of key psychological concepts, designed to provide a foundation from which to understand human beings and human behaviour. In Chapter 4, some themes covered in earlier chapters are applied in practice in relation to a number of 'core' skills, namely communication, listening and assessment skills, observation and decision-making skills.

The second section of this text identifies 50 generalist skills used within social work on a regular basis, giving a name to many of the skills practitioners already use but may not have labelled or conceptualized in this way. This list is not designed to cover all skills and interventions used in social work and some readers may be disappointed not to find certain skills included, such as the range of specialist skills and interventions linked with particular practice approaches. It was not possible to do this without changing the nature of the text, although whenever possible I have tried to give references to further reading. Similarly, it was not always possible to include the theories that underpin all the skills and interventions covered. Hopefully, such a text will one day be written. The perspective I stress throughout this section, and in the text as a whole, is that every intervention should have a clear, specific and identified purpose – a purpose that should be central to the agreement we establish with service users and carers and with other professionals and key individuals. If we fail at the outset to find agreement or to identify a *common purpose,* this omission is likely to emerge as a difficulty later on. This clarity on our part enables us to assess the appropriateness of specific social work practice approaches, perspectives, skills and interventions in terms of their effectiveness in bringing about desired and agreed outcomes.

A final section includes 11 appendices, some of which are revised versions whilst others are new to this edition. Six practice approaches are described, plus three practice perspectives. Also included is a section on the *Stages of Change* and an extract from the National Occupational Standards (NOS) on the knowledge base of social work. Once again, I decided to include these appendices at the end of the book in order to enable the reader to locate and photocopy them easily. Each appendix lists a number of references to guide the reader to other articles and texts. In this edition, behavioural and cognitive approaches are covered in separate appendices. This is because many of the accounts of cognitive-behavioural approaches are largely behavioural, and often written by academics who are more expert in the field of behaviourism, having already published on this subject (Hudson and MacDonald 1986; Sheldon 1982). Although a number of cognitive concepts may also be included, such as Ellis's ABCDE model (1997), these are not always incorporated in a way that gives a coherent and integrated practice account or adequate weight to cognitive concepts. For these reasons, since both practice approaches are important to effective social work practice, I felt that it would help to have a more detailed, separate account of both. In this way, practitioners and students reading this text can appreciate their relative merits and arrive at their own strategy to combine these two approaches.

Some points of clarification about the text are worth noting. The focus and examples given are based on work with individuals because the individual is located in other social formations, namely the family, group, community and organization. However, the skills described are transferable and can be related to other practice orientations and to work with service users and carers in different settings. In this regard, the interventions identified do not solely refer to work with service users or carers, but can include others that we encounter during the course of our work (England 1986: 25). Sometimes our colleagues, managers or other professionals need to be supported and challenged in ways that require the same skills and interventions that we draw on when working with service users and carers.

Throughout the text, I have described people who come within the remit of social work as *service users*. This term is not ideal, but nor are others (Brammer 2003: xix; Dominelli 2002b: 19; Sheldon 1995: xiv; Stevenson and Parsloe 1993: 6). This dilemma is made more complicated because, in my experience, none of the terms used – service user, customer, consumer, recipient of services or client – draw on a language commonly used by people in receipt of social work services. The suggestion that the word *client* should refer to 'those who have social work imposed upon them' and *service users* to denote 'recipients of social work intervention voluntarily entered into' is an interesting differentiation (Wise 1995: 116), but not always an easy distinction to draw. Nevertheless, this conceptualization is helpful because it highlights the importance of language and its limitations. Being critically reflective about the words we use is essential, but this can sometimes be taken to suggest that we have fundamentally altered the stigma and oppression that travels with some oppressed groups. This is often not the case, and this fact can become obscured if we fail to focus on the bigger picture and the discrimination that some groups continue to experience, on a daily basis, within society as a whole.

Staying with the subject of language, it is remarkable to note how often the male pronoun *he* is still inappropriately used in some texts. On occasion I have chosen to highlight this incongruity by adding the adverb *sic*. Also on this theme, a differentiation is made in this second edition between the verb *to practise* and the noun *practice*. In the USA, the word practise is rarely used, but this is not the case in the UK and in countries that have been influenced by UK English usage. However, since competent social work practice does not depend on an awareness of this grammatical distinction, I would not want this issue to be given more attention than it deserves.

As an academic-practitioner, I have used the pronoun *we* to refer to the fact that I have written this text as a practitioner, and the case examples used draw on my experience in a range of different settings. Most case examples relate to my work with children and families and in the field of mental health. More recent examples draw on my work as a groupwork consultant and trainer for South Gloucestershire Social Services and my work with women who are caught up in 'street prostitution'. Most of these 'working women' are on drugs, are homeless and rootless and experience serious deprivation and discrimination.

For practitioners working in other fields of social work, my examples may seem far removed from their practice experience. I am aware of this limitation but the notion of transferability is important in this regard. In the case examples used, all names and other identifiable characteristics have been changed to protect service users' identities, and unless stated to the contrary, readers can assume that the situations described refer to individuals who have sought a social work service on a voluntary basis.

1 THE KNOWLEDGE BASE OF SOCIAL WORK: THEORETICAL, FACTUAL AND PRACTICE KNOWLEDGE

> ... to practise without a theory is to sail an uncharted sea;
> theory without practice is not to set sail at all ...
>
> (Susser 1968: v)

Our ability to draw on – and to use – knowledge is central to effective practice. It is also a requirement laid down in the guidance documents relating to social work training and practice. For these reasons, it is essential to understand what is meant by the term 'knowledge' and, most importantly, to understand how this relates to practice. This chapter begins with a brief account on what constitutes knowledge, which is followed by three sections each dealing with different areas of knowledge: theoretical, factual and practice knowledge. The section on theoretical knowledge includes an account of how theory is defined and conceptualized in social work and covers the role of ideology. The section on factual knowledge provides a number of examples covering the kind of issues where factual information is relevant to social work. The third section on practice knowledge looks at a range of themes, such as critical reflection, reflexivity, critical thinking, practice wisdom and developing hypotheses, and examines how these relate to practice effectiveness. The coverage of these three areas of knowledge ends with an example of how this knowledge might be used in practice. The final section explores the importance of research-informed social work practice, including the way that evidence based practice has been conceptualized, and the difficulties encountered when attempting to apply knowledge to the problems regularly encountered in social work practice.

Knowledge

We seek and use knowledge in order to understand ourselves, others and the world around us. A central aspect of this quest or exploration is the search for truth – the desire to know what constitutes reality or, as Karl Popper states, 'the shaping of reality through truth' (1994a: 7). Thus an exploration of what constitutes knowledge naturally leads to a discussion of what constitutes truth or reality. This in turn gives rise to an important dilemma, namely the difference between *subjective* and *objective* interpretations. What may be true or real for me may not be true or real for others. As a result, how people interpret their lives, and their interaction with others and the world they inhabit, can vary greatly. This can lead to important differences in the way that people perceive events and the understanding and meaning they give to experiences. These issues can seem to be far removed from contemporary social work, yet what constitutes truth or reality lies at the heart of the assessment process and other aspects of our work. This highlights the multiple perspectives gathered from a range of different sources (Paterson 2002: 45) that we attempt to negotiate in our efforts to develop a sound knowledge base, as exemplified in this quote:

> Social work bases its methodology on a systematic body of evidence-based knowledge derived from research and practice evaluation, including local and indigenous knowledge specific to its context. It recognises the complexity of interactions between human beings and their environment, and the capacity of people both to be affected by and to alter the multiple influences upon them including bio-psychosocial factors. The social work profession draws on theories of human development and behaviour and social systems to analyse complex situations and to facilitate individual, organisational, social and cultural changes.
>
> (IASSW/IFSW: 2000)

The reference to 'indigenous knowledge' is important because it can include the knowledge that service users and carers bring to the encounter. This source of knowledge has been seriously overlooked in the past both in social work (Croft and Beresford 2002: 388) and in other areas of health and welfare provision. This is sometimes referred to as *subjugated knowledge* (Hartman 1992), that is, knowledge that derives from people in their everyday contexts who, unlike professionals, are not considered *experts* (Penna 2000: 220). It is this lack of expert status that can lead to people's experience and knowledge being ignored or considered less relevant. As a result, what constitutes legitimate knowledge – and whose knowledge is privileged or given significance – is controversial and contested (Zubrzycki 2003).

The attempt to identify what is 'real' or 'true' in a given situation often takes us to the realm of belief, which for some people carries much the same weight as truth. In this context, *belief* is defined as: 'The acknowledgement that a proposition is true in the absence of demonstrable proof as required by scientific method' (Bullock and Trombley 2000: 72). Sheldon describes beliefs as 'settled views of experience' that we seek to preserve and have confirmed (Sheldon 1995: 153). The notion of *proof* can be defined as 'an attempt to convince people of the truth of what you are saying' (Bullock and Trombley 2000: 692). The emphasis in this account is on persuasion, whereas for Popper it lies in its resilience and testability: 'proposed proof must be able to stand up to critical discussion' (1994b: 13). From this perspective, an assertion can be considered to be true 'if it corresponds to, or agrees with, the facts' (Popper 1994b: 174).

It is important to realize that we experience life through our histories but that these histories are always in the making. It is for this reason that we look for factors that can be verified by reference to external objective evidence, in the hope that hard facts can lead us to a degree of accuracy. Yet we know from the work of Kuhn (1970) and others that the search for objective knowledge, including new data gained through research, is highly influenced by human factors – by the fact that our assumptions and hypotheses are blinkered by ideology and by the thinking of our times (Howe 2002a: 86).

It is this relationship between objective and subjective truth, and the role of belief, proof and evidence, that remains complex and problematic in social work because it can be difficult to know what is real or true amid conflicting realities and people's differing understandings of events and experiences. From this place, it seems important to acknowledge that what constitutes knowledge is a complex issue, and so too is the task of applying that knowledge to contemporary social work practice. In order to address some of these complexities, and to begin to classify the knowledge used in social care, including social work, the Social Care Institute for Excellence (SCIE) commissioned a knowledge review, entitled *Types and Quality of Knowledge in Social Care* (Pawson *et al.* 2003: 73). Its remit was to 'consider what types of knowledge SCIE should draw on, and how to distinguish good quality knowledge from that which should not be relied on in policy making and practice' (Fisher 2003: vi). This proved to be a difficult task because of the diverse and fragmented nature of the social care knowledge base and different interpretations and tensions among academics and employers as to what should constitute the knowledge base of social work. To understand this tension, it is important to look in some detail at how social work knowledge, particularly social work theory, has been defined and conceptualized in order to draw a map of the territory that the subject covers and to provide some directions and signposts through this vast terrain. Without these signposts, we might easily become lost or give up the hope of understanding this difficult subject, yet it is important to remember that:

To travel at all is to hold ideas about the behavioural and social terrain over which we journey. To show no interest in theory is simply to travel blind. This is bad practice and unhelpful to clients.

(Howe 1987: 9)

Three areas of knowledge: theoretical, factual and practice knowledge

The following account looks at the knowledge base of social work under three interconnected sections. Although all three areas are important, considerable weight is given to the first section, theoretical knowledge or theory, because of the importance of the link between theory and practice and the considerable literature that has been written on this subject. These three sections are:

1 theoretical knowledge (or theory)
2 factual knowledge
3 practice knowledge (knowledge in practice).

Each section includes a number of different headings: these will be indicated at the beginning of the section. Some of the themes that have been covered in the different sections are brought together when we look at the use of knowledge in practice, towards the end of this chapter. We return to some of these subjects in Chapter 2 when we look at how we might apply knowledge in practice.

Theoretical knowledge

This first section on theoretical knowledge begins with an account of how theory has been defined within social work. This is designed to provide an understanding of the different terms that are sometimes referred to in social work texts – but not always defined – in the hope that explaining these terms will demystify the subject and make the use and discussion of these ideas, concepts and theories more accessible. It then explores the different themes that this subject covers under three headings, namely:

• knowledge drawn or 'borrowed' from other disciplines
• theories that analyse the task and purpose of social work
• practice theories or practice approaches.

To avoid confusion, it is important to note that there is no fundamental difference between the term theoretical knowledge and the term theory. I have used the term theoretical knowledge because it fits into the framework used in this text, namely the relationship between theoretical, factual and practice knowledge. The term also emphasizes the word knowledge and encourages us to think of theory as one aspect of knowledge.

How theory is defined

Barker defines theory as: 'A group of related hypotheses, concepts, and constructs, based on facts and observations, that attempts to explain a particular phenomenon' (Barker 2003: 434). These theories may take the form of a 'single concept or idea' or attempt to explain 'interrelated concepts' (Fook 2002: 38). An important characteristic of a theory is that it goes beyond the descriptive to include explanations of why things (phenomena) happen. Thus we use theory in an attempt to make sense of the world or particular events. It is also useful because it predicts what is likely to happen in a given situation and can, therefore, guide our decision-making. Sheldon emphasizes this point:

> it is psychologically impossible not to have theories about things. It is impossible at a basic perceptual level, at a cognitive and at an emotional level. The search for meaning, as a basis for predicting behavioural success and avoiding danger, appears to have been 'wired' into our brains by evolution.
>
> (Sheldon 1995: 8)

However, the way we attempt to understand and organize our explanations can shift and change. For this reason, the theories we formulate need to be seen as tentative, so that 'a theory always remains hypothetical, or conjectural. It always remains guesswork. And there is no theory that is not beset with problems' (Popper 1994b: 157). As such, it is essential to avoid seeing theory/theories in terms of *absolute notions* or as *knowledge set in stone*:

> Theories are not absolute notions of the way things really are, but, so long as they account for what appears to be happening in a particular way that satisfies the observer, they are retained. Theories provide 'workable definitions' of the world about us. They make it intelligible. In a very real way, theory-building is reality-building. ... Our theories define what we see.
>
> (Howe 1987: 10)

The notion of 'theory as explanation' places theories and theorizing at one end of a spectrum as something accessible: something that we all do, whether intentionally or not. This category could include *anecdotal experience* (Gambrill 1997: 77), those involving a more *experiential* approach (Pawson *et al.* 2003: 13), *common-sense* notions (England 1986: 33) or *lay* theories (Gambrill 1997: 77). All these terms describe explanations that are primarily gained from direct experience. A different way to describe this is in terms of *bottom-up* explanations, which in relation to social work means theories or explanations that are generated from practice. Theory building of this kind in social work involves refining existing theories or formulating new ones. This form of theorizing falls into the category of practice knowledge, a subject that is covered in greater detail later in this chapter.

At the other end of the spectrum from bottom-up explanations lies a more *top-down* test of applicability, which refers to the way that research or different theories are applied to practice situations. Top-down approaches are more likely to draw on theories that have been classified in terms of *grand theory* or *middle-range theory* – that is, theories based on scientific criteria. The term grand theory was first used by C. Wright Mills (1959) to attack conceptualizations formulated at a highly abstract level, sometimes referred to as 'grand narratives' (Fook 2002: 12), which purport to explain more or less everything in society (e.g. Marxism, psychoanalysis). Lesser claims are made under the heading middle-range theories, which attempt to explain only a limited range of phenomena, such as social inequalities or oppression (Thompson 1995: 23). Postmodern and poststructural 'discourses' also challenge the status and validity of grand narratives and the universal truths and version of reality put forward in the name of science or reason. Instead, grand narratives are seen as 'a mass of conflicting ways of making sense of different experiences from different perspectives' (Fook 2002: 12). Postmodernism occupies an important position in the current evidence based climate. Indeed, some see postmodernism as being hostile or 'antithetical to evidence based policy and practice' (Pawson *et al.* 2003: 13).

There has been, and continues to be, a great deal of debate and controversy among social work academics in relation to which theories are considered to be the most important and applicable to social work. These differences have been conceptualized by some authors in terms of whether social work is 'either a science or humanist endeavour' (Camilleri 1999: 31; Shaw 1996: 2). However, in the realm of theory and theorizing, it can be easy to be drawn into abstract conceptualizations and to lose sight of the fact that for any theory to be relevant it needs to be able to 'speak' to the dilemmas and complexities regularly encountered in social work practice. In this regard, Howe identifies five key areas where the use of theory can illuminate our understanding of people and their circumstances:

1 Observation: it tells us what we see and what to look out for
2 Description: it provides a conceptual vocabulary and framework within which observations can be arranged and organized
3 Explanation: it suggests how different observations might be linked and connected; it offers possible causal relationships between one event and another
4 Prediction: it indicates what might happen next
5 Intervention: it suggests what might be done to bring about change.

(Howe 2002a: 82)

This description provides a clear general account of the way that the use of theory can help us to unravel what is happening and why. These five points are equally relevant and transferable in relation to assessment. Whether drawing on general or specialist theories, the task of theory is to provide a framework from which to explain and understand what is happening and why, so that we can recommend appropriate courses of action. To do this well requires us to draw on the perceptions, explanations and understanding of all people involved, such as service users, carers, other significant individuals and other workers/professionals. It also involves learning how to communicate what we know – our knowledge base – in ways that illuminate others' understanding, and to do this without becoming lost in abstractions or lured off course into enticing avenues that lead nowhere:

> social work theory should never become an end in itself ... a truly useful theory would provide guidance towards a more effective practice, giving a measure of confidence so that we do not feel totally at the mercy of our working environment; if we build on and record effective strategies and techniques, then we build transmittable knowledge by directing others to what is common and regularly occurring in human experience.
>
> (Coulshed 1991: 8)

Having looked at how theory is defined, this section now considers the theoretical knowledge under three headings:

- knowledge drawn or 'borrowed' from other disciplines
- theories that analyse the task and purpose of social work
- practice theories or practice approaches.

Knowledge drawn from other disciplines

Under the first of three headings on the subject of theoretical knowledge, we explore the knowledge that social work has drawn and adapted – or 'borrowed' – from other disciplines (Payne 1997: 44). This has produced a potentially rich and diverse knowledge base. However, like other professions, social work is prone to fashions and, as a result, knowledge that is drawn from too many diverse sources can lead to fragmentation and an incoherent knowledge framework – leading to a 'knowledge pile' rather than a 'knowledge base' (Sheldon 1995: 6). Some theories are presented 'at a highly abstract level' (Stepney 2000b: 21) and, as a result, are not easy to apply to contemporary social work practice. Consequently, *transferability* is lost, that is, 'the ability to remake knowledge for relevance across different contexts' (Fook 2002: 156). Some theories are applied in ways that are confusing, unrigorous or based on an inaccurate understanding of a particular practice approach. For example, it can be difficult to apply a client/person-centred approach outside counselling, particularly in statutory social work or where risk is involved, because this may require social workers to use their statutory powers and to override the principle of service user self-determination. Similarly, Thorne argues that a client/person-centred approach 'has no role' in an environment where market forces and behaviour modification dominate the agenda (2002: 175). One reason for this difficulty is the fact that most practice approaches taught on social work courses do not derive directly from practice. Indeed, the only practice approach to be developed by practitioners is said to be task-centred work (Camilleri 1999: 30).

Social work 'borrows' knowledge from a number of disciplines, outlined below. Some, such as psychology, are more influential than others and more could be added, but the disciplines identified are those that contribute significantly to the knowledge base of social work. It is important to note that these disciplines were originally developed, and continue to be framed, in Western assumptions about human behaviour and the way we live our lives. They tend, therefore, to be *eurocentric* (Robinson 1995, 1998), that is, they 'undermine the importance of nondominant cultural patterns, beliefs and expectations' (Robinson 2000: 222) and can fail to give sufficient weight to the fact that we live in a multicultural society (Thompson 2002c: 78). In terms of their patriarchal or gendered assumptions, some more than others have been the focus of feminist scrutiny (Dominelli 2002a: 99–100; Pierson and Thomas 2002: 338). These disciplines have other limitations in terms of the assumptions they embody and the way these assumptions limit our understanding of what it means to be a human being at this particular point in time.

Each discipline has several 'schools' or specialist lines of enquiry that reflect specific areas of interest or a certain set of principles or methods of investigation. A detailed account of these schools goes beyond the scope of this text, although it is worth noting that some common themes emerge across these disciplines, such as a preoccupation with human motivation and behaviour change.

1 *Psychology*. Psychology is defined as 'the science of behaviour and mental processes' (Hockenbury and Hockenbury 2002: 2). It is the most borrowed discipline within social work and one that embraces six psychological perspectives: biological, psychodynamic, behavioural, humanistic, cognitive and cross-cultural perspectives (Hockenbury and Hockenbury 2002: 10–11). This subject is covered in detail in Chapter 3.
2 *Sociology*. Alongside psychology, sociology has been described as 'one of the defining academic disciplines of social work' (Pierson and Thomas 2002: 452). Sociology focuses on the relationship between the individual and his or her social context or social world. 'Fundamen-

tally, sociology is concerned with examining how people order their lives within the structural constraints of their setting' (Allan 2000: 335).

3 *Law*. Social work is regulated by legal mandate, which means that the law 'determines the powers and duties with which social work is endowed' (Roberts and Preston-Shoot 2000: 183). Much of the coverage of law can be categorized as factual knowledge, such as the difference between regulations, codes, guidance, duty and powers, which is covered in the Introduction. These link to assumptions that underpin the legal system, such as notions of rights and responsibilities. It is important to note that the legal system in the UK is based on an adversarial model, as opposed to the inquisitorial model adopted in other countries, such as the USA (Brammer 2003: 97).

4 *Social policy*. This describes 'government policy in the area of welfare, and the academic study of its development, implementation and impact' (Pierson and Thomas 2002: 441). 'The social policy which emerged from social administration initially focused on the institutional areas of housing, health, social security, education and the personal social services (or social work)' (Stewart 2000b: 322), although with the impact of globalization and international market forces, its focus is changing.

5 *Medicine*. The influence of medicine, and the *medical model* or *biomedical model*, has become more pronounced in recent years, although its benefit is limited where illnesses fall outside a disease model (Wade and Halligan 2004). The medical/biomedical model is based on several assumptions:

- The mind and the body can be treated separately; this is referred to as mind-body dualism
- The body can be repaired like a machine and consequently the merits of technological interventions are often overstated
- Explanations of disease focus on biological changes to the relative neglect of social and psychological factors; this is referred to as reductionist
- Such reductionism also assumes that every disease is caused by a specific, identifiable agent.

(Nettleton 1995: 3)

6 *Politics/political science*. According to Giddens, 'politics concerns the means whereby power is used to affect the scope and content of governmental activities' (2001: 420), whereas political science is 'the study of the organization and conduct of government' (Bullock and Trombley 2000: 661), particularly how governments negotiate and balance competing interests (Colebatch 2002: 135). Political decision-making 'directly impacts on the responsibilities of social workers' (Jordon and Parton 2000: 258).

7 *Economics*. Economics is the 'study of the production, distribution and consumption of wealth in human society' (Bannock *et al.* 1998: 122). Its

importance since the 1990s is evident in the 'marketization' of social work and the development of *managerialism*: 'Managerial priorities associated with the three E's (effectiveness, economy and efficiency) now permeate almost every aspect of the care management task' (Stepney 2000a: 2).

8 *Organizational theory*. The QAA Benchmark Statement cites 'organizational policies and procedures' and 'social science theories explaining group and organizational behaviour, adaptation and change' as subject areas in the new degree. Organizational theory relates to social services departments, community and voluntary agencies, and other organizations and institutions, which are vital to the delivery of services (Hepworth *et al*. 2002: 459). An organization's structure and culture directly influence service delivery.

9 *Philosophy*. 'All men and all women are philosophers' (Popper 1994b: 179). Philosophical investigation includes epistemology, semantics, metaphysics, logic and ethics. These subjects are relevant to social work in terms of the theory of knowledge and how knowledge is acquired and used (epistemology); the meaning communicated in terms of language (semantics); how we come to 'be' and 'know' and to understand reality (metaphysics); the reasoning used in thought processes and decision-making (logic); the professional and personal moral values that we, and others, adopt in our work and everyday lives (ethics). (For an interesting article on the relevance of philosophy to social work, see Aymer and Okitikpi 2000.)

The role of ideology

Whilst the disciplines outlined above may adopt a different language, or draw on different assumptions, it is important to stress again that the different lines of investigation they pursue overlap and interweave. For example, ideological influences shape the context within which different disciplines are located and the different ways that knowledge is sought and used. These assumptions influence the way we see the world and our part within it: 'an understanding of the ideological function of ideas ... allows us to make links between the social structure and individual lives, by explaining how people internalize thinking about the social structure and their place within it' (Fook 2002: 56). Giddens has argued that ideologies often serve to legitimate social and power inequalities and 'to justify the interests of dominant groups' (2001: 691). This legitimating can take many forms: the 'subtle, often unquestioned, workings of ideology can be far more effective in maintaining power structures than the overt and explicit use of power' (Thompson 2000b: 56). An example is the way that the medical model has become more influential in recent years. This has led to the *medicalization* of problems, that is, the tendency to describe behaviour in terms of medical labels. This term is 'used by critics of modern medicine who argue that doctors have too much political influence in issues where they are not in fact professionally competent to make judgements' (Abercrombie *et al*. 2000: 222).

On the other hand, it is our ideological position that informs the 'values and perspectives that social work practitioners use to guide and steer their practice' (Frost 2002: 53). Thus the ideological assumptions we adopt in relation to social work practice can 'function to maintain (or upset) the social order' (Fook 2002: 57). However, one of the problems social work faces – particularly in recent years – is that as a profession we can be too influenced by the ideology of governments rather than remaining true to the ideology of social work, such as the 'principles of human rights and social justice' (IASSW/IFSW 2001) (see page 1 of this text). For example, it could be argued that the ambivalence that exists as to whether welfare rights work is a legitimate part of the social work task (Bateman 2000: 370) could be seen as a reflection of the way that social work has been influenced and mobilized by ideology, and the way that the rights and status of people on benefit have been eroded by successive UK governments. For example, there has been a fall in the take up of benefits among older people (Palmer *et al*. 2004: 3). Does this reflect a lack of concern for the rights of older people among social workers, as well as the government (Richards 2000)? The 'welfare to work' programme and the tagging of children as young as ten years of age present similar ethical and moral dilemmas for social workers (Drakeford 2002: 291), remembering that more than any profession we are likely to have daily contact with people who come from these disadvantaged sectors of the population. Yet I can recall a time in the late 1970s when probation officers picketed outside the newly created 'short sharp centres' (similar to 'boot camps'), with placards objecting to the inhumane treatment of young offenders in these units. I have campaigned on similar issues – and still do. Again, these issues are important because they shape the face of social work.

Perhaps one of the best examples of the impact of ideology is the way that dependency is seen within the welfare state. In my experience, it is not possible for some people to move forward in situations of adversity unless they are allowed to become dependent on professionals in an organized and planned way, that is, in a way that is informed by theory (Winnicott 1965: 83–92), thereby avoiding the dangers of creating an unhealthy or growth inhibiting dependency (Trevithick 1995). I look again at this subject in Chapter 3 when the work of Winnicott is explored. Service users and carers know a great deal about dependency and many would share my perspective. Important opportunities for moving forward are lost, at huge cost to the welfare budget, due to the ill-conceived way that dependency is perceived. For this reason, we need a 'compassionate recasting' of the way that dependency is viewed in health and welfare contexts (Froggett 2002: 122) and to look closely at the reasons that underpin the anti-dependency culture that we have created (Hoggett 2000: 176).

Yet as a society we do allow certain types of dependency. For example, according to statistics available for the UK from the National Institute of Clinical Excellence (NICE) for the year March 2002 to March 2003, there were 26 million NHS antidepressant prescriptions written, costing over £380 million in total. Furthermore, 'the number of children in the UK being prescribed antidepressants, stimulants and other mind-altering drugs is soaring faster than anywhere in the world' (Boseley 2004). For example, the number of prescriptions for all psychotropic drugs to children rose from around 400,000 in 2000 to more than 600,000 in 2001 and to more than 700,000 in 2002. It is argued that there is not enough funding to pay for more and better direct services for people in need. However, what these figures indicate is the vast amount of funding that goes to the pharmaceutical industry – an important issue that warrants greater public debate.

I have described the theories drawn from other disciplines in some detail in order to stress the richness and diversity of our knowledge base and the difficulties this can create in terms of establishing a coherent framework. To know more about 'parent' theories can help us to recognize their 'offspring', such as the link between humanism as a philosophy and a person/client-centred approach. The perspective adopted in this text emphasizes the importance of social workers developing a vital and ongoing dialogue with the social sciences in order to develop a more rigorous, intellectual approach to knowledge in order to be able to apply this knowledge in practice. This dialogue has not always been a focus within social work: 'Mainstream social work has rarely looked into the social sciences purely in a spirit of genuine intellectual enquiry or exploration, searching for new insights and understandings which might in turn lead to new forms of practice and intervention' (Jones 1996: 194). It is hoped that the new social work degree will provide an opportunity to engage with the social sciences in a more in-depth way.

Theories analysing the task and purpose of social work

Under this second heading on the subject of theoretical knowledge, we look at the task and purpose of social work. This is an area 'hotly contested since its inception' (Dominelli 2002b: 3) and one that is fraught with confusion, both for individual social workers and social work agencies (England 1986: 68). All actions, including the implementation of particular practice approaches, perspectives, skills and interventions, are intellectual in character. For some authors, the difficulty in identifying the task and purpose of social work is not so much about role confusion as about disagreement. Should social work be about reform or revolution? Should we be seeking to 'fit' people into the system, or to change the system – or do both? Will social work be overtaken by its control function, at the expense of being able to care for people? The following is an account of some of the major theories used to analyse social work practice. Some explicitly attempt to relate the knowledge gained from other disciplines to practice situations.

Howe's influential categorization divides social work into four paradigms, where a paradigm constitutes 'all assumptions, theories, beliefs, values and methods that make up a particular and preferred view of the world' (Howe 1987: 22).

- *functionalists – the fixers* (e.g. psychosocial approaches; behaviourism)
- *interpretivists – the seekers after meaning* (e.g. client-centred approaches)
- *radical humanists – the raisers of consciousness* (feminist and radical social work)
- *radical structuralists – the revolutionaries* (e.g. Marxist social work).

(Howe 1987: 49)

This framework, and later revisions, remains influential (Payne 1997: 64; Stepney 2000b: 23-4) but is open to question, particularly the relevance of this conceptualization, and those that follow, to contemporary social work practice. Also, some categories do not sit easily together. For example, there is an important overlap between radical humanists and radical structuralists paradigms, which I would tend to group together, and many commentators would not place psychosocial approaches and behaviourism within the same category (Payne 1997: 64).

Payne covers some of the same territory in his *three views of social work*:

- *reflexive-therapeutic views* ('promoting and facilitating growth and self-fulfilment')
- *socialist-collectivist views* ('seeking cooperation and mutual support in society so that the most oppressed and disadvantaged people can gain power over their own lives')
- *individualist-reformist views* ('meets individual needs and improves services' but sees individual and community growth as unrealistic or unachievable).

(Payne 1997: 4–5)

Dominelli divides the role and purpose of social work into three types. These roughly correspond with Payne's categories, which are included in brackets:

- therapeutic helping approaches (Payne's *reflexive-therapeutic views*). Counselling exemplifies this approach, particularly the work of Carl Rogers (1951, 1961). The main focus is on the individual and his or her psychological functioning.

- maintenance approaches (Payne's *individualist-reformist views*). This approach links to Davies's (1994) analogy of social workers as maintenance mechanics. Davies argues that the main task of social work is to ensure that people can cope and manage their lives.
- emancipatory approaches (Payne's *socialist-collectivist views*). This approach links to radical social work (see Appendix 10) and later writers who adopt a more critical or activist perspective (Fook 2002; Healy 2000). 'Those endorsing an emancipatory approach to social work have an explicit commitment to social justice and engage in overt challenges to the welfare system if it is seen to thwart this goal' (Dominelli 2002b: 4).

What is missing from the above list is an explicit mention of social work's role as an agent of control, although this is implied. Parton looks at this important area and at whether social work is primarily a rational-technical activity or a practical-moral one. He argues that 'social work is much better characterized in terms of "indeterminacy, uncertainty and ambiguity", (Parton 2000: 460). In a later article, Howe (1994: 518) simplifies the activities involved in social work, which he summarizes in terms of:

- care
- control
- cure.

This conceptualization is helpful because it highlights the shift that has taken place in recent years away from notions of *care* and *cure* towards those involving *control*. One of the best examples of this shift can be seen in the way that anti-social behaviour among young people has been reconceptualized – and criminalized – under the heading 'youth offending' (Yates 2004). 'Control measures' may be justified in order to provide 'protection' where risk is deemed to be involved. However, control can be exercised in other, more subtle ways. This may involve controlling the availability of resources and services or controlling the activities of employees through the implementation of quality control inspection and procedures (Sinclair 2002: 434–5).

Howe's conceptualization also reminds us of the central place that caring holds within social work: that caring for people can help bring about positive change, recovery or reparation – or cure (Winnicott 1986: 116). It states that where people have been cared for too little, particularly in childhood, or where we find that basic human needs have not been met, this can lead to emotional insecurity, dependency needs and a limited ability to deal with the complexities of everyday living. This can sometimes (but not always) result in a range of distressed and disturbed behaviour. The hope is that by providing care for people who have not received enough, for whatever reason, we will be able to compensate for the lack of original care and, ultimately, help them to move on independently, and without the continued involvement of health and welfare services. In my experience, the act of caring for others has to be thought through very carefully. To be effective in bringing about positive change, reparation or recovery, it has to be the right kind of care, delivered in a way – and at a time – that maximizes the benefits of that care (Trevithick 1998). This kind of change and reparation is brought about in situations where, through our knowledge and intervention skills, we support the developmental task or growth process to start up again and to have its own momentum and motivation (Weick 1983; Winnicott 1986: 120).

Practice theories or social work approaches

Under this third and final heading on the subject of theoretical knowledge, we look at the development of practice theories – also known as *social work methods* (Stepney and Ford 2000), *social work approaches, practice approaches,* or simply as *approaches* (Marsh and Triseliotis 1996; Milner and O'Byrne 2002; Payne 1997: 58; Pierson and Thomas 2002: 477). Again, the absence of a common language is evident. Social work approaches are described by Payne as *practice theories* and are defined as follows:

> Practice theories are relatively discrete sets of ideas prescribing appropriate social work actions in particular situations. Psychological or social explanations of human behaviour are applied to social work situations, and actions are prescribed, based on the worker's assessment of the situation. Practice theories are usually informed as separate, relatively complete and coherent sets of ideas. However, aspects of them are often used eclectically, in combination.
>
> (Payne 2000: 332–3)

This understanding of what constitutes a practice theory was not evident in research undertaken by Marsh and Triseliotis. For example, when newly qualified social work/probation practitioners were asked to identify those theories that they found useful, and were still using in their work, over 80 theorists and theoretical approaches were cited (Marsh and Triseliotis 1996: 51). These findings suggest that the practitioners interviewed were confused about how to define an 'approach' in relation to practice and that the theories and methods taught on social work courses are wide ranging. 'A number of respondents simply referred to single rather idiosyncratic theories and practice models, such as "the Stanley Cohen Model", "alcohol and drugs", or the "Prochaska and Diclemente's Model for Change"' (Marsh and Triseliotis 1996: 52). Of the 80 theorists/theoretical approaches mentioned, seven 'core models' emerged. Most of these were derived from psychology, that is, from humanist, behaviourist and psychoanalytic theory, described in more detail in the next chapter. Interestingly, none of the 'models' identified in this research derived from a sociological perspective, which may reflect the individualization of problems, as well as the emphasis given to psychology on social work programmes. It is interesting to note that in 1957, Germain identified only three major approaches and that by 1983, he had identified 15 approaches (Germain 1983). It would be fascinating to map the number of 'approaches' used in practice today.

Most of the core models identified in Marsh and Triseliotis's research are covered in the practice approaches located in the appendices of this text and, therefore, are not explored in detail in this chapter. These seven practice approaches are:

1 behavioural approaches
2 cognitive approaches
3 crisis intervention
4 person/client-centred approaches
5 psychosocial approaches
6 task-centred work
7 *Stages of Change* (also known as the *Cycle of Change*).

The appendices also include three further perspectives, which draw on a more sociological perspective to varying degrees, namely:

• ecological perspectives
• feminist perspectives
• radical social work perspectives.

To summarize, in this section on theoretical knowledge three areas have been explored: knowledge 'borrowed' from other disciplines; theories analysing the task and purpose of social work; and practice theories. We now turn to look at the role of factual knowledge in social work.

Factual knowledge

This section looks at the second area of knowledge, namely factual knowledge. Again, it is important to stress that the three types of knowledge identified in this text overlap and interweave, sometimes making any distinction difficult and somewhat arbitrary. Common terms used under this heading include facts, data, statistics, figures, records, research findings or evidence, and proof; that is, facts that are verifiable in some way and 'capable of falsification' (Gambrill 1997: 144). Factual knowledge is often used to confirm or refute theories, or to describe theories in ways that are accessible, provable and applicable outside the domain of theory. For example, theories on the widening gap between rich and poor can be confirmed or refuted by referring to statistics for and against this argument. In situations where new factual knowledge has emerged to challenge knowledge once thought to be true, there is a necessity to create new theories or explanations. Again, this stresses the tentative nature of our knowledge base and the fact that knowledge should always be open to review and change in ways that can confirm or refute hypotheses developed or conclusions drawn.

I would argue that our professional credibility can be seriously undermined if we do not have certain facts at our fingertips. The best example of the importance of factual knowledge is evident in relation to the different laws that regulate contemporary social work practice, and the powers and duties within which social work operates. However, it is an area where concern has been expressed both in terms of the extent and quality of law teaching on social work programmes (Ball 1997: 37–8) and the way that practitioners use the law to influence decision-making. This gap in our factual knowledge base is not confined to law. Others have argued that since 1975, 'there has been an on-going process of theoretical stripping out of the social work curriculum' and that in its place we have seen social work values being used as 'a substitute for knowledge and understanding' (Jones 1996: 190–1). This supports the myth that our intentions are enough: the view that if we mean well, we will do well. Similar concerns about the factual knowledge base of social workers have been expressed in relation to welfare rights, as well as the extent to which students are familiar with UK statistics on poverty and social inequalities and their impact on people in terms of life chances (Gordon *et al*. 2000; Gordon and Spicker 1999).

This kind of information can make distressing reading, yet factual information of this kind is essential to effective practice. There is no shortage of research and statistics on the impact of poverty, yet in recent years this knowledge has not influenced practice to any marked degree (Jones 2002a: 8). For example, although it is well documented that not all claimants receive their full benefit entitlement (Walker and Walker 2002: 52), we are still not at a point where all practitioners engage in benefit checks as a matter of course. These subject areas – the law, welfare rights and poverty – are all mentioned in the guidance document in relation to the new degree. It will be interesting to see the weight given to these subjects and to see how they are covered on social work training programmes and integrated into contemporary social work practice. (A source of factual information can be found in *Social Trends*, which every year publishes statistics on general issues relevant to social work, such as health, housing and homelessness, unemployment and income inequalities between men and women.)

Knowledge that has a more factual basis can be described in different ways: as *specialist knowledge* (Fook 2002: 37); *technical knowledge* (Healy 2000: 79); *content knowledge* (Gambrill 1997: 120); *professional knowledge* (Fook 2002: 25); or *formal* or *product knowledge* (Sheppard *et al*. 2000; Sheppard *et al*. 2001; Sheppard and Ryan 2003). These terms imply specialist knowledge and expertise. For some authors, they can place the professional in the role of an 'expert', where professional knowledge is placed in a potentially 'privileged' position (Fook 2002: 37) in relation to the knowledge that service users and carers bring to the situation. Again, a key question in this context is what knowledge is deemed relevant, and who decides (Jones 1996; Webb 1996)? This leads to further questions about when, where and how this knowledge should be taught and in what context – in universities or in practice, or in both (Richards *et al.* 2005)?

Some knowledge is given – that is, it is formal, written, researched and ready for use. For example, the policy and practice guidelines that social work agencies lay down indicate what knowledge is required and expected of practitioners in certain situations. Sheppard *et al.* (2001: 864) describe this as *formal* or *product knowledge*, because 'it refers to existing knowledge, which may be applied' (Sheppard and Ryan 2003). In this conceptualization, product knowledge is linked to *rule based* behaviour; that is, the principle that when you encounter a particular situation, you act in a particular way. Sheppard *et al.* describe this as follows:

> if research findings indicate approach B is the most effective with problem A, and problem A is the one confronted by the practitioner, then approach B should be adopted.
>
> (Sheppard *et al.* 2000: 466–7)

Evidence based practice is given as an example of this kind of rule based approach, albeit one that is criticized because it 'tends to view the process of knowledge application as unproblematic, in that little reference is made to the complexities of such application, or the intellectual procedures involved' (Sheppard *et al.* 2000: 466–7). That is not to deny 'the potential significance of using rigorous evidence in practice' (Sheppard *et al.* 2000: 466–7), but it is to stress that we are on dangerous ground if we allow abstract rules and codes to become an end in themselves (Penna 2000: 220). The perspective put forward in this text argues that when confronted with the complex problems and the range of variables regularly encountered in social work, this kind of rule based 'technical rationality' (Schön 1991) is rarely possible. Instead what is needed is a knowledge base that can provide a range of different options in ways that 'offer guidelines for action in the average daily situation, rather than complete rules about what to do' (Payne 2002: 125). Whether knowledge is given or assumed, the ability to think critically and reflectively when involved in the task of problem-solving is essential (Gambrill 1997: 144). This is a theme we return to in the following section on practice knowledge.

A major difficulty encountered when attempting to identify the knowledge base of any profession is how best to order and classify that knowledge. One way to do this would be to refer to classifications that have already been created, such as the requirements laid down under the heading 'Indicative Knowledge Base' in the National Occupational Standards for Social Work, which call for practitioners to 'understand, critically analyse, evaluate, and apply' knowledge in their specific area of practice across a number of subjects (see Appendix 11 for a full list of subjects). The following example explores a section of the occupational standard's knowledge requirements, in order to help us to identify the kind of factual issues that could be significant, either as background information or as information that may be relevant to a particular piece of work. For example, if we take the first heading cited in NOS (1d), the following knowledge is required:

1. The legal, social, economic and ecological context of social work practice
d.   Theories of poverty, unemployment, health, impairment and other sources of discrimination and disadvantage and their impact on social exclusion

All the topics listed cover a vast subject area and for this reason, it is only possible to provide a snapshot of the kind of factual information that might be relevant. Nevertheless, this task is important because social workers are involved with people from some of the most disadvantaged sectors of the population – which makes it crucial that we know something about the nature of that disadvantage, and what it means in terms of life chances.

General population statistics

The population of the UK was 58,789,194, according to the 2001 Census. Of this total, the ethnic minority population constituted 4.6 million, or 7.9 per cent of the total population of the UK; that is, 92.1 per cent of the population labelled themselves as 'White' in 2001 (*Social Trends* 34). The female population slightly outnumbered the male population (51.4 per cent) (Goring and Thomas 2004: 21).

Poverty

In 2002/03, 12.4 million people, or 22 per cent of the population, were living in low-income households. Of these, 3.6 million were children and 2.2 million were pensioners. The figure for both these groups has fallen in recent years (Palmer *et al.* 2004: 3).

In 2000/01, 58 per cent of families in Great Britain received some form of social security benefit or tax credit (*Social Trends* 33).

Unemployment/employment

Around 7 million workers, 4 million women and 3 million men, earn less than £6.50 per hour. Of these working women, over 43 per cent earn less than £5.00 per hour. Half of all women in full-time jobs and 80 per cent of part-time women workers fall below the Council of Europe's decency threshold of £6.31 per hour (Equal Opportunities Commission).

The gap between men and women's pay is evident at all levels. According to the Equal Opportunities Commission, it is estimated that women still earn on average between 20 and 25 per cent less than men.

Health

Some 10.3 million people aged 16 or over, or 17.6 per cent of all people living in the UK, said they suffered from limiting long-term illness (Goring and Thomas 2004: 137).

In 2001, there was one qualified dentist in England and Wales for every 2,500 people (Goring and Thomas 2004: 179). A similar figure exists for doctors in general practice.

The Registrar General's Classification of Social Classes

The Registrar General's classification of socioeconomic classes is important because these descriptive distinctions are used in official statistics, particularly health statistics. The different occupational categories are often used to highlight 'occupational advantage and disadvantage in British society' (Giddens 2001: 288).

Social class		Examples of occupation
Non-manual		
I	Professional	Dentist, doctor, accountant, lawyer
II	Intermediate	Teacher, manager, farmer, nurse, social worker
IIIN	Skilled non-manual	Secretary, clerical worker, shop assistant
Manual		
IIIM	Skilled manual	Electrician, cook, carpenter, builder
IV	Semi-skilled manual	Agricultural worker, assembly worker, bus conductor
V	Unskilled manual	Laundry worker, cleaner, labourer

Without a knowledge of this classification, it is not possible to understand concepts such as the *inverse care law* (Hart 2004; Shaw and Dorling 2004). This describes the extent of class based health inequalities and the fact that those areas of the UK with the greatest need, due to poverty, pollution, poor housing, urban and rural neglect and decay, are the areas with the lowest levels of health care provision.

Impairment

In 2004, the number of long-term claimants who were sick or disabled had increased by one-third since 1996 and stood at 2.4 million (Palmer *et al.* 2004: 3).

Some 1.5 million people who want paid work are economically inactive – chiefly lone parents and people who are sick or disabled.

Other sources of discrimination and disadvantage and their impact on social exclusion

- In 2001/02 over 10,000 children in Great Britain were permanently excluded from school. This was around 4 per cent higher than the previous year. Boys outnumbered girls by nearly 5:1 (*Social Trends* 2004).
- In 2003, around 200,000 households were accepted as homeless by their local authority, more than double the figure for 1997 (Palmer *et al.* 2004: 6). (A definition of a 'household' is: 'A single person or group sharing living accommodation. For many purposes of sociological analysis, this is a term preferable to the more widely used *family*' (Abercrombie *et al.* 2000: 166).)
- In 2001, 3.5 million pensioners, or 6 per cent of the population, lived alone in the UK, the large majority being women who had been widowed (Goring and Thomas 2004: 16).

Fact sheets that summarize key issues and recent research are useful in providing practitioners with up-to-date information. For example, the *Highlights* produced by the National Children's Bureau (NCB) in relation to children and young people, are helpful in this regard. A list of the themes covered in *Highlights* can be found on the NCB website and purchased for a small fee. However, fact sheets of this kind should not be considered a blue print – all information gained still needs to be related to the specific situation and individual circumstances, a task that calls for reflection and critical thinking.

With the development of information technology runs the problem of information overload, as well as the difficulty of processing information in ways that lead to effective action. Accessing relevant factual information can be a time consuming and skilled activity and it can also be difficult to select and order facts in ways that contribute to problem-solving and effective interventions. Knowledge gained has to be capable of being utilized, sometimes described as 'knowledge utilization' (Fisher 2002: 42), 'utility' or 'fit for use' (Pawson *et al.* 2003: 39). This is particularly relevant in inter-agency work and interdisciplinary practice contexts where knowledge may extend across a broad framework (Lupton 2000: 173–4). Finding a common conceptual and practice language can be difficult where professionals adopt a different knowledge and value base: these and other practice constraints can limit the extent to which factual knowledge is acquired and used (Sheppard *et al.* 2001: 864). For example, few statutory social workers currently have access to online research data, and have had only limited training in how to implement or apply research or research-based technologies (Walter *et al.* 2004: 40). The use of factual information in this way is a central feature of evidence based practice, covered later in this chapter.

Practice knowledge

This third and final section on the knowledge base of social work – described in this text as practice knowledge – looks at the way that knowledge is implemented in practice. Again, this subject overlaps and interweaves with the areas of knowledge already covered, although its focus is not on abstract theoretical and factual issues but on direct practice. It describes how knowledge can be used in different practice situations to produce sound judgements and effective decision-making. In particular, this section looks at a number of different terms that have been used to identify and to enhance practice effectiveness. These terms include coverage of the professional use of self, critical reflection, critical thinking, practice wisdom and the importance of developing hypotheses. The section then goes on to look at some of the ways that practice has been conceptualized by authors such as Gambrill and Sheppard. It asks 'what knowledge do practitioners draw on?' and reminds us that our knowledge is limited in relation to the theories and practice approaches that social workers regularly use in their work. This calls for further and better research, particularly research that is capable of identifying theories that practitioners formulate which are generated from practice, sometimes referred to as *practitioner-generated* knowledge.

Professional use of self: the importance of self-knowledge and self-awareness

One aspect of knowledge is based on our self-knowledge and self-awareness as people, that is, it draws on what we already know about ourselves, what we continue to learn when we encounter new experiences and what we learn through our contact with others. The maxim 'know thyself' goes back to antiquity. For example, it was central to the writing of the Greek philosopher Socrates (Hadot 1995: 20). A second aspect of this capacity for self-knowledge is sometimes called the *professional use of self*, which states that 'the reference point for an understanding of others is one's self. ... to know oneself is to know the other and to know the other is to know oneself' (Howe 1987: 113). This links to our use of empathy and intuition, a theme we return to in Chapter 4. For example, England argues that 'the intuitive use of self' is the central process in social work (1986: 32).

In the course of our lives, we may acquire a rich pool of experience but it is our capacity to reflect on our experiences that leads to self-understanding, self-awareness and self-knowledge – the sense that we know 'what we are doing, why we are doing it, how we are presenting ourselves' (Lishman 1994: 145). An ongoing development of self-knowledge leads to *self-identity*, 'through which we formulate a unique sense of ourselves and our relationship to the world around us' (Giddens 2001: 698). Again, this process is dependent on the ability to conceptualize and intellectualize our experiences in ways that create meaning and understanding. Gibbs and Gambrill link self-knowledge to critical thinking and *meta-cognitive* levels of thought, that is, knowledge about the reasoning process, which they describe in terms of tacit, aware, strategic and reflective levels of thought (1996: 11).

According to Dominelli, *self-knowledge* of this kind is 'a central component of the repertoire of skills held by the reflective practitioner' (2002b: 9). Its importance is also noted in relation to assessment: 'In addition to knowledge of personal and social problems and the assessment process, a good understanding of oneself is also required' (Crisp *et al.* 2003: 32). It describes how we work with people – how we communicate our knowledge, skills and understanding in ways that are helpful and not demeaning, and how we communicate our values in terms of the care, concern and respect we hold for other people. I sometimes describe this as working from our *best self*, which involves working from a place in ourselves where we are disciplined, open to other people and prepared and available to engage in the experience. It can be hard to be our *best self* over a long period, which is an issue that residential workers know well, as do other professionals who are required to adopt high professional standards over a considerable length of time.

For example, it is sometimes the case that, as professionals, we are made to become what Winnicott (1965) describes as a *reliable hate object* – that is, we become the target of a host of negative feelings that others ascribe to us. (I am assuming here that we have not behaved 'hatefully'.) Our professional status, the roles we are required to take up or even our personal characteristics can be sufficient grounds for some people to project or to load their negative feelings on to us. When we are acting from our professional *best self*, we are aware that an appropriate response is not to retaliate, or even to reject the projection, but instead is to try to understand what we have become for this person and why they might need to react to us in this way. Some people choose their reliable hate object quite wisely and seem to know that the person they have chosen is reliable in terms of their reaction. Having offloaded negative feelings in this way, some people can feel a degree of relief.

One of the best places to observe this kind of reaction is at the school gates at the end of the day. Some children, once they recognize a safe person – their parent/carer – can give that person 'hell'. Having done this, they contentedly get on with doing what children do, much to the amazement of the bewildered parent/carer, who is still trying to recover from the onslaught. Some parents/carers might think it wise to contact the school to see if there are problems there, only to learn that the child has been 'an angel' at school, making it difficult to understand the child's reaction except in terms of personal failure as a parent/carer. Some children are very wise in their choice of reliable hate object. Where this involves a person, it is often an individual who, because of his or her reliability, consistency and predictability, gives the child a sense of security and safety (Winnicott 1986: 116). Often it is parents who fulfil this need. If we relate this to social work, intense negative emotions that are targeted on certain practitioners in this way may be providing an opportunity for the service user to work through negative feelings that could not have been projected in this way before due to a lack of reliability and consistency (Winnicott 1965: 228).

To continue to develop self-knowledge and self-awareness of this kind requires the capacity for openness and the ability to be self-critical. However, it can be difficult to be open and honest when we feel threatened or under attack (Kenny and Kenny 2000: 34). Defensiveness can be understood in terms of an individual's personality trait but also in terms of factors in the wider environment that can lead to defensiveness and an inability to think creatively. For example, some people do not live or work in a supportive environment. As a result, there is little opportunity to acquire *wisdom* – that is, the 'ability to think and act, utilizing knowledge, experience, understanding, common sense and insight' (*Collins Dictionary*). The attacks on social work by the media give rise to this kind of defensiveness (Stepney 2000a: 1). It is also an understandable reaction given 'the uncertainty that is an inevitable part of human interaction and decision-making' (Roy *et al.* 2002: 124).

Critical reflection/reflexivity

In recent years, a number of terms have emerged to describe some form of reflection process. These terms include reflection, reflective practice, self-reflection, reflectivity and reflexivity. In addition, another set of terms stress the importance of adopting a critical stance – a task that calls for practitioners to review critically their assumptions and reasoning (Gambrill 1997: 101). These terms include concepts such as critical reflection, critical appraisal, critical analysis, critical reflexivity, critical thinking, critical engagement, critical practice, self-criticality and critical social work. For some writers, the two sets of terms are linked. Given the range of terms that have emerged, it is only possible to cover a few in detail.

Schön (1991), an influential writer in this field and the author of *The Reflective Practitioner*, uses different terms to describe the ways that 'professional practitioners must discover and restructure the interpersonal theories of action which they bring to their professional lives' (1991: 353). These include *reflective conversations with the situation, reflection-on-practice* and *reflection-in-action* (Thompson 2000: 284). Others use the term *reflective practice* to describe 'thinking things through, questioning our guidelines and developing our theories to respond to new situations' (Payne 2002: 128). For Adams, 'reflectiveness is a stage on the way to criticality. It is not enough to be reflective. We need to use the understanding that we gain from reflection to achieve change' (2002a: 87).

Fook also emphasizes the importance of reflexivity (2002: 43) and a reflective approach and a practice that can 'assist us in subjecting our practice to a more critical gaze, at the same time allowing us to integrate our theory and practice in creative and complex ways' (2002: 39). This links to Sheppard's account of the concept of reflexivity:

> The notion of reflexivity emphasises the social worker (i) as an active thinker, able to assess, respond and initiate action and (ii) as a social actor, one who actually participates in the situation with which they are concerned in the conduct of their practice. Thus the reflexive practitioner, in practical terms, is one who is aware of the socially situated relationship with their client(s) i.e. with a clear understanding of their role and purpose; who understands themselves as a participant whose actions and interactions are part of the social work process; who is capable of analysing situations and evidence, with an awareness of the way their own participation affects this process; who is able to identify the intellectual and practice processes involved in assessment and intervention; who is aware of the assumptions underlying the ways they 'make sense' of practice situations; and who is able to do so in relation to the nature and purposes of their practice.
>
> (Sheppard 1998: 767)

Critical thinking

A different way to describe Sheppard's 'active thinker' is the ability to demonstrate *critical thinking*, which Gambrill defines as follows:

> Critical thinking involves the careful examination and evaluation of beliefs and actions in order to arrive at well reasoned ones.... Critical thinking involves clearly describing and taking responsibility for our claims and arguments, critically evaluating our views no

matter how cherished, and considering alternative views.... This involves paying attention to the process of reasoning (how we think), not just the product.

(Gambrill 1997: 125–6)

To apply critical thinking in this way requires us to have acquired considerable background knowledge and some specialized areas of knowledge (Gibbs and Gambrill 1996: 5). For example, I think it is essential for practitioners to have specialized knowledge on the way that poverty, deprivation, disadvantage, social exclusion and ill health impact on specific groups of people, and what role we might play to help alleviate their negative consequences (Sheppard 2002; Stewart 2000a: 263–4). However, the ability to apply this critical edge – or investigative and questioning capacity – is not solely dependent on individual practitioners. So much depends on the context – and whether the opportunity for critical reflection and experimentation is possible, particularly in the statutory sector, where agency policy and practice guidelines often act to constrain innovative and creative practice. Supervision provides an important point of contact from which to explore the assumptions and attitudes that we bring to our work. It also provides the opportunity to link critical reflection and critical thinking with practice effectiveness and continuous professional development (Lishman 2002: 103–4). However, the opportunity to use supervision in this way can become compromised by workload pressures and the use of supervision as a form of managerial control where the focus is on meeting agency targets rather than the quality of the experience and service being provided.

Practice wisdom

A term used by a number of writers is 'practice wisdom', which refers to the 'wisdom derived from experience and personal knowledge about "what works" in a given practice situation' (Stepney 2000a: 21). It is particularly valuable when it is used to indicate the development of 'theory which arises directly out of practitioners' experiences' (Fook 2002: 158). However, it would be difficult to know whether this type of theorizing is taking place because in the UK most practitioners do not find the time or the opportunity to write or to publicize their knowledge, except perhaps informally through their contact with colleagues and other professionals. More commonly, the term practice wisdom is used in a loose way and is often equated with 'common sense' notions (Barker 2003: 334), making it difficult to know whether the wisdom relates to transferable knowledge gained from practice experience or merely 'an anecdotal ragbag of folk remedies' (Pinker 1990: 64). As a result, we have no reliable way to evaluate the extent that practice wisdom contributes to our stock of knowledge, or how applicable or transferable these wisdoms are across different situations.

Developing hypothesis

One way to think about a hypothesis is as a disciplined attempt to link theory and practice. Developing a hypothesis, or 'working hypothesis', is designed to provide a tentative explanation for a group of facts or phenomena that are so far unproven. This is, in effect, a type of 'informal' theory-making (Pinker 1990: 24), where the task is to either accept or refute the hypothesis in the light of further information, facts or other data. Popper states that: 'All scientific knowledge is hypothetical or conjectural' (1994b: 93). Here Popper is stressing the tentative nature of our knowledge and the importance of attempting to refute our theories and to learn from our mistakes. In relation to practice, formulating hypotheses marks an attempt to define, explain and predict certain events, with a view to increasing our understanding in order to arrive at an agreed course of action. For example, in a referral concerning non-attendance at school, we might formulate a variety of hypotheses: that the child is absent from school because s/he is looking after a parent or younger sibling; s/he may be being bullied; s/he finds the teacher frightening; s/he finds the culture of school bewildering; his/her parents do not have the money to buy essential clothing; and so forth. We would then test these hypotheses against any evidence available, remembering that: 'Testability has degrees: a theory which asserts more, and thus takes greater risks, is better testable than a theory which asserts very little' (Popper 1994b: 94).

Formulating hypotheses is an important part of Schön's notion of *reflection-in-action*. Like Popper's formulation, the task is to 'test' different hypotheses against the evidence in ways that either confirm or refute each hypothesis (Schön 1991: 146). The one that 'most successfully resists refutation' is the one to be accepted, but tentatively. Other factors, not yet recognized, may come to light that 'resist refutation more successfully still' (Schön 1991: 143). The importance of seeking verification has to be stressed and is consistent with an evidence based approach to practice. The use of unclarified or unconfirmed data based on intuition or common-sense notions alone is not enough (Coulshed and Orme 1998: 21).

What knowledge do practitioners draw on?

When thinking about the use of knowledge in practice, including the concepts mentioned above, it is important to acknowledge at the outset that we currently know very little about the different types of knowledge that practitioners draw on in their ongoing, daily contact with service users, carers and others (Sheppard *et al.* 2001: 863). This use of knowledge in practice is described by Gambrill as *domain-specific knowledge* or as *procedural knowledge*, which 'includes the skills required to implement content knowledge.... What facts may be important to know? What theories and concepts will be helpful? What skills do you need to use this knowledge effectively?' (1997: 102). For Gambrill, *performance skills* are needed to put useful and relevant concepts, theories and strategies into effect. This involves developing effective problem-solving and decision-making skills and finding ways to overcome the barriers that block the development of these skills (Gambrill 1997: 109).

A different way to conceptualize the application of different types of knowledge in practice contexts is described by Sheppard as *process knowledge*. This refers to 'the processes by which social workers are able to make sense of, make judgements about and act upon situations. In essence, this refers to the cognitive or reasoning processes which are used in practice situations to inform decision-making' (Sheppard *et al.* 2001: 864). This is in contrast to formal or product knowledge, described earlier, which refers to the application of existing knowledge or rules (Sheppard and Ryan 2003). In a number of important papers based on their research, Sheppard and his colleagues describe how practitioners 'make sense of, define and respond to, situations' (Sheppard and Ryan 2003: 157). They tentatively conclude that, whilst there is evidence of an extensive use of legal knowledge, 'there is limited direct evidence of overt employment of research to inform practice' (Sheppard and Ryan 2003: 172).

This problem is not unique to social work but can be found in relation to other professions, such as medicine. For example, the results of an ethnographic study undertaken in general practice found that:

> Clinicians rarely accessed and used explicit evidence from research or other sources directly, but relied on 'mindlines' — collectively reinforced, internalised, tacit guidelines. These were informed by brief reading but mainly by their own and their colleagues' experience, their interactions with each other and with opinion leaders, patients, and pharmaceutical representatives, and other sources of largely tacit knowledge. Mediated by organisational demands and constraints, mindlines were iteratively negotiated with a variety of key actors, often through a range of informal interactions in fluid 'communities of practice', resulting in socially constructed 'knowledge in practice'.
>
> (Gabbay and le May 2004: 1013)

In this context, *tacit knowledge* means implicit, rather than explicit (theoretical/factual) knowledge: that is, 'knowledge gained from watching what colleagues do, trial and error, reflective practice, peer approval, client satisfaction and so on' (Pawson *et al.* 2003: 11). The findings of Gabbay and le May do not sit easily with an evidence based approach, but they do confirm that similar problems to those experienced by social workers also exist in medicine:

practitioners do not have the time (nor usually the skills) to rigorously review all key sources of knowledge themselves. Thus the real skill of the practitioner might be expected to be that of learning reliably from the knowledge of trusted sources either individually or through working in a community of practice.

(Gabbay and le May 2004: 1051)

Practitioner-generated knowledge and research

Concepts such as the professional use of self, critical reflection, critical thinking and practice wisdom have emerged in an attempt to enhance practice effectiveness. However, whilst reflection and criticality are important concepts they tell us little about the type and quality of knowledge that practitioners draw on, or how effectively that knowledge is being used. It is clearly the case that some practitioners do not have an extensive knowledge base, or do not have the abstract or conceptual language to identify the knowledge that they are using in their work, such as theories, facts and concepts. In terms of continuing professional development, it is not possible to value or to build on expertise that does not have a conceptual language. On the other hand, there are times when practice can be ahead of theory, particularly in situations where new social problems have emerged and there has not been the opportunity to describe and to conceptualize these developments. For example, before research was available on the impact of drug abuse, practitioners had to rely on their own practice experience when confronted with problems related to addictions of this kind (Barber 2002).

To provide the opportunity for learning and development, we need to emphasize the importance of 'both reflective and empirical methods' of knowledge development (Fook 2002: 158). In relation to empirical methods, it is easy to ignore the fact that practitioners not only use knowledge but are also capable of generating new knowledge – new theories and new explanations – based on their knowledge in practice. In order to tap into this knowledge, more opportunities and funding needs to be made available to encourage practitioners to research and write about their work, so that the practice knowledge that they hold can be shared, debated and developed further. This links to the notion of the 'practitioner researcher' – a development that is hampered by the fact that 'Practice has not yet been defined as a research site' (Preston-Shoot 2004: 30).

In the USA, the setting up of 'master classes' [sic], where 'experts' describe their practice experience, have proved to be valuable contexts for sharing experiences and ideas in this way. In addition, more bottom-up research is needed where the research question involves exploring, in a more open-ended way, the knowledge base that practitioners actually use, as opposed to the knowledge they are expected to use within their agency context. The work of Sheppard *et al.* and Gabbay and le May, described above, are important examples of this form of research. Research of this kind could help to resolve some of the confusion that exists in terms of the relationship between agency policy and practice and what constitutes the knowledge base of social work. Whilst agency procedures are often based on knowledge, such as policies that meet legal requirements, a sound and critically reflective knowledge base involves more than merely adhering to agency policies and procedures.

Example: linking theoretical, factual and practice knowledge

The following is an example of how we might link theoretical, factual and practice knowledge. The example relates to a service user who is known to social services and who has asked for support to cope with his or her depression. The coverage of factual knowledge focuses on electronic sources because other sources of information on depression are covered in other sections of the example and throughout the text. The different websites mentioned are listed in the notes at the end of this chapter.

Theoretical knowledge

Our theoretical knowledge of depression should include some under-standing of the medical model and biomedical approaches and the symptoms that indicate clinical depression within this model. In addition, we may choose to look at critical perspectives on the medical model, such as those that can be found in social theories of depression (Brown and Harris 1978); feminist perspectives (Trevithick 1998; Ussher 1991); anti-psychiatry perspectives (Langan and Lee 1989: 48); concerns about the 'medicalization' of emotional and social problems as 'diseases' (Giddens 2001: 156–7; Illich 1976; Onyett 2000: 216); recent literature from social work practitioners and academics theorizing in this field (McLeod and Bywaters 2000; Scambler 2003; Sheppard 1997); and, importantly, people involved in the survivor movement (Ennis, J. 2000). This theoretical information gathering is not designed to dismiss or attack the medical model and its adherents, but to place this model in context, in order to think critically about its relative merits and limitations and how this knowledge may inform our work with the person in question.

Factual knowledge

Factual knowledge can be gained from a variety of sources. For example, it may be helpful to refer to statistics on the incidence and prevalence of depression among men and women. (The incidence of a disease indicates the number of new cases of a disease over a specified time period, whereas prevalence indicates the number of people who have a disease.) This kind of factual information on depression can be gained from a variety of electronic sources. For example, the health encyclopaedia at the NHS Direct website[1] has a link to some basic but well-referenced information about depression, such as symptoms, medical diagnosis and treatment options.[2] This information is available via the National Electronic Library for Health.[3] This website is a gateway to a large number of electronic resources and is an important resource for knowledge based decision-making. Current clinical guidelines on the treatment of depression are available from National Institute of Clinical Excellence (NICE).[4] More detailed evidence about a variety of interventions in particular patient groups, such as children or people with other health problems, as well as depression, is provided in the latest edition of the Cochrane Library, which can be accessed from its consumer-friendly site[5] or from the official site.[6] More details about the benefits, dosage and side effects of anti-depressant drugs can be found on the British National Formulary website,[7] and where there may be a 'risk to self or others', reference to the Mental Health Act 1983 would be appropriate.[8]

These references relate to national data. In relation to the help available, local resources and services can be found by referring to the relevant Primary Health Care Trust and to information available from social services. Services provided within the statutory sector may be located in hospitals or in health centres and are likely to be multi-disciplinary. Some funded services may be located in the voluntary sector, perhaps focusing on specific types of provision, such as postnatal depression groups.

Practice knowledge

With regard to experiential knowledge, our starting point might be our personal and practice experience of depression and the current knowledge we have about the different services and resources available. If working in a multidisciplinary context, it would be important to maintain contact with other professionals. Access to other resources could also prove valuable, such as books written about depression (Godfrey 2004; Gut 1989; Rowe 1994), or articles written by academics drawing on a more practice oriented perspective (Sheppard 1994; 1997). A starting point might be to refer to the coverage on depression in one of the excellent compilation texts (Adams *et al.* 2002a; Adams *et al.* 2002b; Davies 2000; Davies 2002; Stepney and Ford 2000). Service user choice must be integral to any problem-solving and decision-making processes. This may involve providing information on service users' and carers' rights under the Data Protection Act 1998 and Freedom of Information Act 2000. This assessment and information gathering process is likely to include a detailed exploration of how the person in question perceives events, including their depression. It should include a focus on any internal and external pressures experienced and on the kind of help that is being sought. If appropriate, it may also be helpful to collect baseline data in order to indicate the severity of the depression, and to monitor changes, using a standard questionnaire such as the Beck Depression Inventory (1987).

Of particular importance is the coping capacity of this individual, and the extent to which he or she is able to be central to their own recovery process. Where self-recovery is limited, it is important to identify other sources of support, both personal and professional. In terms of the kind of help being sought, and choices of the individual in question, it may be possible to offer a range of interventions, based on our knowledge, our own generalist and specialist skills, the capacity of the agency and wider social environment to support this individual and the intervention approach agreed. This may involve negotiating with other professionals or advocating on behalf of the person in question. These are important interventions, particularly when working in multidisciplinary contexts. Sound communication skills lie at the heart of this work (Trevithick *et al.* 2004), as do good listening, observation and assessment skills (Milner and O'Byrne 2002). Information gathering of this kind is a time-consuming activity. However, in relation to the problems regularly encountered in social work, such a knowledge base can be built up over time and will only require updating.

The importance of research-informed social work practice

Research is included under a separate heading within this chapter because it describes how we acquire and produce knowledge, rather than being knowledge in its own right. This final section highlights the way that the findings of research contribute to our theoretical, factual and experiential knowledge base. In particular, it focuses on the way that evidence based practice has been conceptualized within social work, and its advantages and limitations. It also covers the way the certain key terms have been defined, beginning with how research has been defined within social work:

> Research comprises the results from systematic investigations based on planned strategies. This may be primarily research that involves systematic inquiry based on observation or experiment. It may also be secondary research, research that takes primary research studies as its objects of inquiry.
>
> (Walter *et al.* 2004: xiii)

Research may deploy qualitative or quantitative methods of investigation. 'Qualitative research methods aim to understand the dynamics of social phenomena in their natural context, and to generate rich description from diverse perspectives. They produce data in different forms but typically as language' (Walter *et al.* 2004: xi). This may draw on small samples and is often based on interviews. Quantitative research methods 'aim to measure or quantitatively assess social phenomena; to describe representative samples in quantitative terms; and to estimate or test quantitative relationships. They produce data in numeric form' (Walter *et al.* 2004: xi). These may include 'frequency counts, averages and percentages, and which may be analysed by statistical methods' (Fuller and Petch 1995: 200). Qualitative research methods are more established in social work and, whilst some authors advocate the development of 'multi-method research' (Shaw 2000: 291), the relationship between quantitative and qualitative methods has been subject to conflict with regard to 'the status of objectivity, truth and knowledge about the proper nature of scientific enquiry' (Cheetham *et al.* 1992: 139).

Evidence based practice

Walter *et al.* define *evidence* as 'the empirical findings of research' (2004: ix). Although the term empirical is sometimes used in different ways, in this text it refers to findings based on experiment, observation and research (Munro 1998b: 5; Payne 1997: 32) or, more simply, findings based on experience in some way (Gambrill 1997: 94). In recent years, certain concepts have come to dominate the field of research and practice effectiveness. Terms such as *'what works'* evidence (Hudson and Sheldon 2002: 65), which looks at the success of particular interventions or approaches to a particular task, and *evidence based practice* (Sheldon and Macdonald 1999) have come to take on particular meanings. The way that evidence based practice is conceptualized in social work has been influenced by the work of Sackett and its application within medicine:

> Evidence-based medicine is the conscientious, explicit, and judicious use of current best evidence in making decisions about the care of individual patients. The practice of evidence based medicine means integrating individual clinical expertise with the best available external clinical evidence from systematic research. By individual clinical expertise we mean the proficiency and judgment that individual clinician acquire through clinical experience and clinical practice.
>
> (Sackett *et al.* 1996: 71)

As we can see, Sackett *et al.* emphasize the importance of practice experience, or *practice knowledge*, as well as 'external clinical evidence from systematic research'. This differs from the way that some authors conceptualize evidence based practice within social work, which places less emphasis on the 'expertise' and experience that practitioners bring to bear and instead focuses more on the quality of 'current best evidence' (MacDonald 2000: 123) and the availability of 'technically better research' (Macdonald and Macdonald 1995: 61).

> Evidence based practice denotes an approach to decision making which is transparent, accountable, and based on a consideration of current best evidence about the effects of particular interventions on the welfare of individuals, groups and communities. It relates to the decisions of both individual practitioners and policy makers.
>
> (MacDonald 2000: 123)

The position adopted is that judgements based on scientific knowledge, or scientific reasoning, enhance professional decision-making (Gibbs and Gambrill 1996: 17). This supports the view that 'science makes knowledge' and that 'practice uses it' (Darlington and Scott 2002: 1). However, it is important to take a broad view of what constitutes evidence. So much depends on how evidence is conceptualized, acquired and analysed – particularly who defines evidence and for what purpose. Also important is the extent to which research relates to the complexities of social work (Shaw 1996: 173; Shaw 2003: 112). Unless these complexities are acknowledged, evidence based practice can unwittingly represent 'the process of knowledge application as unproblematic' and fail to recognize 'the complexities of such application, or to the intellectual procedures involved' (Sheppard *et al.* 2000: 467).

These points highlight differences in the way that evidence based practice is perceived within social work. For example, Sheldon argues that practice effectiveness is best achieved by using specific methodologies, namely 'systematic reviews of randomized control trials and meta-analysis of controlled trials' (Sheldon 2000: 67). Again, this reflects the view that 'a formal rationality of practice based on scientific methods can produce a more effective and economically accountable means of social care' (Webb 2001: 60). Some researchers argue for a combination of different methodologies (Ferguson 2003: 1012) and avoid the notion of a hierarchy of research methods. However, with regard to intervention research, Sheldon argues for a 'very definite hierarchy (not just a continuum) of methods', with systematic review of randomized control trials (RCTs) or meta-analysis of controlled trials located at the top of this hierarchy and single case designs at the bottom (Sheldon 2000: 67–70). In order to understand these terms, it may be helpful to look at how they have been defined. Most definitions are from the *Cochrane Collaboration Handbook,* but another useful source of definitions can be found on the website of the Centre for Reviews and Dissemination (CRD), University of York.

1 *A review.* This is 'any attempt to synthesize the results and conclusions of two or more publications on a given topic' (Centre for Reviews and Dissemination).

2 *Systematic review.* This describes: 'A review of a clearly formulated question that uses systematic and explicit methods to identify, select and critically appraise relevant research, and to collect and analyse data from the studies that are included in the review. Statistical methods (meta-analysis) may or may not be used to analyse and summarize the results of the included studies' (Cochrane Collaboration).

3 *Meta-analysis.* This describes: 'The use of statistical techniques in a systematic review to integrate the results of included studies. Sometimes used as a synonym for systematic reviews, where the review includes meta-analysis' (Cochrane Collaboration).

4 *Randomized control trial (RCT).* This describes: 'An experiment in which investigators randomly allocate eligible people into intervention groups to receive or not to receive one or more interventions that are being compared. The results are assessed by comparing the outcomes in the treatment and control groups' (Cochrane Collaboration Library).

5. A *single case design* (also known as an N *of 1 design*/N = 1 or **single-subject design**). This describes a research procedure where the behaviour of a single subject, such as an individual service user or carer, is used as a comparison and a control (Barker 2003: 399). These research designs are largely quantitative (Sheldon 2000: 70) and for this reason, provide different research results. 'Many reviews are not systematic but are still valuable and helpful so long as the reader is aware and takes account of this fact' (Light 2003).

It is argued that RCTs are 'the most sure-footed way of piecing together what works', yet it is also acknowledged that RCTs are 'found less frequently' in social work (Macdonald and Macdonald 1995: 49–50). Indeed, to date there have been no large-scale RCTs undertaken in the UK in the field of social welfare for a range of different reasons. Some authors argue that RCTs are not always appropriate in the field of social welfare (Cheetham *et al.* 1992: 22) because of the difficulty in finding two parallel groups, and the fact that it can be difficult to control other variables that are likely to influence the outcome of a study. In addition, professional ethics and the issue of power need to be considered (Everitt 2002: 112), particularly in relation to service user choice, and the fact that to intervene may be a statutory requirement (Cheetham *et al.* 1992: 22).

Perhaps in response to the way that evidence based practice has been promoted within certain quarters, some academics have chosen to use different terminology to link theory and practice – and to stress the important relationship between research and practice effectiveness. These include terms such as *knowledge-based practice* (Fisher 1998), *research-based knowledge* (Parton 2000: 453) and *critical best practice perspective* (Ferguson 2003: 1005). A fourth term, *research-informed practice,* is preferred by some for the fact that it recognizes 'the diverse and often subtle ways in which research can impact on practice, and the fact that there are other influences on practice' (Walter *et al.* 2004: xii). It is worth noting that articles published in some medical journals, such as the *British Medical Journal,* increasingly question the use of RCT methodology in relation to complex interventions (Prideaux 2002). Thus, for Sackett *et al.*: 'Evidence based medicine is not restricted to randomized control trials or meta-analyses. It involves tracking down the best external evidence with which to answer our clinical questions' (1996: 72).

When considering the link between research evidence and social work, it is important to examine whether the populations and settings of the research are similar to those encountered in contemporary social work practice in the UK. One of the most researched practice approaches is described under 'the range of techniques known collectively as CBT' (Sheldon 2000: 70). In research studies on the use of this collection of approaches, the vast majority produce 'significantly positive results against comparisons with either no intervention or with other commonly employed methods' (Sheldon 2000: 70). However, other factors need to be brought into the picture. For example, Sheldon acknowledges that much of the research to support the effectiveness of behaviourist and CBT approaches originates from psychologists and the work of clinical social workers based in North America. The extent to which this research is transferable and relevant to the work of UK practitioners when it originates in a different profession – and in different countries – is open to question. Or again, the claims made tend to be based on 'discrete problems in somewhat protected settings' (Sheldon 2000: 70). In other words, they are based on behaviour that has been broken down in ways that can be researched under clinical situations, where the impact of other variables can be controlled. This context can be far removed from the problems regularly encountered in contemporary social work in the UK, a point acknowledged by Sheldon who states that 'extending the use of CBT to routine settings (where things are a whole lot messier) is undoubtedly the next challenge for this discipline' (Sheldon 2000: 70).

It is clear that behaviourist or cognitive approaches, whether used separately or in some combination, are important and I believe that both should be taught on all social work programmes. For example, both approaches encourage the gathering of baseline data at the outset, making it easier to monitor changes and to evidence effectiveness – a task that other approaches could usefully adopt. However, greater caution is called for when claiming that certain practice approaches are more effective than others until we have more and better research on this subject. The reality is that, at present, we do not have an extensive body of research in social work to draw on. One reason for this may be due to a sense of ambivalence, in certain sections of social work, about the value of our knowledge base. This ambivalence is usually described in terms of a theory–practice divide, a theme summarized in the following account.

The ambivalent relationship between theory and practice

For many years there has been an ambivalent and troubled relationship between theory and practice within social work. This has been described in different ways: as an 'anti-theoretical' stance (Coulshed and Orme 1998: 3) and as an 'intellectual purge' (Jones 1996: 204). This links to Bion's notion of 'anti-thought' (Bion 1967). For some commentators, the tension does not lie in the difficulty of translating theory into practice but more in terms of who is to control the shape and future of social work: should it be practitioners, academics, employers, the government through those it selects to regulate social work or a partnership of all? A range of factors contribute to these tensions, including the lack of agreement among academics about which subjects should be taught. Also, the attitude adopted in the past by CCETSW, and some state employers, in relation to social work academics and training programmes has at times had a negative impact on the way that social work is organized, both in practice and in universities. As a result, these factors have tended to reinforce the divide between theory and practice and led to further tensions and fragmentation, leading Jordan to conclude that we need to 'pull together':

> the profession has not been well served by its 'theorists', nor has it always been helped by its research community. Theory has been offered as a menu of choices between ideologies, all derived from outside practice (such as feminism, anti-racism and socialism), and none embracing the essential features that unite all aspects of expertise.... Theory should seek to pull together the defining characteristics of the profession, and to explain apparent inconsistencies and contradictions in particular research findings.
>
> (Jordan 2004: 17)

On the other hand, it has been said that 'social work needs to articulate, celebrate and broadcast the theoretical frameworks which inform, structure and facilitate its operation' (Coulshed and Orme 1998: 3). We may be moving towards this kind of recognition, and an end to this 'intellectual purging', with the current emphasis given to knowledge in the Post Qualifying Award and the new degree and masters in social work. However, serious tensions remain in relation to the current organization of social work, particularly in the statutory sector. A 'managerialist' approach does not necessarily need social workers who are creative and innovative, with a good knowledge base and sound intellectual abilities. Yet this kind of creativity is integral to critical thinking (Gibbs and Gambrill 1996: 5), reflexivity and, ultimately, to practice effectiveness. Social work may never have a genuinely exclusive knowledge base (England 1986: 33–4), and this is also true of other professions. However, its 'distinctive identity and expertise lies in its emphasis on the *social* aspects of problems and their resolution' (Jordan 2004: 17), and in the fact that 'those who practise social work are committed to the task of making life more bearable for those whom others might prefer to forget – or choose to condemn' (Davies 2002: 2).

Conclusion

This text takes as its starting point the view that all actions, including the implementation of practice approaches, perspectives, skills and interventions, are intellectual in character. In order to understand the intellectual nature of our work, I have categorized the knowledge base of social work in terms of three types of knowledge – theoretical knowledge, factual knowledge and practice knowledge – and have described these areas in some detail. I have done so in order to show that social work draws on a substantial and rich knowledge base. This has clear advantages but can also create problems when attempting to select and apply this knowledge in ways that lead to effective social work practice. I have also written in detail in order to encourage discussion and debate about our knowledge base, and the purpose of social work, because we need to explore, criticize and use the concepts described in this chapter if we are to be able to relate these themes into contemporary practice in ways that are relevant. This task remains important because we cannot shape the future of social work until we know where we are currently located and where we have already been.

In terms of our location within the wider social and welfare picture, I have argued that we need to have an ongoing relationship with the social sciences in order to engage with current developments and debates. I believe that social work has much to contribute to these debates, as well as much to learn. We take up these themes again in the following chapter, which looks at the link between knowledge and practice, particularly in relation to social work skills, competence, interventions, transferability and other terms relevant to practice.

NOTES

1 NHS Direct website homepage – http://www.nhsdirect.nhs.uk
2 For depression, NHS Direct website link – http://www.nhsdirect.nhs.uk/ en.asp?TopicID = 154
3 National Electronic Library for Health website – http://wwe.nelh.nhs.uk
4 National Institute of Clinical Excellence (NICE) – http://www.nice.org.uk/ page.aspx?o = cat.diseaseareas
5 Cochrane Library's consumer friendly website – http://www.informedhealth online.org
6 Cochrane Library's official website – http://www.cochrane.org
7 British National Formulary website – http://www.bnf.org
8 Mental Health Act 1983 – see http://www.dh.gov.uk/PolicyAndGuidance/ HealthAndSocialCareTopics/MentalHealth

2 SOCIAL WORK SKILLS, INTERVENTIONS AND PRACTICE EFFECTIVENESS

This chapter describes how the knowledge base of social work, covered in the previous chapter, is applied in practice. Again, it is important to stress that the points covered do not relate solely to work with service users and carers. A great deal of our contact in social work is with other professionals and with others who may play a significant role in relation to service users and carers. Therefore, the application of theoretical, factual and experiential knowledge needs to encompass all situations where, as practitioners, we are interacting with others in some way. The perspective emphasized in this section, and in other parts of this text, is that practice is an intellectual activity, as well as a practical endeavour.

The chapter looks at a range of practice terms and how these have been defined, beginning with what we understand by *competence, skill* and *intervention*. It argues that for these abilities to be *transferable*, they have to be linked to a sound knowledge base. In particular, considerable coverage is given to interventions, and how to demonstrate their effectiveness. The second half of this chapter looks at differences in practice terminology and identifies how these terms are used in this text. It then goes on to apply these concepts in practice, taking ten common choices that arise in relation to direct work and applying these concepts to a case example. One point that emerges from this account is that, as a profession, we do not share a common language. As a result, there is a tendency for social work academics, educators, practitioners, students and others to use practice terms differently. This confusion about terminology can make it difficult to give a coherent and 'intellectual account' of ourselves (England 1986: 56). It can also mean that the effectiveness of our interventions may be lost if the terms we use have no agreed and precise meaning, or if they are not used in a rigorous way. And if we are confused, then it is likely that service users, carers and others are also confused, which once again places notions such as empowerment, partnership or service user/carer involvement on shaky foundations.

Competence

When looking at the notion of *competence*, it is important from the outset to sort out the difference between this and *competences* because the two are not the same. The term *competences* was first introduced into the new Diploma in Social Work by the Central Council for Education and Training in Social Work (CCETSW) in 1989 but, interestingly, it does not appear in the dictionary. A more accurate way to describe competences is as a competency based approach (Coulshed and Orme 1998: 8). The appropriateness of this approach within social work has been the subject of a great deal of debate and criticism, which is well documented (Ford and Hayes 1996). For example, it has been argued that competences miss all that is complicated in the interaction between social worker and service user because it follows a 'prescriptive account of social work education' (Coulshed and Orme 1998: 8), thereby moving the focus from 'reason to rote' (Howe 1996: 2). A different range of criticism states that competences stand in opposition to a reflective approach to practice (Payne 2002); ignore the central importance that process plays within a given interaction (Adams 2002b: 258); and impede the development of anti-oppressive practice and a values based approach within social work (Dominelli: 2002b: 8–9). Howe summarizes the concerns expressed by many academics and practitioners in relation to competences:

> Such an outlook seeks to establish routines, standardized practices and predictable task environments. It is antithetical to depth explanations, professional integrity, creative practice, and tolerance of complexity and uncertainty.
>
> (Howe 1996: 92)

I agree with many of these criticisms. It seems to me to be a fundamentally flawed approach to reduce a series of actions to simple sequences and then to attempt to apply these sequences in ways that cannot fully embrace the complex and interrelated nature of many of the situations encountered in social work. Many of the essential capacities, interpersonal skills and personal qualities that we bring to our work – such as our compassion, concern and care for others – are integral to the interaction and the quality of service provided, but these essential attributes can be overlooked where the focus is on a superficial conceptualization of behaviour.

However, if competences or a competency based approach is not appropriate for the complexities inherent in social work, we need to arrive at a different and better format from which to evaluate effectiveness – that is, some way of being able to know for ourselves, and to demonstrate to others, that our efforts have been worthwhile in terms of what has been achieved. If we do not do this, others will. Some argue that the knowledge requirements written into the National Occupational Standards (TOPSS 2002) are an attempt to reconcile some of these differences:

> The development of holistic models of competence encompassing higher-order abilities of cognition and reflection offers some reconciliation of the positions, although underlying disputes remain about curriculum priorities, for example, as between critical theoretical content and learning for efficient service delivery.
>
> (Whittington 2000: 107)

The argument that has been centred around competences links to differences of opinion in relation to social work education and training, covered in greater detail in Chapter 1. Should the focus of social work courses be primarily oriented to *training* students in terms of what they need to know to ensure efficient, effective and economic service delivery? Or should the primary orientation be towards education and providing a broader understanding, and the ability to acquire and apply knowledge when confronted with new or complex situations? Howe takes up this point:

> Without a knowledge of underlying theory and principles, the practitioner is confined to performing surface responses according to pre-coded procedures. Information checklists, problem categories and recommended responses do not need the knowledge, skills and discretionary powers of the autonomous professional.
>
> (Howe 1996: 92)

These concerns are very real, yet we also need to recognize that the notion of *competence* is now embedded in UK government policy. For this reason, it is important to revisit this concept to see if we can reconcile some of the tensions between 'reason' and 'rote'. It seems possible to do this if we look at the way that competence was originally defined by CCETSW:

> Competence in social work is the product of knowledge, skills and values. In order to provide evidence that they have achieved the six core competences students will have to demonstrate that they have: met practice requirements; integrated social work values; acquired and applied knowledge; reflected upon and critically analyzed their practice; and transferred knowledge, skills and values in practice.
>
> (CCETSW 1996: 17)

Interestingly, the NHS Competency Framework for Primary Care Trusts describes competence in terms of knowledge, understanding and skills –

that is, the values requirement for social work is replaced with that of understanding. It seems to me that the inclusion of all four features – knowledge, understanding, skills and values – can provide a valuable framework from which to evaluate and enhance practice effectiveness. However, it is important that the concept of competence is broadened to include not only the abilities of individual practitioners but also the knowledge, understanding, skills and values that service users and carers bring to the encounter, and the way that these four features are supported in the wider social and environmental context. This emphasizes the interrelationships between structural and individual factors in relation to the context in which services operate and are delivered.

Skills

A central feature of competence is the notion of *skill*. However, it is a word that is often used interchangeably with concepts such as competence, intervention and techniques (O'Hagan 1996: 12), or defined in terms of 'social work values, ethics, and obligations' (Cournoyer 2000: 5). To explore this subject more thoroughly involves drawing on authoritative writers outside the field of social work. For example, in Welford's conceptualization, skills have three characteristics:

1 they involve 'an organized and co-ordinated activity in relation to an object or situation' in ways that underlie performance;
2 skills are learned gradually, through repeated experience; and
3 they involve actions that are ordered and coordinated in a 'temporal sequence' or in chronological order.

(Welford 1958: 18)

'Within any skilled performance these characteristics are closely bound together, and in order to gain an adequate view of the nature of skill all must be considered' (Welford 1958: 18). For example, the skill of driving a car involves a pre-set collection of actions that need to be carried out in sequence or in chronological order; that is, we generally put the gear stick into neutral, switch on the ignition, press the accelerator, press the clutch and so on. In time, these tasks can be performed without conscious thought, although at the outset considerable mental concentration is required before we can drive in a reliable and safe way. The interrelated nature of different actions supports the argument against a competency based approach, which separates out different actions or activities into their component parts. Driving would have no meaning if we only focused on one aspect of the task, such as switching on the engine. Similarly, the NOS requirement that 'social workers must be good at timekeeping' has no real meaning without a sophisticated understanding of human psychology and of why reliability and consistency is an essential attribute when working to establish significant working relationships.

As human beings, there are huge individual variations in relation to the skills we learn – and do not learn – and how easy we find this learning. In general terms, one factor that enables a skill to be learned is a degree of innate or developed ability that an individual possesses. In this context, ability is defined as something 'inborn and relatively stable, while a skill is easily modifiable by practice' (Schmidt 1975: 120–1). From this perspective, abilities can enable the development of other abilities and a number of skills. For example, the ability to speak one foreign language often signals the ability to learn other languages. Similarly, acquiring basic skills can lead to the development of intermediate and advanced skills with additional training and/or practice. This learning is best acquired where time is set aside to prepare for the performance of a particular skill – and where guidance is provided beforehand and feedback available afterward (Legge 1970: 235). In addition to guidance and feedback from others, the capacity for self-reflection and self-criticism are important. Interestingly, there has been some debate within medicine as to whether certain attributes and qualities, such as empathy, can be taught. One view, which I would support, is that empathy can be improved and successfully taught if it is embedded with students' actual experiences with patients (Mercer and Reynolds 2002: 9), or service users and carers.

If we define skills in terms of what we learn, then interventions describe how we put that learning into practice, that is, the actions we perform to influence events. However, it is not always easy to separate the two concepts because they overlap. For example, we do not know how well a skill has been learned until we try to put that skill into practice, as an intervention. Because of this complex interconnection, at times I have grouped skills and interventions together in this text. The following section attempts to categorize the different levels and types of skill that are important within social work, so that we can identify, order and conceptualize the level of competence and performance that we bring to our work. These same categories can be used to identify and analyze the effectiveness of our interventions.

Level of skill

The level of skill that can be learned, through training and experience, can range from basic to advanced skills:

- *basic skills*: these relate to skills that are required in many social work situations, such as the use of open and closed questions or providing information on resources. Many of the skills and interventions described in this text begin as basic skills.

- *intermediate skills*: these relate to the skills that are needed to deal with more difficult situations, such as working with service users who we find difficult to engage, or who come across as withdrawn and unresponsive.
- *advanced skills*: these skills relate to being able to work with problems that are multifaceted and intractable or in situations involving conflict, hostility or high levels of distress.

Generalist and specialist skills

In broad terms, skills can also be categorized into generalist and specialist skills. These can be practised at a basic, intermediate or advanced level.

Generalist skills. All practitioners use generalist skills, such as the 56 skills described in this text. These can be categorized as basic, intermediate or advanced skills and interventions, again depending on ability, experience and training. In the past, generalist skills of this kind have tended to be associated with a generic practice approach – a term used to describe an approach that 'assumes a common core of knowledge, values and skills underpinning all practice' (Parsloe 2000: 145). Between 1970 and 1990, a generic approach dominated much of social work, but in recent years we have seen a move towards greater specialism. Some writers also link generalist skills with an eclectic approach, a theme covered later in this chapter. In the USA, this broader range of skills is sometimes described in terms of the 'generalist' social worker, that is, 'a practitioner whose knowledge and skills encompass a broad spectrum and who assess problems and their solutions comprehensively. The generalist often coordinates the efforts of specialists by facilitating communication between them, thereby fostering continuity of care' (Barker 2003: 176).

Specialist skills. Parsloe sees specialist practice as indicating 'either a division of labour or superior knowledge and skill about a client group, problem area, methods or settings' (Parsloe 2000: 145). For example, the specialist skills used by practitioners who are adopting a behaviourist practice approach are likely to demonstrate significant knowledge and experience in relation to systematic desensitization, contingent management and so forth (Sheldon 2000: 74–6). Specialist skills can also describe the use of specific skills in relation to a particular service-user group, such as the use of Makaton with people with learning difficulties (Pierson and Thomas 2002: 263) or the specialist skills required to work with the grief that accompanies bereavement (Worden 2000). Specialist skills imply that additional training has been undertaken, although Parsloe notes that: 'There has been little research into whether the different practices have different outcomes. A question, of particular relevance for social work education, concerns the stage at which social workers should specialize' (2000: 145).

It is important to avoid placing generalist and specialist skills, and basic, intermediate and advanced skills, in any hierarchy. In some situations, the use of basic skills is all that is required: to use advanced skills could complicate our efforts and lead to confusion. This framework can also be useful when attempting to understand the skills that service users, carers and others bring to the encounter and the extent to which they feel able to act with confidence on their own behalf. Some practice approaches, particularly behaviourist and cognitive approaches, give considerable emphasis to the task of teaching people new skills, particularly social skills – interventions that could be useful in relation to other practice approaches.

Interventions

The word *intervention* is used a great deal, but is rarely defined. It comes from the Latin *inter* (between) and *venire* (to come) and means 'coming between'. As such, interventions lie at the heart of everyday social interactions and 'inevitably make up a substantial majority of human behaviour. They are made by those who desire and intend to influence some part of the world and the beings within it' (Kennard *et al.* 1993: 3). Thus interventions are not confined to professionals. In any given encounter, different people may intervene at several points, on their own behalf or on the behalf of others, in an attempt to influence the course of events in some way. The social work interventions described in this text refer to the purposeful actions we undertake as professionals in a given situation, based on the knowledge and understanding we have acquired, the skills we have learned and the values we adopt. Interventions are, therefore, knowledge, skills, understanding and values in action. In social work, the term is thought to be 'analogous to the physician's term *treatment*' (Barker 2003: 226; Epstein and Brown 2002: 34).

In social work, the context for our intervention may focus on individuals, families, communities, groups or organizations and may take several forms, depending on their purpose and the generalist and specialist nature of the work described earlier. In broad terms, interventions can be categorized as directive and non-directive (Coulshed and Orme 1998: 216).

Directive interventions. In general, interventions that are directive attempt to purposefully change the course of events. In this task, they may be highly influenced by agency policy and practice or by the practitioner's perspective on how to move events forward. For example, they can involve offering advice, providing information and prescriptive suggestions about what to do, or how to behave, in certain circumstances. This range of interventions can be particularly important, and a professional requirement, where immediate danger or risk is involved.

Non-directive interventions. In non-directive interventions, 'the worker does not attempt to decide for people, or to lead, guide or persuade them to accept his/her specific conclusions' (Coulshed and Orme 1998: 216). Instead, the task is to work with service users, carers and others in ways that enable individuals to decide for themselves. This may involve helping people to problem solve or to talk about their thoughts and feelings and the different courses of action open to them (Lishman 1994: 107). Counselling skills can be important in this regard (Thompson 2000b: 302–3).

Often our work involves both directive and non-directive elements and, once again, it is important to see both types of intervention as having something to offer in particular situations, since both have advantages and disadvantages (Mayo 1994: 71–2). Certain practice approaches may be better suited to certain individuals or types of problem and may involve being more directive. For example, behaviourist, cognitive and psycho-social approaches are generally considered to be more directive, but subject to some differences in emphasis depending on the perspective adopted with an approach and the disposition of the practitioner. On the other hand, community work tends to be non-directive, while person/client-centred approaches almost always fall within this category.

Time periods and levels of intensity

Different types of intervention, and practice approaches and perspectives, are likely to involve different time periods and levels of intensity depending on the point at which the work is staged, the setting where the work is located, the problem presented, the individuals involved and agency policy and practice. For example, some practice approaches have a time-limited factor incorporated into their way of working, such as task-centred work, crisis intervention and some behavioural approaches, and may be preferred by agencies for this reason. However, even for practice approaches that were originally set up to work with people for a considerable time – or in an open-ended way – such as psychosocial approaches, the current trend is towards more planned short-term, time-limited and focused work (Fanger 1995: 323–34).

Whilst we are required to negotiate with service users and carers, and to take account of their needs and expectations in relation to the different options we might recommend, it is still not common practice in my experience for social workers to offer service users and carers a choice as to whether they might prefer a more directive or non-directive approach (Lishman 1994: 107). The same lack of choice can be seen in relation to the practice approach adopted. This situation is likely to change with the involvement of service users and carers in social work training programmes and in decision-making processes in relation to agency policy, practice and service delivery (Barton 2002: 401–6; Croft and Beresford 2000: 385–93).

The focus of interventions

There is some disagreement among social work academics, and some practitioners, about the purpose and use of different interventions. Some authors argue that 'the term intervention is oppressive. It indicates the moral and political authority of the social worker to invade "the social territories" (Payne 1996: 43) of service users' (Dalrymple and Burke 2002: 56). Others share the concern about the potentially 'invasive' nature of interventions and the way they can be used to control others (Langan and Lee 1989: 83) and to support 'the assumption of specialist knowledge' (Fook 2002: 37). Jones is similarly concerned about power differences, and the attitude of social workers, particularly in relation to people living in poverty: 'the working-class poor have been generally antagonistic toward social work intervention. They have rejected social work's downward gaze and high interventionist and moralistic approach to their poverty and associated difficulties' (Jones 2002a: 12). Whilst it is true that any intervention in the 'wrong hands' can be oppressive, or delivered in ways that have no clear purpose or in-depth understanding, in my experience 'the working-class poor' – and other service user and carer groups – do not speak with one voice in terms of how they experience social work. Depending on the nature of the problem for which our help is being sought or offered, some look for – and sometimes find – interventions that are warm, empathic, caring and non-judgemental, where practitioners demonstrate 'relevant experience and show appropriate knowledge' (Lishman 1994: 14). For some social workers, these attributes are an essential feature of any intervention. They come from our humanness – from the way we communicate our commitment, concern and respect for other people – and describe qualities that many service users and carers value (Cheetham *et al*. 1992: 6; Wilson 2000: 349).

A second main area of disagreement is focused on whether interventions should be targeted on personal change or wider societal, environmental or political change. Once again, so much depends on the kind of help that is being sought. Some people may want help accessing a particular service, or other forms of help, and may not welcome the use of interventions that are designed to steer them in a particular direction – in this case, towards social action (Payne *et al*. 2002: 9). On the other hand, some problems are likely to recur – or become worse – if no collective action is taken. For example, I worked on a council estate a number of years ago where the electricity tariff was set at an unacceptably high level by the electricity board for that region. Helping these tenants to set up a Tenants Association, and to take collective action, resulted in the tariff being significantly lowered. Similarly, the changes directed at people on benefit, such as the 'welfare to work' schemes adopted in the USA and in the UK (Halpern and Bates 2004: 32), are likely to impact negatively on the quality of life of a considerable number of people unless these policies are challenged and modified.

We do not yet live in a fair and just society and it may be our moral duty to draw attention to the 'social ills' that disadvantage certain sectors of the population, namely people who are poor, sick, frail or disadvantaged and discriminated against in some way. Advocacy skills may be important in this context, but so too is the voice of 'users', remembering that 'user involvement can also be seen as an aspect of social action' (Thompson 2002b: 303). Lishman takes up this point: 'We need to acknowledge with our clients the social, political, economic and structural pressures which disadvantage them, and to promote collective action. We need to work in ways which are empowering and do not individualize structural problems' (1994: 108). Within this picture, the danger of individualizing problems is profound. For example, it is likely that the practice approaches, skills and interventions described in this text will be mainly used by practitioners in one-to-one work. This need not be the case, because most can be adapted to include working with groups, including working with communities, but these options are rarely used or preferred. Yet it is clear that the use of groupwork approaches, alongside one-to-one work, offers an important opportunity to focus on both personal and social change, based on collective action (Doel 2005).

When and how to intervene

The GSCC's concept of 'minimum sufficient intervention' (GSCC 2002) has added a further complication in relation to whether, when and how to intervene, and how to do so in ways that are purposeful and effective. What is meant by the words 'minimum' and 'sufficient' is difficult to know and even harder to measure. The absence of clear guidance in this area runs the risk of placing social workers in a *double bind*, where we are damned if we do – and damned if we do not – purposefully intervene to influence the direction of events. As we can see when we examine the findings of the inquiries into the deaths of children known to social services, the inability to intervene, or the inability to intervene purposefully, drawing on a sound knowledge base, can have tragic consequences. This was true in the case of Victoria Climbié (Department of Health 2003) and in other inquiries into child deaths (Gough 1993; Munro 1996). A failure to intervene can be as serious as an ill-timed, poorly expressed or purposeless intervention. When we hold back, we may hope that by not intervening we will not be held responsible for any 'real or fantasised damage resulting from the intervention' (Kennard et al. 1993: 11). For example, I recall working with a colleague who felt it was inappropriate to intervene to stop two boys from fighting – that the boys 'needed to sort it out themselves'. I took the position that fighting was the only behaviour the boys knew and could rely on and that it was our professional responsibility to stop the fight and to help them to find new ways to resolve their differences.

If we decide that we must act, it is important to ensure that we have a mandate to so and that our involvement is justified (Doel 1994: 24). As stated earlier, for the most part this is derived from social work's legal mandate (Roberts and Preston-Shoot 2000: 183). Establishing a mandate for our involvement is important in all situations, but particularly where we have a statutory responsibility to intervene, which may be the case when children or adults are at risk. In addition to our legal mandate, other decisions may influence our involvement, such as:

1 the urgency of the problem;
2 the consequences of not alleviating the problem;
3 the chances of success in alleviating the problem;
4 the ability of the worker and agency to help with the problem;
5 the motivation of the client to work on the problem;
6 the support which the client will receive from other people; and
7 the specific nature of the problem.

(Doel 1994: 27)

Writing in a groupwork context, Kennard et al. (1993: 6) provide a guide to the kind of questions that we might ask ourselves before making an intervention. I have adapted and extended this guide for use in different social work contexts as well as groupwork, such as one-to-one work, work with families, groups, communities or organizations.

What is the situation that I am observing or have encountered?
↓
What data/evidence is there to confirm/refute my hypothesis?
↓
What factors or processes are contributing to this situation?
↓
Do I judge the situation/interaction to be constructive, destructive or neutral?
↓
Would it be advantageous to change this situation/interaction?
↓
Is it possible to change it?
↓
What intervention(s) might influence this situation/interaction?
↓
Is the necessary intervention within my repertoire?
↓
Is the time/opportunity ripe for an intervention?
↓
What measures can I use to assess the effectiveness of my intervention?
↓
What measures can I use to assess the effectiveness of my work overall?

Clearly, it would not be possible to ask ourselves this range of questions in all situations, particularly those that call for immediate action, but questions of this kind can be useful when preparing for an interview, when reviewing what happened after the event and when attempting to explore the impact of our interventions. The ability to deliver immediate, on-the-spot interventions is an important skill and one that becomes less daunting with practice and experience. Nevertheless, on-the-spot interventions can still be stressful, particularly when we feel nervous, pressured, tired or when confronted with complex problems or confusing situations.

Whenever possible, it is helpful to draw on documentary evidence to support our subjective observations, hypotheses and assessment of the situation. Gathering baseline data before the work begins, and as it progresses, is essential if we are to be able to monitor and evaluate the effectiveness of our work. However, collecting baseline data is not always an easy task for practitioners or service users and carers to undertake, which may be why this task is so often overlooked. Asking service users and carers to record behaviour or events when they already feel weary, or overwhelmed, can feel like 'one task too many' – and a job that can be easily forgotten when confronted with other pressures. It can also be difficult to analyse this data – making data collection feel like 'one task too many' for practitioners. Similar difficulties can emerge when we ask service users, carers and others to evaluate our work. This too can be a time consuming activity but, nevertheless, an important one (Cheetham *et al.* 1992: 53). Until these activities are built into the social work task and process, they are likely to be seen as secondary to other activities – a situation which is far from ideal.

Three factors influencing intervention effectiveness

In this section, we look at how to measure the effectiveness of our interventions. For the most part, effectiveness tends to be evaluated solely in terms of the performance of practitioners. However, in this section I return to themes covered in the Introduction and in Chapter 1, where I suggest that two other factors need to be included in this analysis, namely the capacities that others bring and those that the environment fosters, because these influence the outcome of a particular intervention.

If we look at the effectiveness of particular interventions from a 'capacities perspective', three factors are important. First, and centrally, the capacities that we bring to the situation as social work practitioners, in terms of our knowledge, skills, understanding and values. Second, the capacities that others bring to the encounter and the knowledge, skills, understanding and values that they operate within. Finally, the resources and barriers that exist in the wider social or cultural environment or system, and the extent to which these may enhance or inhibit the success of an intervention. From this perspective, practice effectiveness involves the ability to accurately 'read' or conceptualize and match these different capacities in ways that enable contact to be made and realistic objectives to be agreed. It is our responsibility, as practitioners, to do this 'reading' and to recommend appropriate courses of action. The following describes these features in more detail.

Practitioner's knowledge, skills, understanding and experience

Effective interventions involve being able to use our knowledge to describe the mandate for our involvement, that is, whether we are invited or required to be involved in some way. Effective interventions also involve being able to recommend appropriate courses of action, an appropriate choice of generalist skills and the specialist interventions associated with a particular practice approach. For example, our first intervention may be to clarify the purpose of our involvement or visit. This includes being able to pitch the intervention in ways that address the needs and expectations of the other person, that is, the abilities and understanding – or the capacities – that the person brings to the encounter. For both practitioners and others, these capacities are not fixed but can vary, depending on other influences, both positive and negative. In this regard, it is important to have a degree of self-knowledge about our own capacities as practitioners, particularly the extent to which we can be resilient under difficult circumstances, such as when working with people who are offensive or aggressive.

At the same time, it is important to remember that pitching our interventions is a highly skilled activity, and one that draws on our theoretical and factual knowledge and practice experience. This includes developing an understanding of the interplay between external (sociological) and internal (psychological) factors, as expressed in the capacities that others bring to the encounter and the capacities that the environment allows for and supports. Identifying users' and carers' needs and expectations is central to a needs-led approach and a perspective encouraged in some assessment frameworks (Department of Health 2000). Similarly, we are encouraged to adopt a *strengths perspective,* that is, a perspective that is based on the principle of empowerment and that takes as its starting point the view that people possess 'the inherent capacity to adapt, learn, grow, change, and use their inner resources to confront and respond to daily challenges in their lives' (Kisthardt 1992: 60). This perspective runs counter to one that adopts a *deficit perspective,* that is, one that focuses on 'the supposition that clients become clients because they have deficits, problems, pathologies and diseases: that they are, in some critical way, flawed and weak' (Saleebey 1992: 3). A strengths perspective is central to some task-centred approaches (Marsh 2002: 110) and a feature of solution focused therapy (Milner 2000: 336). It is also one that can be incorporated into other practice approaches.

Recipient's knowledge, skills, understanding and experience

The knowledge and understanding that service users and carers bring to a situation has been seriously overlooked in the past (Adams 2000a: 293; Croft and Beresford 2002: 388). This picture is changing with the involvement or 'participation' of service users and carers, and other 'consumers', in policy and practice decisions in relation to the planning, design, delivery and evaluation of services, in both health and welfare contexts (Pierson and Thomas 2002: 334–5). These developments challenge the view that social workers' judgements are necessarily superior to those held by the individual in question. Clearly, not all service users are in a position to enact decisions for themselves, such as 'involuntary clients' or people who have serious impairments or who 'lack capacity' (Munby 2000: 37). Yet despite these exceptions, it is increasingly recognized that most service users and carers have expectations and a view about the kind of services they need and want. Where their confidence is lacking or knowledge is limited, practitioners can play an important role – working in partnership – to help to meet specific needs and to work to extend people's potential or capacities in key areas (Neville 2004). Again, a 'capacity' perspective and a 'strengths perspective' are linked. The kind of questions that may be asked using both perspectives, adapted from Cowger (1992: 142), Kisthardt (1992: 71–2) and Weick (1983), could include:

- What capacities, knowledge, skills, understanding and values does this individual bring to the situation, and how can they inform and guide future actions and strategies?
- What meaning is ascribed to the problem?
- What actions have already been tried to resolve the problem, and with what success?
- What is expected or desired from the help being sought?
- If some capacities or resources are unused or poorly used, what help is needed to enhance capacity development?

These interventions enable us to focus on the knowledge, understanding and other capacities that service users, carers and others bring to the encounter and to identify specific strengths and expectations. They are framed to acknowledge an understanding of the value base that people bring and to take account of the importance of cultural diversity (Egan 2002: 51). A capacity perspective emphasizes the way that needs can drive desire. It is the experience of need and the desire to have those needs satisfied that motivate people to take risks in the hope that this will give rise to new possibilities, or yield new opportunities, that can provide the necessary impetus to help them to move forward. From this perspective, it is desire that gives rise to a feeling of hope and possibility (Phillips 1988: 84).

Environmental factors

Given the complexities inherent in social work, before we can evaluate the effectiveness of social work interventions we need to take account of the 'limited means of relief' (Cheetham *et al.* 1992: 6) available in terms of resources, services and other forms of support. This links to the concept of social capital, which provides a framework to map what is present and absent in a given community and how these relate to wealth production. This concept attempts to map the degree, range and quality of social support networks and their impact on the emotional and physical health of a particular community or neighbourhood. 'Social capital typically diminishes if it is not regularly renewed or replaced. Such depreciation is often marked by the shutdown of places where people spontaneously congregate, e.g. churches, schools, pubs and clubs' (Fuller 2000: 798). The absence of adequate funding for front-line services, and how this impacts on the services and resources available, can mean that the success or effectiveness of some social work interventions is not possible.

This takes us back to the important questions raised earlier about where our interventions should be focused. Should they focus solely on those tasks that are possible and achievable within the structural constraints that agencies face? This course of action does not challenge the status quo, but it does mean that within these limits we may be able to meet some needs – and to demonstrate effectiveness (Allan 2000: 336). On the other hand, should our interventions focus on working with others to advocate for more resources to be made available, while doing what we can to address people's needs? Since it is acknowledged that political, social and environmental factors have a significant influence on the development of certain types of problems, such as those due to the impact of poverty, deprivation and disadvantage (Jones 2002a: 7–18; Palmer *et al.* 2004), then it seems important to focus some of our knowledge and skills in this area. Indeed, as social workers we have a mandate to act in this area – that is, to 'empower individuals, families, carers, groups and communities in decisions affecting them' and to 'challenge discriminatory images and practices affecting individuals, families, carers, groups and communities' (TOPSS 2002: 4). This is a considerable undertaking when we consider the plight of people living in poverty.

> the fact remains that a significant proportion of the British population are living on incomes substantially below the average for the rest of the population and are, as such, at risk of malnutrition, hypothermia, homelessness, restricted educational opportunities, poorer health, earlier death and of being the victims of crime. For example, a child

born into a poor family is four times as likely as a child from a better-off family to die before the age of 20.

(Walker and Walker 2002: 52)

We are also encouraged to work from an ecological perspective, yet it is unclear how these requirements can be met within a climate that individualizes problems and solutions and where we have lost some of the skills and interventions required for collective action. For example, interventions that focus on wider social and cultural factors, such as advocacy (Bateman 2000) or the skills needed to bring people together, are not within the repertoire of all social work practitioners. To intervene effectively in this area not only involves good communication, observation and listening skills. It also involves, importantly, an in-depth knowledge and understanding of the way that organizations, such as health, welfare, education, housing, social services, operate – or are supposed to operate – in terms of the legal, policy and practice requirements placed on them. Although there is considerable emphasis on the importance of advocacy in relation to the new degree, in the past this has not been the case. Nor has the nature of our class-bound society been fully acknowledged and translated into specific social work skills and interventions (Smith 2002: 327).

Drawing on a capacity perspective, I have argued that three factors influence the effectiveness of particular interventions, namely the capacity of individual practitioners, those of service users and carers, and those located in the wider environment. However, it is important to stress that responsibility is not evenly spread and that, as practitioners, it is our professional responsibility to work with these factors and to frame and negotiate our recommendations and interventions accordingly. In the final analysis, 'the ultimate responsibility for organizing and delivering excellent, affordable services rests with staff' (Adams 2002a: 292), although the extent to which we can achieve specific goals may sometimes lie outside our control. It is also important to note that any skill that is not used can cease to be a skill – and that this is as true for service users and carers as it is for practitioners. Nevertheless, we may achieve more than we realize, remembering that the absence of evidence does not necessarily mean the absence of benefit.

Transferability of skills

The importance given to the transferability of skills can be seen in the fact that this subject is mentioned in all guidance documents governing social work education and practice. For skills and interventions to be transferable, they have to be related to a sound knowledge base and an understanding of human beings in their particular social contexts. They also have to be reliable and enduring across different, often difficult, situations, and to be capable of being used in ways that demonstrate a degree of accuracy and efficiency. This transition can be seen in two ways. First, it describes the way that we translate the skills we have learned into different interventions, both directive and non-directive. Second, it describes the ability to transfer the skills and interventions we have acquired to different and new situations, in ways that involve being able to:

> explain in a coherent, comprehensive and convincing manner how their practice is informed by their knowledge base, and be able to apply their knowledge and learning to new situations through appraising what is general and what is particular in each situation.
> (GSCC 2002)

This knowledge base includes an understanding of sociology and psychology, as well as other relevant theories in relation to human behaviour: 'The final factor for skill development which is reliable and transferable is an understanding of theories of human behaviour so that skills are related to individual clients and not just routine behaviour' (Parsloe 1988: 8). If theoretical and factual knowledge is central to transferability, so too is experience: 'Practice activity is also a source of transferable learning in its own right. Such learning can transfer both from a practice setting to the "classroom" and vice versa. Thus, practice can be as much a source of intellectual and cognitive learning as other modes of study' (QAA 2000: 11–12). However, it is important to state that transferring our knowledge from one situation to another is not always as straightforward as sometimes implied (Matthews et al. 2003). This is particularly true in relation to those practice approaches that have been mainly developed in clinical settings, such as behavioural approaches, where other variables can be controlled to a degree. The point to be stressed is that the transferability of skills is, like practice effectiveness, in essence an intellectual activity, as well as a practical one. For example, skills and interventions cannot be transferred if they have not yet been named – which is an intellectual activity. Or again, when confronted with complex human behaviour, such as an encounter where someone is being aggressive, it is important to have a body of knowledge and concepts to draw on to help us to understand what might be happening and why. Linking our knowledge to practice in this way means that both are constantly in dialogue, each informing the other in ways that 'invigorate, fascinate and professionally uplift' (Howe 2002a: 87).

Practice terminology

The knowledge base of social work, particularly the 'theory-practice divide' (Camilleri 1999: 30), is not helped by the absence of a common language. This can be seen in the different way that the same practice terms are used by social work educators and practitioners, a point taken up by Sheldon: 'It is often surprising how little definitional work has gone into concepts which are in everyday use in social work' (1995: 10). This confusion continues to create considerable uncertainty in ways that can undermine our intellectual and practice credibility. In order to understand these differences, the following section looks at how some of these terms have been described, and how these terms are defined within this text. These terms include in alphabetical order: electicism/eclectic approaches; methods; models; practice approaches; and practice perspectives.

Eclectic approaches

Eclecticism can be seen as a response to the diversity and complex nature of many of the problems that social work embodies (Cheetham *et al.* 1992: 51) and has important advantages. 'Eclecticism enables different ideas to be brought to bear, helps to amalgamate social work theories when they make similar proposals for action, deals better with complex circumstances and allows workers to compensate for inadequacies in particular theories' (Payne 2002: 133). Although many practitioners describe themselves as 'eclectic', not all can identify a specific practice approach or the interventions linked to this approach. In fact, the use of the term eclecticism can confuse what is happening in practice and blur the fact that some practitioners have not had sufficient education and training, practice experience or guidance in supervision to give them the knowledge and confidence to be able to dip into a range of practice approaches. Also, some practice approaches do not sit easily with one another, which can make a 'pick-and-mix' or 'salad bar' (Sheldon 2000: 65) approach less appropriate than is sometimes implied (Thompson 2002: 293). On the other hand, it is clear that some practitioners possess the knowledge, skills and experience that enable them to draw on a range of practice approaches in ways that are effective, rigorous and consistent with an eclectic approach. Social work will always involve a degree of eclecticism in order to deal with the range of different individuals and problems that fall within our orbit (Payne 1997: 53). However, too often eclecticism is used in a way that is vague, and for this reason it is not included as a distinct practice approach within this text unless cited by other authors.

Methods

Perhaps the greatest confusion surrounds the use of the term *method*. In some texts, particularly those from the USA, methods refer to the four general types of practice (Haynes and Holmes 1994). These are:

- work with individuals/one-to-one work (sometimes involving counselling)

- work with groups/groupwork (sometimes called social groupwork)
- work with families/family work (including family counselling and family therapy)
- work with communities/community work (sometimes called community organization or community development)
- work with organizations (sometimes called organizational or management consultancy).

Thompson includes the same four categories when he describes different 'methods of intervention' (2000: 65) to which I have added a fifth category which is listed above, namely work with organizations.

In an earlier, working copy of the National Occupational Standards (2002), the term method is defined as covering 'tested, accepted and recognized social work procedures and practices' (TOPSS 2002: 34). However, it is not clear what is meant by the terms 'procedures and practices'. In a later version of NOS, no definition is included. Instead the two concepts, methods and models, are placed alongside without explanation as to what these terms cover. Other uses are also evident. For example, some authors use method to describe activities that are termed practice approaches in this text, such as 'behaviourist methods' (Sheldon 2000: 65) and task-centred 'practice methods' (Doel 2000: 343). Additionally, method is sometimes used quite loosely to describe a way of doing things, such as 'reflexive methods' (Fook 2002: 122). The term *methodology* tends to be more rigorously applied and is most often used in relation to research:

> The systematic and specified procedures by what a social worker or other investigator develops hypotheses, gathers relevant data, analyses data acquired, and communicates the conclusions.
>
> (Barker 2003: 272)

Of the different terms used, 'method of intervention' is perhaps the clearest, and for this reason this term will be used in this text to describe these five types of practice.

Models

Howe differentiates between a *model* and a theory. He does so by identifying a model as a *description* rather than an explanation of phenomena, acting not as a perfect representation but as an initial attempt to order, or simplify, information by illuminating the pattern of relationships or phenomena observed:

> Models, acting as analogies, can be used to order, define, describe phenomena. They do not explain the things seen, but they do begin to impose some low level order on what is otherwise a jumble of information. Models act as bricks in theory building.
>
> (Howe 1987: 10)

This links to a dictionary definition, where the word model is used to describe a 'standard to be imitated' or a 'representative form, style or pattern' (*Collins Dictionary*). However, the word is used differently by other authors, such as the term *models of practice* (Payne 2002: 137), which again I would describe as practice approaches. Its most consistent use can be seen in terms such as the medical model (Marks 2002: 50–1), biomedical model or biopsychosocial model (Bailey 2002: 172), or again in the coverage of the social model of disability. The work of other authors could be added to this range of uses. In order to avoid further confusion, I have tried to avoid using this term in this text.

Practice approaches

As we have seen, what I have termed *practice approaches* can be described in a variety of ways – as approaches, models or methods. However, Payne's definition of practice theories comes the closest to the way the term is defined in this text:

> *Practice theories* are relatively discrete sets of ideas prescribing appropriate social work actions in particular situations. Psychological or social explanations of human behaviour are applied to social work situations, and actions are prescribed, based on the worker's assessment of the situation. Practice theories are usually informed as separate, relatively complete and coherent sets of ideas. However, aspects of them are often used eclectically, in combination.
>
> (Payne 2000: 332–3)

Practice approaches draw on a coherent body of theory that is often used in a systematic way. They often include particular interventions that are associated with that practice approach, such as the concept of transference in a psychosocial approach (see specialist practice interventions). The practice approaches described in this text include:

- behaviourist approaches (see Appendix 1)
- cognitive approaches (see Appendix 2)
- crisis intervention (see Appendix 3)
- person/client-centred approaches (see Appendix 4)
- psychosocial approaches (see Appendix 5)
- task-centred approaches (see Appendix 6).

The extent to which practitioners use these practice approaches in a rigorous way is unclear. It is likely, as Payne notes, that some concepts that derive from specific practice approaches are used in everyday social work practice, but their theoretical origins may not always be known.

Practice perspectives

The word 'perspective' is often used but not often defined in social work texts. It describes a partial 'view of the world' (Payne 1997: 290) and is often used to attempt to order and make sense of experiences and events from a particular and partial viewpoint. In the framework I am describing, practice perspectives do not adhere to a particular theory, or adopt specialist practice interventions, such as those associated with different practice approaches. For example, while *consciousness raising* may be a term associated with a feminist perspective, other perspectives may focus on raising people's awareness, such as a radical social work perspective. The perspectives included in the appendices of this text include:

- ecological perspectives (see Appendix 7)
- feminist perspectives (see Appendix 8)
- radical/progressive/activist perspectives (see Appendix 9).

Some ways of analysing and working with problems could be viewed as a practice approach or a perspective – ecological approaches or perspectives being a case in point. However, I have categorized this as a perspective, even though it has a range of specific concepts within its conceptual framework, because I know more practitioners who use this as a perspective than as an approach. Other main perspectives include:

- anti-oppressive perspectives (Payne 1997: 238–65)
- anti-discriminatory perspectives (Payne 1997: 238–65)
- empowerment perspectives (Dominelli 2000: 125–38)
- anti-racist/black perspectives (Goldstein 2002: 407–14)
- service users' perspectives (Croft and Beresford 2002: 385–93)
- carer's perspectives (Barton 2002: 401–6)
- survivor's perspectives (Ennis, J. 2000: 341)
- disabled people's movement perspectives (French and Swain 2002: 394–400)
- anti-ageist practice (Phillipson 2002: 61)
- children's rights perspectives (Jackson 2000: 62).

Not enough is known about the ways in which particular perspectives influence practice or about how effective this work is in bringing about desired change. However, it seems to be the case that most practitioners undertake assessments from one perspective or another and that, at times, different perspectives can clash. For example, a user perspective may clash with an agency perspective (Lishman 1994: 87). In addition, the partial nature of any perspective can mean that it leads to a 'blinkered' or biased understanding. It could be argued that this difficulty is inherent in any judgements we make. Our only safeguard, therefore, is to be aware of this danger and to be critically reflective about the perspectives we adopt. We can sometimes see the partial nature of our understanding if we attempt to look at the situation, problem or phenomena from a variety of perspectives. In this text, I use the term practice perspective to denote a partial but important way to think about, observe and order phenomena.

Knowledge based practice: ten practice choices

The following account brings together many of the points covered earlier in this chapter. Drawing on a case example, this framework describes ten common practice choices in relation to direct work with service users and carers.

Method of intervention

This involves making a choice in relation to the most appropriate practice options and includes five choices:

- work with individuals/one-to-one work
- work with groups/groupwork
- work with families/family work
- work with communities/community work
- work with organizations.

Practice approaches

The practice approaches covered in this text, to which others could be added, include:

- behaviourist approaches
- cognitive approaches
- crisis intervention
- person/client-centred approaches
- psychosocial approaches
- task-centred work
- *Stages of Change* (or *Cycle of Change*).

Practice perspectives

Three practice perspectives are covered in this text:

- ecological perspectives
- feminist perspectives
- radical/progressive/activist perspectives.

Other perspectives illuminate factors from a particular viewpoint and include:

- anti-oppressive perspectives
- anti-discriminatory perspectives
- empowerment perspectives
- anti-racist/black perspectives
- service users' perspectives
- carers' perspectives
- children's/young people's rights perspectives
- survivors' perspectives
- disabled people's movement perspectives
- anti-ageist practice.

Skills and interventions

This work may draw on a range of skills that include:

- planning and preparing for the interview
- creating a rapport and establishing a relationship
- welcoming skills
- empathy and sympathy
- the role of self-knowledge and intuition
- open questions
- closed questions
- 'what' questions
- paraphrasing
- clarifying
- summarizing
- giving and receiving feedback
- sticking to the point and purpose of the interview
- prompting
- probing
- allowing and using silences
- using self-disclosure
- using homour
- ending an interview
- closing the case and ending the relationship
- giving advice
- providing information
- providing explanations
- offering encouragement and validation
- providing reassurance
- using persuasion and being directive
- providing practical and material assistance
- providing support
- providing care
- modelling and social skills training

- reframing
- offering interpretations
- adaptation
- counselling skills
- containing anxiety
- empowerment and enabling skills
- negotiating skills
- contracting skills
- networking skills
- working in partnership
- mediation skills
- advocacy skills
- assertiveness skills
- being challenging and confrontative
- dealing with hostility, aggression and violence
- providing protection and control
- managing professional boundaries
- record keeping skills
- reflective and effective practice
- using supervision creatively.

Level and type of skill

These issues are covered in greater detail earlier in the chapter. The level of skill required can range from basic to advanced:

- *basic skills* – foundation skills
- *intermediate skills* – the skills for dealing with more difficult situations
- *advanced skills* – superior skills for working with problems that are multifaceted and intractable.

Skills can also be categorized as generalist and specialist skills:

- *generalist skills* – such as the 50 generalist skills described in this text
- *specialist skills* – specialist skills associated with a particular practice approach.

Duration

Depending on the problem presented and the individuals involved, the time-span for the work can vary. It will vary according to agency policy and can include involvement that is categorized as:

- short-term (up to 12 weeks)
- medium-term (falling between 12 and 26 weeks)
- long-term (stretching beyond 26 weeks).

Stage of the work/practice emphasis

Our contact can vary depending on the stage of the work, agency policy and practice, as well as the duration of the work. In general terms, most work can be categorized to cover three stages:

- the beginning phase
- the middle phase
- the end phase.

For example, our emphasis at the beginning phase may be on relationship-building; in the middle phase the focus may be on consolidating the relationship and strengthening trust; and at the end it may involve forming links with family members or neighbourhood groups to enable the work to end and progress to continue.

Level of intensity

Some referrals require a different level of intensity, depending on the problem(s) presented and the circumstances of the individual. These can roughly be divided into three levels:

- *Non-intensive* (fortnightly/monthly) – this relates to work that is less intensive, where contact with service users is likely to be fortnightly, perhaps because the work is near to completion and the case is coming to a close or because the work cannot proceed at a quicker pace
- *Moderate* (weekly) – this is where work is ongoing and contact with the service user, family members and other professionals is likely to take place at least once a week. Providing weekly relationship counselling, family work or individual counselling would normally fall within this level of intensity
- *Intensive* (twice weekly) – this is where the work is demanding and the problems presented are multifaceted, severe, enduring and complex. This may involve two or more points of contact with the service user, different family members and/or other professionals during the course of a week.

Practice setting

We may be called on to work in a range of different practice settings. These could include:

- a workplace/agency setting
- a person's home
- a residential setting
- a prison or day centre
- a community centre

- a hospital
- a school
- a more natural or spontaneous setting, such as a café or car journey.

Supervision

An important feature in relation to all aspects of practice, particularly practice effectiveness, is the availability of quality supervision, as well as the capacity to use that supervision effectively. Supervision features strongly in guidance documents relating to social work training and education because it is in supervision that close attention can be paid to the way that knowledge, skills, understanding and values are used, and analysed critically, to support and improve practice (TOPSS 2002: 47). Further coverage of supervision can be found in Chapter 8.

Case example: Sarah

Sarah, aged 12, was referred by the school when it was found that she was self-harming, using a razor blade to score her arm. From the limited information that the school was able to gather, Sarah's mother had recently remarried and Sarah described feeling 'pushed out' by her mother and step-father. Sarah failed to come home on two occasions. Her mother was said to be at her 'wits end' because of Sarah's self-harming behaviour and her 'impossible moods' at home. The situation appeared to be deteriorating and family breakdown appeared to be a real possibility. The following ten practice decisions were proposed in relation to work undertaken with Sarah. (The section in italics indicates the practice choices adopted in relation to this case example.)

Implementation

Practice choices	*Practice decision*
1 *Method of intervention*	• To work on a *one-to-one basis* with Sarah, mainly using counselling skills (Rogerian).
	• Other options that were considered included the possibility of *family work* once a sound relationship with Sarah had been established and if all parties agreed with this proposal.
	• If this recommendation was not considered appropriate or acceptable, it may have been helpful to offer *groupwork*. The school ran a young women's support group and it may have been appropriate to consider this in

	order to help reduce Sarah's isolation from her peers and to build her self-confidence and self-esteem.
2 *Practice approach*	• To work from a *person/client-centred approach*.
3 *Practice perspective*	• To work from a *young people's perspective*, together with a *feminist perspective*.
4 *Skills and interventions*	• *Generalist skills and interventions*: when the work began, the skills and interventions adopted focused on assessment, particularly information gathering; observation skills; listening skills; the judicious use of open and closed questions; and providing information and explanations. • *Specialist skills and interventions*: these were focused on building trust and included interventions based on the concepts of congruence, unconditional positive regard and empathy – but communicated in every-day language.
5 *Level and type of skill*	• A range of different skills and interventions were required, some focusing at a *basic* and *intermediate* level. In addition, *advanced* and specialist skills and interventions were required to address Sarah's self-harming behaviour and to work with her in the counselling sessions.
6 *Duration*	• *Medium term*. Early in the assessment process, the risk of family breakdown was confirmed. Other problems relating to Sarah's self-esteem and relationship with her mother and step-father were also revealed. Proposed duration for work: six months.
7 *Stage of the work/ practice emphasis*	• *Beginning phase*. Initially, the focus was on practical issues in relation to the counselling sessions, such as travel arrangements and trying to identify Sarah's expectations and choices in relation to the work being planned.
8 *Level of intensity*	• *Initially intensive (twice weekly) contact* with Sarah in order to work on her self-harming behaviour and to avoid family breakdown. • In time, working towards *weekly* contact.

9 *Practice setting*	• *Agency counselling room.*
10 *Supervision, training, consultation and support structure*	• *Monthly line management supervision.* • Also the opportunity to attend a training course on working with young people who self-harm. • If required, it may be possible to have some consultancy from a local women's therapy centre.

Critical reflection and analysis

This example is drawn from my work and illustrates how we might use different methods of intervention in order to work effectively with Sarah. The decisions made reflect a range of different considerations. In terms of the method of intervention, it was clear from my initial contact with Sarah and the school that the referral had to be dealt with carefully and required one-to-one work. Sarah was described as a shy and reserved young woman with no friends. The school was concerned that every effort should be made to ensure that Sarah continued to attend. Sarah had no friends and proved difficult to engage, but if she had a close friend I would have suggested to Sarah that we include her friend in the counselling session. However, before asking a question of this kind, I would have needed to be sure that Sarah had the capacity to say 'no' if she viewed this suggestion as unhelpful.

The same degree of sensitivity needed to be exercised in relation to decisions about which practice approach to suggest. Sarah had no previous experience of counselling or social work and, therefore, did not know how to differentiate between the different practice approaches that could be considered appropriate. I recommended a person/client-centred practice approach because I felt that Sarah would benefit from an approach that stressed the importance of empathy, congruence and unconditional positive regard. I initially found it difficult to explain these terms, and why they were important, in 'ordinary' language.

Sarah appeared to have little confidence and a profound despondency about the future and what life had to offer her. Adolescence can be a difficult time, but particularly hard for young people who do not come from a stable home environment (Herbert 2002: 359). The generalist interventions I used focused on a range of skills to enable me to establish a rapport and form a trusting relationship and, at the same time, to arrive at an assessment, including the extent to which Sarah might be at risk of harming herself further or being rejected by her family. An assessment of this kind can take a considerable amount of time, particularly when working with someone who may be difficult to engage. Listening, observation and information gathering skills are important in this regard, as is the ability to ask 'good' questions. At regular intervals, I explained to Sarah my reason for choosing a particular line of questioning and what I hoped this might achieve. In particular, I was attempting to identify why, when and how often Sarah harmed herself and what triggered this behaviour, in order to establish the severity of the problem and to use this baseline data to monitor and evaluate progress. I also wanted to see the extent of Sarah's self-understanding and the extent to which she felt she had some control over her need to self-harm.

In choosing a children's rights perspective, I was attempting to ensure that I remained sensitive to power differences and that Sarah's best interest remained my primary focus (Jackson 2000: 62). By incorporating a feminist perspective into my work, I was attempting to understand whether Sarah's gender, including her relationship with her mother, might be playing a part in her self-harming behaviour. Research indicates that young women predominate in statistics in relation to self-inflicted injuries (Coleman *et al.* 1995; Hawton *et al.* 1996). The setting for the counselling session needed to be considered carefully and be prepared and protected from unnecessary interruptions or distractions. In terms of the time period needed for this work, because of the degree of emotional distress that Sarah was exhibiting, and the fact that she was still harming herself, it was agreed that we would work together for six months initially, with a review at three-monthly intervals and the opportunity to continue the work if necessary. In order to 'contain' Sarah's self-harming behaviour and the threat of family breakdown, and to give Sarah the opportunity to talk in detail about her thoughts and feelings, it was felt that the counselling sessions should be twice weekly until the situation stabilized, working towards weekly contact.

Throughout this work, I had regular contact with Sarah's family to elicit their support and to help them to deal with Sarah's 'difficult' behaviour at home. This contact also ensured that I did not set myself up as the 'good parent' in ways that might deepen the rift between Sarah and her mother. At the outset, we considered how the work could be supported and consolidated within Sarah's wider social network. These details were worked out in monthly supervision sessions with my line manager. Other ideas and suggestions came from my colleagues and I also attended a training course for practitioners working with young people with self-harming behaviour.

Conclusion

In this chapter, I have looked at the way a number of key terms are used within social work, as well as how these terms are used within this text. Without this kind of clarity, it is not possible to develop a common language from which to discuss crucial issues in relation to practice effectiveness. In the previous chapter, I stressed the importance of social work's knowledge base. In this chapter, I have stressed the importance of applying and using that knowledge in practice and have argued that action is an intellectual, as well as a practical, activity. I have argued that for skills and interventions to be transferable not only depends on the knowledge, skills, understanding and values that service users and carers bring but also on the part played by the wider environment and the social and political context within which the work is located. More than ever we are being called upon to justify the practice decisions we make. These cannot be based on our own preferences alone but must include an awareness of practice approaches that have been shown to be effective in particular contexts. Some of this knowledge may come from research or reading, but it may also be drawn from our own practice experience.

At every point, the expectations and preferences that service users and carers bring to the encounter, or to the work, need to be included in our recommendations and practice plan. The capacity for critical thinking is important in this regard because, despite claims to the contrary, 'we are still a long way from possessing comprehensive empirical knowledge to guide treatment selection' (Hepworth *et al.* 2002: 360). Further research is needed to understand the process and context of particular interventions in relation to certain groups of people, problems and situations. Service users and carers bring their own understanding and meaning to any encounter – their capacities and 'expert' knowledge – and we do the same. It is in this collaboration, based on the principle of partnership, that we help bring about the kind of changes that are being sought. There are barriers in this collaboration, perhaps the most serious being located in the wider social and political context and the fact that social services departments are seriously underfunded for the requirements they are being asked to meet. As a result, too many social workers, particularly in the statutory sector, are working in circumstances that are stressful, demoralizing and prescriptive and that deny the opportunity to explore the concept of practice effectiveness in ways described in this chapter and text. This need not be the case and there are hopeful signs, and new opportunities, in the changes being implemented in the organization of social work.

3 UNDERSTANDING HUMAN BEINGS

This chapter looks at some of the main theories that are relevant and useful in contemporary social work. In this task, it is not my purpose to sketch a comprehensive review of different psychological theories but to provide a foundation from which to begin to formulate answers to key questions that are important to social work. Why, for example, do people behave in certain ways, sometimes becoming 'stuck' or locked into 'self-destructive scripts' (England 1986: 16)? What enables people to keep going, sometimes in the face of extreme adversity or demoralizing experiences (Howe *et al.* 1999: 30)? How do these experiences differ, if at all, for people who carry additional oppressions because of their gender, race, class, age, disability, sexual preference, culture, religion and/or health? Above all, how can we effectively help people to move their lives forward?

Many of the concepts described in this chapter are based on the belief that emotional development is a continuous process, and that the capacity to develop – to grow and to change – is present in human beings throughout our lives (unless there are biological or neurological conditions to impede this process). The theories outlined here also seek to address a complex issue, that is, to identify the factors – environmental and internal to the individual – that influence the possibilities for growth and development. The study of the 'life-long process of change' (Reber and Reber 2001: 196) is usually undertaken within the discipline of developmental psychology. However, this term is often taken to refer to child psychology, rather than an investigation of human development throughout the whole of life from the cradle to the grave. Within this discipline, two major fields of investigation have emerged: stage theory and life span developmental psychology.

Stage theory includes: Freud's stages of psychosexual development; Maslow's hierarchy of needs; Erikson's eight stages of man (Erikson's work is also described as belonging to life span developmental psychology); Piaget's stages of cognitive development; and Kohlberg's stages of moral development. These theories assume that each stage must be completed more or less successfully before the next stage can be negotiated. 'Grand' theories of this kind have serious shortcomings in terms of whether they can provide a 'complete explanation of developmental processes' (Rutter and Rutter 1993: 3). Nevertheless, they have contributed a great deal simply by conceptualizing the different processes and influences involved in development.

Life span developmental psychology argues that continuities and discontinuities both exist within the growth process, and that psychological functioning and development change throughout the course of our lives. 'We are social beings and our psychological functioning is influenced by the interactions and transactions we have within our social environment' (Rutter and Rutter 1993: 6). It looks at the effects of people's behaviour, past experiences and the social structure in shaping experiences and how, for example, risk and protective factors operate in terms of the developmental process and those factors that influence attachment. It also touches on social learning theory: how people, particularly children, develop through observing and imitating the behaviour of others. For further reading on life span psychology, see Sugarman (1986).

The following is a brief summary of some of the main psychological theories important within social work. It looks at theories in relation to: need, human motivation and self-actualization (Maslow); the search to reach our 'true' potential (Rogers); the learning we can gain from observing human behaviour (Skinner 1974); the relationship between conscious and unconscious thoughts, feelings and actions (Freud); the impact of life stages on human beings (Erikson); attachment theory (Bowlby); and the struggle of human beings to achieve independence (Winnicott). It then looks at other important developments within psychology, particularly the work of feminists in relation to women's emotional development and oppression, and explores the issue of change. I finish the chapter by highlighting the limitations of these theories, particularly in relation to minority groups.

Psychology's three 'forces': humanism, behaviourism and psychoanalysis

Psychology is sometimes described as having three 'forces': psychoanalysis, behaviourism and a 'third force' – humanistic psychology. Psychoanalysis is based on the belief that as human beings we are born with the capacity for good and evil and that much of our life is determined by the tension and conflict between these two elements. Behaviourism, on the other hand, is based on a belief that feelings of distress or neurosis come about through faulty conditioning and that what needs to be changed is maladaptive behaviour. It stresses the importance of observable, testable, measurable, reproducible and objective behaviours:

we are as we behave. As such, unlike psychoanalysis and humanism, behaviourism is not primarily concerned with the meaning and understanding that human beings ascribe to their thoughts and feelings.

Finally, humanistic psychology emphasizes a belief in the essential goodness, wholeness and potential of human beings (Feltham and Dryden 1993: 84). This school of psychology, sometimes described as the 'human potential movement', stresses the importance of individuals exercising freedom of choice in relation to their lives.

Psychoanalysis, behaviourism and humanistic psychology have all had an impact on social work, although psychoanalysis has had a particularly marked influence (Yelloly 1980: v). More recently, behaviourist theories, particularly cognitive-behavioural approaches, have become important, although many social workers gravitate towards humanistic approaches, primarily because of their theoretical accessibility, their 'holistic' approach, their adaptability and the sense of hope they engender. The practice approaches covered in the appendices of this text highlight how these three main theories, psychoanalysis, behaviourism and humanistic psychology, relate in practice.

Humanism

Maslow's hierarchy of needs

Maslow (1954) is often described as the founder of humanistic psychology. His quest to understand human behaviour and motivation led him away from psychoanalysis, which he found too absorbed with neurosis and disturbed behaviour, and away from behaviourism, which he found too mechanistic, remarking after the birth of his first child that anyone who had seen a baby born could not be behaviourist. Instead, he put forward the concept of a *hierarchy of needs* where the need for *self-actualization*, that is, the need that human beings have to realize their full potential, can only be fulfilled once other needs have been met. Self-actualization describes an inborn tendency for human beings to grow and to maximize innate talents and potentialities.

According to Maslow, the first level includes basic physiological needs for food, shelter, clothing and so on. Once these needs have been met, the actualization process creates a momentum for the next level of needs to be realized, namely for security and safety and to feel free from danger. Again, once these have been met, there is an innate motivation to move on to the next stage, and so forth. This is represented as shown in Figure 3.1.

Maslow's concept has serious limitations. Some people address their needs in ways that do not fall within Maslow's conceptual framework. Creative people have been known to sacrifice basic physiological needs

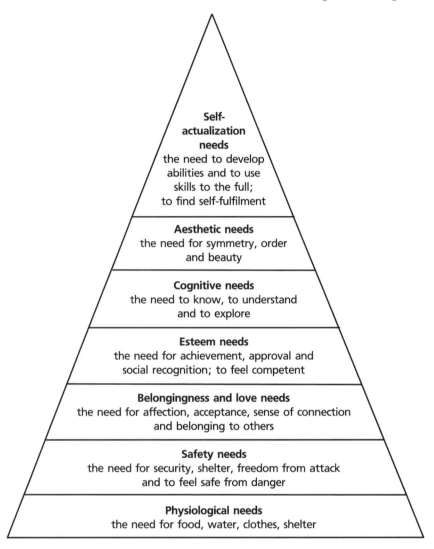

Figure 3.1   Maslow's hierarchy of needs. Fundamental or basic needs must be met or satisfied, at least partially, before other 'higher' needs can be met.

for, say, food and rest, in pursuit of their creativity. Similarly, some people who appear to have satisfied their basic needs somehow fail to move on to address higher needs. For reasons that this theory cannot explain, they somehow become stuck. However, in his conceptualization of a hierarchy of needs, Maslow was one of the first people to analyse human needs and to relate the meeting of needs to a notion of human growth and development, motivation and the maximizing of human potential. As such, 'Maslow's model may provide a rough working generalization about most people in most situations, but it is not really adequate as an explanation of human motivation' (Hayes 1994: 435).

In social work we encounter situations where it appears very difficult for some individuals to move their lives forward beyond the first two levels. The energy spent on trying to survive in the face of adversity necessarily means that emotional resources or energy are not free to be used on other courses of action, such as finding a job, sorting out school problems or meeting other needs. This has important implications for our work because it could mean that providing the right kind of practical or material assistance, or emotional support for service users, could release the momentum and motivation towards self-sufficiency and independence (self-actualization). Without this understanding, we run the risk of providing resources and services into a bottomless pit, where fundamental change does not happen.

Rogers's client-centred approach

Carl Rogers, an American psychologist and founder of client-centred therapy (sometimes called person-centred counselling), shared Maslow's view that human beings have an innate drive or motivation to develop and maximize their inherited potential. Rogers described this as an *actualizing tendency*, a term similar to Maslow's terminology. However, unlike Maslow, whose theory is descriptive and speculative and located at the level of ideas, Rogers formulated not only a complex theory of human growth and development, but also a practice approach: client-centred therapy (1951). Its aim was to help create the conditions for individuals to overcome the constraints placed on them from the impact and internalization of negative and invalidating experiences and criticisms.

Rogers stressed the need for positive self-regard. He noted in detail the impact of adverse conditions on the capacity of individuals to be self-directing, to trust their innate abilities and resourcefulness, and to be in touch with their own 'locus of evaluation', that is, their ability to trust their thoughts and feelings in relation to decision-making and choosing particular courses of action. For Rogers the actualizing tendency is motivated by the drive for emotional and intellectual growth, but this growth is only normally possible in situations where the individual is released or freed from the fear of punishment, coercion, inhibiting social pressures and other negative or constraining experiences. Central to Rogers's theory is the belief that individuals know more about themselves and their lives than anyone else and, because of this, are in the best position to deal with personal problems that emerge. The role of the therapist or practitioner is to create the conditions necessary for people to find their way to a new self-concept and self-regard. From this new position, it is hoped that people can develop the capacity to solve their own problems and to function in ways that feel satisfying, so that any opportunities for growth and development that emerge can be explored and maximized.

From this theory of human growth and development, Rogers went on to develop a practice approach to help individuals to overcome these constraints. This involves a therapist or practitioner creating a particular kind of relationship using *congruence, unconditional positive regard* and *empathy* in order to understand an individual's subjective experience. The therapist's or practitioner's aim is to get alongside the client in ways that show a willingness to enter the world of another human being and to provide an experience and presence that is validating, releasing and restorative. Through this process, individuals are presented with a different way of perceiving and experiencing themselves, so that a new self-concept can emerge and, with this, the capacity to solve their own problems. This is not easy to achieve because it requires a huge level of commitment, skill and discipline on the part of the counsellor. It also requires the individual to recognize and work with the qualities that the counsellor brings to the relationship, so that trust, a particular kind of intimacy and a degree of mutuality can be reached (Thorne 2002: 178). Although not without its critics or shortcomings, Rogers's theory stands out for its profound optimism and belief in the capacity of human beings to embrace difficult experiences, to take hold of their lives and to move forward, and for the important role that others, including social workers, can play within this process (for a more detailed account of Rogers's work, see Thorne 1992).

Behaviourism

The behaviourist school of psychology is based on the theories of Pavlov (1927), Watson (1970), Skinner (1974) and others. It attempts to explain behaviour in terms of observable and measurable responses and starts from the position that behaviours are learned, which means, therefore, that behaviours can be unlearned. Thus neurosis is considered to be the result of faulty conditioning, which means that when people feel distressed, what needs to be changed is the maladaptive behaviour. This places the focus on the behaviour itself, as opposed to analysing the underlying conflicts or causes. The view is that 'introspection and the unconscious are unscientific hypotheses' (Barker 1995: 34). As a therapy, it is considered to be particularly effective in relation to fears and phobias and also for obsessional states such as compulsive hand-washing.

Most behavioural perspectives share the following characteristics:

- Reliance on empirical findings rather than speculation to inform

assessment and intervention
- Identification of personal and environmental resources that can be drawn on to attain desired outcomes
- Description of baseline levels of relevant outcomes and skills
- Clear description of assessment and intervention procedures
- Close relationship between assessment and intervention
- Clear description of desired outcomes
- Concern with evaluation.

(Gambrill 1985: 184)

Behaviourist approaches include four major techniques – systematic desensitization, aversion therapy, operant conditioning and modelling – although therapists may use these interventions differently. Desensitization is often used as an effective means of alleviating fear and anxiety by attempting to weaken the anxiety response to a given stimulus through exposure to a series of similar anxiety-provoking situations until a more relaxed response is reached. Aversion therapy is, in some ways, the opposite of desensitization because it consists of administering unpleasant, painful or punishing stimuli to individuals whose 'unacceptable' behaviour is in some ways felt to be gratifying, with the intention of altering this reaction and behaviour pattern. The use of this technique on certain groups of people, such as 'sex offenders' and people who are alcoholic, has been criticized. Also, it has proved less successful than anticipated (Bullock and Trombley 2000: 70). As a result, aversion therapy tends to be less popular than other behavioural techniques. Operant conditioning is a technique where 'the environment has been specifically programmed to support certain behaviours and discourage others' (Sheldon 1995: 62) by altering the consequences that follow. The reinforcement may take the form of a reward, such as those found in token-economy schemes. Finally, Bandura (1969) emphasizes the importance of modelling as an effective way to bring about behaviour change. This involves encouraging an individual to acquire behaviour by imitating the actions or behaviour of others.

According to Gambrill, several characteristics distinguish behaviourist approaches:

Several characteristics distinguish the behavioural approach from other social work frameworks. A behavioural approach constrains social workers to draw on empirical research in selecting assessment and intervention procedures. For example, if research demonstrates that the observation of behaviour in the natural environment offers valuable information that can complement and correct impressions given by self-reports concerning the interaction between clients and significant others, then this kind of information would be used if feasible and ethical. If the literature shows that one kind of intervention is more effective than another, then within ethical and practice limits, social workers would use this approach regardless of personal theoretical preferences.

(Gambrill 1985: 185)

It is probably true to say that behaviourism itself has had little impact on social work, although behaviourist theories and practices have had a considerable influence, particularly since the 'marriage' that led to the development of cognitive-behavioural approaches. According to Sheldon, the bringing together of cognitive and behavioural approaches has meant that 'behaviour therapy and applied behavioural psychology have undergone a "cognitive revolution" in the past decade' (1995: xii). As the term implies, cognitive-behavioural approaches attempt to link behaviour with how human beings organize and understand their worlds and how these beliefs become known, perceived and understood. Two concepts that link behaviour and thoughts in this way are learned helplessness and locus of control.

Learned helplessness

A particularly valuable concept, based on social learning theory, is learned helplessness (Seligman 1975). This describes the generalized view that helplessness is a learned state, brought about when individuals are exposed to unpleasant, harmful or corrupting situations where there is no avoidance or escape. Such individuals learn through experience that there is nothing they can do to bring about change or to modify their situation, that is, they become powerless. Seligman's view, and that of cognitive-behaviourists, is that if behaviour can be learned, it can also be unlearned 'in a sympathetic, step-by-step way, by teaching the skills necessary for the reassertion of some control over their unpredictable environments' (Sheldon 1995: 61). Working alongside service users in this way can help them to overcome doubts and fears that they harbour. This concept is particularly useful and adaptable within a social work context because it helps us to understand why some people fail to take action or fall victim to events (Cigno 2002: 186).

Locus of control

A different way to conceptualize the degree to which an individual has internalized a sense of helplessness and powerlessness would be to explore the extent to which they believe they can control their destiny and behaviour. This helps us to understand where the individual is located in relation to the process of change. The locus of control (Lefcourt 1976) is measured along a scale from a high internal to high external locus. Individuals with a high internal locus of control tend to accept responsibility for their actions and to believe that it is possible to influence or control ('master') their circumstances and lives. At the other end of the spectrum, individuals with a high external locus of control believe that control is located elsewhere and that 'things happen to them' – both positive and negative – over which they have little or no control. The usefulness of this concept is that it helps to identify whether, when presented with a new situation or dilemma, individuals will consistently and spontaneously perceive a situation as something over which they can or cannot exercise a degree of control. This has important implications when, as practitioners, we are attempting to assess the degree of responsibility that service users can take on and what role we should play. For a further account of the use of behaviourism within social work, see Hudson and Macdonald (1986) and Cigno (2002) on cognitive-behavioural social work.

Psychoanalysis

Like many writers, Freud described people's tendency for growth and emotional development as innate: as an 'instinctual propelling force' (Freud 1924: 396). Some people have sufficient inner emotional resources to set in motion this opportunity for growth and development, whereas others do not feel they have enough emotional resources 'inside them', mainly because of depleting experiences in childhood. This means that any movement forward will depend on the quality and nature of help given.

Freud developed his theories from listening to his patients. As a technique, psychoanalysis and some of its theories are not easily applicable to social work. However, Freud's writings on the unconscious (i.e. mental processes of which we are not aware), and concepts such as the superego, ego and id, are important hypothetical constructs that help us to understand human behaviour. Behaviours driven by the id are largely unconscious and describe impulsive behaviours that can lead to all kinds of difficulties; for example, when a young person steals but in explaining their motivation, they can only say 'I felt like it'. The ego mediates between the conscious and the unconscious, and it too is partly unconscious. Its primary function is to deal with external reality and to make decisions. Enhancing the capacity of the ego to deal with stress and conflicts is another way to describe our attempts to extend people's capacity to *cope*, which is an important activity within social work. Such strategies are central to ego psychology, popular in the USA (Parad 1958). Finally, the superego is conceptualized as the 'conscience' of the mind, where rules or moral codes are harboured to control behaviours, punishing transgressions by arousing feelings of guilt. Individuals with an overdeveloped superego can be racked with feelings of guilt, responsibility and blame that are inappropriate to the situation. If the id is concerned with pleasure and the ego with responsibility and reality, the superego is concerned with idealism, often based on an internalization of parental attitudes.

In order to protect the ego – or the self – from thoughts, feelings or actions that are felt to be too threatening (Jacobs 1999: 98), defensive strategies are employed, often unconsciously. For example, events may be forgotten or repressed in order to protect the individual from memories that would produce anxiety or guilt if they became conscious (Reber and Reber 2001: 625). Defences can also distort what is remembered, which makes it difficult for the individual or others to gain an accurate picture of experiences and events. On the other hand, defences serve to protect the individual and, as such, it can be counterproductive to confront them head-on or to attempt to break them down. Traditionally, interpretations are used to help individuals to gain insight into their behaviour or to help them to become aware of defensive or unconscious reactions. This is a skill that requires specialist training (McLeod 2003: 501), because if used inappropriately, interpretations can increase defensiveness and inhibit progress.

The importance of the relationship between practitioner and service user lies at the heart of psychoanalytic approaches, not only as a basis for helping people to move forward but also as a way of understanding inner conflicts that are unconscious. These are communicated through transference and countertransference reactions, in other words, in the ways we are experienced by service users and what we represent: who we have become for service users or what part we are being invited or expected to play. For example, a mother whose child is refusing to attend school may experience us as being critical (negative transference), when in fact our reaction is deeply sympathetic and uncritical. Or again, we may end an interview feeling despairing, having picked up feelings of abandonment and rejection communicated unconsciously by the service user. Picking up negative or troubling feelings in this way is inevitable: these are the reactions on which 'hunches' or intuition are built. Supervision can help us to understand these experiences. However, it is important to stress that being able to work directly with transference and counter-transference reactions, rather than just understanding them as concepts, requires specialist training. Even with such training, we must always check that we are not bringing our own unresolved feelings into the encounter or into the relationship. For further writings about the application of psychoanalytic concepts within social work, see the *Journal of Social Work Practice*.

Erikson's eight stages of man [sic]

Erik Erikson (1965), a German immigrant to the USA in the 1930s, built on Freud's theory of psychosexual development (oral, anal, phallic, latency and genital phases) and the impact of biological and social and cultural influences on human development. His theory was one of the first to emerge as part of the discipline of 'life span psychology'. This framework attempts to categorize human experience from the cradle to the grave and to understand how human beings operate, find an identity and meet the demands placed upon them within a changing social and cultural context.

Erikson's proposition was that the ego – the self – of the infant is not fixed at birth, nor during childhood, but that the infant has all the elements necessary for development to take place at different stages. From this basic premise, Erikson saw development being moulded throughout life, as part of a lifelong response to the demands and challenges placed on individuals. These demands provoke 'crises', where difficult challenges or problems have to be confronted and successfully resolved, from which 'vital strength' is gained. Although it is not essential for each stage to be fully resolved, failure to meet these challenges can be damaging to development and self-esteem and can result in developmental stagnation or a 'stuckness'. This can, however, be overcome with help.

The eight stages identified by Erikson are not based on clinical or scientific evidence but they do describe in general the kinds of concerns that human beings encounter at different points in their lives. They are represented in Table 3.1.

Erikson's work continues to be influential, particularly in relation to adolescent psychosocial development and the ageing process. For a more detailed description and critique of Erikson's different stages, see Craib (1989: 84–6); for the use of Erikson's work in relation to adolescence and the problems of identity, see Kroger (1996) and for an exploration of how his work has been adapted within the field of adult development, see Levinson (1978, 1996) and Gould (1999).

Attachment theory

John Bowlby, a British psychiatrist and psychoanalyst, was commissioned after the Second World War to investigate children orphaned or separated from their parents as the result of war. In 1951, Bowlby produced a report in which his research concluded that human beings have an innate and fundamental need to form meaningful attachments with others, particularly in childhood but also throughout life, and that within this process mother-child relationship or 'bond' is of central importance. Bowlby later revised his views on the prominence given to mothers to include other significant adults (Bowlby 1988: 27).

According to Bowlby, the *affectional bonds* created between the mother and baby help to establish a secure base, particularly in the first year of life, where positive and trusted attachment figures foster feelings of confidence and self-worth and act as a source of emotional stability and security (Bowlby 1979: 130). From this secure base, children

Table 3.1   Erikson's eight stages of psychosocial development (eight stages of man)

Approximate age (chronological ages are not always clear)	Stage	Psychosocial crisis	Favourable outcome (potential 'new virtue')
0–1 year	Infancy	Trust v. mistrust	Trust, optimism, hope
1–6 years	Early childhood	Autonomy v. shame and doubt	Sense of control, adequacy, self-confidence
6–8 years	Play age	Initiative v. guilt	Direction and purpose
10–14 years	School age	Industry v. inferiority	Competence in social, intellectual and physical skills
14–20 years	Adolescence	Identity v. role confusion	Fidelity; an integrated sense of being a unique individual
20–35 years	Young adulthood	Intimacy v. isolation	Love; ability to form close relationships and to make commitments
35–65 years	Maturity	Generativity v. stagnation	Care and concern for family, society and future generations
65 years +	Old age	Integrity v. despair and disgust	Wisdom; a sense of fulfilment and satisfaction with life and a willingness to face death

develop self-confidence, self-reliance, trust and cooperation with others (Bowlby 1979: 117). On the other hand, negative attachment figures who are inaccessible, unreliable, unhelpful or hostile can result in children feeling anxious, insecure, rootless and mistrustful and lacking in self-confidence. Within this process, Bowlby emphasized the importance of children being able to recognize and collaborate with attachment figures in ways that feel reciprocal and rewarding (Bowlby 1979: 104), stressing that a healthy personality involves both self-reliance and reliance on others.

He also stressed that the pattern of relationships that are established first will tend to persist throughout life, although therapy can help to bring about change. These models are internalized, to become *working models* of the self, from which children hold an inner picture of themselves: their self-image, self-esteem and sense of worth. These may be positive or negative, depending on the nature and quality of a child's past and present internal and external experience (Bowlby 1979: 118). They lead to a range of expectations being established and a particular outlook on life and the future.

Bowlby's work (1980) revealed that infants formed different kinds of attachments, influenced by the behaviour of the parents/carers, as well as the situation and social context. He identified three stages of reaction to separation from an attachment figure, namely:

- *Protest*   At this stage, children demonstrate clear signs of being tearful, upset and agitated, sometimes calling for the attachment figure or searching for them.
- *Despair*   When the protest fails to bring the attachment figure back, children enter a period of despair, characterized by withdrawn behaviour, tearfulness, refusing to eat, bed-wetting and soiling.
- *Detachment*   At this stage children become detached, appearing to have adapted to the situation and to be disinterested in the attachment figure. They have learnt to fend for themselves and may use thumb-sucking, rocking or masturbation in an effort to comfort themselves.

Alongside Bowlby, others have studied infant–parent relationships, including James Robertson and Mary Ainsworth, and developed new theories based on their observations and classifications. For example, the research of Ainsworth *et al*. (1978), particularly the 'strange situation' test (Howe *et al*. 1995: 79), led to the development of a different attachment classification system: secure attachment; insecure attachment: avoidant; and insecure attachment: resistant. To this, Main (1995) added a fourth category known as insecure: disorganized attachment. (For a more detailed description of these different categories of attachment and their impact on psychosocial development, see Howe 2002b: 174–7; Howe *et al*. 1999.)

Over the years, the work of Bowlby and others has been important within social work in making links between children's emotional development and behaviour and the quality of their relationships with their parent(s) and other attachment figures. As a result, attachment theory has been used extensively, in day care settings, in residential establishments and fostering, and was once a central feature of the Assessment Framework used in relation to children (DoH 1988). It continues to be particularly useful in mapping continuities and discontinuities in care and the degree to which a lack of permanence or consistency can have an impact on children's emotional development and on their capacity to relate to themselves, to others and to their wider environment (Rushton 2000: 250–2).

Winnicott's writing on dependence and points of failure

Winnicott was a paediatrician and psychoanalyst whose work had a significant influence on social work and teaching, as well as medicine, in the 1950s and 1960s. Winnicott wrote extensively but this section will focus on his writings on the journey we must all make from dependence to independence, and finally towards interdependence. It will also focus on a brief account of Winnicott's writings on the points of failure.

The journey towards independence begins with the almost absolute dependence of the newborn baby, whose needs must be responded to and adapted to almost totally in order to enable physical and emotional growth. This leads to the possibility of moving towards a state of relative dependence, where the mother or carer introduces less adaptation to ensure that the child can begin to look outwards to have their needs met, to look to themselves and their wider social environment. This time of great exploration is marked by infants and toddlers being able to leave the security of their parents/carers and to venture further afield in search of new experiences. If all goes well at this stage, a movement towards independence begins to develop, marked by a desire on the part of the child to find ways to do without actual care and to undertake more things for themselves (Winnicott 1965: 84). This stage should not be confused with premature self-sufficiency, which occurs when individuals are failed and forced into a false independence before they have the emotional resources or maturity to manage for themselves (Winnicott 1986: 21). This kind of failure can result in the development of a 'false self', designed to protect the individual's 'true self's core' from the impact of further failures, trauma or 'impingement' (Winnicott 1958: 291–2).

In relation to the movement in and out of dependent states, the concept of interdependence is important because it describes the capacity of the individual to give and to receive from others without undue anxiety. This can lead to the individual being able to engage in more reciprocal relationships with others, and to be able to relate with a degree of confidence to their wider environment and to society. This conceptualization stresses the fact that as human beings, we need one another. For this reason, Winnicott regarded independence more as an illusory ideal than a realizable, or even desirable, goal: 'Independence is never absolute. The healthy individual does not become isolated, but becomes related to the environment in such a way that the individual and the environment can be said to be interdependent' (Winnicott 1965: 84). This involves being able to seek help and the company of others without feeling compromised or depleted by the experience. The fact that for some service users this is not a possibility helps in part to explain why they do not take up services that are offered. This journey can be represented diagramatically (see Figure 3.2).

Points of failure/failure situations

Neglect in infancy can result in 'delays and distortions' in development. One way to attempt to understand when and where the developmental process has become delayed or stuck could be to look at how past failures are continuing to have an impact. 'Failure situations' or 'points of failure' (Winnicott 1958: 281) describe experiences of being disappointed, 'let-down' or failed by others in crucial ways. These unthinkable memories and failures remain 'frozen', but they are waiting for a safe and reliable situation where they can be 'unfrozen'. The most severe and enduring failures often occur in childhood, and the involuntary revival of these memories can catapult service users into a different, often earlier, time-zone and 'space'. From this place it can be difficult to distinguish between past and present, primarily because unresolved and painful feelings of the past are experienced in the present, often becoming merged with present-day events. For example, the ending of a significant relationship can revive unresolved feelings of grief from the past about the death of a loved one or the loss of an earlier relationship, no matter how long ago this occurred. Whatever triggers a return to these points of failure, and this may never be fully known, the fact that they have come back into prominence – into our memory or half-awareness – is significant on two accounts:

- these feelings take up emotional energy and reserves in ways that exhaust service users and threaten their capacity to cope; and
- they provide an opportunity to recover from earlier failures and for the developmental process to start up again where this has become stuck.

This perspective sees all behaviour as providing important clues. For example, repeating harmful or self-destructive behaviour can be seen quite

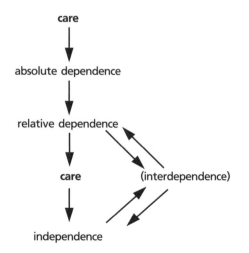

Figure 3.2 Winnicott's stages of dependence

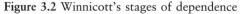

simply as a manifestation of distress, which it clearly is. However, it can also be seen as a return to previous traumas or points of failure in a service user's attempt to become free of their constraining impact. The energy that is taken up trying not to feel the pain of these earlier experiences – to forget, to control or to repress difficult feelings or failures – can be freed up and used creatively in other areas of our lives.

Too often, these points of failure are left unhealed or unresolved, which means that the developmental process can become locked or 'frozen' at these points. As a result, certain aspects of an individual's emotional development can become stuck. An example of this uneven development can be seen when an individual communicates a balanced perspective until we touch upon a painful, unresolved issue, when suddenly the dialogue takes a different, less rational tone. Sometimes it can feel as if the individual has gone back to a younger age. For those areas where growth has become stuck, it can be difficult for people to work through these painful experiences without help because they may be unaware of them: that is, they are unconscious.

Alongside these aspects of developmental delay or 'stuckness' exist pain-free areas, that is, areas where an individual has not been hurt or where there has been the opportunity to resolve painful issues that they may have experienced. In these areas of resilience and strength there remains the possibility to grow, to change and to embrace the challenges that life brings. Experiences of success and achievement can expand an individual's emotional reserves. These resilient aspects of the personality can help compensate for those areas where a person feels hurt and vulnerable, perhaps by guarding or steering the individual away from the experiences, thoughts and feelings that are likely to trigger difficult emotions. But sometimes this vigilance is not possible, because the ongoing experiences of adversity are too severe and also because it takes energy to continuously protect those parts of the personality that are vulnerable. Life has its own way of intruding into the best laid plans and deepest defences. Again, the death of a loved one is an example of an experience that is likely to 'throw' most people, but particularly those who are already carrying a great deal of unresolved grief and loss. (For a more detailed account of the relevance of Winnicott's writings to social work, see Applegate and Bonovitz 1995.)

Other developments within psychology

The developments within psychology that are most relevant to social work practice concern those concepts that illuminate, in developmental terms, our understanding of the difficulties that some service users experience in relating to others and to their wider social environment. For some writers, this has led to an exploration of how, as human beings, we develop a sense of self, because it is through this notion of the self (sometimes referred to as individualization) that we come to know and understand ourselves and interact with others (Howe 1996). However, we can neither relate with confidence nor establish a meaningful identity with other individuals, or with our community, if we do not have a coherent sense of self. This 'social self' is developed in relation to others. This has led to an exploration of the importance of 'relatedness', which is a concept where, according to Portnoy (1999), humanistic and psycho-analytic psychotherapy converge. The socially based nature of personality development is taken up by Howe, who states that: 'The poorer the quality of people's relationship history and social environment, the less robust will be their psychological make-up and ability to deal with other people, social situations and emotional demand' (Howe 2002b: 172).

These theories help us to understand the difficulties that some service users experience in their relationships with other people and especially in their capacity to empathize. This is particularly important in relation to parents' capacity to empathize with their children and can be seen in situations where parents fail to react to their children's tears or pain because they cannot feel what it is like to be that child at that moment. As a result, they do not know what weight to give to pain or how to react in ways that are comforting and reassuring. For the parent, what is often absent in this situation is any personal experience of being empathized with and comforted as a child. They do not have or cannot recall positive experiences that they can draw on and use in relation to their own children: they cannot give what they did not have themselves. The same can be said for parents who have not received good quality care and attention in childhood. This is sometimes described as parents failing to understand their children's needs. However, the implications are more far-reaching because an inability to empathize with children can leave children unprotected and unable to relate to others, particularly their peers, in ways that feel satisfying and mutually rewarding. This can lead to isolation and personal and social fragmentation: 'Those who are not embedded in social relationships find it more difficult to realize a coherent sense of self' (Howe 1996: 95). These social relationships are more difficult to establish where people come from 'adverse environments which lack love, mutuality and empathy' that have inhibited the 'formation of secure and confident personalities' (Howe 2002b: 172).

Different theories attempt to understand these reactions, in the hope of being able to effect change. The emphasis on relationships and relatedness links to object relations theory, a British school of psychoanalysis, which takes as central the interrelatedness between people (Kohon 1988). This emphasis can be found in the work of Balint, Fairbairn, Guntrip, Klein, Winnicott and others. Similar concepts are described in the USA under different theories, such as self theories or self-psychology, and can be seen in the works of Kohut (1971), Mahler *et al.* (1975) and Kernberg (1969,

1984). Through the work of Kohut, self theories are linked to another American psychoanalytic approach, namely ego-psychology, popularized through the work of Hartmann (1958), Parad (1958) and Kohut (1971, 1977) and the casework approach of Florence Hollis (Hollis 1964). Towards the end of the 1950s, ego-psychology had become very influential in psychoanalysis in the USA. However, within social work, this approach is now less influential, except in relation to crisis intervention (Parad and Parad 1990). (For a more detailed summary of different psychoanalytic theories in relation to self and others, see Brearley 1991.)

Feminist writings on psychology, psychoanalysis and feminist therapy

One of the most important developments in relation to psychology, particularly psychoanalysis, can be found in feminist writings on these themes, both in the USA and in the UK. The focus of feminist writings has been twofold: firstly, to challenge male dominated and sexist assumptions about women's lives and emotional development that reinforce inequality; and, secondly, to create a new and different women-centred theory and practice, loosely labelled 'feminist therapy' (Mitchell 1974, 1984; Chodorow 1978, 1989, 1994, 1999; Flax 1981, 1991, 1993; Benjamin 1990, 1995; Seu and Heenan 1998).

The challenge posed by feminists, particularly in the 1970s and 1980s, to psychology, psychoanalysis and the mental health system was formidable. For psychoanalysis, it focused on an attack of Freud's concept of penis envy and his revision and dismissal of women's accounts of sexual abuse. In the field of psychology, assumptions held by professionals who effectively saw women as being less well adjusted than men were also challenged (Broverman et al. 1970). Similar analyses were made in relation to research, particularly the assumption that girls' experience could be understood in terms of boys' experience. For example, Carol Gilligan identified a clear gender bias prevalent within certain developmental theories. A former student of Kohlberg, Gilligan challenged particularly the work of Kohlberg (1969) and Piaget (1932) because, within their research, girls were not included: 'the child' is male and 'females simply do not exist' (Gilligan 1993: 18). Gilligan goes on to state that Kohlberg's 'six stages that describe the development of moral judgment from childhood to adulthood are based empirically on a study of eighty-four boys whose development Kohlberg followed for over twenty years' (Gilligan 1993: 18). The absence of girls from the study meant that: 'Prominent among those who thus appear to be deficient in moral development when measured by Kohlberg's scale are women' (Gilligan 1993: 18).

The attempt to create an alternative field of feminist theory and practice in relation to women has led to many interesting developments. For example, Gilligan's work led her to explore the ways in which women and men approach experiences differently, with men seeking to 'protect separateness' and women to 'sustain connections' (Gilligan 1993: 44–5). She explains that 'the failure to see the different reality of women's lives and to hear the differences in their voices stems in part from the assumption that there is a single mode of social experience and interpretation' (1993: 173).

Gilligan's concepts form part of the theoretical framework for the Stone Center, a feminist initiative based in Boston, Massachusetts (Jordan *et al.* 1991; Jordan 1997). The work of this centre exemplifies the quest among feminists to develop a theory and practice based on women's experiences of oppression and social inequality. This exploration draws on the work of a range of feminist writers, particularly Jean Baker Miller's classic text *Toward a New Psychology of Women* (1976) and also, among others, the work of Kohut (1971, 1977), Klein (1975), Guntrip (1977), Stern (1987) and Winnicott (1958, 1965). The theoretical and practice perspective of the centre stresses the importance of the interconnectedness between people. This has led to a radical reappraisal of the concept of dependency as a necessary and important element in relating. It has also led to a critique of concepts such as mutuality and the central place that empathy plays in terms of establishing a sense of relatedness and connection. These concepts have resulted in important developments in terms of the relationship between therapist and service user and have challenged whether the distance between the two works well for women.

Much of the development of 'feminist therapy' within the UK in the 1980s focused on the work of Luise Eichenbaum and Susie Orbach (1982, 1984), which drew on psychoanalysis, particularly object relations theory. It also focused on a broader theoretical and practice framework that could be seen in the development of women's therapy centres, particularly the work of the London Women's Therapy Centre, where feminists were exploring how to make available a range of different therapeutic approaches – gestalt, bio-energetics, psychodrama – and how to ensure they spoke to women's experiences. In addition, a whole range of different responses were developed in relation to difficulties previously ignored, such as group and individual therapy for women with eating disorders, or who had been sexually abused or undergone abortions. The experiences of women from minority groups – black, lesbian, working class – were also explored (Hibbert and van Heeswyk 1988; Trevithick 1988). These developments, and the awareness they stimulated in terms of women's oppression and how to address the impact of social inequalities, have been far reaching, and continue to be so, particularly in relation to social work. (For a further account of feminist writings on these themes, see Howell and Bayes 1981; Ernst and Maguire 1987; Seu and Heenan 1998.)

Further thoughts, reservations and criticisms

So far, I have largely described the strengths of these theories. I have done so purposely because of the tendency within social work to cast aside concepts that are considered to be flawed or inadequate in one way or another – described earlier as the 'theoretical stripping out' of theory from the social work curriculum (Jones 1996: 204). In doing so, my intention has been to keep alive the opportunity to explore and debate whether these theories illuminate our understanding of human beings and our current, day-to-day experiences as social work practitioners. They may not, but it seems important to arrive at this viewpoint from examining their strengths and limitations personally, rather than relying on other writers to do so on our behalf. The perspective I am taking is that no one theory can speak to all aspects of the human condition or to every situation that we face. Also, theories have to be located in their own history and the cultural influences and limitations prevalent at particular times. We may believe our current awareness to be superior, but who knows? Future generations may not be so kind.

There are other reasons for continuing to explore the value of the different theories described. First, these and other psychological theories form part of the knowledge base of other disciplines. Within a climate that emphasizes the importance of inter-agency collaboration and multidisciplinary work, we place ourselves in a disadvantaged position if we are not familiar with theories commonly referred to in health and education settings. Second, it seems important for us to engage in a dialogue within social work about whether a 'normative' standard of human behaviour is a helpful way of understanding human beings, given the fact that generalizations of this kind can be dangerous in relation to minority groups. If, for example, we were to develop Lena Robinson's (1995) views about the limitations of psychology with regard to black people, we must be prepared to commit ourselves to developing new theories, or revising those that already exist, so that they describe black people's experiences more accurately. Third, where theories have shortcomings, some can be built on in the light of current knowledge and experience. As a profession, we have much to contribute in this area, and this is particularly true of practitioners. One area worthy of further exploration within psychology, and one to which social work has much to contribute, concerns the impact of oppression on the emotional and material life of service users and what we can do, if anything, to strengthen people living in situations of adversity (Sheppard 2000).

It seems important at this point to highlight the main criticisms and reservations that have been made about some of these theories. One major problem relates to the assumptions made about how the experiences of different groups are represented in terms of 'normal' development. Robinson takes this point forward in relation to the assumptions made about black people:

A main feature of Eurocentric psychology is the assumption among psychologists that people are alike in all important respects. In order to explain 'universal human phenomena', white psychologists established a normative standard of behaviour against which all other cultural groups were to be measured. What appeared as normal or abnormal was always in comparison to how closely a specific thought or behaviour corresponded to that of white people. Hence, normality is established on a model of the middle-class, Caucasian male of European descent. The more one approximates this model in appearance, values and behaviour, the more 'normal' one is considered to be.

(Robinson 1995: 12)

In the case of women and black people, and in relation to all minority groups, the problem in establishing norms based on the values and assumptions of a dominant group is that they reinforce *their* reality *as reality,* leaving those at odds with this reality to be seen as deviant or deficient. Robinson goes on to describe three models that have been used to describe human development. These are:

- *the inferiority model*, which maintains that black people are 'intellectually, physically and mentally inferior to whites – due to genetic heredity' (Robinson 1995: 13)
- *the deficient (deprivations) model*, which states that black people are deficient in terms of intelligence, cognition and family structure, 'due to lack of proper environmental stimulation, racism, and oppressive conditions' (Robinson 1995: 13)
- *the multicultural model*, which differentiates between the difference and deficiency by acknowledging the strengths and limitations that all cultural groups possess. Like Gilligan's work, it emphasizes the importance of minority groups defining themselves.

The conclusion that Robinson draws is that 'social work policies and practices are fundamentally Eurocentric' (1995: 3), based on middle-class values and made up of 'mostly white middle-class people who are very much removed from the black population' (Robinson 1995: 4). This view does not accord with my experience of social workers, but I would agree that 'traditional principles and theories in psychology have not had sufficient explanatory power to account for the behaviour of black people in Britain' (Robinson 1995: 5). This criticism could be extended to include other minority groups because none of the theories described in this chapter explore their relevance in relation to differences of class, race, gender, age, disability, sexual orientation, culture and creed.

This leads to a second major criticism of a more psychologically oriented approach, which is that it can individualize problems and fail to place sufficient responsibility on to social factors. This has been termed the *psy complex*. Individualizing problems in this way can lead to a range of dilemmas:

> Because psychology is based heavily upon the construction of norms, there is a danger that people who deviate from the norm are considered to be 'abnormal', even though a norm is only an average of the spread of possibilities. When the norm becomes that which is desired and normative there is a danger of labeling people as deviant, even when they represent a part of the natural diversity of human beings.
>
> (Daniel 2002: 340)

These dangers highlight the importance of trying to look at the wider picture – at the sociology of particular groups as well as the psychology. To do this well involves being clear about what we mean when we use certain terms. For example, the term *deprivation* is used in this text to denote 'a lack of welfare, often understood in terms of material goods and resources but equally applicable to psychological factors' (Gordon and Spicker 1999: 36). It can mean the absence or loss of a secure home, family life, opportunities: in fact, the loss or absence of something generally held to be desirable within society. Deprivation of any kind, such as those losses relating to material possessions, physical attributes or emotional abilities, can happen to anyone and may be due to a range of different causes – an accident of birth, a stroke of bad luck or personal failings. But disadvantage describes the way that the absence – or the loss – of key resources or experiences can lead to the narrowing of people's life chances:

> The disadvantaged are those whose access to a range of goods or desirable life chances is restricted because of some characteristic or condition. The function is similar to that between disability, an inherent impairment of function or sensory capacity, and handicap, the extent to which a disabled person is prevented from achieving a satisfactory life, economically, emotionally and socially.
>
> (Brown 1983: 4)

In this definition, people who are disadvantaged 'are consistently exposed to the highest risks of being deprived. Put crudely, the disadvantaged are those whose deprivations occur not because they are foolish or unlucky but simply because they belong to a particular social group' (Brown 1983: 5). Within this picture, social disadvantage is the result of the way that inequalities are built into the fabric of our society. As a result:

> Certain groups are consistently exposed to deprivation in income, health, education, housing, employment and family life. This systematic deprivation means that such groups occupy a permanently disadvantaged position in society. One deprivation is associated with another, they interlock to form patterns of multiple

disadvantage which trap vulnerable groups in the misery of constant deprivation and ramify adversity across the generations.

(Brown 1983: 11)

It is most often the case that people who are economically poor or weak or frail in some way are likely to experience adversity and, as a result, to suffer. Again, the word *poverty* is used a great deal in social work and not always defined. In this text, it is defined as follows:

Poverty is the enforced lack of those material items which a majority of people accept as essential for participation in society. People who do not already have, or because of low income are unable to purchase, the goods and services which would allow them to participate fully in society are living in poverty.

(Stewart 2000a: 263)

This definition is sometimes called *relative poverty,* that is, where poverty is defined 'in terms of its relation to standards which exist elsewhere in society' (Gordon and Spicker 1999: 113). The relationship between psychology and sociology can be seen very clearly in the psychological consequences of social injustice (Sheppard 2002).

Conclusion

Understanding human beings is not easy because we are complex and diverse – and so too is the social world to which we belong. Yet there is something deeply satisfying about finding some kind of order in the midst of chaos and confusion, when a sense of meaning emerges from situations that seem to deny this possibility or when, sometimes against great odds, there are positive changes. These experiences highlight the importance of the reciprocal nature of our relationship with service users and carers, as well as how much we learn and gain from being given the opportunity to understand another human being. It leads to a certain kind of personal understanding, sometimes at a deeper level than is normally possible. Without this opportunity to learn, we cannot extend our knowledge and understanding of human experience, particularly our understanding of the unique experiences that individual service users bring. Nor can we develop the skills needed to address more complex problems, which, in turn, can affect our confidence.

Uncertainty is endemic to social work and it is unlikely that we will ever be able to differentiate with confidence those areas of human behaviour that are knowable and those that are not. It is for these reasons that it is important to commit ourselves to exploring a range of explanations, positions and theoretical underpinnings in order for us to gain a greater understanding.

4 COMMUNICATION, LISTENING

AND ASSESSMENT SKILLS

This chapter applies some of the points covered in earlier chapters to the knowledge and skills required in relation to communication and assessment skills. The first section begins with a brief account of the types of problems that social work is asked to deal with on a regular basis and what this means in terms of the solutions sought and the services provided – and how these relate to the 'role and purpose of social work' (Dominelli 2002b: 3). The second section looks at the importance of communication skills within social work, focusing in particular on the importance of verbal and non-verbal forms of communication, observation and listening skills. (Interviewing skills belong to this 'family' of core skills but are covered separately in Chapter 5.) The final section covers the important role assessment plays within social work and how different emphases and approaches influence the assessment process. The importance of problem-solving and decision-making skills in the assessment process is emphasized.

Common problems

From the difficulties inherent in living, problems emerge. Some problems experienced by service users occur with worrying regularity. In order to understand the nature of these problems, some writers have attempted to categorize them. For example, Reid's influential categorization identifies nine 'unsatisfied wants' (Reid 1978: 25–30). These are:

1 Interpersonal conflict
2 Dissatisfaction in social relations
3 Problems with formal organizations
4 Difficulties in role performance
5 Decision problems

6 Reactive emotional distress
7 Inadequate resources
8 Psychological or behavioural problems not elsewhere classified
9 Other and unclassifiable

(Reid 1978: 309–14)

Reid's categories remain important because they describe problems that lie behind most referrals to social services (Coulshed and Orme 1998: 118). The ninth category, other and unclassifiable problems, can be used to categorize problems that defy classification, as well as new problems that emerge, such as those related to drug addiction.

When attempting to conceptualize how problems arise, Popper sees this in terms of a disturbance: 'The problem arises when some kind of disturbance takes place – a disturbance either of innate expectations or of expectations that have been discovered' (1999: 4). Watzlawick *et al.* (1974) analyse the nature of the problems that emerge differently. In most texts, the words 'problem' and 'difficulty' tend to be used interchangeably. Watzlawick *et al.* use 'difficulties' to refer to everyday, undesirable or unbidden events that can be resolved through common-sense solutions. 'Difficulties' can also describe dilemmas that have 'no known solution and which – at least for the time being – must simply be lived with' or accommodated in some way (Watzlawick *et al.* 1974: 39). The idiosyncratic and irritating behaviour of some family members is an example of a difficulty that must be endured and tolerated. 'Problems', on the other hand, are situations, thoughts, feelings or experiences that are too troublesome, perplexing, distressing and complex to be dealt with, solve or overcome. Often several difficulties occur together, sometimes resulting in a transition from difficulties to problems. Within this conceptual framework, people with problems seek help (or are offered help) because they cannot keep going, or are unable to move the situation forward, without help.

Sometimes, difficulties have become problems, or problems have been made worse, by the fact that unhelpful solutions have been tried, leaving people feeling demoralized and defeated. Watzlawick *et al.* (1974: 39) identify three unhelpful problem-solving actions likely to produce negative results:

- A solution is attempted by denying that a problem is a problem; '*action is necessary, but is not taken*'.
- Change is attempted regarding a difficulty which for all practical purposes is unchangeable (e.g. the generation gap, or a certain percentage of incurable alcoholics) or non-existent; '*action is taken when it should not be*'.
- Action is taken which does not address the problem at the correct level. For example, this may be manifest by our asking service users to tackle certain problems for which they are ill-prepared – because they are too

frightened or lack appropriate skills or confidence. Watzlawick *et al.* describe this as action '*taken at the wrong level*'.

Interestingly, Sheldon takes a similar view in his differentiation between help and support. Before deciding what form our help should take, we need to analyse whether we can be of help at all: some service users 'are beyond therapeutic help as are some medical patients, and so care and support are the best we can offer, whilst others are not, but will become so if we do not intervene' (Sheldon 1995: 125). This highlights the importance of preventative measures. In some sections of social work, such as children's services, there is a renewed interest in early intervention. For example, family support services are often described as being preventative (Little 2000: 133). However, this emphasis is not present throughout social work, where the concept of risk can be given more weight than the concept of need (Stepney 2000a: 7). We return to the concept of risk assessment later in this chapter.

Solutions and services

What help is offered will depend on a range of factors, such as where the referral stands in terms of eligibility, statutory or legal obligations, the availability of staff and resources, the priority in relation to other cases, government targets and so forth. Cheetham *et al.* identify the diverse tasks and goals as:

> attempting to help vulnerable individuals to improve their quality of life or social functioning; to maintain these at an acceptable level or to arrest deterioration; to influencing systems within and outside social work, sometimes by playing a gatekeeping role; to performing some kind of controlling function, by rationing access to scarce resources, by trying to change deviant behaviour in the interests of 'society' or of deviant individuals themselves, or by using compulsory powers of removal from home.
>
> (Cheetham *et al.* 1992: 13)

In order to understand that diversity, different writers have attempted to analyse the different ways that social work responds to the human dilemmas presented. They include, for example, Dominelli's therapeutic helping, maintenance and emancipatory approaches (2002b: 3–4); Payne's reflective-therapeutic views, socialist-collectivist views and individual-reformist views (1997: 4); Davies's maintenance mechanic (1981: 137); and Howe's concepts of care, control and cure (1994: 518). Another way to understand how we respond to problems and difficulties would be to analyse these in terms of the shift that has occurred within social work from:

- doing things *to* service users; to
- doing things *for* service users; to
- doing things *with* service users.

The concept of partnership is important in this regard; that is, the means by which people are encouraged and enabled to take part in ways that influence problem-solving and decision-making, and policy and practice procedures that underpin those activities. In recent years, there has been a marked shift in the importance given to the part played by service users and carers in the decision-making process (Beresford and Croft 2000: 355). However, whilst this shift is important, it does not guarantee more and better services. Also, participation may lead some service users and carers to opt for having more things done for them – perhaps because they are weary of having to do things for themselves – thereby becoming more dependent on state resources rather than less dependent. Such choices could present a difficulty for a government which is looking at ways to reduce the cost of welfare services. Yet without access to these services, we could find that difficulties turn into problems, and lead to further hardship and suffering, particularly for vulnerable people who have no other resources or security other than state resources (Pringle and Thompson 1999).

Whether working with individuals or groups, families or communities, the activities of social workers cover a vast range, such as:

> assessment; providing information, advice, and sometimes counselling designed to alter behaviour or attitudes or to increase understanding; arranging service provision or arguing for it with other agencies; providing personal care in residential and day care settings; offering general support to clients and their carers; mobilizing community resources.
>
> (Cheetham *et al*. 1992: 13)

The assumption that our work will have a positive impact can neither be taken for granted nor easily evidenced (Fischer 1973: 19; MacDonald *et al*. 1992; Myers and Thyer 1997), leaving some commentators to advocate practice approaches and interventions likely to produce 'small successes' rather than 'large failures' (Doel 2002: 192).

COMMUNICATION SKILLS

Good communication skills, particularly listening and interviewing skills, lie at the heart of effective social work practice. Communication has been defined as: 'The verbal and nonverbal exchange of information, including all the ways in which knowledge is transmitted and received' (Barker 2003: 83).

Like other interventions, it is through our capacity to communicate with others that we reveal the knowledge, skills and understanding that we are working from. We also use these skills to communicate an 'ethically sensitive practice' (Thompson 2002b: 307); that is, to combine being both sensitive and purposeful with being able to acknowledge the uncertainty that is inherent in looking across into another person's world. To understand another person, and their world of meaning, we need to start by acknowledging our ignorance of that person and their social world. We also need to learn to ask good questions, in ways likely to provide information that is both relevant and sufficiently detailed, and to watch for clues. Interestingly, according to one piece of research, 50 per cent of people seeking help do not return for a second interview (Marziali 1988). We know little about why people do not return but the reason(s) may not always be negative. More follow-up studies are needed in this area.

As human beings, we are always communicating something, although this may not be in words. For this reason, communication lies at the heart of social work. The young person who is disruptive in school, the person addicted to alcohol or drugs, the mother too depressed to get out of bed, the person whose strategy for getting what s/he wants is to steal, lie or cheat, and the old person too fiercely independent to seek help when needed are all communicating something about how they feel about themselves, their lives and the hardships and adversity they have experienced, and may still be experiencing. For this reason, learning to understand what people are communicating, and to put our own thoughts and feelings into words, is a crucial skill within social work.

These skills involve being able to communicate across a wide spectrum, from those located at the 'higher end' of the professional ladder, such as magistrates, doctors, consultants, solicitors, assistant directors or directors, to those who are struggling to survive at a different, often 'lower end' of the social ladder. My guess is that most social workers feel more comfortable talking to service users than people in senior positions. Our own reactions when we feel nervous or intimidated can be a valuable reminder of how intimidated some service users or carers may feel in relation to us. However, it is important that our own lack of confidence is not allowed to disadvantage the people we work with, remembering that: 'Professionals are less effective on their clients' behalf if they cannot communicate precisely and persuasively' (Clark 2000a: 181).

A different way to describe communication skills is as interpersonal skills, which Egan sees as 'the principle skill for just about everything we do' (2002: 70). Similarly, Dickson and Bamford describe interpersonal skills as the capacity of 'the worker to engage meaningfully with the client' in ways that demonstrate 'skilled professional interaction' (1995: 85). It is a term most commonly used in counselling (McLeod 2003: 480) and often linked to the work of Carl Rogers (Chui and Ford 2000: 44). In social work, interpersonal skills, 'people skills' or 'personal effectiveness skills' (Thompson 2002c: xv) refer to the quality of contact, rapport and relationship that is made between social workers and service users, carers, colleagues, other professionals and interested parties. Most of the skills and interventions described in this text could be described as interpersonal skills.

Language

We use language – and our capacity to communicate – to shape our lives and to relate to others. As professional social workers, it can be our choice of words and the gestures, meaning and understanding that accompany the words we use that enable relationships to be formed and work to be done. The important part played by language is captured in the following quote:

> language informs the way we think, the way we experience, and the way we interact with each other. Language provides the basis of community, but also the grounds for division. Systematic knowledge about language and practical awareness of how it works is fundamental to the process of building mature communities.
> (Montgomery quoted in Thompson 2003: 36)

There is an ongoing struggle within social work about which words to use, or what language to adopt, to describe certain situations or categories of people. The hope is that by changing the words we use there will be some fundamental shift in the nature of the oppression that certain groups experience. A new word can give us hope, and help us to identify one another, but it cannot guarantee equality or justice. This can only be achieved through our commitment to social justice and by being honest with ourselves, and others, about the real differences that exist and the difficulties we encounter when trying to establish more equitable relationships. In relation to our own language, and the language that others adopt, this calls for a 'linguistic sensitivity' so that we are aware of our language and can explain to others what we might find problematic or discriminatory about their choice of words (Thompson 2003: 118), rather than use it as an opportunity to 'put them down'.

An example of the confusion caused through differences in language is demonstrated very clearly in *Getting the Message Across* (Social Services Inspectorate 1991), where one member of the project group circulated a questionnaire to 100 service users listing a range of words frequently used within social work. Others from the project consulted service users with a variety of special needs. The following shows how this group of service users understood certain terms, shown in italics:

- *voluntary agencies* – people with no experience, volunteers
- *maintain* – mixed up with maintenance – money paid for children in divorce settlements
- *sensitive* – tender and sore
- *encompass* – a way of finding direction
- *agencies* – second-hand clothes shops
- *common* – cheap and nasty (it is not advisable to talk about 'common' values)
- *eligibility* – a good marriage catch
- *allocation process* – being offered re-housing
- *function* – wedding (party), funeral
- *format* – what you wipe your feet on at the front door
- *gender* – most did not know this word
- *criteria* – most did not know this word
- *equitable manner* – most did not know this term
- *networks* – no one knew this word
- *advocacy* – some users thought this word meant that if they did not agree with the assessment they would have to go to court. They wondered who would pay the bill.

(Social Services Inspectorate 1991: 20)

For these reasons, the Social Services Inspectorate recommends that agencies should develop a local glossary of terms likely to be misunderstood and to involve service users in this task. For example, the term 'common purpose' used within this book – as well as other terms – may need to be clarified in this way.

For the most part, our coverage of this theme has been based on the assumption that we have the abilities required to communicate with others and to use language without difficulty. However, some people have specific communication needs. For example, people who have a hearing impairment may need the support of a trained competent British Sign Language (BAL) interpreter. Loop systems can also be important for people with hearing difficulties. People who are sight impaired (Irvine 2000: 364–5) or who have communication problems, perhaps due to a disability, may require specialist support to aid communication, such as Makaton – a system of signing often used with people with learning disabilities (Pierson and Thomas 2002: 263). The use of Braille for people who are visually impaired tends to be less popular than other low-vision aids (Pierson and Thomas 2002: 262).

Non-verbal forms of communication

The importance of non-verbal forms of communication, sometimes described in terms of body language, should not be underestimated. For example, in the classic study by Birdwhistell (1970), it is estimated that in a typical encounter involving two people, the actual spoken or verbal content is likely to carry only one-third of the social meaning in any given event, whereas the non-verbal forms convey roughly two-thirds of the meaning. In addition, it is estimated that more weight is given to non-verbal forms of communication, particularly when there is a conflict between verbal and non-verbal forms, because the assumed meaning, once picked up, cannot easily be accessed or refuted (Mehrabian 1972). The following quote highlights the ambiguity of our non-verbal communication in relation to interviewing:

> Detailed studies have identified many items in the nonverbal vocabulary, including five thousand distinctly different hand gestures and one thousand different steady body postures. Precise observation of nonverbal behaviour is important, but it is only a first step. The interviewer still has to infer some valid meaning from the data. Accurate observation is a necessary but insufficient requisite for understanding the psychological relevance of the gesture.
>
> (Kadushin and Kadushin 1997: 315)

The analysis of what is being communicated non-verbally is a complex undertaking and one prone to 'common-sense' interpretations that may not be accurate. For example, I once worked in a residential situation where the self-injuring behaviour of a young woman, Anna, was described by a staff member as 'attention-seeking'. Another understood the same behaviour to be an indicator that Anna was feeling 'safe'. One had a negative understanding, the other a positive, but I felt both to be wrong. Anna's own understanding, which had not been sought, was that she had 'had enough', having been let down by her parents and foster carers. She had every reason to be distressed, but this information was not sought and, as a result, her behaviour was not understood. This example illustrates a tendency within social work to attribute the behaviour of service users to personality characteristics rather than outside forces, while they themselves are likely to cite external causes and situational variables as responsible for many of their problems and choices. In all communication, but particularly non-verbal forms, there can be a miscommunication between the message sent and the message received. This is more likely to happen when we are operating from a set of assumptions. We see and hear through our histories and this can have advantages and disadvantages. Our best safeguard is to check our perceptions directly with the person in question, but this too may fail if the person is not able – for whatever reason – to reveal his or her true thoughts and feelings.

Lishman (1994: 20) divides non-verbal communication into two broad areas: proxemics (distance and physical closeness) and kinesics (movements, gestures, expressions). For Kadushin and Kadushin (1997: 287–320), non-verbal communication includes the following:

- chronomics (time keeping, such as the likelihood of people being too early or too late; preparedness)
- artificial communication (the language of the physical setting, such as how the home is arranged, and personal presentation, such as personal dress, choice of clothes)
- smell (emotional states communicated through subtle changes in body odour)
- touch (handshaking, hugs; these tend to be defined according to the situation and cultural norms)
- paralinguistics (cues that depend on hearing and how words are said in terms of their tone, pitch, volume, speed, emphasis, intonation, articulation and intensity)
- proxemics (communication through space and distance; the distance people need in order to feel comfortable)
- body language kinesics (visual communication through the face, eyes, hands and arms, feet and legs).

Lishman also includes the importance of 'symbolic communication': 'punctuality, reliability and attention to detail can be symbolic of the worker's care, concern and competence' (1994: 18). For example, I would describe returning telephone calls to service users, carers and other professionals as 'symbolic communication', because it communicates the sense that we are organized, disciplined and rigorous in our professional approach. It communicates that other people, and their communications, are important. How we dress can be significant: 'The way we dress communicates symbolically something of ourselves, and will have symbolic meaning for clients (and colleagues) depending on age, culture, class and context' (Lishman 1994: 18). I recall a social worker being bewildered by a service user who complained when he had arrived to introduce himself wearing dirty jeans and a combat jacket. Or again, I recall my own shortcomings when I have let children and young people down by cancelling appointments or failing to turn up on time. My explanations felt insignificant compared to the distress I caused. Our mistakes can make learning a difficult experience but perhaps a worthwhile endeavour if we allow ourselves to be changed by our errors.

Observation skills

Our understanding of non-verbal forms of communication is usually gathered through our observations. These help us to understand and to formulate hypotheses about what is actually happening and why, and to check out the reliability of our perceptions against those of other people and other information available. Gambrill stresses the importance of observation skills in social work:

> Observation in real-life settings may be required to clarify problems and identify related circumstances. Without a fine-grained (detailed) description of problem-related contingencies based on careful observation, you may make inaccurate assumptions about maintaining conditions. You may overlook problem-related behaviours of misapplied and unapplied contingencies. Each individual is unique. Only through careful observation may interaction patterns between clients and significant others be understood.
>
> (Gambrill 1997: 375)

Observation skills can be used quite generally or as a specific intervention. Inviting another colleague to sit in on a particular meeting or interview in order to gain a different perspective would be an example of using observation as an intervention. Whether used as a general or specific tool, to understand both the content and process of a particular interaction, observations are 'of particular relevance when the interest lies in the nature of the interaction between individuals or the styles of intervention adopted by social workers' (Cheetham *et al.* 1992: 44). In addition, our capacity for self-observation, although always somewhat limited, provides us with an opportunity to analyse our own role and impact (Sheldon 1995: 132–3).

If an observer is to be invited to 'sit-in', it is important to explain the purpose of the observation and to seek the permission of the service user before the session, so that they have the chance to refuse without feeling 'put on the spot'. This is important for the person being observed, because it can be quite unnerving to be watched by another human being, particularly when the observation is in silence and undertaken by a professional. As human beings, we all have parts of our personality that we do not want to be seen by others. Also, being observed can give rise to a range of worries and fantasies about the observer, particularly what the observer is thinking: some people interpret silence as someone being critical. Again, these concerns need to be addressed. Where part of the process involves giving feedback, unless the purpose is to be more confrontational, it can help to be more descriptive than interpretative in the observations offered, thereby allowing the individual to form their own conclusions and inferences. Finally, it is worth remembering that when observing a session in silence, particularly when it involves the disclosure of abuse, the observer can sometimes leave the session feeling distressed if they have been exposed to feelings in an unguarded way. These difficulties need to be explored beforehand and discussed in supervision so that the benefits of direct observation are not lost.

LISTENING SKILLS

Listening skills are essential in a whole range of different situations – when listening to colleagues, attending meetings, engaging in inter-agency collaboration – in fact, in all situations where communication is a central theme. There are several reasons why, as people and as professionals, we listen to others:

- to acquire information;
- to empathize;
- to discriminate;
- to evaluate;
- to appreciate;
- to derive other benefits (for example, it can be time consuming to ask a person to repeat what they have said because we failed to listen carefully).

(adapted from Smith 1986: 252–5)

Different authors stress different aspects of the listening process. For Egan, active listening is about being present in ways that identify key messages and feelings, attempting to understand the client in terms of his or her context, being tough minded when listening and processing what is being said and musing on what is missing (2002: 85–8). 'People want more than physical presence in human communication; they want the other person to be present psychologically, socially, and emotionally' (Egan 1990: 111).

This is sometimes called *active listening*, which describes a special and demanding alertness on the part of the listener (Lishman 1994: 63), where the aim is to listen closely to the details of what is being conveyed and to ensure that the person is aware that this is happening. It is sometimes termed *credulous listening*, which is about believing what is being communicated (Feltham and Dryden 1993: 105). This description aptly fits much of social work where, in the face of evidence to the contrary, we might doubt the evidence before we would doubt the individual. While this might be the correct initial approach to follow, we must always be open to reviewing our judgements in the light of new information. *Non-selective listening*, sometimes called non-directive listening or evenly suspended attention, is where listening occurs at several levels: to what people say; how they say it; at what point they say certain things; whether certain themes recur; and to what they do not say. This is sometimes described as 'listening with the third ear'. This form of listening allows us to be sensitive to the wider social and cultural context from which an individual speaks. The following is a list of the 20 basic skills involved in listening:

- being as open, intuitive, empathetic and self-aware as possible
- maintaining good eye contact

- having an open and attentive body orientation and posture
- paying attention to non-verbal forms of communication and their meaning
- allowing for and using silence as a form of communication
- taking up an appropriate physical distance
- picking up and following cues
- being aware of our own distracting mannerisms and behaviour
- avoiding making vague, unclear and ambiguous comments
- being aware of the importance of people finding their own words in their own time
- remembering the importance of the setting and the general physical environment
- minimizing the possibility of interruptions and distractions
- being sensitive to the overall mood of the interview, including what is not being communicated
- listening for the emotional content of the interview and adapting questions as appropriate
- checking out and seeking feedback wherever possible and appropriate
- being aware of the importance of timing, particularly where strong feelings are involved
- remembering the importance of tone, particularly in relation to sensitive or painful issues
- avoiding the dangers of preconceptions, stereotyping or labelling, or making premature judgements or evaluations
- remembering to refer to theories that are illuminating and helpful and also, where appropriate, to explain, in an accessible language, theories that may aid understanding
- being as natural, spontaneous and relaxed as possible.

By adopting a non-selective or non-directive approach when listening to others, the intention is often to try to minimize our own personal bias and stereotypical assumptions. It also helps us to follow the speaker's lead. The importance of creating a safe environment, free from distractions, when listening to others has to be stressed. Listening provides a creative opportunity to demonstrate our commitment and care; it is an essentially respectful undertaking, particularly if done with generosity. When listening in silence, this commitment, warmth and concern must be conveyed through our body language which, if done well, may speak so clearly that the individual never realizes that we have said nothing in words.

Most people think that listening is an easy activity. As a result, for many it is considered an innate skill that comes naturally and, therefore, needs no training. This is not the case. The essence of good listening is learning about how to reach the emotions and thoughts of others – this is not a skill that can easily be taught. The misconception that listening is easy can be based on a confusion between listening and hearing. We may hear what is being said, but this may be a passive activity, whereas listening requires a more active involvement. Kadushin and Kadushin differentiate between the two by describing hearing as a physiological act, the appreciation of sound, whereas listening is seen as a cerebral act, that of understanding (1997: 50).

It is estimated that something like 45 per cent or more of our waking lives is spent listening. However, where listening performs part of our professional role this figure is higher. Smith (1986: 261–2) divides poor listeners into three categories:

- *pretend listeners* – are 'not actually listening at all but only pretending to'. They have learnt to respond in appropriate places, thereby giving the impression of listening
- *limiting listeners* – practise 'a type of partial listening where the listener consciously determines that he will attend only certain portions of the speaker's remarks', often those aspects considered more interesting
- *self-centred listeners* – 'are concerned only with themselves and pay little or no attention to others'.

(Smith 1986: 261–2)

Egan takes up some of the same points but uses different terms to describe inactive or inadequate listening (2002: 75–6), such as non-listening, partial listening, tape-recorder listening (merely repeating the client's words) and rehearsing (where the interviewer stops listening in order to rehearse a response). To this list, Egan adds: filtered listening (where the interviewer selects in and selects out aspects of the communication); evaluative listening (where the interviewer judges what the interviewee is saying in terms of good or bad); stereotype based listening (where stereotypical labels replace understanding); fact-centred rather than person-centred listening (where facts are substituted for understanding); sympathetic listening (where the interviewer 'takes side' out of sympathy); and interrupting (where the interviewer interrupts in ways that break the communication flow, often to ask questions that are untimely) (Egan 2002: 90–2). There are times, particularly when we are tired or preoccupied, when we are all prone to being poor or inadequate listeners. However, to become locked into the habit of not listening is serious because these patterns can be difficult to shift.

ASSESSMENT

There has always been an acknowledgement of the essential role of assessment within social work. However, its significance took on a new meaning in the 1980s and 1990s following several public inquiries into the deaths of children known to social services. Other negative media coverage in relation to people discharged from psychiatric hospitals also called into question the role of social workers and our capacity to make professional judgements. This led to a stronger emphasis on the importance of assessment, particularly where risk is involved – an emphasis which has remained central to much of the legislation that has been passed in recent years (Milner and O'Byrne 2002: 14–18). Of particular importance is the guidance on assessment that has been written into the *Framework for the Assessment of Children in Need and their Families* (DoH 2000). This document, which replaced the more checklist based approach of the *Orange Book*, emphasizes the need to have a full picture of the child's circumstances and the importance of adopting a child-centred approach (Brammer 2003: 156). It also incorporates an ecological perspective, using a helpful diagram to illustrate the range of factors that could be explored.

Assessment has always been a key feature of social work education and one that continues to be central in guidance documents in relation to the new degree. However, it is interesting to note that the SCIE Knowledge Review on assessment found that 'there is no singular theory or understanding as to what the purpose of assessment is and what the process should entail' (Crisp *et al.* 2003: v). In addition, the review found that the assessment skills taught on social work programmes tend to be grouped with other subjects, rather than being taught as a distinct subject in its own right. One reason for this may be due to the fact that assessment covers a broad spectrum of activity, such as work involving individuals, families, carers, groups and communities, and takes a different form depending on the way that legislation has framed the assessment task within children's services, adult care and the criminal justice system. The development of specialist training in these subject areas may make it logical to teach assessment skills under these headings. Another reason may relate to the fact that an assessment can be undertaken for a range of different reasons, although 'traditionally in social work, assessment has been about identifying deficits or difficulties rather than strengths, with an emphasis on matching needs with eligibility for services' (Crisp *et al.* 2003: 2).

The purpose of assessment

In general, most service users seek our help in relation to themselves, others, their current living situation or wider social network for three main reasons:

- to help and support individuals to *maintain* the quality of life they currently have and to avoid a deterioration

- to help and support individuals to introduce *limited changes* (first-order change, where the system itself remains unchanged)
- to help and support individuals to introduce more *radical change(s)* (second-order change where changes occur to the system itself).

For a fuller account of first- and second-order change, see Watzlawick *et al*. 1974: 10–12. One of the clearest general definitions of assessment is provided by Coulshed and Orme:

> Assessment is an ongoing process, in which the client participates, whose purpose is to understand people in relation to their environment; it is a basis for planning what needs to be done to maintain, improve or bring about change in the person, the environment or both.
>
> (Coulshed and Orme 1998: 21)

This definition emphasizes the collaborative nature of the relationship between practitioners and service users and carers, as well as the importance of incorporating social and environmental factors within the assessment process.

Assessment involves a range of activities in which practitioners, service users and carers:

- describe
- explain
- predict
- evaluate
- prescribe

(Coulshed and Orme 1998: 22)

Some academics and practitioners describe the assessment task as a one-off event, whereas for others it is an ongoing process. However, the difference may be one of terminology since most acknowledge the importance of monitoring events, updating information and responding to new developments. A complex issue in assessment, and one that is important to all practice approaches, relates to the extent to which we need to understand a particular problem – and its causes – for us to be able to work effectively with others to help bring about change. A second complexity relates to service user and carer participation in the assessment, decision-making and policy process. These judgements are even more difficult where the problems encountered are complex, multidimensional, severe and enduring.

Past causes

In relation to the past, Sheldon regards with suspicion the 'search for long-lost causes', except in the case of major trauma, for the following reasons:

(a) there is no guarantee that they will ever be found;

(b) because the exercise is costly in time and resources;

(c) when views as to the original causes of problems *can* be elicited they are not always agreed upon by the protagonists, nor are they necessarily valid;

(d) dwelling on the history of problems can sometimes serve to intensify bad feelings and can distract from the necessity of doing something positive in the here and now.

(Sheldon 1995: 112–13)

This last point is important. Sometimes we may focus on the past because we do not know how to address the problem that has been presented. On the other hand, it is sometimes clear that service users want to explore past events, and it can be unhelpful and overprescriptive to steer them away from their natural inclination. Also, some approaches use a service user's self-selected 'story-telling' as a particular intervention and approach to assessment. For example, a psychosocial approach tends to use this form of narrative, but others have also found it a helpful way to understand how service users see their lives and the difficulties they have encountered. 'People live stories, and in the telling of them reaffirm them, modify them, and create new ones' (Clandinin and Connelly 1994: 415). The attraction of a narrative approach is that this intervention is 'client/person-centred' and people often greatly appreciate the opportunity to describe themselves in this unhurried way. However, it can be a time-consuming activity and needs to be well thought out if we are to take full advantage of the opportunity it provides to work closely with service users.

Service user and carer participation and involvement

Although frequently grouped together, it is important to note that the needs and concerns of service users and carers can often differ. However, both groups share some common concerns and interests. For example, 'both may be equally in need of a service, and both can equally contribute to an understanding of the situation that they share' (Barton 2000: 3). Or again, both groups can be disadvantaged in the way that professionals treat them. This difficulty can be even more pronounced for women and people from ethnic minority groups. User participation has been described as follows:

User participation implies active involvement in the social sphere and refers to a range of involvements which individuals and groups may have in organizations, institutions and decisions affecting them and others. These extend from having control to being a source of information or legitimation. Participation is crucially judged by the extent to which people can exert influence and bring about change.

(Beresford and Croft 2000: 355)

In recent years, there has been a commitment to eliciting feedback on how service users experience the services provided and the importance of our 'seeking and actively responding to [service users'] perceptions and evaluations' (Lishman 1994: 4). To fail to do so can easily lead to the mistaken view that the assumptions we make are shared by service users, when clearly they are not (MacDonald *et al.* 1992: 624). We cannot hope for positive outcomes if we side-step individuals, whether service users or other significant individuals, no matter how difficult or stressful their inclusion might be (Thoburn *et al.* 1995). However, many authors encourage caution about using service user feedback or evaluations as the only or main indicator of practice success, without considering the context within which the evaluation takes place (Cheetham *et al.* 1992: 53; MacDonald *et al.* 1992: 631; Fuller and Petch 1995: 41).

In relation to carers, it is estimated that there are roughly 6 million carers in Britain, some of whom provide care for a few hours per week whilst others may be providing 24-hour care. Social workers' obligations in relation to carers are embodied in the Carers (Recognition and Services) Act 1995. This act does not apply to all carers: in effect, the care provided has to be 'substantial and regular' (Brammer 2003: 320), but the act places a duty on social services departments 'to assess the needs of carers independently of those of the person they support' (Petch 2002: 224). The Carers and Disabled Children's Act 2000 extended the C(RS)Act 1995, making it an 'absolute duty to assess but not directly to provide services' (Brammer 2003: 320). Many carers face difficulties accessing services:

> Another consistent observation is that resources are not allocated fairly. Carers often express the view that they have to fight to get anything.... Longstanding inequalities in the allocation of scarce resources are likely to be exacerbated as service users and carers become more aware of their rights.
>
> (Barton 2002: 405)

In the past, there has been a marked absence of the carer's voice in research relating to users (Barton 2000: 43). However, the requirements laid down in the UK government's White Paper, *Realising our Potential* (Cabinet Office/Office of Public Service and Science/Office of Science and Technology 1993), are intended to ensure that research designs take account of the views of the people who might benefit from the research (Everitt 2002: 116). The task of organizations such as INVOLVE, a national advisory body funded by the Department of Health, is to ensure that the public – *patients* or *consumers* – are actively involved in public health and social care research, rather than being used as the 'subjects of research' (Buckland and Gorin 2001).

Needs-led versus resource-led assessments

> Needs-led policies seek to respond to identified need, either at the individual or collective level. They are frequently contrasted with service-led responses, determined by available provision rather than specific need.
>
> (Petch 2000: 228)

As a result, a tension exists between needs-led and service-led assessments. Identifying the needs of service users and carers is included in some of the legislation that regulates social work practice, such as the needs-led policies defined under the National Health Service and Community Care Act 1990, the Carers (Recognition and Services) Act 1995 and the Chronically Sick and Disabled Persons Act 1971 (Munby 2002: 438–47). An example of the shift in thinking in relation to meeting the needs of service users can be seen in the enactment of the Community Care (Direct Payments) Act 1996, where local authorities were given powers to make cash payments to enable service users to purchase their own assistance. However, in 1997 the 'Gloucester Judgement' changed the grounds on which to press for more resources, when it was stated that local authorities have the right to take resources into account in the provision of services (Horder 2002: 116). Yet despite the setback of this ruling, some service user and carer groups continue to make considerable progress in terms of having their voice heard, although this representation is not available to all people from marginalized and excluded sectors of society, such as people in prison or mental hospitals, or young people whose behaviour is increasingly being criminalized (Yates 2004).

This tension is likely to persist where demand for resources exceeds supply. The question of who gains access to resources and what happens to those who fail to qualify – perhaps because they do not know how to use the 'system' to their advantage or because they have been designated ineligible – is a crucially important issue (Jordan 1990: 87). This is an ongoing concern for practitioners and policy-makers committed to creating a more equitable allocation of resources. For our purposes, the degree to which an assessment is needs-led or service-led will affect the range of information sought and the overall focus of the assessment. This can be seen in the different assessment formats identified by Lloyd and Taylor (1995: 700), which include:

- third party assessments (for example, pre-sentencing reports, case conference reports, social history assessment)
- investigative assessments (for example, risk assessments in relation to child protection and mental health)
- eligibility/needs assessments (for example, in relation to community care and children in need)

- suitability assessments (for example, in relation to prospective child-minders, foster carers, adoptive parents)
- multidisciplinary assessments (for example, in relation to hospital discharge, statementing in education).

Finally, it is worth noting that there are different ways to undertake an assessment. These include:

- *practitioners working alone*, which is the most common format;
- *joint assessment*, which mainly refers to two practitioners working together. This is particularly valuable where the situation is fraught or the problems are complex;
- *group or team assessment*, where everyone who has had contact with the family or group contributes what they have experienced or perceived; and
- *multidisciplinary assessment*, which involves professionals from different disciplines working together, sharing their knowledge and expertise in ways that effectively meet the different needs of service users. This way of working is central in community care.

Multidisciplinary and inter-agency work has many advantages but it also has serious disadvantages, particularly where the theory and practice model and value base differ markedly (Bywaters 1986) and where differences in status limit the contributions of some professionals. Tensions that emerge in relation to professional roles, boundaries and practice autonomy need to be addressed if a sound collaborative framework is to be established (Lloyd and Taylor 1995: 701). This involves finding a balance between conflicting demands, because time spent communicating with other professionals is likely to lead to less time being available for direct contact with service users. A final danger in relation to multiprofessional collaboration relates to the assumption that the bigger and more varied the group making decisions, the better the decision-making. Compliant decision-making or *groupthink*, sometimes influenced by a dominant individual or representative of a profession, can lead to assumptions not being questioned and, ultimately, the wrong decisions being made (Milner and O'Byrne 2002: 177). This danger has already been noted in relation to child protection case conferences and is likely to emerge in other settings given the government's commitment to inter-professional collaboration (Bywaters 1999).

These tensions become heightened where the system for controlling the intake and allocation of work is inadequate. This can lead to agencies becoming defensive and adopting a range of different strategies. As a result:

> they keep a low profile in their communities; they draw back from them, dilute the standard of the services, set up queues, use deterrents such as leaving telephones and offices unmanned, give a

more privileged service to certain service user groups (such as children) or spend time fighting invisible enemies.

(Coulshed 1990: 70)

One way to ensure that service users can access services easily would be for organizations to accept responsibility for introducing a system for monitoring referrals and prioritizing cases and access to resources. This can ease the 'irreconcilable demands' made on social workers in relation to the number of cases that can be worked with effectively at any one time (Macdonald 1990: 541).

In relation to assessment, the expectation that practitioners are able to work from a range of different practice orientations, approaches and perspectives, and a sound knowledge base, is important. However, this involves moving away from choosing practice approaches that suit our personal preferences and styles and instead choosing ways of working that best meet the needs of service users or the particular problem presented. This requires us to be more rigorous and creative in the way we approach our work and the relationship between knowledge, practice and research. This subject is likely to remain important and part of the ongoing debate about how we can work more effectively, efficiently and collaboratively in relation to the range of problems for which our help is sought.

Practice emphasis

Within some practice approaches, the assessment task may have a different focus. Some give weight to certain factors or problems more than others, and propose different solutions (Milner and O'Byrne 2002). For example, following a cognitive-behavioural approach to assessment, Sheldon focuses on a more here-and-now approach by attempting to identify the factors that influence problems. These include three elements: 'cognitive patterns, emotional accomplishments and behaviour itself' (1995: 158). This practice approach stresses the importance of attitudes and observable behaviour ('in excess, in deficit, inappropriate in relation to time and place') and being able to assess changes based on before and after comparisons of events, behaviours or difficulties (Sheldon 1995: 111–13).

Other assessments analyse problems presented differently. For example, some attempt to assess service users' coping capacities (England 1986: 14; Perlman 1986: 261; Howe 2002b: 177) and how these can be strengthened in order to help people through difficult times. The part that protective factors play in helping individuals, including children, to deal with adversity is important (Boushel 1994: 173–90). Other approaches are interested in people's coping capacity but may describe this in different terms. For example, task-centred approaches attempt to assess what service users can achieve in terms of specific tasks designed to meet agreed objectives (Marsh 2002: 106). This may involve attempting to identify what problem-solving activities have already been tried, and to what effect, in order to avoid situations likely to produce negative results (Watzlawick *et al*. 1974: 39). The focus may also be one that acknowledges the particular strengths and motivation that service users bring to the encounter (Miller and Rollnick 2002). Where an approach includes, or incorporates, an anti-discriminatory/anti-oppressive perspective (Doel 2002: 193), more weight is likely to be given within the assessment process to the positive and negative influence of social or environmental factors (Dominelli 2002b: 5) and the dangers of our adopting discriminatory assumptions and oppressive practices. In this regard, 'the power of language to reinforce existing power structures' is important (Thompson 2002c: 94). Despite the different emphasis given to certain factors over others, all practice approaches and perspectives, in their different ways, emphasize the importance of practitioners being warm, genuine, respectful and caring in their contact with service users (Cheetham *et al*. 1992: 51).

Evaluating outcomes

We cannot know whether our assessment of a given situation or problem was sound and accurate without finding some way to measure the outcome. However, it is important to identify what we are trying to evaluate and to differentiate between:

- evidencing our own practice effectiveness; and
- evaluating the overall success of a piece of work in terms of the final outcome or result.

The reason for this is that it is possible to be successful in terms of the interventions and skills used in a particular situation and yet to find that the overall results or outcome is negative. This may be due to the impact of factors relating to the individual in question or the context within which the work is taking place. Two broad outcome categories that are important in this regard are:

- outcomes of a particular service (service-based outcomes) that is, 'the nature, extent and quality of what is provided';
- outcomes for service users (client-based outcomes) that is, 'the effects of a particular provision on its recipients'.
                                                    (Cheetham *et al*. 1992: 63)

Thus an evaluation 'goes beyond the identification of effectiveness ...[and] may conclude that an intervention has been successful in terms of the objectives, but argue that these are either trivial, inappropriate or misconceived. To evaluate social work, therefore, involves assessing it within the broader context' (Cheetham *et al.* 1992: 10). As with measures of effectiveness, evaluations have to be related to context and the many variables that influence a particular outcome or result. Some variables are predictable and need to be acknowledged in the objectives and outcome statements agreed. Information that has been systematically gathered and analysed as part of the ongoing format for monitoring developments should help to indicate how well the work is progressing and what decisions need to be taken.

Task and process

Another differentiation within the evaluative process involves distinguishing between the task and the process. There is a danger that the task and process elements of our work may be placed in competition with one another or made to appear mutually exclusive, rather than being viewed as an integral part of the whole. For example, Howe emphasizes the importance of process: 'it is not the specific technique that is important but the manner in which it is done and the way it is experienced' (Howe 1993: 3). However, external constraints and poor agency policies and procedures can mar our progress, and these factors need to be taken into account, particularly where the work involves an 'outcomes approach': that is, an approach that works backwards from an outcome statement. For example, if an outcome statement, agreed by all parties, is for a child to be rehabilitated with his/her family, it is hopefully incumbent on the agency – social services – to provide the necessary resources to ensure this outcome is possible. Otherwise, as practitioners we can easily be left with tasks or outcomes that are impossible to implement. These points link to those covered in Chapter 1 on practice knowledge and the role of research based practice in social work.

There are several ways to evaluate: through our own perceptions and through asking for feedback from service users, colleagues, supervisors, other professionals or individuals involved in a particular piece of work. We can also seek evidence from external events. For example, if we have helped a service user to complete a benefit form, the success of this intervention should be evidenced in the benefit being received. This information can be gathered from a variety of sources: direct observation; feedback from service users and others; information from other agencies, such as hospital or education records; or feedback from colleagues and other professionals. However, this raises the issue of service user confidentiality. It also raises questions about the validity of evidence gathered.

It is sometimes assumed that 'involuntary clients' who come within our remit unwillingly are always resistant to change. This may not be the case. For example, research undertaken by O'Hare (1991) suggests that the difference between voluntary and involuntary service users in terms of willingness to change is not as marked as often assumed. Important breakthroughs can occur with individuals who do not seek a service voluntarily or who demonstrate the greatest resistance, but we are more likely to be successful in initiating change if we are optimistic and can communicate a sense of hope and possibility (Trotter 1999: 116).

Problem-solving and decision-making skills

Problem-solving

Central to the task of assessment is problem-solving. Increasingly, there is the expectation that social workers will not attempt to problem-solve on the behalf of others unless there is a sound reason for doing so, such as some form of impairment that hinders this possibility. According to Howe:

> Theories which appeal to clients' rational capacities and cognitive strengths tend to adopt a problem-solving approach.... Social work theories that fall into this category include task-centred approaches, cognitive-behavioural theories, and many forms of family therapy, brief solution-focused therapy and some aspects of systems theory.
>
> (Howe 2002a: 85)

However, helping people to play a central role in the problem-solving process can run into difficulties where people lack the emotional resources that are needed to be able to cope with responsibility, or lack the necessary confidence, knowledge and/or skills to act on their own behalf. Also, time constraints can sometimes make it easier to undertake the problem-solving ourselves, thereby running the risk of creating an unhealthy dependency. The search for solutions is implicit in problem-solving, but these need to be seen in terms of *experimental* or *attempted* solutions, that is, possible solutions that need to be tried out to see which works and which does not (Popper 1999: 3).

Decision-making

If problem-solving activities work out well, it should be possible for individuals to arrive at helpful decisions. These are sometimes described in terms of sound and effective decisions. However, O'Sullivan differentiates between these two terms: 'Decisions are sound when appropriately made according to established criteria, while effective decisions achieve the decision makers' goals' (2000: 85). In this conceptualization, sound decisions imply the ability to gather information – or 'best evidence' – from a variety of sources and to use that information and understanding judiciously, whereas effective decisions imply a more focused and goal oriented course of action.

Professional decision-making can take many forms. The extent to which service users and carers are informed, consulted and involved in decision-making can be categorized as follows:

- decisions that should be made but are *not made*
- decisions that are made where service users and carers are *not informed*
- decisions that have already been made where service users and carers are *informed*
- decisions that are yet to be made where service users and carers will be *consulted*
- decisions that are made in partnership where service users and carers are *jointly involved*
- decisions that service users and carers *make for themselves*.

Developing the kind of practices, goal setting and service provision that support user involvement involves:

- encouraging users to describe their own needs through the construction of jointly constructed problems, goals and tasks;
- sharing the assessment with the user (including the written assessment) and explaining why particular services are being offered, giving users the right to refuse what is being offered; and
- ensuring that users have sufficient information both about the decisions made, and the services available.

(Coulshed and Orme 1998: 62)

Making judgements

Also inherent in the problem-solving and decision-making process is the ability to arrive at some kind of judgement. However, forming judgements can sometimes be confused with being judgemental, that is, with being critical or oppressive, or holding prejudicial or stereotypical views. This confusion can result in practitioners failing to take decisions for fear of being considered judgemental, yet:

There is a very important distinction, however, between 'making a judgement' and 'being judgmental'. Social workers are required to face the challenge and responsibility of the former in order to be helpful; they need to avoid the prejudice, closed-mindedness and blaming implicit in the latter. The avoidance of making a moral judgement remains in itself a moral judgement.

(Milner and O'Byrne 2002: 169–70)

This concern about being judgemental has, according to Lloyd and Taylor, led to practitioners failing to explore key areas of enquiry and 'to operate in a narrow, blinkered way and at a very superficial level' (1995: 706). In relation to child protection, part of the problem is that: 'Our understanding of human nature in general and of child abusers in particular mean that we are always making decisions based on imperfect knowledge' (Munro 1996: 793–4). Nevertheless, the findings of the child abuse inquiries indicated that a 'closer study of these reports shows how resistant social workers are to changing their minds and how powerful an influence this has on the conduct of a case' (Munro 1996: 794). For these reasons, it is essential to highlight the importance of being able to form independent, balanced, courageous and sometimes unwelcome judgements, based on critical thinking and the 'best evidence' available to us at that time.

Organizational and administrative skills

It is estimated that as practitioners we spend approximately one-third of our working week in direct work with service users, although some would put the figure lower. This means that roughly two-thirds of our time is spent dealing with 'indirect' tasks, such as liaising with other agencies, mobilizing resources, attending meetings and training, and so forth. The multiple roles we perform, amid competing pressures, call for sound organization and planning skills if we are to be efficient and effective in our work. Too often, we are not. Instead, we can become caught up being 'busy' – where we are 'too busy to think and at times of confusion this state has advantages' (England 1986: 2).

By establishing good organizational and administrative systems, we are in a position to ensure that we make the best use of whatever time and resources we have available to us. This involves devising a personalized administrative system for planning, organizing, monitoring and reviewing our work to ensure that we are keeping to agreed programmes, action plans, targets, aims and objectives, and that these are consistent with the expectations of our agency in terms of its policy, practices and administrative structures. The emphasis is on an administrative system that aids practice, but this requires discipline. It also requires that the demands of the agency in terms of form-filling and other administration do not detract from practice. The disruptions caused by constant agency reorganization are a case in point.

For example, it would be helpful for practitioners to be given feedback about data collected. However, I know of situations where the data collected has not been looked at but has instead been left to gather dust: practitioners know this is the case and feel rightly demoralized and reluctant to engage in further form-filling exercises. Some of these tensions could be avoided if agencies, senior management, managers and practitioners could establish clear priorities and expectations, so that feedback could be built in and work planned and organized accordingly (Howe 2002a: 82–3). Otherwise, we run the risk of our work being dictated to by the urgency of the latest 'crisis' or being allowed to drift in an 'anything goes' attitude (Payne 1997: 55). The importance of planning and preparation in relation to interviewing is looked at again in Chapter 5.

Conclusion

In this chapter I began with a general account of the problems and difficulties that emerge in social work and highlighted a number of concepts used to analyse these dilemmas and the different courses of action that can be taken. The second section looked at communication skills, focusing in particular on the importance of language, non-verbal forms of communication, observation and listening skills – skills that are central to the task of assessment and effective practice. The third section explored the importance of assessment in social work: its purpose; the different types of assessments that can be undertaken; the place that service users and carers now hold within the overall picture; and how we might evaluate the effectiveness of our work. In the final section, the skills involved in assessment are broadened to include problem-solving and decision-making skills, and the importance of organizational and administrative skills.

We are all confined – to some extent – by what is possible and achievable within the funding available, workload pressures and other constraints on resources, but these limitations are made more restrictive when we fail to explore in a rigorous way the opportunities and possibilities that exist. However, more than ever, the part we play in helping to bring about lasting positive change is located within a collaborative framework. This has clear advantages but it can also be difficult to implement. The challenge lies in our being able to form a collaborative and inclusive partnership with service users, carers and others, so that together we can successfully address the dilemmas for which our help is sought.

On a final note, it is important to remember that it is not always easy for people seeking help to state their needs or put words to their thoughts and feelings, particularly when these are tangled amid feelings of confusion, fear, humiliation, anger and despair. At these times, it can be hard for people to remember their strengths and abilities – the courage and determination that have enabled them to get this far. Within this mass of jumbled experiences, misunderstandings between people and agencies can occur, sometimes with tragic consequences, as the inquiries into the deaths of children known to social services attest (DHSS 1982; Gough 1993; Munro 1996; Laming 2003). As practitioners we still have more to learn about how to work with people in ways that communicate the purpose of our work, clearly and sensitively – in ways that shine a torch on what is happening and why, that illuminate possible ways to move things forward and provide evidence of effectiveness, or otherwise.

This learning is an ongoing process and never complete. Indeed, one way to view every interaction is as a learning experience for both parties. Some service users may add to our learning by testing our resilience, particularly those who have a different value base, or who 'have no interest in being helped' and are not motivated to change (Trotter 1999: 1). Others may teach us how to pose questions in ways that lead to greatest openness and honesty, and the chance to take things forward. Or we may learn how to listen to what is *not* being said, rather than what is actually said, and to be able to hypothesize from this experience. At the same time, through the process of actually putting thoughts, feelings and experiences into words, service users and carers may be able to order events and emotions in ways that are helpful. And, in this process, they may learn more about their strengths and limitations – their capacity to cope or the limits of this coping ability – when faced with too many demands or too much stress. As stated earlier, what we gain from this involvement is that we too can grow and be changed by the encounter. It is this, and the benefits that others reap from our best efforts, that is our ultimate reward.

5 BASIC INTERVIEWING SKILLS

This chapter looks in some detail at 20 interviewing skills and describes how our theoretical knowledge can be put into words to aid effective communication. This includes being able to communicate our understanding, and the meaning given to experiences, and being able to respond in ways that foster action and the opportunity for people to move forward. However, our communication and interviewing skills extend beyond our direct contact with service users and carers to include being able to communicate with other professionals, family members, neighbours and the general public. Within social work, interviewing plays a vitally important role: 'Although social work involves a great deal more than interviewing, social workers spend more time in interviewing than in any other single activity. It is the most important, most frequently employed, social work skill' (Kadushin and Kadushin 1997: 3).

One way to see an interview is as a conversation with a purpose that is designed to meet a 'specific and usually predetermined purpose' (Barker 2003: 227). For this reason, good planning and preparation are the hallmarks of a successful interview: 'failing to plan is planning to fail'. The purpose of many interviews is laid down by the type of task being undertaken. For example, the primary purpose of some interviews may be to give or gain information or to ascertain whether the particular help being sought falls within the remit of social services. This may be the primary task of the initial (screening) interview or assessment. In recent years, there have been important developments in relation to information gathering and giving described under the heading 'information technology', which could have 'radical implications, opportunities and risks for social work' (Shaw 1996: 5). For further information on this theme, see Shaw (1996).

This information gathering and giving is central to the assessment and decision-making process and can be roughly divided into more formal interviews, such as child protection 'investigations', mental health or community care assessments, and those less formal interviews more common to everyday problems presented (Doel 1994: 26). Skills have to be developed in both areas because the two can overlap and the balance shift between one and the other. Also, the demands made on practitioners can change because interviewing is sensitive to and influenced by developments within social work. For example, in relation to children and families, since the 1990s, there has been a shift away from an emphasis on investigation and surveillance, prevalent from the mid-1970s, towards attempting to include and involve parents and children in the problem-solving and change process (Waterhouse and McGhee 2002: 267). This links the interviewing skills to concepts of 'partnership' and 'empowerment', because the interview may be the medium through which important connections and relationships are developed.

One way to see the task of gathering information is as a sort of detective – a Sherlock Holmes or Miss Marple – where our purpose is to find out as much as possible in ways that open up the possibility for an honest and respectful dialogue and 'partnership' to be created. This process can touch on the lives of a wide cross-section of people – service users, carers, their families, friends and neighbours (Lishman 1994: 71) – yet it is sometimes worrying to see how narrowly we cast our net when exploring the problems placed before us. For example, absent fathers tend to be ignored (Munro 1998a: 93), as do other family members deemed to be hostile to social work or to the particular service user in question. We can learn a great deal from people who have an axe to grind, although it is important to be careful about how, if at all, this information can be used. Although it is quite natural to want to avoid people who may prove 'difficult', this selecting out of key individuals can seriously limit our understanding and the options available. It is a shortcoming that should reveal itself in supervision.

For example, I once worked with a six-year-old girl, Alice, who was allocated to me at the point where she needed to be found a new placement while the adoption process was in motion. Alice had been made the subject of a care order due to her father's cruelty. Tragically, this had resulted in her being brain-damaged but, because of her trauma, it was not clear to what extent. Almost by accident I found an old reference to her paternal grandparents in her case file, dating back several years. We had no address but the case notes stated that Alice's grandfather worked for the local gas board. With this information, through a range of informal networks, I was eventually able to track down the grandparents' whereabouts. They had lost contact with their son because of his threatening behaviour towards them and, as a result, had also lost contact with Alice (in fact, their son was by then in prison). They did not know of her abuse or that she was now in care but they were pleased to hear of Alice and delighted at the prospect of seeing her again. To cut a very long story short, Alice's grandparents eventually adopted her. She now attends a special school and, as can sometimes happen, she appears to be less permanently disabled than originally thought (Sinason 1988). Her grandparents love her enormously and I believe that for the first time in her life she knows what it means to live in a peaceful, secure and permanent environment. Not all children are so fortunate and it may be quite rare for us to bring about this kind of change because too much is working against us. Nevertheless, most social workers can describe situations where they felt truly helpful and, amid the doom and gloom of everyday practice, it is important to remember that positive outcomes are sometimes possible, but may call for us to be imaginative and determined and to cast our nets wide.

Transferability of skills

It is difficult to transfer skills and interventions from one situation to another if they do not have a name. Therefore, an important feature of this chapter, and the chapters that follow, is to give a name to the range of skills and interventions regularly used in social work. However, once a skill has been named, it can prove difficult to describe its key features because words alone cannot convey all that is being communicated. For example, good communication skills also involve the thoughtful use of tone, timing, body language and the ability to choose words that can convey the information and meaning we want to communicate. Clearly, it is not possible to include these elements in a text of this kind; these skills and interventions are best learned in role-play exercises and in practice. The examples given in this chapter, which are drawn from my own experience as a practitioner and from encounters that actually occurred, stress the importance of using more direct and accessible language. In a book of this kind it seems fitting to give examples whenever possible in order to bring to life the skills and interventions being described. This makes it possible to analyse the quality of our communication and whether we have been able to 'get through'.

Our poor ability to explain the reasons for our involvement or why we have chosen a particular course of action has been criticized in public inquiries (DHSS 1982; Hill 1990; Gough 1993) and continues to be a source of concern (Munro 1996, 1998a). Without this clarity of purpose – the language to describe what we are doing and why – and the skills to help service users and carers to be clear about their needs, we cannot properly evaluate or research the appropriateness of specific interventions in terms of what is being communicated, both verbally and non-verbally. Nor can we evaluate how effective we and others have been in our efforts to bring about desired and agreed outcomes.

As stated earlier, we know that a skill has been acquired when it is enduring, that is, when it is reliable even under difficult, if not impossible, circumstances. I am reminded of this fact regularly when I ask students to role-play an interview. Some students respond by claiming that they can normally conduct a good interview but not when they are being observed by me or other students. My reply is to remind them that, firstly, we have no evidence of competence if we cannot allow our work to be observed and, secondly, being put off-stride in this way can be an indicator that the specific skills and interventions being demonstrated are not yet fully acquired because they are not reliable, resilient and enduring under pressure. Although the development of our knowledge and skills – and we perfect these attributes in our interventions – is a lifelong learning process, once we have acquired certain skills, they are available to be transferred across different service user and carer groups and adapted to fit different settings and circumstances. To do this well involves linking the knowledge we have acquired to practice, particularly our understanding of human behaviour and the uniqueness of every human being and the exceptional nature of every experience (Parsloe 1988: 8). It also involves using the findings of research to influence practice. For example, the importance of our being reliable and consistent in our contact with service users cannot be stressed enough. Punctuality is particularly important (Lishman 1994: 18–19). So too is the importance of returning phone calls at the first opportunity. These skills may seem trivial but they communicate a great deal. Failing to attend to these details can severely limit our ability to establish a good 'working alliance'.

The skills covered in this chapter include:

- engaging with the task and purpose of the interview
  - planning and preparing for the interview
  - creating a rapport and establishing a relationship – welcoming skills
  - empathy and sympathy
  - the role of self-knowledge and intuition
- questioning
  - open questions
  - closed questions
  - 'what' questions
- confirming what has been said and heard
  - paraphrasing
  - clarifying
  - summarizing
  - giving and receiving feedback
- sticking to the point and probing deeper
  - sticking to the point and purpose of the interview
  - prompting
  - probing
  - allowing and using silence
  - using self-disclosure
  - using humour
- endings: disengaging and termination skills
  - ending an interview
  - closing the case and ending the relationship.

Engaging with the task and purpose of the interview

Engaging skills have, as their starting point, the importance of taking seriously the weight given to problems by service users, but doing so within a context where there is a critical awareness of information that appears to be inconsistent or incomplete or to have been omitted. This process also entails social workers being explicit about what we are doing and why (Munro 1998a: 89). Our willingness as practitioners to engage with the difficulties people are experiencing can be one way that we communicate the values we hold, such as a belief and confidence in people's ability to change their lives, the importance of self-determination (Clark 1998) and people's right to be given help in times of hardship. Our success in this communication can be seen when individuals leave the interview with an increased sense of self-confidence, self-respect and energy because they feel that they have been heard and that the meaning they give to their experiences has been understood. People who feel positive about themselves and their capacity to influence others, including their ability to influence us, are more likely to be successful in changing their lives.

However, not all interviews can be a positive experience. Some involve setting clear boundaries, whilst others may be about 'breaking bad news' (themes that are covered later in the text). It is also important not to overemphasize the degree of influence that we can exercise. This same limitation can be present for service users and carers (Dominelli 2002b: 8). Limitations are particularly difficult to overcome in relation to structural inequalities, such as the hardships and oppression encountered by people who are weak and frail, or who are poor (O'Sullivan 1999: 15). For O'Hagan, this means that 'in social work, the task of communicating and engaging is often more complex and hazardous than it is in everyday life' (1996: 4–5).

Planning and preparing for the interview

Before beginning an interview, it is important to think carefully about its purpose and what we hope to achieve in the time allotted. Good planning and preparation are most important, and the interview should be considered within its widest context, which involves taking into account the particular needs and/or expectations of:

- the individual or group of people seeking our help
- other people involved with this individual or group of people (e.g. neighbours and other family members)
- ourselves as practitioners, in terms of our personal and professional expectations
- agency policy, procedures, practice, resources and requirements of us, as employees or representatives of the agency

- other professionals connected to this individual or group of individuals.

There are essentially two ways of preparing ourselves for this task. Both cover many of the same issues but in different ways. One could be called a *reflective* approach, where information is gathered up in a less systematic but more empathic and intuitive way. This is my preferred approach, and involves using our empathic skills to 'enter imaginatively into the inner life of someone else' (Kadushin and Kadushin 1997: 108) through the thoughts and feelings, fears, expectations and fantasies of the person attending the interview, and the reality of their situation in terms of their home life, financial situation, journey to the locality office and so on. If, for example, we imagine that the service user might feel nervous, what evidence would we look for to confirm or deny this hypothesis? At what point will we combine 'intuition and analysis' (O'Sullivan 1999: 89)? If confirmed, what can we put in place to help this individual to feel at ease?

Another way of preparing for an interview involves using a checklist, made up of a list of the tasks or issues that need to be considered (an interview checklist is included in the first edition of this text (Trevithick 2000). Both a reflective and checklist approach require that we familiarize ourselves with the case notes and update our knowledge in terms of recent events, particularly in relation to others involved in the case. It is important to note that in relation to the 45 public inquiries into child abuse cases between 1973 and 1994, a major omission noted was the family's past history: 'eight reports noted that social workers failed to read their own files and so overlooked important facts such as previous child abuse' (Munro 1998a: 91). Finally, it is essential for us to make a note of our own thoughts and feelings, particularly whether we are harbouring negative stereotypical attitudes or beliefs about the individual in question. For any interview or interaction to be successful, service users and others involved in the work need to feel that, as professionals and as people, we are competent and caring human beings, capable of understanding their concerns and worries, both from a general and a specific standpoint. Here it is worth remembering that some service users approach their contact with professionals harbouring a range of fears that include worries that they may be blamed, criticized or turned away. For these reasons, it is important to be aware of these concerns and to think about how they can be addressed (Lishman 1994: 17).

These considerations help to give the interview some structure and establish a clear role in terms of the boundaries of the task, time and territory. Once having scanned these factors, it is then important to concentrate on being as open, relaxed and natural as possible in order to ensure that a rapport can be created and a relationship established with the person seeking our help. Every individual is unique and every interaction different and these facts must be conveyed in our planning and preparation. Otherwise the interview runs the risk of being perceived as a cold, uncaring, impersonal experience, which hinders the possibility or quality of future contact. Being able to respond with flexibility and adaptability to an individual's needs is also a sign of a successful interview. However, agency policies and the constraints placed upon resources may limit the options available to us, particularly in relation to the availability of services.

The difference between service users' and carers' expectations and what is possible in terms of agency policy and resources is an ongoing tension within social work and the interview is often the setting where these tensions are aired. Careful planning and preparation can be one way to open up new possibilities. For example, Braye and Preston-Shoot make the point that social workers could make greater use of legislation and policy guidance to ensure that service users' and carers' needs are met and their voices heard in the unsympathetic climate of 'top-down hierarchical bureaucracy' (1995: 109). A similar point is made in relation to the list of services available under the Children Act 1989 designed to support families: 'Surveys (Aldgate *et al.* 1994) have shown considerable discrepancy in the way in which these provisions have been implemented. Some authorities have adopted a minimalist approach, whilst others provide a much wider range of services' (Thoburn 2002: 196). These points stress that interview planning and preparation involve more than focusing on ourselves, but need to be extended to include drawing on information from a wide range of sources, particularly using our knowledge of the law and government guidance to push for more and better services.

Interviews in different settings

From time to time our work involves undertaking interviews in other settings, sometimes called 'secondary settings' (Lishman 1994: 141), which can include:

1 social services/probation office interviews
2 the home (including foster homes/adoption placements)
3 residential settings
4 prisons
5 schools
6 hospitals (psychiatric and general hospitals)
7 day centres
8 community centres
9 informal, transitory or detached settings (e.g. conversations in cafés, car journeys)

Every setting has its own characteristics and idiosyncrasies. A useful description of some of the above can be found in Davies (2002). These accounts include community care settings, the hospital, probation settings, the psychiatric unit, foster care and adoption settings, the community childcare team and divorce court welfare settings. Kadushin and Kadushin give an interesting account of interviews that take place in the home, where service users can defend themselves through the intelligent use of 'arranged distractions':

> The interviewee can exercise a measure of self-protection by using 'arranged distractions' – letting a radio or TV blare at full volume, giving a warm welcome to neighbours who drop in, or vigorously rattling pots and dishes while washing them during the interview. Because the setting is the interviewee's home, the interviewee has to take the initiative to turn down the radio or TV, although the interviewer can request this. Of course interviewers can, somewhat more subtly, gradually lower their voices until the interviewee is prompted to turn down the radio in order to hear.
>
> (Kadushin and Kadushin 1997: 83)

Another interesting account of more informal interview settings is provided by Davies (1981: 176–9) in his description of 'detached work'. These interviews often happen spontaneously and can take place in a range of different situations: while driving in a car, going for a walk, playing sport, washing up, fixing a bike, playing a computer game. All can provide opportunities for people to explore their thoughts and feelings in ways that do not feel too focused or overexposing. However, it is important that honest and clear professional boundaries are maintained because in more natural settings it can be easy for people to be taken off-guard to the point where they find themselves revealing more than they wish.

Creating a rapport and establishing a relationship

For any interview to be successful a rapport must be established. In relation to the social work interview, rapport is described as 'the state of harmony, compatibility and empathy that permits mutual understanding and a working relationship between the client and the social worker' (Barker 2003: 359). Sometimes the word rapport is used instead of the word relationship, or they are both used interchangeably, but they describe different experiences. To establish a relationship implies a type of contact that is ongoing, or a connection that continues over time. The best known example of a relationship is friendship. We may not see our friends often, but that may not diminish the quality of the contact and how much we care for one another. A professional relationship is different and is sometimes described as a 'working alliance' between two or more people.

To establish a rapport implies an interaction that is meaningful. Taken from the French, it describes the quality of a particular interaction at a point in time and the way that ideas, thoughts and feelings have been shared and understood. As such, it is possible to establish a good rapport quite quickly with a complete stranger, as if by chance. 'Hitting it off' or 'clicking' with someone in this way, which is often intuitive, can be the basis from which a relationship can begin. On the other hand, it is possible to have a good working relationship yet fail to establish a meaningful rapport or to 'hit it off' during a particular interview or encounter. For these reasons it is important that the word rapport is used rigorously to denote a genuine and meaningful point of contact and is not allowed to slip into an idealized version of events.

Establishing a rapport involves creating a climate where the interviewee can begin to gain confidence in our personal and professional integrity. This is important because it creates the favourable conditions necessary for people to be able to discuss and reveal problems or difficulties, successes or failures, and strengths or weaknesses in ways that aid understanding and allow for a realistic plan of action to be created. However, for a rapport to be created requires that both parties are active and willing participants in this process. This may not be achievable, particularly when working with people who are mistrustful or reluctant or who have been coerced into making contact or attending certain events. For this reason, Feltham and Dryden state that 'there are limits to the therapeutic effectiveness of spontaneous and genuine rapport' (1993: 192).

The relationship

The relationship we build with service users and carers is central to the social work task, and often forms part of what is being described in the term *social work process*. The following description captures the importance of the relationship we strive to create:

> While it is true that people do not come to social work looking for a relationship, and while it is no substitute for practical support, nevertheless social workers are one of the few groups who recognize the value of relating to others in a way which recognizes their experience as fundamental to understanding and action.
>
> (Coulshed and Orme 1998: 3)

However, in some practice contexts there is confusion about why relationships are important, and also their purpose. I have encountered situations where establishing a relationship is cited as the sole focus of the work or an end in itself. This can lead us nowhere in terms of the changes being sought. However, there are situations where relationship building is central to the task of establishing a 'corrective relationship': a reparative experience that is created to compensate for previous unsatisfactory or painful relationships and failures (Payne 1997: 81). But even then the ultimate aim of this work should be to restore lost confidence in order for the individual to be able to explore relationships with others, particularly with their peers, or to rebuild lost relationships.

The relationship is 'the communication bridge between people' (Kadushin and Kadushin 1997: 100). It is the boat in which we travel together towards agreed and desired destinations; that is, a vital part of the repertoire of skills we require in order to be effective and to arrive at some agreed outcome. The quality of the interaction, the trust and understanding that are held within the relationship, act as a vital thread. It is a thread that opens up the possibility for defences to be lowered, for the truth to be faced, for doubts and fears to be worked through and change to be integrated and embraced in ways that are not possible without this connection to another trustworthy and reliable human being.

In terms of the importance of relationships within social work, we still know little about their specific characteristics and benefits. This is partly because every relationship is unique and made up of intangible factors that are difficult to identify (Cheetham *et al.* 1992: 12). Yet establishing sound working relationships is essential to many activities that we value. It can be seen in the way we build partnerships and create alliances and in the practice approaches, skills and interventions that we adopt. It can also be seen in the commitment we demonstrate to support mutuality, reciprocity and power sharing as important activities that enhance the possibility of empowerment, self-determination and independence.

Feminists working and writing from the Stone (Women's) Center in Boston, USA, see building relationships as central to the empowerment and growth process (Surrey 1991: 167). Within this theoretical framework, it is the experience of connection that leads to growth – a growth that is based on *mutual empathy* and *mutual empowerment*:

> We use the word *connection* to mean an interaction between two or more people that is mutually empathic and mutually empowering. (We) use *disconnection* to mean an encounter that works against mutual empathy and mutual empowerment ... (and) the word relationship to mean the set of interactions that occur over a length of time. A relationship may be composed on connections and disconnections, usually a mixture of both.
>
> (Miller and Stiver 1997: 26)

According to Miller, positive relationships can lead to psychological growth. This can be recognized in terms of five observable phenomena:

- feeling a greater sense of 'zest' (vitality and energy)
- feeling more able to act and being able to act
- acquiring a more accurate picture of herself/himself and of other people
- feeling a greater sense of worth
- feeling more connected to other people and a 'greater sense of

motivation for connections with other people beyond those in the specific relationship'.

(Miller 1986: 3)

This description captures the heightened feelings of self-worth and sense of well-being that a good relationship can foster. For example, I recall working with Sally, who had a long history of depression. For much of her life, she had lived with her ageing mother on a council estate, with very little contact with family or friends. This was partly because her mother still carried a profound sense of shame about Sally being illegitimate. From this lonely childhood, Sally had little opportunity to learn important social skills. As a result, she developed a strange mode of communication, which led to further social exclusion. It became clear that a major focus of our work involved helping Sally to establish relationships with others. Her relationship with her mother provided a sound foundation from which to build a relationship with people involved in the project, including other women suffering from depression. In order to track Sally's progress, we paid close attention to changes in her outlook, both in relation to herself and in terms of how she saw the possibilities and opportunities available to her within her social sphere. These changes formed part of our discussions with Sally. This involved using Jordan's account of the 'relational model', which stresses the importance of using the professional relationships we created as a way to help an individual 'achieve and maintain a sense of contact and connection' (Jordan 1991: 283) with others. It involved 'normalizing' reactions, thoughts and feelings, which Sally tended to exaggerate because of her lack of experience of social settings and being with other people.

The skills involved in creating a rapport and successful relationships overlap. In relation to those central to forming a relationship, these include (Kadushin and Kadushin 1997: 103–27):

- conveying an acceptance of the individual
- demonstrating an empathic understanding
- conveying a sense of genuineness and authenticity
- demonstrating a concern for the issue of service user self-determination
- showing the professional ability to decide which information needs to be kept confidential and which does not
- demonstrating a respect for the service user's individuality
- showing an interest, conveying warmth, generating an atmosphere of trust.

Welcoming skills

One way to establish a rapport is to ensure that the welcome people receive is warm and respectful. This helps to allay some of the fears and uncertainties that may exist. For some service users and carers, these anxieties may be due to the difficulties inherent in asking for help: some may have never asked for help before. For others, it may be their first experience of social services, the probation service or a voluntary agency. As a result, they may have little idea of what to expect – or what help can be offered – and this kind of uncertainty can be worrying. A different group of people may be wary because they have had contact with social services, the probation service or similar agencies in the past and these experiences have left them feeling negative about the prospect of future contact. Whatever the concerns, to provide a warm welcome on all occasions can be one way of working towards establishing a good rapport and sound 'working alliance'.

Shaking hands

Although shaking hands is becoming less popular, in the UK it is still used as a formal gesture in some circles. This is particularly the case in professional settings, where the encounter or meeting may begin with people shaking hands as they are introduced. This makes it important that we know how to shake hands. It can be an important means of communication and shows that we are not reluctant to make contact in this more formal way when the situation requires it. Some people place great store on how people shake hands.

In relation to service users and carers, the picture is more complex and subject to wide variations according to individual preference and cultural influences. For example, women tend to shake hands less than men and children almost never offer their hand unless they do so for fun. Generally, men tend to be more at ease and practised in this type of physical contact but even among men there are wide variations according to class, race and age.

Deciding whether or not to shake hands can be a test of our intuitive skills because we are often asked to gauge what is needed on little evidence. Clearly, no one should ever be coerced into shaking hands. However, if a service user or carer comes across as relatively relaxed and able to manage this more formal contact, my preference is to shake hands because it marks a clear beginning and end to the encounter. I also find it helpful to have the opportunity to 'touch' a person physically and to gain some impression, however tentative, about where they are coming from, although I would exercise great caution before drawing any firm conclusions from a handshake. Shaking hands also creates the need to say a few warm words of welcome or farewell. This too can be quite revealing. Whatever our personal preference in relation to handshaking, the point to stress is that it is important to think about how to welcome or bid farewell to people we encounter. However, it is also important to note that not all interviews can end on a positive note.

Other forms of physical contact

A question that constantly arises is whether or not it is appropriate for service users, or others being interviewed, to be touched during the course of an interview. As a general rule, this is not wise, although there are some exceptions to this rule. For example, if someone is crying it can feel inhuman and unprofessional not to offer some physical contact: perhaps tap the shoulder, touch their hand or offer a cup of tea. However, a word of caution is needed because what we consider comforting may not be the same for all people. Some people who have been abused find any kind of physical contact difficult. For some people, any form of touching or accidental physical contact, including being hugged, can feel like a violation and can run the risk of awakening earlier abusive memories. Similarly, to touch individuals when they are crying can make some people feel guilty or inhibited about expressing emotions in this way, and may have the effect of closing them down. They may worry that they have upset us; here it is important to offer reassurance that this is not the case.

These complexities are difficult to unravel and call for us to be intuitive. They highlight the importance of self-knowledge and the distinction that needs to be drawn between our personal reactions and our professional responses as a person-in-role. One of the most useful things we can do is to try to 'be with' the feelings being expressed and to provide comfort in ways that feel appropriate. Another is to encourage the expression of emotion by talking to the individual who is upset. A soft, gentle voice offering realistic reassurance can feel like a blanket, wrapping itself around someone to keep them safe. However, the ability to soothe in this way cannot be learned because it must come from a different, more sensitive and intuitive part of our personality – and is all the more important for this reason.

Informal opening conversations ('social chat')

Another way of providing a relaxed welcome might involve starting up an informal conversation. This frequently involves talking about uncontroversial subjects, such as the weather or the journey. Again, our intuitive skills are needed to gauge how long a discussion of this kind should last. To be too brief can leave people feeling hurried and rail-roaded. On the other hand, it can create unnecessary anxiety if these informal conversations are dragged out longer than necessary. This kind of conversation, sometimes called a 'social chat', should not be trivialized because it allows people to gain an impression of us before the interview begins. As practitioners, it gives us the opportunity to create a climate that makes it possible for people to ask for help or to discuss difficult subjects. For some individuals, initial impressions are important and are formed within the first few moments of contact, hence the phrase 'you only get one chance to make a good first impression'.

Service users and carers can feel welcomed and respected by the kind of reception they experience when first walking into an agency (Lishman 1994: 17). Some of this is communicated by the receptionist, who can do a great deal to create a caring environment. Over the years, I have seen some shameful behaviour on the part of receptionists and, whenever possible, I have communicated my concern. But more often, particularly in recent years, I have seen some very sensitive and kind interactions between receptionists and visitors to the agency. I can think of a locality team that I visit regularly where the receptionist goes out of her way to ensure that she is warm and caring in the welcome she provides. I am sure that this person's skills make it easier for people to visit this agency and to keep in touch with the practitioners who work there. Too often these gestures of kindness and concern go unnoticed, particularly in relation to so-called 'junior' or 'support' staff.

Another way to think about the reception a service user and carer might receive relates to the actual physical decor of the reception area in relation to whether:

- it is too formal or informal
- it is comfortable, tidy and well decorated
- it has an appropriate range of seating (comfortable seats, including seating appropriate for older people, chairs and a desk if needed)
- it is private and confidential, and located in an area where interruptions and disruptions can be avoided
- it reflects the multiracial, multicultural, age and gender composition of people seeking a social work/probation service
- it is wheelchair accessible and can accommodate children's buggies and prams
- it provides enough sufficiently current and interesting magazines to help pass the time away if service users and carers have to wait to be seen.

As practitioners, it is our professional responsibility to ensure that the reception and welcome that service users and carers receive when they first visit our agency is, as far as possible, a warm and welcoming experience.

Empathy and sympathy

Empathy

Creating good working relationships involves being able to empathize with others. It describes an attempt to put ourselves in another person's place, in the hope that we can feel and understand another person's emotions, thoughts, actions and motives. Empathy involves trying to understand, as carefully and as sensitively as possible, the nature of another person's experience, their own unique point of view and what meaning this carries for that individual. It goes beyond sympathy (passive understanding) in conveying a willingness to 'enter imaginatively into the inner life of someone else' (Kadushin and Kadushin 1997: 108).

Shulman divides the skills involved in empathy into three sections:

- *reaching for feelings*, which involves 'stepping into the client's shoes', thereby coming as close as is humanly possible to another person's experience;
- *displaying understanding of client's feelings*, which entails suspending disbelief or similar reactions and instead 'indicating through words, gestures, expression, physical posture, or touch the worker's comprehension of the expressed affect'; and
- *putting the client's feelings into words*, which is particularly important when clients are unable to articulate certain feelings, because they do not fully understand the emotion or because 'the client might not be sure it is all right to have such a feeling or to share it with the worker'.

(Shulman 1999: 158–60)

Being empathic is not a request for practitioners to be perfect or mechanical in our responses, but to present ourselves as real human beings, reliable and consistent in our contact with service users and carers, capable of conveying 'interest, warmth, trust, respect' (Kadushin and Kadushin 1997: 124). At times it can be difficult to differentiate empathy from those attributes that are about being concerned professionals. Egan addresses this dilemma by differentiating between empathy as 'a way of being and empathy as a communication process or skill' (1990: 123). For Egan, the effective use of empathy is dependent on the 'skill of the helper and the state of the client' (1990: 135). The skills that both bring to the encounter link to the point made earlier in this text, when I have described the capacities of practitioners and service users and carers.

Some authors describe 'an empathy which goes beyond placing oneself in another's shoes by daring to put these on and wear them for a while' (Dominelli 2002b: 9). This begs the question about whether it is actually possible to experience another person's reality in this way, which it clearly is not. To do so runs the risk of our intruding uninvited into another person's world. For this reason, Rogers (1957: 4) is correct in stressing the importance of our exercising great caution about where we tread, always taking our lead from service users and carers and not from our own desires, however caring and honourable.

The ability to be empathic is one of the most important skills used when interviewing and is central to client-centred approaches. It involves attempting to understand thoughts, feelings and experiences from another person's point of view in order to understand how they might be feeling. It can be difficult to put into words a sensitive and accurate understanding of another's experience. Our own subjective experience is a useful starting point. However, in some ways, our attempts to understand the meaning others give to their experiences will always be elusive, although our failures may be forgiven and bridged by our willingness to try to understand. For this reason, such a crossing over of meaning and understanding can have a profound impact and one that may be remembered for a lifetime. As stated earlier, the importance of being understood by another human being is enormously important, not least because it can lead to self-understanding. Self-understanding can last a lifetime: longer than our professional involvement, which may be fleeting. Nevertheless, our role in this process of self-discovery may be deeply significant.

The actual words used to convey empathy need to be easily understood and consistent with the mode of communication with which the individual is familiar. For this reason, it is important to avoid seeing empathy as an opportunity to indulge in philosophical ramblings or personal statements about the meaning of life or how much we admire the individual in question. Empathy is based on self-knowledge and self-reflection and an ability to reach into and to communicate that knowledge, in words and/or body language. One way to see this two-way communication is as a conversation using two mirrors, where the reflection of another person is always seen alongside our own reflection. Sympathy, on the other hand, is more about looking solely at the mirrored reflection of another person.

Examples: Empathic response

Service user: My husband died last year. It's been hard without him.
Practitioner: You seem very sad. How have things been since he died?

Asking a general question, such as 'How have things been?', is sometimes preferable to asking a more specific question, such as 'Are you still finding it difficult to adjust to life without your husband?' General questions allow the individual to self-select the issues and concerns they choose to include in the word 'things'. However, closed questions are often preferable if someone is distressed.

Service user: I had to take to the streets when I left care because I had nowhere else to go.
Practitioner: I think that this must be one of the worst experiences that we can have as human beings – to feel that we have nowhere to go, no home. How did you manage to keep going?

Sympathy

Sympathy is about being moved by another human being. It is sometimes described as feeling *for* another person (passive) as opposed to empathy, which is described as feeling *with* another person (active) (Shulman 1999: 156). In some social work texts, this emotion is seen as inferior to empathy, being viewed as a form of pity and/or as implying an unquestioning acceptance of an individual's experience (Egan 1990: 139). However, sympathy can be, and often is, a genuine, human response to another person's experience of hardship or suffering. We cannot be empathic all the time. That would be exhausting and fail to do justice to the unique features of this emotion. But we can allow ourselves to feel sympathy with the plight of others. It is, therefore, a particularly important skill when we meet someone for the first time, where the need to convey a sense of concern, warmth, interest, care and compassion is paramount.

***Example*: Sympathetic response**
Service user: My husband died last year.
Practitioner: I am very sorry to hear that. How are you managing?
Service user: I had to take to the streets when I left care because I had nowhere else to go.
Practitioner: That must have been a difficult experience.

The role of self-knowledge and intuition

The use of self-knowledge or self-awareness in professional practice involves the conscious employment of social work skills, knowledge, values and personal experience in ways that are illuminating to the work at hand. Shulman describes this self-knowledge as follows:

> The capacity to be in touch with the service user's feelings is related to the worker's ability to acknowledge his or her own. Before a worker can understand the power of emotions in the life of the client, it is necessary to discover its importance in the worker's own experience.
>
> (Shulman 1999: 156)

It implies the ability to be open and available, to become involved but not merged with service users and to be sensitive and intuitive about the verbal and non-verbal communication taking place. It is about allowing ourselves to be affected by the experiences and hardships that people face in ways that 'move us'. In the case of injustice, it can encourage a healthy sense of outrage, which can act as an impetus and driving force in our efforts to help bring about change. However, it is important that this impetus does not slip into a need to 'rescue' people (Karpman 1968), perhaps by taking on too much responsibility or promising more than we can deliver. One example of the professional use of self can be seen in the appropriate and judicial use of self-disclosure. Another can be seen in the way we create and maintain professional boundaries. In personal terms, it is where we take up an appropriate position of separateness while also maintaining a clear connection to service users, so that we are not too distant or inflexible on the one hand, nor too merged or inappropriately accommodating on the other.

Self-knowledge is not easy to acquire but is central to good practice, including anti-oppressive approaches, because the 'importance of knowing oneself in order to engage effectively with others who are different is . . .essential to carrying out anti-oppressive practice but immensely difficult to do' (Dominelli 2002b: 9). We may only begin to know the limits of our self-awareness when presented with problems that trigger reactions inappropriate to the situation. For example, we may feel we have come to terms with childhood experiences of rejection until we encounter a service user who is deeply rejecting of us, and we find ourselves shaken unexpectedly by our reactions. Once we realize our vulnerability, we have a professional responsibility to attend to these unresolved emotions so that we can continue with the work at hand. Our personal commitment to sort out and work through these personal dilemmas can be an invaluable source of knowledge in helping others in similar situations to work through similar feelings. Unless we do this, we are forever vulnerable to falling into pockets of distress or anxieties 'that lead to inattention, poor listening and inappropriate responses and actions' (Lishman: 1994: 60).

Intuition

Linked to the professional 'use of self' is intuition. England strongly emphasizes the importance of intuition, imagination and experience as central components to good practice but within a framework where these attributes can be evidenced and measured: 'the practice of social work must be evaluated . . . . and . . . subject to a description and analysis which can determine quality' (England 1986: 139). Other more recent publications also stress the importance of intuition (O'Sullivan 1999: 87; Seden 1999: 128, 133), but with well-founded reservations. Hypotheses or actions based on 'intuitive reasoning' or 'intuitive judgements' should always be rigorously tested against other sources of information available (Munro 1996: 795). We still know so little about how to bring about positive change or the part played by intuition within this process. Where theories and methods are cited, 'we can find numerous conflicting or complementary theories, many of which are highly speculative and little researched' (Munro 1998a: 96). Further research is needed on the place of intuition within social work: ' "Hard" knowledge such as facts are pertinent, but so too are thoughts and feelings and the worker's own clarified intuition' (Coulshed and Orme 1998: 21).

The use of intuition relates to our being able to read non-verbal forms of communication accurately. It refers to the ability to understand or to perceive something in ways that are not gained through conscious reasoning or 'explicit deliberation' (O'Sullivan 1999: 87). This links to Schön's concept of *tacit recognitions* (1996: 50), where we are involved in making sense of communications that come in the form of thoughts, hunches, instinctive reactions, impressions, associations, insights, impulses and guesswork. For example, in the Jasmine Beckford inquiry practitioners had formed 'hunches' but felt unable to act on them (London Borough of Brent 1985). There are times when it is only a 'hunch' that tells us that something is wrong or that alerts us to the possibility that a dangerous situation is developing. It is from this place that the impetus to gather evidence or 'hard facts' emerges, but until our intuition can be clarified in this way, our ideas must continue to be considered as hypotheses (tentative propositions) or as possible indicators (a sign, warning or a pointer to a particular direction, event or outcome).

Case example: Bee

As a fieldworker I once worked with a group of eight- to ten-year-old girls, all of whom were experiencing difficulties likely to result in their being brought into care. One member of the group, Bee, displayed particularly disturbing behaviour. She seemed oblivious to the social conventions in relation to when and where to touch other members of the group and bewildered or unaffected by the hostility her behaviour provoked in the other girls. This provocative behaviour felt out of keeping with the fact that, in most encounters involving adults, Bee demonstrated a worrying level of compliance and desire to please. It was as if she was trying to read our minds. This situation was made more complex because Bee had been assessed as having learning difficulties and it was not always clear she had understood what was being communicated.

One night, I was asked to drop Bee off at home because her social worker was unwell. As we drove nearer to her house, Bee appeared to become more agitated and quite bizarre in her behaviour. Her father was waiting for us at the door, arms folded. We arrived late and as I moved to get out of the car to offer my apologies, Bee began to panic. She hurriedly gathered her belongings together, insisting that I drive off. I did as she asked, but on my way home I felt deeply confused and concerned about Bee's behaviour. I felt frightened and felt that I had picked up this fear from Bee. The following day I mentioned this to her social worker who reassured me that Bee was 'always like that' and that the behaviour I had witnessed was quite 'normal for Bee'. Apparently, her father had a profound mistrust and dislike of social workers and the agreement was that Bee could attend the group on the proviso that this did not involve having contact with social services or the group leaders. When people communicate a profound mistrust in this way, it is important to wonder why this is the case. What past contact has this individual had with social workers and other people in authority, and why?

Bee never found her way to the group again. Over the weeks and months that followed, I continued to feel concerned and encountered the same reassurance from her social worker that she was fine. Several months passed until it came to light that Bee's 16-year-old sister was expecting a baby by her father. A careful investigation of this situation led to questions being raised about Bee's relationship with her father. It transpired that she had been the victim of physical and sexual abuse, not only by her father but by other men invited into the home. The father was eventually sent to prison and Bee and her sister received into care. This experience serves as a reminder that attempting to differentiate between learning difficulties and the effect of sexual abuse on children can be a complex and difficult undertaking. In order to survive, and to keep alive any good feelings in relation to parents who abuse, some children learn to develop behaviours in order to protect themselves: they 'have to smile or become stupid or blind to what is happening' (Sinason 1988: 99). This case example reminds me also of the importance of revising our judgements and decisions in the light of new events and of seeing this as a sign of strength not weakness (Munro 1996: 799).

Questioning

Asking a range of different questions is central to interviewing. Different authors highlight the qualities that practitioners need to demonstrate in order to frame questions in ways that are helpful, illuminating and empathic (Lishman 1994: 24–5; Seden 1999: 30; Nelson-Jones 2000: 183). Most stress that *before asking a question we must be interested in the answer*. This goes back to the point made earlier, that most people intuitively know whether they are being listened to and whether their thoughts and feelings are being given the importance they deserve. It is important to note that questions can be used as a way of stimulating self-reflection – as a way of returning people to their own thoughts and their own knowledge base – because it is here that the kernel of self-determination and empowerment is located.

On the other hand, Kadushin and Kadushin describe five forms of unhelpful questions (1997: 248–58):

- leading or suggestive forms of questions
- too many 'yes'/'no' questions
- garbled or unclear questions
- double or multiple questions
- too many 'why' questions.

It can be very easy to think that as practitioners we know how to ask questions, but the above dangers need to be considered seriously, particularly the point about avoiding leading questions or 'putting words into other people's mouths' (Seden 1999: 31). Most of us come to the task of interviewing with fixed patterns of behaviour of which we are largely unaware. Some of these behaviours may be facilitating, but others may be off-putting or unhelpful. Hence the value of watching ourselves on video. For example, how well do you think you can tolerate silences? Many practitioners think they can manage silences without difficulty until presented with a situation where they are required to remain silent or to work with someone who is silent. Here the compulsion to speak is almost unbearable and can lead to all kinds of strange questions being asked simply in order to break the intense discomfort that silence can engender.

Open questions

These are designed to give freedom of choice, enabling service users to express their thoughts and feelings in their own words and in their own time; to choose or to ignore certain concerns. However, it is important to set aside sufficient time for this kind of exploration.

It is suggested that open-ended questions should form a major part of an initial interview or first encounter. However, these can feel threatening or overwhelming for service users who are not used to formulating their thoughts and feelings into such an open space. Some individuals try to address their confusion and anxiety by trying to guess the response we are looking for. This kind of mind-reading can seriously detract from the purpose of the interview unless it is addressed. Other people find difficulty answering open questions because they do not yet have words with which to explain what has happened to them.

Some fear is due to a worry about coming across as 'stupid' or of being judged. It may be possible to overcome any difficulties by addressing them directly or by stressing what we are hoping to achieve and how this will benefit the individual concerned. It may help to ask a range of open and closed questions. These different approaches require that we are flexible and able to change the form or content of the interview in ways that enable people to tell their stories and to gather their thoughts and feelings with greater freedom. When people remain agitated and defensive, the only option may be to stop the interview or to spend time explaining in greater detail why it is important for us to ask these questions. At this point, and at other points in this and other interviews, it is important to inform people of their rights and of agency policy in relation to information that is recorded about them or other members of their family.

Examples: Open questions for initial interview or assessment
Practitioner: How can I be of help?

Practitioner: I've got some information about what happened [shows charge sheet] but I want you to tell me what happened – in your own words.

Example: Life-story work

Practitioner: One way for me to get to know you would be for you to say something about yourself. How does that sound? [Nod]. Where would you like to begin?

For an informative description of life-story work with children, including the use of play, life-story books and Fahlberg's (1991) ecomap, see Brandon *et al.* (1998: 18; 154–62). Garbarino *et al.* (1992) provide a helpful account of how to elicit and evaluate information from children.

Closed questions

Closed questions can often be answered 'yes' or 'no', or with other responses that only require a few words, such as asking a person's name, address, age and so on. This form of questioning is useful when trying to elicit factual or detailed information, particularly when time is limited. It can also be used to keep the interview focused, to open up new areas, to change the direction of the interview, to draw the interview away from or towards sensitive or emotional topics, to slow an interview down and to allow missing details to be covered. However, this does place more responsibility on the interviewer, who must both choose and formulate relevant questions and listen carefully to the answers so that questions follow on naturally. This can require a great deal of concentration and is one reason why interviewing can be so tiring. On the other hand, closed questions can foreclose exploration. For example, doctors seeking to diagnose a patient quickly are more likely to ask closed questions (Corney 1991: 5).

Closed questions can be particularly valuable when working with people who do not have a great deal of confidence, perhaps because they feel reticent or mistrustful or find it difficult to formulate their thoughts and feelings. People involved in accidents or who have been traumatized in other ways may find themselves uncharacteristically unable to answer open questions but able to manage closed questions relatively well. People vary, and all situations are different, so it is important that we are able to adapt.

The main disadvantage when using closed questions is that they may steer the interview in the wrong direction by being too focused. This can lead to a sense of frustration on the part of the interviewee, who can easily feel that their experiences are being disregarded or categorized and squeezed into little boxes. Here, it can be helpful to spend time before and after the interview talking about the difficulties involved in having to answer questions in this way and reaffirming why it was important. It is sometimes assumed that open questions are more in keeping with anti-discriminatory/anti-oppressive practice than closed questions. This implies that all people are the same and that all interviews can be conducted in the same way. This is clearly not the case.

For some people, 'why' questions can be experienced as accusatory or authoritarian (Seden 1999: 31). Thoughtful wording, accompanied by careful tone and timing, can ensure that this danger is avoided. In most circumstances it is unhelpful to ask combined questions, but where a great deal of factual information is being sought, to avoid the interview feeling like an interrogation, combined questions may be necessary. For example, rather than ask 'Are you on medication?', which, if affirmed, will require a second question ('What are you taking?'), it may be better to ask a combined question: 'If you're on medication, can you tell me what you are taking?'

Example: Gathering basic information

(Choice of words, tone and timing are important when trying to gather information of this kind. It is also important to say why the information is needed and who will have access to it.)

Practitioner: I'm afraid I have a number of rather boring questions that I have to ask. What I'd like to do is to get them over with quickly so that we can talk about things that you want to look at. Is that okay? Right, can I have your name and address, please?

Service user: Okay. Michael Smith, 37 Baron Street, Newtown.

Practitioner: Thanks. What's your date of birth, Michael?

Service user: Fourth of September 1983.

Practitioner: So you're sixteen?

Service user: Yes.

Example: Clarifying the reason for the referral

Practitioner: I see from the letter from your doctor that she thinks you need a social worker to help you to sort out some problems you're having at home. Is that how you see the situation?

Service user: No. I didn't know that my doctor had written. I came because I got a letter from you asking to see me.

Practitioner: Okay. I think it would help to take a step back and start at the beginning so that I can understand why your doctor has referred you to us. Is that okay?

Service user: Yes.

Practitioner: When did you last see your doctor?

Service user: Last week.

Practitioner: What was that for, Mrs Day? ['What' question]

'What' questions

This form of questioning is particularly popular in family therapy and in certain types of brief therapy. Its main advantage is that it is quite unspecific in terms of what constitutes the 'what' implied in the question, thereby leaving the interviewee free to define for themselves the issues or concerns that they wish to focus on. Another advantage is that its emphasis is on the present rather than the past, but with an opportunity for additional questions to be asked relating to the past, if that is considered necessary (Lishman 1994: 77).

Sometimes there is insufficient time, and it is not always useful, to explore the past or the cause of a problem, because this may not help us to formulate what the current impact of the problem is and how it might be rectified or solved (Watzlawick *et al.* 1974: 84). Indeed, an exploration of the past can be a way of avoiding what is actually happening in the present. However, some 'why' questions can come across as accusatory or blaming, although this difficulty can be overcome when a sensitive and caring tone of voice is used.

'What' questions are immensely adaptable, particularly when attempting to explore wider issues and the part that other individuals or factors play in the perpetuation of the problem encountered. This emphasis is consistent with a systemic perspective that stresses that no one person is solely responsible for a problem or a difficulty that exists, although as human beings we are all responsible for our actions. For example, 'what' questions can be asked in most situations: 'what is going on?'; 'what plays a part in perpetuating this problem?'; 'what part does this problem, individual or family play in relation to the whole (system, family, community, etc.)?'; 'what needs to happen to bring about change or a solution to this problem?'; 'what is needed to keep the momentum for change alive?'; and 'what would tell us that the intervention, approach or work has been effective?'

Examples: **Initial interview**
Practitioner: What's happening – as you see it – Mr Black?
Practitioner: What do you think will happen if we leave things as they are?
Practitioner: What can I say or do to make a difference?

Asking a purposely vague question, such as 'what is happening?' allows the individual to decide what they see to be 'happening'. This can include anything and take us to some unexpected places. This in turn can enable us to judge whether different parties see the situation in the same way and, if not, to explore what these differences are and, if important to the task, how they can be bridged and a common purpose agreed.

Confirming what has been said and heard

These interventions are designed to ensure that we have understood the content and meaning of what has been communicated so far. This is sometimes referred to as 'tracking'; that is, the 'skill of listening intently and empathetically to the moment-to-moment explorations of the client, with an ability to reflect back and/or to summarize what is said' (Feltham and Dryden 1993: 195). It combines creative listening with responding to and reflecting back what is being communicated (Seden 1999: 29).

The skills include paraphrasing, clarifying, summarizing and giving and receiving feedback. Each offers a different way to ensure that we have understood what is being communicated and provides an opportunity to demonstrate that understanding in words. This allows for misinformation to be corrected and for knowledge and expertise to be returned to the individual concerned. Putting our observations into words also allows the individual to hear their own comments and statements but in a different way. This can be both illuminating and thought-provoking, sometimes enabling new and different options to be explored. When feeding back in this way, it can be easy to slip into jargon: 'what I hear is' or 'I want to share with you what I hear'. Some people find this kind of language off-putting, which makes it important to choose words that are in everyday use and easy to understand (Social Services Inspectorate 1991: 20).

Paraphrasing

In paraphrasing, the essence of the person's statement is restated, although not exactly as an echo. It is a selective restatement of the main ideas with words resembling those used by the individual, but that are not the same: 'para' means 'alongside'. Its main purpose is to ensure that we have grasped the sense and meaning of what is being communicated. Sometimes the only sure way to know this is for us to put in words our own thoughts and impressions. In doing so, practitioners:

> demonstrate they have heard the client, they offer their under-standing of what they have heard (to be confirmed or otherwise), and their use of paraphrase casts a slightly different light on the original statements, allowing the client to hear their own statements in a way which itself can powerfully move her (or him) into new personal perspectives.
>
> (Feltham and Dryden 1993: 130)

Paraphrasing is not the same as imitation, repetition or mimicking, which can be experienced as humiliating and should be avoided. We seldom have permission to be familiar in this way, although sometimes this permission is assumed if the service user is young or 'unequal' in other ways: this is inappropriate. Paraphrasing carries other dangers. Restating points already covered can make some people feel that their own words are not adequate or clear. This can elicit the response, 'What was wrong with the way I said it?' Some people come from a history of being taunted for their style of speaking or choice of words. This is particularly true of ethnic minority groups and young people, who may find paraphrasing offensive or undermining. Where this is the case, paraphrasing should not be used unless it is to enable service users to recover from the inhibitions they feel about their capacity to communicate (Seden 1999: 50). Another danger with paraphrasing is that it can be used to change the meaning of what was said into something different. This kind of trickery can be deeply alarming because it 'sets people up' by making it seem they said something that they did not say. Nevertheless, despite these dangers, the ability to relate accurately or restate another person's words is an important skill and the basis of good report writing.

***Example*: Putting what has been said into your own words**

Practitioner: Let me put what you have said into my own words so that it is clear that I've understood you properly. Please interrupt me if I get anything wrong. You want John to live at home but only if he behaves himself properly. You are prepared to put up with his laziness, late nights and loud music but you draw the line when he smokes or truants from school ...

Service user: [Interrupting] I don't like the fact that he smokes but I can't stop him. What I won't have is John smoking in the house in front of the other kids. That's different.

Practitioner: Right. So the line you draw is that for John to live at home he has to agree not to smoke in the house and he has to go to school. Is that right?

Service user: Yes.

Clarifying

Clarifying is primarily used to sort out confusions and to ensure the listener has an accurate grasp of what is being conveyed. It is also used to put words to thoughts and feelings in a language that can be easily and clearly understood, but without falsifying and changing the original meaning. More generally, clarifying can help the individual to identify, confirm and rank the problems that are currently most troubling. This is particularly useful where individuals have many problems and need to focus on those that could have the greatest impact on them. Clarifying can also be used to extend an individual's knowledge base or deepen their understanding of themselves and others they are close to. It differs from paraphrasing because, when clarifying, we frequently choose the same words used by the individual whereas, when paraphrasing, the emphasis is on putting some of the points covered into our own words. A further and different role that clarifying can play is in relation to checking out assumptions and expectations that may be present, on the part of either the interviewee or interviewer (Lishman 1994: 14). This allows for differences to be addressed and, it is hoped, worked through.

Like many of the skills described in this chapter, clarifying can have advantages beyond the technique itself. It can reveal that we are listening carefully and giving importance to what is being said. This can be a particularly important and validating experience for people who have rarely had their thoughts and feelings confirmed in this way. However, clarifying what has been said can interrupt the flow of the interview and, like paraphrasing, can make some people feel ill at ease because it can feel like a veiled criticism or imply that they are communicating poorly. If these concerns emerge, they need to be addressed before the interview can proceed further.

Example: Identifying and confirming events

Practitioner: Let me see if I have this right. Tell me if anything's wrong. You went into the Women's Refuge with your children in May 1998, where you stayed for six months? When your husband tracked you down there, you then went to your sister's in Nottingham where you were for three months until your husband followed you there. Then you returned to the refuge, where the workers there helped you to take out an injunction. Is that right?

Service user: Yes.

Example: Ranking problems/crisis work

Practitioner: We've covered a lot of different things – your worries about your husband, the school, neighbours and debts – but from what you've said, and correct me if I am wrong, the problem that seems to worry you the most is the fact that you've got no money and a lot of debts – debts that you can't pay. [Pause] Is that right?

Service user: Yes. I'm up to my neck in debts and I can't bear it – I can't cope [begins to cry]. I owe money all over the place – to my neighbours, at the local shop. I can't go out 'cause I'm frightened I'll bump into my neighbours. I daren't go to the door in case it's someone looking for money. I nearly didn't answer the door to you because I thought you were the bailiffs. I've taken to stuffing any bills that come through my door behind the settee – it sounds crazy but I just can't bear to see them.

Practitioner: It's not crazy but that's a terrible way to have to live. What can I do to help?

Service user:	Don't know. I feel I've run out of ways to keep going – there's no let-up.
Practitioner:	[When it is absolutely clear that this person cannot move the situation forward without urgent help and where it is known that there is no specialist help easily available, such as debt counselling or welfare rights advice] How would it feel if you came back next week and I go through all the bills that are stuffed behind the settee. I'll add up what you owe and then we can have a look at which are the most pressing and then we can sit down together to see what can be done. How does that sound?
Service user:	It would feel such a relief to hand over the problem to someone – anyone.
Practitioner:	Okay. In the meantime, try not to worry. Why not go and see your neighbours and tell them what's happened so that they know that you are trying to pay them back. Did you used to see quite a bit of them in the past?
Service user:	Yes. We got on well – always have.
Practitioner:	The way things are right now, they miss out twice. They don't see their money and they don't see you – maybe they miss you? Why not make contact – invite them in for a cup of tea?

There are several points to note in relation to this second example. First, it is often preferable to refer financial problems of this kind to a debt counsellor, welfare rights advice centre or the Citizen's Advice Bureau. However, given the level of anxiety and strain that this service user is experiencing, I would only consider a referral to another agency if I knew for certain that the referral would be picked up quickly. This involves telephoning the appropriate agency to see whether they could see the service user in question and when. It is worth noting that some firms and utilities, such as gas and electric companies and water boards, will under special circumstances consider spreading payments over a longer period or on occasion even consider waiving debts.

Second, when we know that someone is frightened to answer the door, perhaps because they are hiding from debtors, it is important to state the day and time we will be returning and to keep to this rigorously. I recall working with a young mother, Ali, who refused to answer the door to anyone. This raised alarm bells among professionals and resulted in regular visits being made to her house, although these were in vain. Then, one day, quite by chance, I managed to meet Ali on her doorstep and she let me in. I assumed she had left her two small children alone but I was wrong: her boyfriend, Tony, was with them. I was also wrong in assuming that her children were not well cared for. Fortunately, I managed to keep these concerns in check and, as a result, I encountered two young people who were eager to talk about the difficulties they were facing. The story that unfolded was that Ali was frightened to answer the door because Tony was absent without leave from the army and the couple were terrified that the army might track him down. They lived in fear that Tony 'could be put away for a long time'. The more that professionals called to the door, the more frightened they became. After a difficult start, I was able to do some good work with this family who lived in council housing that was appalling and dangerous to their health. They were eventually rehoused in a different area of the city and, I believe, settled down well.

Summarizing

Summarizing can be useful in a number of ways. First, we can begin a new session by drawing together and summarizing points covered in earlier sessions. Second, it can provide an accurate and succinct partial or detailed breakdown of what has been covered so far. This allows us to gather together the disparate strands and central themes of what has been covered and to check out that the understanding we have is the same as that of the individual being interviewed. Again, this can help service users to clarify their own thoughts and perceptions, and sometimes lead them to look at the issue from a slightly different angle. 'Often, when scattered elements are brought together, the service user sees the "bigger picture" more clearly. Thus, summarizing can lead to new perspectives or alternate frames of reference' (Egan 1990: 258). Third, a well-timed, brief and accurate summary can be particularly useful when the discussion has started to drift or the session to lose direction. It can be used to draw one line of enquiry to a close so that a new one can be opened. Finally, summarizing is used to draw the session to a satisfactory end. Within this process, summarizing what has been covered can highlight issues that have not been explored and provide a useful opportunity to plan future sessions.

Example: Summarizing issues still to be covered in relation to a young person being prepared for independent living

Practitioner: Let's look at what we've discussed so far. You've talked about your experiences of being in care, your foster parents, how you got on at school. Is there anything I've left out? [Service user shakes head] What we still need to look at with the time we've got left is where you plan to live when you leave care. Is that okay? [Service user nods] Where would you like to start – what ideas have you already had?

Example: Final summary of the points covered in an initial interview

Practitioner: I think that's all we can cover today. What we have looked at is your childhood, your history of going in and out of hospital, your current living situation and how you are coping right now. We can talk more when we meet again next week. Does that sound all right?

Service user: Yes, that's fine.

Giving and receiving feedback

Giving and receiving feedback, both negative and positive, has advantages for both practitioners and service users. First, clear and honest feedback can have a practical application as a way of ensuring that a particular course of action is 'on course' in terms of achieving agreed objectives. Second, feedback can be used as a way of noting the emotional content of the communication, 'reflecting feelings entails responding to clients' music and not just to their words' (Nelson-Jones 2000: 130). This can help service users to learn more about themselves – how they come across – which can be important in ensuring the success of a particular endeavour. For example, where someone is approaching a particular task with a sense of defeat or pessimism, feeding back these impressions may be essential to avoid the task being sabotaged and effort being in vain.

In practice, giving and receiving feedback is a difficult undertaking because it requires the ability to deal with the feelings that this brings up in ourselves and others. Some service users find any form of feedback, positive or negative, difficult and upsetting. People who have been hurt in the past by negative feedback can easily become worried that they are going to be 'got at' again. To allay these concerns, at the outset it can help to stress that the 'purpose of feedback is not to pass judgement on the performance of clients but rather to provide guidance, support, and challenge' (Egan 1990: 389). Egan goes on to describe three purposes of feedback:

- *confirmatory* when it lets clients know when they are on course, that is, moving successfully through the steps of an action program toward a goal;
- *corrective* when it provides clients with information they need to get back on course if they have strayed;
- *motivating* when it points out the consequences of both adequate and inadequate program implementation and includes suggestions for improving performance.

(Egan 1990: 389)

Positive feedback can also create problems, particularly where people have been tantalized and lured into painful or humiliating experiences through the use of kindness and flattery. For example, I once worked with a young woman who had been sexually abused. She associated any compliments or words of appreciation as an attack because before abusing her uncle would 'woo' her with flattering comments. Her response to kindness was to ask, quite spontaneously, 'What do you want?' or 'What's the payback?'

Given the way that some people have been hurt in the area of giving and receiving, before giving feedback it is vital to think about how they might react and to adjust our comments accordingly. Although it is always important to be honest and truthful (Clark 2000: 51), the balance between being honest and being facilitative can be a difficult one to find. When faced with this tension, it can help to remember that some things can be left for another time and that feedback is more likely to be taken on board if it is brief and to the point, and if it focuses on behaviour as opposed to statements about the individual (descriptive rather than interpretative). It also helps to give sufficient time and opportunity for service users to comment and to invite disagreement, reminding them that our views can be wrong and are not 'gospel'. To encourage self-evaluation and self-reflection can be far more valuable in terms of facilitating change than feeding back our perceptions.

So far, the focus has been on our giving feedback to service users. However, many of the same points apply to practitioners receiving feedback, because we too can feel apprehensive and behave defensively, particularly if we think the feedback we are about to be given is negative or critical. In terms of quality assurance, service user feedback is becoming increasingly important and, as expectations rise, complaints and complaints procedures are likely to become important (Adams 1998: 115). As practitioners accountable to our agency and to maintaining professional standards, we can find negative feedback worrying. For this reason, it is always helpful to raise these concerns in supervision.

Sticking to the point and probing deeper

The following skills describe some of the ways that we can keep to the point and purpose of the interview. This may be necessary to fulfil a specific purpose, such as to acquire information for assessment purposes, or to ensure that we have explored the issues to be discussed, some of which may be difficult to talk about. A common problem is when the interview is allowed to drift and people are left to ramble across topics that are not relevant. This purposelessness is a problem within social work that extends beyond the interview setting. For example, we know that some children 'drift' into care and, once there, plans are not always properly executed. This is evidenced in the poor educational achievement among children 'looked after' (Aldgate 2002: 27).

There are times when this 'drifting' is important and has to be allowed to happen. It can be a form of story-telling, but even in this context the 'story' is likely to need some direction if the account raises more questions than answers. Sometimes interviews being left without a clear structure, content or purpose may be justified on the grounds that it is in keeping with service user self-determination and a client-centred approach, or is consistent with an anti-discriminatory perspective. None of these justifies an interview being left to drift, but this issue raises an important question: whose responsibility should it be to ensure that the agreed purpose of the interview has been kept to? The presumption is that this responsibility lies with the practitioner, as the person employed to fulfil certain tasks and to ensure that interventions are effective in reaching specific outcomes (Clark 2000: 56).

Sticking to the point and purpose of the interview

The ability to ask questions that change the pace or direction of an interview, or that probe deeper, is an important skill, particularly when interviewing people who are reticent, confused, anxious or unable to give a clear picture of what they want and why. Some responses may stem from a deliberate desire to mislead but most occur because, as human beings, it is natural for us to feel guarded to some extent about what we are prepared to reveal about ourselves, particularly to strangers. In fact, I am often surprised and sometimes quite troubled by how much service users are prepared to reveal, sometimes to complete strangers.

It can be difficult for some people to broach certain issues and, where this is the case, we need to be able to offer reassurance that these subjects can be discussed, and discussed in ways that are not without clear boundaries. However, this reassurance will feel hollow if we ourselves do not possess the ability to address difficult topics. This is an example of the importance of self-knowledge. We must be able to deal with fraught situations in a professional manner, either because we have 'sorted out' and 'worked through' sensitive issues, or because we have learned the capacity to manage these in ways that do not interfere with the quality of our work and our rapport with service users. Avoidance can be as much a defence for practitioners as it can be for service users. For example, it can be an abdication of responsibility for practitioners to adopt 'a non-questioning, non-directive style', where information is gathered in a piecemeal manner and based on service users being left to 'identify and address their problems themselves' (Munro 1998a: 99).

Our attempts to stick to the point or purpose of an interview can be experienced as either helpful or coercive, depending on the individual and our skills in drawing people away from issues that are less relevant. The skill here is to be able to return to the purpose without disturbing the rapport and trust that has been established. There are several reasons why we might want to intervene in this way:

- the discussion has become overly focused on one issue at the expense of others;

- the content has been exhausted and the communication is becoming repetitive;
- the discussion has moved on to peripheral issues or irrelevancies;
- it has moved away from difficult issues and needs to be brought back; or
- the discussion has become emotionally charged and a sense of calm and balance needs to be introduced.

Examples: Sticking to the point by focusing on issues not fully covered

Practitioner: I now have a good picture of your mother's health problems so I wonder if we could leave this issue here, so that you can say some more about the housing problems you mentioned?

Practitioner: If I can return to something you mentioned in passing, can you say more about your children's contact with their father? How often do they see him?

Example: Steering the interview away from an upsetting issue

Practitioner: I can see how upset you are about being separated from your daughter – let's hope that this need not be for long ... Since this is a difficult situation for you, perhaps we should leave this discussion about her foster home for now, so that you have the chance to take it all in and to feel less upset. What do you normally do to help to calm yourself when you feel upset in this way?

Service user: I usually have a cup of tea and a cigarette – that's what helps.

Practitioner: Well, I can offer you a cup of tea – and am happy to go and make this for you – but I'm afraid you'll have to go outside if you want a cigarette but that's okay. I can bring your tea to you outside. What do you want to do? Do you want to go outside and have a cigarette and cup of tea? Can we talk again when you've had a break?

It is helpful to speak slowly and distinctly when addressing someone who is visibly upset because the capacity to take in information when we are emotionally distressed is often severely limited. When speaking slowly in this way, it is important not to use a tone that is patronizing. In my experience, people tend to remember the tone we use more than anything else.

Prompting

Prompting is used to encourage the person being interviewed to begin speaking or to continue. It can take many forms such as inviting further comment through direct suggestion, by providing a link between one statement and another in order to encourage further dialogue or by helping the individual to return to unfinished sentences or comments. The need to prompt can sometimes be reduced by our making it clear why we need certain information. If a person's reticence is due to anxiety about what the information will be used for, it helps to address this concern by stating openly where information is recorded, who has access to it, where it will be kept and how service users can access their records (see Chapter 8 on record keeping skills).

When prompting, there is a temptation to finish off another person's sentence. This should be avoided at all cost because it is important that people find their own words to describe their thoughts and feelings. Like paraphrasing and other skills described earlier, prompting someone to continue speaking can be experienced as encouraging or coercing. Timing, sensitivity, a kind tone and caring approach are crucial in helping people to differentiate between the two.

Example: **Inviting further comment**

Practitioner: Earlier, you said that prison 'was hell' but then moved on to talk about problems finding work. How do you know what prison is like?

Example: **Unfinished comment**

Practitioner: That's twice you've started to say something about having no money but stopped. It's always hard to talk about money issues – particularly when there isn't enough to go round – but what do you mean when you say you have no money?

Service user: Don't get me wrong – I'm not saying I am bad with money. I make sure the kids always have enough to eat but they have to do without other things like new shoes, school trips, you know ... that kind of thing.

Example: **Linking**

Practitioner: If I can go back to something you mentioned earlier, you said that Peter doesn't get on with your new partner. Later, you also said that Peter now wants to live with his father. Is there a link between these two comments?

Service user: [Silence] I don't know what you mean – what you're getting at?

Practitioner: I am trying to find out whether Peter wants to leave because he is unhappy about your new partner – perhaps he feels put out. You lived alone together for a long time, didn't you?

Service user: He probably is – but so what. What can I do about that?

Practitioner: Well, it depends on whether you feel you can do something about it – and what Peter really wants ...

Probing

Probing is used to elicit more detailed or specific information and can be a useful intervention when trying to gather information from individuals who are prone to adopt more misleading patterns of communication. It is a skill central to risk assessments. Probing can take the form of questions, statements or interjections (Egan 1990: 141) and can be an invaluable skill in providing information that helps to make sense of people's experience or to provide a fuller picture of the total situation. Egan describes this as the 'magic bit of information' that helps to make sense of what has happened so far: 'prompts and probes are the salt and pepper of communication in the helping process' (Egan 1990: 147). However, probing must be undertaken skilfully so that the person in question does not become more defensive and guarded. To avoid meandering into areas that are private and personal, it helps for probing questions to be linked to a hypothesis or line of enquiry and, if possible, to explain why certain questions are being asked.

***Example*: Asking more in-depth questions**

Practitioner:	You seem to know your way round this office. Have you been here before?
Service user:	What makes you say that?
Practitioner:	You seemed to know where the interview room was without my having to lead you. Have you been here before?
Service user:	Yes.
Practitioner:	When?
Service user:	About three years ago.
Practitioner:	What brought you here then?
Service user:	Just a little misunderstanding. [Changing the subject] Are you going to help me with my benefit problem or not?
Practitioner:	Yes, in a minute. What was that misunderstanding?
Service user:	My daughter hurt herself.
Practitioner:	Hurt herself in what way?
Service user:	She slipped and fell down the stairs.
Practitioner:	Why did that involve this office?
Service user:	I can't remember – it was so long ago and all a misunderstanding. Can we talk about my benefit?
Practitioner:	Let's start at the beginning, Mrs Wood. Tell me what happened from the beginning so that we can move on to look at your benefit problem. Where do you want to start?

***Example*: Making a statement to encourage a response**

Practitioner:	You appear to be troubled about the contract we have just agreed.
Service user:	Yes, I never realized that I would be expected to do so

much myself. I thought you'd do it all for me and I don't know whether I am up to it.

Practitioner: Okay. Maybe I'm expecting too much of you but I'm trying to find the right balance. It's important that you play your part because otherwise, you won't feel that any headway we make was because of you. Let's take a step back, shall we? What is it that bothers you the most about the things you have to do?

Example: Picking up an interjection

Service user: When I left your office last week I felt a bit upset about what we had talked about.

Practitioner: A bit upset?

Service user: Well, very upset really.

Practitioner: What upset you? Can you remember?

Service user: I hate it when you're late. When you leave me sitting in that horrible waiting room with those useless old magazines. I hate it.

Practitioner: I'm sorry. That's my mistake and something that should not have happened. I'll do all I can to make sure it doesn't happen again and I'm sorry it upset you. [Pause] It's good you're able to tell me – is there anything else that I do, or don't do, that bothers you?

Allowing and using silence

Silence can generate difficult feelings both for service users and practitioners, so much so that it is not always easy to know who is feeling the most uncomfortable. This section explores some of the assumptions that are made about silence and how we can best work with this 'period filled with lack of speech, in which both interviewer and interviewee participate' (Kadushin and Kadushin 1997: 214).

The assumption is that talking is better than not talking and that nothing is being communicated when silence prevails. That is not the case, because words can be used to create or kill real dialogue, to conceal rather than to reveal. Other assumptions include the view that silences should always be broken; that the interview is not successful if there is too much silence; that it is mainly inexperienced practitioners who feel uncomfortable with silences; and that silences indicate poor communication skills or are a sign of failure on the part of the practitioner to engage with the interviewee. In addition, silence within English culture can easily be confused with a lack of politeness, incivility or poor social skills. Silence can also be used as a sign of rejection or disapproval. Although there will be times when these assumptions ring true, they may also be far from accurate.

For these reasons it is important to attempt to identify what is being communicated through silences – how silence is being used. This in turn helps us to understand how long we should allow the silence to run for. What might be called 'creative silences' describe a period of non-speech that is communicating something meaningful and important about the individual and his or her situation. Creative silences indicate that the individual is happily preoccupied with his or her own thoughts and feelings. This stands in contrast to a more 'troubled' form of silence that indicates a feeling of anxiety, embarrassment or confusion on the part of the interviewee, or a withholding or punishing withdrawal. Troubled silences can also reveal that the individual is too upset or too fearful to speak, perhaps because they feel overwhelmed or feel that they need to protect themselves or others.

Several points need to be emphasized. First, it takes two to create a silence in an interview: the service user and the interviewer. If a service user is silent, we need not be – unless we decide to be so. Second, we often do not know for certain what is being communicated through the use of silence – and this includes our own silence – and whether it is a 'productive silence' or not. One way to overcome this difficulty would be to ask the person in question what their silence means but, of course, we may not get a response! In relation to our own silence, it can help to think about what we are communicating in our silence and what our silence means to us. Third, it is crucial to remember that the briefest silence can appear to be a long time. This very quickly comes to light if we have the opportunity to do a time-check. One 'trick' I use cautiously – as a 'last straw' – when trying to communicate with children and adolescents who are determined to remain silent involves planting a deliberate error in my soliloquy. The one most likely to produce a response is when I purposely describe them to be younger than they actually are (see example below). Once a silence has been broken, it may be wise not to try to analyse immediately what the silence meant. For some service users, this can feel like they have lost control or that they are being manipulated. This is particularly important to remember when working with children and adolescents.

The ability to be calm, silent and still in an interview is an important skill and one that every competent interviewer needs to acquire. One way to see a pause is as a brief silence – a resting place – that allows time to gather thoughts and feelings. However, like silences, we can find long pauses difficult to bear. Where a person is known to have a pattern of being silent, it can help to sit facing a clock, so that we can check the time without interfering with the flow of the interview. This allows for silence to be measured against reality, rather than our own internal clock, which tends to tick very slowly in an interview where silence is present (see Kadushin and Kadushin 1997: 213–18).

Example: Speaking into the silence of a young person determined not to speak

Practitioner:	Well, you're a very silent 12-year-old ...
Service user:	I'm not 12, I am 13! So there!
Practitioner:	Sorry – my mistake. So you're 13 – not 12?
Service user:	Yeah. Do I look like a 12-year-old? [said with contempt]
Practitioner:	No, you don't. When's your birthday, Jake?
Service user:	In December.

Example: Speaking into the silence

Practitioner:	You have been silent for some time now Jenny. I wonder why you don't want to talk today?
Service user:	[Silence]
Practitioner:	[Pause] I wonder if you are afraid that I might be angry because you didn't manage to turn up last week?
Service user:	[Silence]
Practitioner:	[Pause] I'm sure that you came all this way for a reason ... but at this point in time, it's not easy for me to see what help I can be ... why you feel you cannot speak. Has something happened?
Service user:	[Silence]
Practitioner:	[Pause] Are you angry with me?
Service user:	[Silence]
Practitioner:	[Pause] Maybe it's best if I don't ask you any more questions. Maybe I should fill this silence with my words and tell you what I think has been happening – and you can tell me if I'm right or wrong. My guess is that last week, you couldn't come to see me because you were grounded again. I think you had another row with your mother – maybe you both said some tough things – and she said you had to stay in your room until you apologized. Apologies are difficult for you and this meant you missed seeing me. I'll bet that since the row, you've felt very confused and hurt. Maybe you've said to yourself that it's better not to talk at all since talking gets you into trouble. Instead, you're left talking to yourself but the problem is that it's very hard for any of us to sort things out without talking. I think you have found talking helpful in the past and it can help you now. I am here to help you.
Service user:	[Silence]
Practitioner:	My guess is that you are talking but you are not talking out loud. I think that you are talking to yourself. Am I right? I wonder if you can bring yourself to tell me what is going on in your head – what you are saying to yourself so

	that you don't feel so alone with these feelings? These feelings can be so ...

Service user: [Interrupting] Oh, I can't stand it when you go on and on. How come you know all this?

Practitioner: Because it's happened before and I remember things that happen to you.

Using self-disclosure

Self-disclosure highlights the importance of our being able to draw on our own personal knowledge and history to gauge what course of action is appropriate and necessary in order to be effective in a particular situation or encounter (Lishman 1994: 145). However, this self-knowledge and 'professional use of self' is taken one step further because self-disclosure relates to revealing present or past personal information about ourselves. *The general rule is that self-disclosure should not occur unless it is in the interest of the individual seeking help.* For example, it can be invaluable for people who feel isolated and alone in their suffering, or who worry about revealing themselves in any way, for us to reveal that it is all right to be *known* in certain ways. This can help to break down feelings of shame, guilt or self-blame – the feelings that say 'I'm not like other people', when in fact many reactions that people may experience as 'odd' or 'strange' are common to much of the human race. This can bring an enormous sense of relief. For example, if we have been bereaved it can help to disclose how we overcame our feelings of devastation and grief at the death of someone we loved.

Sharing thoughts and feelings through self-disclosure can help service users to see us as 'ordinary human beings' as well as professional workers. Similarly, it can help us to feel more empathic and in touch with what is being said and felt. However, self-disclosure must be handled sensitively because it carries many dangers. For example, I recall an incident where a social worker shared his history of sexual abuse with a service user. He did so for many reasons but none related to the best interest of the service user, who was left feeling bewildered, confused and powerless to help. This is an extreme but true example and one that highlights how inappropriate it can be for us to share our personal or professional problems or history in this way. Or again, it is important to avoid using certain phrases that are not accurate, such as 'I know what it's like' or 'I know what you're going through.' We can have some idea of what it is like, but all human beings are unique, which means we cannot know from our own experience what another person's experience is actually like. For this reason, it is often better to be quite vague and to keep our comments to a minimum, unless there are good reasons to do otherwise.

Example: Self-disclosing past experiences (**truanting**)

Practitioner:	I never used to like going to school so I know a bit about what it's like to have to go somewhere that you don't enjoy. In my case, I managed to keep going because I found a teacher who I could really talk to. Is there any teacher, or pupil (student) that you like or get on with quite well?
Service user:	There's a few people I like the look of but I don't come across them.
Practitioner:	Well, maybe it's our task to ensure that you do come across them. How does that sound?
Service user:	Dunno ...

Example: Self-disclosing past experiences (**depression**)

Practitioner:	I have had bouts of depression in the past and so I have some idea about how you're feeling but people experience depression in very different ways. Can you describe what this depression is like for you and when it started?
Service user:	Do you still suffer from depression?
Practitioner:	No, I'm fine now. It may be important to say that depression can and does lift. What we have to look at is what will help you to overcome this depression.

Some practitioners would not feel comfortable disclosing personal information of this kind and that is a valid position. There are no hard-and-fast rules. However, it is important to use self-disclosure thoughtfully. If there is any indication that it may not be received well, I would avoid it.

Using humour

The sensitive and judicious use of humour can be helpful in a range of situations. However, for the most part it is a subject that is rarely covered in social work texts. When used well, humour can introduce issues that may be potentially awkward, anxiety provoking or embarrassing. It can enable us to introduce uncomfortable issues in ways that are tentative, and to back off if we encounter difficult reactions. Humour can also place the interaction on a more normal, ordinary footing and help us to reveal our humanness:

> Humour is an equalizer. It deflates pomposity. Workers' capacity to laugh at themselves without embarrassment or shame communicates genuineness in the relationship. It introduces a desirable element of informality and spontaneity into an essentially formal encounter.
>
> (Kadushin and Kadushin 1997: 225)

Some of the best use of humour focuses on all that is ridiculous about life, and the human condition – and the 'trials and tribulations of everyday life' (Foot 1997: 263). From this perspective, it is about being playful in situations that allow this kind of light-hearted and good-natured interaction. However, such playfulness is influenced by important social and cultural differences that need to be acknowledged. Without this knowledge and sensitivity, it can sometimes be difficult to tell whether someone is *laughing with* or *laughing at* another person. When used appropriately, humour can lead to a sense of enjoyment and fun, and can also be an energizing experience. Laughter can be particularly energizing, depending on its function. For example, Foot looks at the social functions of laughter and describes several types: humorous laughter, social laughter, ignorance laughter, evasion laughter, apologetic laughter, anxiety laughter, derision laughter and joyous laughter (Foot 1997: 271–5).

However, humour can backfire when it is used in ways that are not appropriate to the situation or to the individual in question. Some people can confuse a more playful interaction or the use of humour with humiliation and can become defensive if there is the slightest hint that they are being laughed at or ridiculed. This may not indicate that the individual has a poor sense of humour but that he or she has been wounded or humiliated in the past by the use of humour and is sensitive in this area. Situations that we find amusing may not amuse others – and this is particularly true of people who are caught up in these situations. Where we have misread a person's capacity in this way, the best course of action is to apologize. It is, therefore, important that we are thoughtful about our reasons for using humour to ensure that it is being used appropriately. For example, the use of humour and certain kinds of jokes can sometimes belittle other people's suffering, hardship or oppression. A more subtle misuse can occur when humour is used as a way to communicate ambivalent or hostile emotions that we are not prepared to own, such as the fact that we do not like or respect the person in question. These forms of communication can be deeply confusing and disarming, and leave people in a situation where they do not really know what is being said and, therefore, how best to respond.

A sense of humour is an important attribute for professionals, and also for service users and carers. However, just as we may use humour in a range of different ways, so too may service users and carers. For example, some people may use humour against themselves, or against others who share their oppression. This may help them to cope with difficult experiences or it may indicate that they have internalized their oppression, and come to believe negative comments about themselves and others who share their oppression. Similarly, some service users and carers may use humour to express prejudicial views about other groups of people, making it difficult for us to know how to react, particularly when our agreement is sought. As professionals it is important that we do not endorse comments that reinforce negative, stereotypical or oppressive attitudes but instead think of ways to challenge these comments. However, interventions of this kind need to be undertaken carefully if they are to be effective in helping to change people's beliefs and attitudes, and if we are to avoid defensive reactions, and oppressive attitudes becoming entrenched even further (Payne 1997: 226). Sometimes our attempts to solve problems can become part of the problem (Preston-Shoot and Agass 1990: 55). Therefore it is important to remember that the use of humour can be a very vital aid to communication but only if used with considerable caution, and in ways that are culturally sensitive and appropriate to the situation and individual in question.

Endings: disengaging and termination skills

According to Kadushin and Kadushin, 'preparation for termination [of the interview] begins at the start of the interview' (1997: 271). This perspective encourages us to think of our contact with people as complete experiences: as encounters that have a beginning, middle and end, all of which should be considered at the planning and preparation stage of the work we are about to undertake. For example, work that has a focus and purpose should mean that we are able to identify how long the work will run and what outcome we are seeking when we reach the end.

One reason why significance is given to endings is because they provide an opportunity to do a great deal of important work. For service users who have experienced painful, abrupt and sometimes traumatizing endings in the past, experiencing a good ending can provide the chance to begin to sort out and work through any issues that inhibit them from moving forward. Some of these painful experiences may be due to unresolved grief at the premature death of someone close to them. Other experiences may be due to social workers and other significant figures leaving them without saying a proper good-bye. Children 'looked after' describe poignant experiences of feeling abandoned and their trust betrayed by social workers who never came to say good-bye, or who came only once, thereby giving them virtually no time to prepare for the fact that they may never see this important individual again.

For example, I once worked with Diane, who felt she had a special relationship with a particular health visitor: she felt understood and accepted by this individual in ways that were important. However, one day the health visitor did not turn up as agreed. In fact, she never turned up again. The reasons for her departure were never revealed to Diane but this experience continued to haunt her. It acted as a barrier when Diane encountered other professionals, despite the years that had elapsed, so much so that at the beginning of my work with Diane, the focus had to change (but not the overall purpose) in order to address the grief and anger that she felt about being abandoned in this way. Perhaps something untoward happened to this health visitor. We will never know. What we do know is that it is likely that Diane could have adjusted to her health visitor's untimely departure had she been offered some kind of explanation – something that said to Diane that she was important. This example shows how crucial it is that we do not forget or underestimate our importance to the service users we come into contact with.

To provide a good ending allows the opportunity for individuals to work through what it feels like to be left or to be left behind. It also provides an opportunity for people to experience what a good, well thought-out ending should involve. For example, a good ending can allow the understanding, knowledge or wisdom gained to be reviewed and consolidated in ways that can be built on and used in the future. However, some individuals find endings very hard, perhaps because they come from a history of being 'let down' and failed. As a result, changes of any kind, but particularly endings, can feel very final and devastating. For this reason, it is essential to remember that endings can give rise to a whole range of unexpected emotions. These include feelings of bewilderment, helplessness, fear and a terrifying sense of aloneness, abandonment and rejection. These reactions can happen, perhaps less intensely, when we go away on holiday or are absent for other reasons, but may remain hidden because it can be difficult for service users to reveal how much they have come to rely on us. It is therefore important that we do not underestimate our significance, nor the impact that an ending can bring about.

Ending an interview

Interviews have enormous variations and so too do their endings. Where a clear time boundary has been stated at the beginning with regular but unobtrusive time-checks and reminders, one can assume that most people will feel ready to end the interview. However, despite these boundaries and safeguards, it can be hard for some service users to 'let go' and to move on. Some desperately try to get all they can out of the interview – right up to the end. As a result, the interview can end up being drawn to a close in a way that feels rushed, with insufficient time to review what has been covered or to work through any feelings triggered by our departure.

One way that people reveal a difficulty working within boundaries can be encountered in the form of 'doorknob revelations'. These occur where significant or painful information is revealed at the end of the interview, as we are about to leave. As a practitioner, these revelations put us in a difficult 'no-win' situation. To extend the time boundary could mean we have lost control of it, and could also make us late for other appointments, but to be too rigid could involve missing an opportunity to understand the service user better. Also, on occasion it can be very important to show that we are willing to change the time boundary – to be flexible and to adapt – in order to meet the needs being expressed. Whether we decide to respond or not, the request and our response should be reviewed and considered in terms of the overall purpose that has already been agreed. There are no easy solutions to these difficulties except to provide an opportunity early in the interview for service users to talk about what it feels like when the end of an interview is in sight.

Example: An uncomplicated ending to an interview

Practitioner: Okay. We've got ten minutes left and I wonder how you would like to use the rest of the time we have?

Service user: Can we talk about what will happen when my husband comes out of prison?

Example: A difficult ending to an interview ('doorknob revelations')

Practitioner: It's 10.20 which means we have ten minutes left. I wonder if we could use the time remaining to look at what we've talked about and then to decide what we plan to cover when we meet again next week. How does that sound to you?

Service user: Okay but there's something I want to tell you before you go. You know I said my mother died of cancer when I was seven. Well that wasn't right. My aunt told me last year that she killed herself. That's why I went to live with my aunt – there was no one else to take care of me. [She begins to cry]

Practitioner: I'm sorry. [Pause] I did not realize that your mother died in that way. That's very upsetting for you to hear. You said your aunt told you this last year. What prompted her to tell you then, Sarah? [This ill-timed question is ignored]

Service user: [Sarah begins to sob]

Practitioner: It's okay ...'. Keep going. It must have been a real shock to you to hear this. [Pause] I'm glad you've found a way to tell me.

Service user: [Still sobbing deeply]

Practitioner: [After a reasonable time has elapsed and Sarah's sobbing has begun to be less intense] I can see that you're very upset and I feel for you but I'm afraid I have to go in a minute because I have to be elsewhere.

Service user: [No reply]

Practitioner: Sarah, is there anyone you would like me to contact who could come over now to be with you?

Service user: [No reply]

Practitioner: [Pause] Sarah, would it help if I asked your aunt to come across? How does that sound?

Service user: No. I don't want my aunt. I'm dead angry with her for not telling me sooner.

Practitioner:	Okay. I understand. But who can I ask instead? Who would be better?
Service user:	Peter, my boyfriend.
Practitioner:	Okay. Can I have Peter's phone number so that I can contact him? [After contacting Peter] Before I go, let me get my diary and we'll make another time to meet before next week.

It is important to note that the sense of time we feel when someone is crying is very similar to the time we feel when people are silent. It can seem that the individual has been silent or tearful for longer than they have in reality. Unless deeply distressed, most people tend not to cry for long periods, but this does not make the experience of crying any easier to bear for everyone concerned. It is important to check how people are feeling after a prolonged tearful experience. Some may feel physically sick or have a headache. Others may appear bewildered, as if in an altered state. Where this is the case, it is important to ensure the individual arrives home safely.

Closing the case and ending the relationship

Closing a case appropriately where we are ending the prospect of future contact can be one of the most difficult yet important skills to acquire (Kadushin and Kadushin 1997: 271–84). It is made more difficult to achieve when, through lack of resources, other forms of help are not forthcoming. This is particularly troubling when working with people who do not have the emotional, practical or material resources needed to manage without support of a particular kind. These concerns are very real. Sometimes this can lead to a situation where we continue to work with service users longer than is appropriate. We may be justifying these in sophisticated ways but, nevertheless, extending our involvement longer than is appropriate can create a situation where our work becomes purposeless and devoid of direction. It can also result in an unhealthy dependency being created, based as much on our own concerns as those of the service user. This is not the hallmark of a competent practitioner. Focused, thoughtful and sensitive supervision can be enormously helpful in addressing these difficulties.

Under ideal circumstances, cases should be terminated at a point that has been mutually agreed: when goals have been reached or the time allocated for the work has come to an end and the service user feels ready to end the contact. Well-planned endings often involve a tapering down of services, for example extending the length of time between appointments. This then also allows for the progress to be properly evaluated against agreed goals, aims and objectives. This may include identifying how to build on what has already been learned and achieved, perhaps by referring the individual to other appropriate agencies, as well as providing the opportunity to work through difficulties, such as those triggered by separation and loss. It also allows the service user the chance to look ahead and to propose appropriate courses of action, including where to find additional help if this is needed.

One of the most valuable skills in relation to endings involves encouraging people to bring other people into their lives to replace us, by helping them to turn to others who can provide the care, concern, guidance and support that they need. However, for a range of different and complex reasons, in practice many endings are not mutually agreed nor carefully planned and prepared. As a result, they do not leave either party with a sense that there has been a satisfactory completion of an important and valuable piece of work. Closing cases at an inappropriate point does little to enhance the reputation of social work. However, where resources are limited, cases may have to be closed in less than ideal circumstances. Other agencies may request our continued involvement but do so without taking into account the fact that resources allocated to one case necessarily involve those resources being unavailable elsewhere. This highlights the complexities involved in social work and the difficult decisions we have to make. It can leave us in a 'no-win' situation and vulnerable to attack, which in turn can affect our judgement about whether or not to close a case.

Example: Preparing for the contact and relationship to end

Practitioner: Greg, You may recall that our agreement was to work together for six months. You may also remember that three months into our work, when we'd reached the half-way point, we agreed to review our progress. We now have eight weeks remaining, which means that we will meet eight more times before we stop meeting. Endings can be difficult but they can be made easier by talking things through and by looking at what it will be like when we stop seeing one another. What comes to your mind when I say that our work will be ending in eight weeks' time?

Service user: I don't think I'd realized that we only have eight weeks left. I have been thinking in terms of months and two months seems a long way off. But eight weeks, or eight more meetings, seems like no time at all. I am already feeling that I would find it difficult to manage without your help.

Practitioner: It's good that you're in touch with how you're feeling. Let's look at this a little more. What do you think you will miss most about not seeing me?

Service user: Having someone to talk to. I know lots of people but it's

	hard to talk. You let me say whatever comes into my head and you never tell me off or say that I am wrong or stupid or tell me to shut up.
Practitioner:	That's right. Part of our agreement was to work together to help you to trust your thinking. When you're not scared or worried about being criticized, you think very well. You know what you want even if you don't always know how to get it. The question we must now think about is who would be the best person for you to turn to when our work and relationship comes to an end?
Service user:	No one.
Practitioner:	Let's try that question again. We need to be sure that there definitely isn't someone out there before we look at the possibility of finding new friends and relationships. Of all the people you know, who is the easiest person for you to talk to?
Service user:	My friend John.
Practitioner:	Right. What is it about John that makes it easy for you to talk to him?
Service user:	He never puts me down. My parents put me down all the time but John doesn't.
Practitioner:	So, what John and I have in common is that we don't criticize you or put you down?
Service user:	Yes.
Practitioner:	Who else do you know who doesn't put you down?
Service user:	No one.
Practitioner:	Let me put this another way. Who do you know who doesn't like being put down?
Service user:	My sister. She hates being put down and my parents have done that to her a lot.
Practitioner:	Good. Now you are able to name two people who you think might be good to talk to about things that are important to you when our work comes to an end: John and your sister. You have also been able to say why these people might be good to talk to – because they are less likely to put you down or to criticize you. What you have said is very important. Over the next eight weeks, I want to suggest that one of our tasks will be to spend some time trying to help you to strengthen your links with John and your sister – and any other relationships that come to mind that may be valuable to you – so that when the time comes for us to end our work together, you have other people to turn to.

If Greg's contact with John and his sister does not work out well, it may be worth considering meeting them. The purpose of this meeting would be to try to sort out and work through issues that inhibit Greg from forming a relationship with them. It is likely that difficulties encountered here happen in other situations.

Before ending this chapter on basic interviewing skills, it is important to include an account on motivational interviewing. This approach is one of the most influential and effective ways of working with complex problems and behaviours, particularly those associated with addictions.

Motivational interviewing

An important technique for enhancing people's motivation to change their behaviour is motivational interviewing. This approach is 'built on a fundamental objection to the traditional, disease-oriented model of motivation' (Barber 2002: 92), which sees addiction as a 'disease' or as an illness. This disease model is based on the medical model, covered in Chapter 1, and a belief that underpins the thinking of organizations like Alcoholics Anonymous: 'One does not become an alcoholic, one is born an alcoholic.' This states that alcoholism is incurable – an irreversible condition and deficit of the individual. It argues that change is not possible until people's lives have deteriorated to the point where they have reached 'rock bottom'; it is at this point that denial and resistance break down. This more traditional and accepted view of addiction is argued against for several reasons. First, there is no evidence to support the view that alcoholics have an inherently deficient personality. Second, many people change for positive reasons, without hitting 'rock bottom'. Third, the actions of individuals are not the only factor that gives rise to change: external factors can inspire or inhibit change. Finally, the role played by practitioners and counsellors, and the knowledge and skills that they use in their work, can be hugely influential (Barber 2002: 92).

In opposition to the disease model, and its emphasis on 'blaming and shaming' people to change their behaviour, motivational interviewing adopts 'a client-centred and empathic counselling style' (Miller and Rollnick 2002: 37). Motivational interviewing is based on four general principles:

- *Express empathy*. This stresses the underlying principle of a client-centred approach which is that acceptance facilitates change. It is therefore important to understand where the service user is coming from and to do this by 'skilful reflective listening' (Miller and Rollnick 2002: 37). This perspective sees ambivalence, that is, the reluctance to change, as normal.
- *Develop discrepancy*. This principle departs from a rigorous use of a

client-centred approach, which is non-directive, because motivational interviewing is directive. Its intention is to help resolve ambivalence so that change can occur. This principle stresses that it is the service user, and not the practitioner, who needs to present the argument for change and that change becomes possible when there is a recognition of a discrepancy between what is actually happening and what the person wants to happen.

- *Roll with resistance.* This principle stresses that: 'Resistance that a person offers can be turned or reframed slightly to create a new momentum' (Miller and Rollnick 2002: 40). Practitioners should avoid persuasion or the desire to argue the case for the benefits that change could bring. Instead the emphasis is on drawing out a person's resistance and encouraging the service user to find their own answers and solutions.
- *Support self-efficacy.* 'The concept of *self-efficacy* ... refers to a person's belief in his or her ability to carry out and succeed with a specific task. Self-efficacy is a key element in motivation to change and is a reasonably good predictor of treatment outcome' (Miller and Rollnick 2002: 40). This principle emphasizes the importance of faith and hope as central elements in the process of change, including the practitioner's belief that change is possible. It stresses that it is the person in question who is responsible for initiating and implementing the changes that they wish to embrace.

William Miller began his career as a therapist using behavioural, self-control techniques with 'problem drinkers'. He developed this brief, directive client-centred approach when his research revealed greater success after adopting this method. For a further account of motivational interviewing, see Prochaska and Norcross (2003: 159) and Barber (2002).

Conclusion: interviews as 'positive experiences'

It is likely that many of the 20 interventions described in this chapter already form part of the skills repertoire of most social workers. In addition, the task of interviewing can be thought of as an intervention in its own right because of the opportunity it provides to gain a greater understanding of people and their situations. This in itself can bring about change. For these reasons, interviewing skills are as important to experienced practitioners as newly qualified staff because they help to ensure that our work has a structure and purpose, with clear objectives located within a meaningful value base. They are also crucial when we encounter difficult or chaotic situations or complex and intractable problems. For example, as an experienced practitioner I still find myself needing to draw on interviewing techniques when I encounter situations that I find overwhelming or frightening, or when I am tired and lacking in concentration at the end of a difficult day. They act as a safeguard – as a compass when I find myself lost in the wilderness of my own preoccupations and fears. The following two chapters continue this theme and explore interventions that can be used to help people to move their lives forward and to bring about change.

6 PROVIDING HELP, DIRECTION

AND GUIDANCE

Unlike in Chapter 5, the interventions outlined in the first part of this chapter describe reactions that are not solely the domain of professionals; family, friends, neighbours, concerned individuals or strangers can be skilled in helping a human being who needs help. As practitioners, our role and responsibilities result in different expectations. Accountability is different. The second part covers skills that are more specialist. The following skills are described:

- giving advice
- providing information
- providing explanations
- offering encouragement and validation
- providing reassurance
- using persuasion and being directive
- providing practical and material assistance
- providing support
- providing care
- modelling and social skills training
- reframing
- offering interpretations
- adaptations
- counselling skills
- containing anxiety.

Providing help

It takes skill to decide what kind of help may be needed and how to offer this in ways that are personally and culturally acceptable to the individual.

These skills are at the heart of social work but are difficult to acquire. Nevertheless, according to England, 'good social workers *know*, through their experience, the value of their helping work with clients. That value cannot be abandoned' (1986: 4, original emphasis).

It is the uncertain nature of the value of helping – what it means to give and to receive help – that must be unravelled, clarified and articulated so that the essential part that help plays in sustaining and creating positive change can be identified and utilized to the fullest. To fail to enter into this dialogue about the value of helping leaves us caught in an ambivalence: trapped between those who desire to care for vulnerable people within a 'caring society' and those who despise and attack vulnerability and who demean those who care for vulnerable people. Without this clarification, we are open to being stereotyped as ineffective 'do-gooders', where our work and the help we offer is characterized as ineffective, coercive and controlling, and beyond scrutiny and evaluation (England 1986: 5).

To begin to unravel what is included in the term 'help' is difficult because there is no uniformity across social work and, as a result, being helpful can involve a range of different interventions. In an attempt to clarify the use of these terms, *practical* and *material assistance*, *support* and *care* are differentiated in this book and used to describe different activities and different skills. However, none of these interventions is mutually exclusive. For example, most problems have an emotional element. Some service users may feel ashamed or embarrassed about asking for practical assistance. In order to ensure that they can take up and utilize whatever practical help is needed, emotional support may be required (Lishman 1994: 7). The converse is not necessarily the case. Emotional support itself may be all that is required. For example, practitioners using counselling skills working with someone who has been bereaved may only work with the feelings of bereavement and loss, if practical support is being provided elsewhere.

Much of our willingness to help may be conveyed quite subtly through our behaviour. Yet, despite our best efforts, some service users may still dislike having to seek or ask for help. These negative feelings may include a concern about how they might be seen by others, or may have their roots in a fierce sense of independence. The possible responses are endless and very much dependent on what it was like for the individual to have to rely on others in the past. Memories of earlier failures, disappointments or humiliating experiences can result in people feeling guarded. Some professionals respond inappropriately, by treating service users like children or as if they are stupid. Others demand compliance, insisting that service users should be grateful, cooperative and deferential. Too often, this can result in people feeling robbed of their self-respect and sense of personal autonomy. It can be difficult for any individual to accept and to benefit from services when these are offered in a demeaning way. Older people are particularly susceptible to this kind of patronizing behaviour. So too are children and young people and others, such as people from minority groups, whose right to be respected does not always come automatically.

All professions are prone to treat people badly, sometimes in ways that are less obvious, such as making people wait for long periods. Citizens' and patients' charters are designed to address these difficulties and inequalities but have limitations because they neither guarantee people's entitlement to certain services nor their right to be treated fairly (Adams 1998: 193). While there is no room for complacency, social work is noticeable in its commitment to embrace practices that demonstrate anti-discriminatory and anti-oppressive perspectives (Thompson 2002a: 91).

According to Howe, 'helping is a test of the helper as a person' (1987: 113). This statement emphasizes that much of our ability to give help appropriately relates to our own personal history of being helped and our ongoing capacity to receive help from others in our everyday lives. It reinforces the importance of self-knowledge and of our being in touch with what we feel when we are at the receiving end of help and the anxieties felt from being beholden to or having to depend on others. Howe's statement also emphasizes the importance of creating and sustaining a more equal, mutual and reciprocal relationship when working alongside or in partnership with service users. For example, I once worked with a social worker who had a remarkable capacity for being able to empathize accurately with service users and to translate that understanding into appropriate and creative forms of help. However, his ability to communicate that understanding was on the whole quite poor. After a time, and some serious misunderstandings, it came to light that the reason for this difficulty lay in the fact that this worker was brought up in a mixed race, immigrant family where the language used took the form of commands: 'do this/do that'. Questions or requests were not the kind of phrases commonly used. Although his language had changed over the years, the legacy of this early form of communication remained, particularly when he felt under attack or nervous. This example highlights how our early experiences can affect our capacity to provide help, both negatively and positively.

Providing help also offers an opportunity to give more than practical services. It allows us to stretch the experience across other needs. For example, in setting up a nursery place for a child, we could use this opportunity to pass over a sense of enthusiasm for the possibilities it opens up for the mother or father, as well as for the child. We could use it as an opportunity to explore what direction this parent might want for their life and for their child. Clearly, encouraging someone to pursue their hopes and desires in this way has to be tempered by the reality of the situation. However, too much realism can be a reflection of our own depressed outlook and can dampen enthusiasm and the opportunity to herald something new and exciting.

Taking hold of opportunities and stretching them in this way can demand a great deal from us and, inevitably, we cannot always put forward our *best self* because there will be times when we do not feel able to respond in this way. For example, when we find ourselves guarding resources as if they are our personal possessions or when we feel too put upon, depleted and empty to be able to give at all, let alone to give generously. Service users may pick up on this fact, and in such a situation it may be wise for us to acknowledge our weariness and temporarily bow out as gracefully as possible, in the hope that we can return soon with renewed energy. This may be preferable to our struggling to give from a depleted part of ourselves. If persistent, difficulties of this kind can mark the beginning of burn-out: that is, a situation where we feel disillusioned, undervalued and exhausted by expectations and demands that feel overwhelming and impossible to process (Feltham and Dryden 1993: 23; Payne 1997: 23).

Giving advice

Advice and guidance are sometimes used interchangeably because both involve recommending something or directing an individual towards one or several courses of action. In a professional context, both can carry the expectation that our views are backed by knowledge and/or experience. However, 'guidance' tends to sound less prescriptive (vocational or career guidance agencies) whereas the word 'advice' tends to have a more definite flavour.

Advice is often sought either to help identify the problem clearly or to help identify possible solutions, but should be offered with the greatest care because we can be inaccurate or simply wrong in the advice we offer. Offering advice inappropriately can also reinforce a sense of personal inadequacy or be experienced as intrusive (Feltham and Dryden 1993: 7). For these reasons, it is important to be judicious and thoughtful about the kind of advice we give, perhaps only offering advice when asked and with the proviso that we may be wrong. These safeguards help to ensure that any advice given is sensitive to an individual's personal situation and expectations, including their cultural and social context.

In recent years some social workers have felt reluctant to give advice. It can be seen as 'imposing our values and morals on our clients' (Lishman 1994: 83); as contradicting the principle of client self-determination (Biestek 1961); as failing to acknowledge the importance of service users taking on the role of 'experts' in relation to their own lives; as patronizing and disempowering; or as discouraging self-sufficiency and personal autonomy by creating an unhealthy dependency. As a result, offering advice can generate anxiety among practitioners, in case we give the 'wrong' advice and are held accountable. One way to manage these anxieties is to be honest and open about what we do and do not know, and to avoid bluffing or hedging our responses. However, certain areas of knowledge are required of us and are essential to the social work task, which means that in certain situations we have a responsibility to offer advice and to provide advice that should include, as a minimum, 'detailed, accurate and up-to-date knowledge about the law, welfare rights and local community facilities' (Davies 1981: 52). This links to the point made earlier about the importance of social workers developing a sound knowledge base.

It is interesting to note that service users do not always share our reservations about being given advice (Lishman 1994: 8–9). As with the offer of explanations, advice can be particularly important for people who feel bewildered and confused or who need to base their decision on our opinions. For example, offering advice to people who have been recently bereaved can help to structure what they have to do and in what order. For this reason, it is important for service users to decide for themselves whether or not they want to hear advice that is on offer, rather than us deciding for them. Most service users weigh up the advice they are given quite carefully and will tend to ignore advice that seems inappropriate. However, the timing of advice giving is important. As a general rule, it should only be offered when other possibilities have been exhausted and the decision-making and problem-solving processes have broken down. It is important that advice is not 'thrown in' at the end of the session, as a parting shot, because this does not give the individual the opportunity to take new information on board and to work through whatever thoughts and feelings have emerged.

Providing information

Recent years have seen the development of specialized information services and centres, such as those in relation to housing, welfare rights and legal rights and those providing information on local resources, such as self-help groups and social networks (Lishman 1994: 78). This development has left some social workers unsure about whether it is appropriate to offer certain kinds of practical help, such as welfare rights checks, where specialist expertise may be more accurate and up-to-date. Nevertheless, even if we do not undertake welfare rights checks ourselves, it is essential that we know where these more specialist advice centres are and the nature of their referral criteria.

In more general terms, providing information can be central to problem-solving and the decision-making process. For this reason, it is important that any information offered is accurate. Updating the information we have on local resources can be a time-consuming task, particularly without proper organizational structures to feed in new information and developments. However, for service users to act on information later found to be wrong can result in a serious loss of trust and confidence in the competence of social work as a profession.

Where the task involves referring people on to other agencies or organizations, it helps to check the accuracy of the information to hand, perhaps by telephoning the agency before referring people on, having ensured first that we have the service user's permission to do so. It is alarming how many service users are given incorrect information at this stage: for some, it must feel like being sent on a wild goose chase, where only the most charmed or most determined get through. Checking disabled access is particularly important.

The following points need to be stressed. Anxiety and fear can interfere with an individual's capacity to listen and to digest information, because emotional energy is being taken up attending to these anxieties. This may be conveyed by the individual appearing to be confused or preoccupied. Where this is the case, it can be helpful to repeat information, using a language that is simple, steady and accessible. This is particularly true when communicating bad news, such as details of an accident or illness. If this does not work and the individual still seems confused and lost, we need to consider ending the session.

Again, it is vital not to give important information right at the end of a session when concentration may have lapsed: sometimes it is essential to be present to see how well information has been processed. Where we suspect that a person might forget the details covered, a follow-up letter may prove helpful, but only where we know the service user has adequate literacy skills and where receiving a letter would not be experienced as daunting.

Leaflets and other written information

The importance of providing written information in the form of leaflets and handouts is likely to depend on the situation and what knowledge the individual already has and needs. This may vary over time. For example, an asylum seeker who has recently arrived in this country is likely to need a great deal of information, which may have to be translated. This may entail explaining basic information, such as how different services and government departments operate and how to access these. For example, it can save a great deal of time and anguish if we explain the difference between social security and social services. Leaflets must be adapted where service users' capacity to understand and to take in information is limited. Special care needs to be taken in relation to differences of age, physical disability, hearing or sight impairments, emotional state, literacy and comprehension skills, and so on. There are many imaginative ways to overcome such difficulties, such as using drawings, pictures, figurines and videos (Lishman 1994: 82–3).

It can be too easy for people to be 'fobbed off' with information, as if by handing out a leaflet we are always giving something useful, helpful and appropriate. Sadly, that may not be the case and, instead, we could be handing out worry or confusion, particularly if the leaflet is not written in a way that meets the needs of the person seeking this information. The test lies in whether they were able to use this information and the best and easiest way to find this out is to ask for feedback. Another way would be to read the information or leaflet as if we were a stranger to the issue being communicated – a visitor from Mars – to see if it is informative. We may find, as is sometimes the case, that too much knowledge is assumed: this can raise more questions than answers.

Information giving, whether given verbally or in written form, can be seen as an opportunity to provide new meaning and understanding. As a symbolic communication, providing advice, guidance or explanations can have far reaching consequences (Lishman 1994: 15–19). Information that is passed over well not only helps people to make an informed choice but can also give confidence in a way that encourages individuals to act independently and effectively on their own behalf in the future (Millar et al. 1992: 108). Therefore, how we communicate information can be as important as the information itself. Leaflets handed out with an attitude of indifference, or as an afterthought, are likely to be treated in the same way. For this reason, it can be helpful to bring the leaflet/ information 'alive', by reading it beforehand, marking those areas considered relevant and important, and by making it personal by adding the individual's name to it. These gestures are important because they reveal a commitment and thoughtfulness: they can also save valuable time.

Finally, it is important to note that under the Disabled Persons Act 1986, social work departments and voluntary agencies have a duty to provide leaflets and information in an appropriate and accessible format for people with disability, such as providing information in Braille or via tape recordings. Equally, it is required that information is provided in the language of the people who use the service. This expectation also extends to information on health and welfare issues. For example, the current Attendance Allowance leaflet (DS 702) is available in several other languages: Bengali, Chinese, Greek, Gujarati, Hindi, Punjabi, Turkish, Urdu, Vietnamese and Welsh.

Providing explanations

Explaining is a core skill in social work, and important in other health and welfare settings, but it is a subject covered very little in social work texts and in communication studies research. Brown and Atkins (1997: 183) propose three reasons for this neglect:

1 explaining is a taken-for-granted activity; a great deal of time is spent explaining in everyday life and in various professional contexts, so it is assumed that everyone knows how to explain.
2 for some professional groups such as counsellors, therapists and social workers, explaining has associations with authority-centred approaches, with telling, instructing and didactics; hence the study of explaining is shunned.
3 explaining, like so many taken-for-granted activities, is a deep concept. Explaining has interconnections with understanding, with language, with logic, with rhetoric, and with critical theory and with culture. It is, therefore, a complex activity and one that has been neglected in terms of research.

Explanations differ from advice and guidance because their purpose is not to offer direction but to illuminate, clarify, reconcile or interpret events with a view to providing greater understanding. They attempt to throw light on the cause, nature and interrelationship of different thoughts, feelings and events. They can be divided into three forms: illustrations, demonstrations and verbal explanations. Of these, the focus of this section is on verbal explanations, which can be seen in terms of three main categories, each addressing a different type of question:

• interpretative explanations – what?
• descriptive explanations – how?
• reason-giving explanations – why?

(Brown 1997: 184–5)

Some explanations may involve all three categories, in an attempt to describe the problem or situation in words that can be understood and absorbed, so that a new understanding can be reached. This endeavour is more likely to succeed if it is, first, sensitive to the service user's thoughts and feelings; second, delivered in a way that is interesting, involved, clear and well structured; and, third, where the communication has been planned in a way that maximizes learning and understanding – 'a little remembered is better than a lot forgotten'.

Responsibility for an unsuccessful communication should lie with us and not be blamed, implicitly, on service users. One way to check whether a new understanding has been reached is to ask service users to recall what they have heard or to ask them to apply this understanding to specific and relevant situations in their lives. This needs to be undertaken sensitively, drawing on points made earlier in the text on the 'nature of helping' and the importance of understanding the meaning given to experiences.

Explanations as a way of addressing emotional needs

In relation to emotional needs, explanations can be profoundly important for people who are confused or who easily become confused because they have little confidence or trust in their own thinking and how to understand and link different experiences. Some of this confusion may be short-term and likely to lift relatively easily. However, for some people this state of confusion is severe and enduring, and in some cases may be the result of discontinuities and disruptions in childhood. For example, I once worked with a young woman, Jo, whose family was always moving house, possibly to avoid debts, although this was never known for sure. Her parents never appeared to offer any explanation about events, which meant that there was never any transition or bridge between one experience and another. This situation reflected a serious lack of consistency and predictability in Jo's life. This difficulty was compounded by the fact that Jo was not a 'wanted child'. She felt this acutely, and it was later confirmed by her mother, who admitted she had tried to have an abortion when she knew she was pregnant with Jo. The result of these experiences meant that Jo lived with the dread, throughout her childhood, that one day she would come home and find her family gone and her house empty; she would be left behind, with nowhere to go and no means of knowing where to find her family.

Jo found it virtually impossible to link events or to bring cause and effect together. She thought 'things just happened' for no reason, or no reason she could work out. The absence of words and explanations from her parents meant that Jo found it hard to sort out one feeling from another or to know which feelings belonged to her and which belonged to others (Howe *et al.* 1999: 145). This profound sense of confusion and bewilderment haunted Jo's struggle in the world and, when she left care, she eventually became rootless, living in doorways, with no sense of belonging anywhere, as if searching for something. One of her greatest joys was to have things explained to her, which she once described as 'a word lullaby', because it attempted to provide some order, certainty and predictability in a world that otherwise felt frightening and beyond comprehension.

The importance of explaining the world and what is happening, for service users who have not had this experience in childhood, needs to be emphasized. It is for this reason that story-telling (Jewett 1997: 119–23) or narrative accounts (Shaw 1996: 62–3) are important. We can recognize these gaps and confusion when, as with Jo, we encounter service users who regularly manifest a profound bewilderment, asking what appear to be naive questions but with little capacity to remember the answer. Such bewilderment can be painful and terrifying. For this reason, the ability to explain situations to service users – to help them to understand past and present events and future possibilities – in a language and tone that is accessible and kind, is one of the most important communication skills that we can develop as practitioners.

Offering encouragement and validation

Offering positive encouragement can be an important intervention within social work. However, according to Lishman, research suggests that these interventions may not be widely used by practitioners:

> There seems [to be] general hesitancy or ambivalence in social work about the value of explicitly conveying approval or positive encouragement. This may reflect in part a cultural bias against giving or accepting positive feedback, an anxiety that giving approval can be patronizing. It may also reflect underlying values and prejudices in social work.
>
> (Lishman 1994: 51)

An exception is where encouragement forms part of a particular practice approach as, for example, in Rogers's (1957) concept of *unconditional positive regard*, or where, as with praise, encouragements are used as 'support interventions' (Kadushin and Kadushin 1997: 205) intended to ensure that certain options are explored or undertakings completed. In relation to cognitive–behavioural approaches, encouragement and validation are described in terms of *positive reinforcement* (Sheldon 1995: 63; Cigno and Bourn 1998: 18).

Encouragement can be seen in two ways: to help service users *towards* or *away from* a particular course of action, experience, thought or feeling. Both can be particularly helpful when individuals have poor self-esteem (Mruk 1999: 153), little self-confidence or limited experience, or when they feel overwhelmed and afraid of what they may encounter. Encouragement can help to smooth the journey towards these experiences or can be a low-key means of drawing service users away from certain actions or activities that may be dangerous or damaging, and/or pose a threat to themselves or to others.

Some practitioners feel reluctant to attempt to steer another person's behaviour in this way. The concern is that they could be used unethically, perhaps as a means of controlling or manipulating individuals in a particular direction: these dangers have to be guarded against. Nevertheless, some people need encouragement to keep them going and give them confidence. Although it may not always be appropriate to respond to these needs, they should not be ignored. A further difficulty is that it can be hard to know how to express our encouragement in ways that do not sound soppy or 'over-the-top'. This skill comes with practice and experience and is not always an easy balance to find.

Validation

Whereas encouragement is oriented to inspire or motivate people to think or act differently *before* an event or experience, validations tend to provide a positive appraisal *after* the event. In this sense they are a form of feedback. However, they often have a more personal orientation because they provide an opportunity to applaud the commitment and effort put into a particular situation and to celebrate any achievements or personal learning that have been gained. Validation of this kind is important when working with people who lack confidence in themselves, perhaps in relation to their appearance or in their ability to make sound decisions and to act independently. However, care must be taken that the validations we give are honest and truthful and not exaggerated or given merely to make someone 'feel better'. Validations sound hollow or patronizing if they are not based on actual abilities or real achievements.

Providing reassurance

Offering reassurance can be an important way to ease anxiety and uncertainty – to smooth troubled waters – and to provide comfort. This can be particularly important for times when an individual has lost touch with a more balanced view of what is happening in their lives and, as a result, needs someone to assure them that, despite their worries, everything is basically in order. However, reassurance should not be offered where we are not confident that our words will come true. To be overoptimistic or overly reassuring when the outcome cannot be clearly predicted or controlled is to run the risk of letting people down and putting our relationship and credibility in danger. If our reassurances are later proved wrong or unfounded, this could seriously – perhaps even irreparably – undermine confidence in our judgement. It is worth remembering that people can feel reassured indirectly by the way we conduct ourselves, including the way we dress (Kadushin and Kadushin 1997: 291–4; Lishman 1994: 18), and by our ensuring that they are treated with respect (Clark 2000: 50).

Some people repeatedly seek reassurance yet somehow they remain agitated, as if the words of reassurance have not been meaningful – have not touched them or 'got through'. Where this is the case, repeating reassurances is unlikely to produce any reduction in the anxieties being experienced and, in fact, can be counterproductive because 'the repeated seeking of reassurance undermines the person's confidence to deal with the problem himself' [*sic*] (Trower *et al*. 1988: 110). Instead, it may help to draw attention to the fact that our words are not reassuring and to ask the individual to explore what is happening to them at this moment, in this 'here-and-now' conversation. The person needing reassurance may not be able to explain or to understand their behaviour, but this line of questioning can help to break into the repetitive nature of the communication and mark the beginning of a real engagement.

In these and similar situations, it can be helpful to ask ourselves 'What is this individual trying to communicate about themselves?' or 'What or who have I become for this person?' and to feed back our thoughts and feelings. For example, it can help to ask 'What do you think I could give you that would be useful or helpful to you right now?' This helps to break into the repetitious nature of the communication and establish a more direct rapport.

Using persuasion and being directive

Persuading service users to behave differently or to see themselves in a different light can be very difficult. People can become very fixed in their ways, and although this intervention attempts to create some possibility for change, it also runs the risk of our being too coercive and influential, sometimes to the point where we persuade service users to do something they are not yet ready to do. This can foreclose exploration and restrict the opportunity for people to find their own way in relation to decisions that affect their lives. Too often the result is failure, which can have a negative impact on a person's confidence and their hopes for the future.

In any attempt to influence others, power differentials have to be taken into account. Being persuaded by someone in authority can feel like an instruction or a command – as a 'should' and an 'ought' – where the only option possible would be to comply. Failing to acknowledge inequalities of this kind can mean that we create or reinforce feelings of poor self-esteem or personal inadequacy. It is important that these feelings, and the reality of power differentials, are addressed (O'Sullivan 1999: 118; Clark 2000: 200).

In some professional circles, such as medicine or dentistry, persuasion is more highly valued than it is in social work, where it tends to be viewed with reserve and suspicion because it involves attempting to influence people. However, this can be a denial of the sometimes uncomfortable fact that, as human beings, we all try to influence one another to lesser and greater degrees, whether this is undertaken in blatant or subtle ways.

Although non-directive approaches seem to be preferred by social work practitioners, particularly those embracing a more client-centred/person-centred approach, there will always be situations that warrant our being directive. For example, there can be risks involved if we do not attempt to persuade someone away from danger, or when we do not use our knowledge and experience to direct someone towards a course of action that could be of benefit. The key is to use persuasion – as with all other directive interventions – judiciously, basing our decision-making on the interest of the service user and on the best information we have about the potential advantages of a particular course of action. There are times when we need to 'respond to a client's need for structure and direction' (Lishman 1994: 116) by being more directive, but this should be undertaken as a short-term intervention. Being directive and persuasive is more likely to be successful where we have a good relationship with the individual in question, where the person is open and responsive to our viewpoint and where we feel we have sufficient knowledge and experience to steer people in the ways suggested. For further reading on the use of more directive interventions, cognitive-behavioural approaches provide good examples, such as those found under the heading *positive* and *negative reinforcement* (see Sheldon 1995: 63–4).

Providing practical and material assistance

One of the ways that we communicate our care, concern and commitment to others is through offering practical and material assistance. Research findings indicate that service users greatly value being given practical help, particularly when it addresses problems they are struggling to deal with themselves, such as writing letters, transportation or acting as an advocate (Mayer and Timms 1970; Fisher 1983; Lishman 1994: 8–11). Equally, being given access to resources that would otherwise be difficult to access – such as day care provision, after-school activities, respite accommodation or laundry facilities – can greatly ease the pressures and stresses that service users experience, often on a daily basis (Dartington Social Research Unit 1995; Thoburn *et al.* 1995; Thoburn 2002). In this respect, the limited financial assistance available to service users remains a serious problem, given the fact that, for many, poverty is the major issue (Clarke 1993; Jones 2002a, 2002b). Sainsbury *et al.* summarize the situation as follows:

> Social workers (compared with their clients) overestimated the relative helpfulness of insight work, the use of authority and giving advice, but underestimated the helpfulness experienced by clients as a result of material and financial help and negotiations with other agencies on their behalf.
>
> (Sainsbury *et al.* 1982: 19–20)

Two problems exist in relation to providing practical and material assistance. First, it is sometimes undertaken without a clear sense of purpose or strategy in terms of a particular outcome or goal: 'rushing about merely "doing" might say more about needing to be helpful as opposed to trying to understand the meaning of someone else's experience' (Coulshed and Orme 1998: 2). Such activity is devoid of purpose and, therefore, prone to having little real impact. For England, more 'active' forms of material and practical assistance should be offered in order to improve a service user's 'coping capacity'; that is, they should form part of an identified strategy and always be related to the service user's 'objective resources' (1986: 14).

The second problem relates to the fact that the request for practical assistance may not meet a response at all. Instead, emotional support or counselling may be offered, perhaps because this accords with the orientation of the practitioner or because practical or material problems, such as those relating to social security benefits, debts, poverty, homelessness, unemployment, ill health and so on, are not given the priority they deserve by the practitioner within the employing agency. Much of the time this shift towards counselling and away from providing practical support goes unnoticed. However, it can become evident when the service user's perceptions of their problems and their preferred solutions are compared to those of practitioners and this difference or discrepancy is noted.

Providing support

'Support' is one of the most imprecise words used within social work. It can mean almost anything from offering assistance, backing, sustenance, reassurance, guidance, encouragement, validation, care, concern and love (Feltham and Dryden 1993: 187). For this reason, it is important that we are clear what we mean when we use the term. In this book, 'support' is used to describe *emotional support*; that is, responding to the need that we all have to be able to turn to a person, perhaps located in an agency, who can give us appropriate back-up during periods of strain, stress or crisis, so that we can continue to cope and to keep going. Talking through problems with a sympathetic listener is a common source of emotional support. This may sometimes be described as social support (Sheppard 1997), which may be preferable because the word 'emotional' may be exposing or off-putting.

Ideally, this kind of support will be met by partners, family, friends and neighbours (Thoburn 2002: 197). However, where this is not the case, individuals may need help to locate appropriate sources of support, such as a support group for parents or mental health 'survivors'. There is much evidence from mental health and childcare research that the availability of support is associated with lower levels of stress and can result in, for example, more competent parenting (Thoburn 2002: 197) and fewer admissions to psychiatric hospitals (Sheppard 1997: 321). For some people, however, this support may not exist or may be too difficult to access. For others, the support may be offered too late or be inappropriate or inadequate, perhaps because their own personal resources and support systems have become seriously depleted. In such cases, service users may look to practitioners for this kind of emotional or social support. This may be difficult to provide on an ongoing basis without adequate back-up in the form of sound, structured supervision and peer and agency support.

The point to be stressed is that where we encounter a serious breakdown in a service user's capacity to cope with everyday tensions, our responses in terms of alternative sources of support have to be both robust and reliable, if we are to avoid a further deterioration in the quality of life for that individual. This involves our being clear about what support is needed, and is being offered, for how long, by whom and for what purpose. It also involves checking that the support is being received in the way intended and that it is helpful. When carers are asked to provide this support, they too can show signs of being unable to cope with the demands placed upon them (Phillipson 2002: 59–60). The consequences of this kind of breakdown in support networks are profound. It can lead to greater marginalization, isolation and loneliness, and to further demands being made of social services to provide alternative back-up. As practitioners, this calls for us to use our skills effectively in order to be able to create or to re-establish support networks and, in the meantime, to find ways to sustain the demands placed upon us by service users who have no alternative sources of support.

Providing care

When related to social work, notions of *care* and *caring* have many meanings, such as care orders, *care and control*, *in care*, care in the community, care assistant, carers, care packages, care planning and care management. Implicit in these different terms is an orientation to provide for the well-being of others. To *care* could be seen as allowing ourselves to be affected emotionally by another human being, while to be *caring* could involve being able to demonstrate a warmth, gentleness, kindness and concern for others (caring *about*) or providing physical help or comfort (caring *for*).

One way to view the relationship between helping and caring is to see helping as relating to the *task* and caring to the *process* of providing for others. Cheetham *et al.*, developing a point suggested by Sainsbury (1987), see *helping* as tangible and *caring* as intangible:

> Some social work is about *helping*, while some may emphasize *caring*. Helping clients seems to imply some observable difference made to their lives; and there are indeed some quite clear-cut, tangible social work tasks, for example providing information or arranging a specific service, the presence of which can be noted as one outcome of intervention. Caring, on the other hand, may involve

the intangibles of a personal relationship without necessarily making an outwardly observable difference.

(Cheetham *et al.* 1992: 12, original emphasis)

The rewards in providing help, whether as a carer or as a professional, can be many. For example, it can be deeply satisfying to know that, through our efforts, we played some part in enabling an individual to keep going, to gain more from life or to move on to new experiences. It is this mutuality and reciprocity that motivates us to want to do our best and to care for others. This mutuality is defined as 'the recognition of mutual obligations towards others, stemming from the acceptance of a common kinship, expressed in joint action, towards a more equitable sharing of resources and responsibilities' (Holman 1993: 56).

The fact that it is predominantly women who care for others, often in difficult and pressured circumstances, has been described as 'compulsory altruism' (Land and Rose 1985). The extent of the lack of understanding in relation to the emotional, physical and social cost of caring for others was starkly demonstrated by the Audit Commission report that described 'the care provided by relatives and friends as "free"' (Audit Commission 1992: 3; Davis and Ellis 1995: 146). An important role we could play as practitioners would be to highlight these gender inequalities and to agitate for better care, practical assistance and support for those who give and for those who receive this care.

The pitfalls in caring

It is not always easy to know how to pitch our care and support and there are many pitfalls. For example, our attempts to be helpful can sometimes come across as and be experienced as patronizing or condescending. Much depends on our intention, choice of words, timing and tone. It also depends on the way in which we ourselves have been cared for in our lives and how comfortable we feel in the role of helper. Where people, practitioners and service users alike, have been hurt in terms of their capacity to give and to receive – to give out and to take in – the 'give and take' that is central to creating a rapport and being empathic can be difficult to achieve without understanding and patience. When these different factors fail to fit together well, we can indeed easily fall into the trap of being patronizing or condescending and find ourselves speaking down to the person in question. When this happens, it is important that we do not become defensive or apologetic to the point where service users feel they must neglect their own issues to care for us. Instead, it is better to try to understand how our words and gestures have been experienced and learn from our errors.

People's rights to help and the way that help is offered are important issues. People who have for years prided themselves on their ability to be self-sufficient can find the offer of help offensive or intrusive. To touch on delicate subjects is a skilful endeavour. For example, I recall once suggesting to an elderly couple living in a second floor flat that they might find a second handrail helpful. Both had fallen down the stairs on a number of occasions, but not seriously. My suggestion was poorly received; in fact it was received as an insult. It took several weeks of gentle persuasion and another fall before they felt able to consider a second rail and then with the proviso that it would be removed if they 'didn't take to it'. Luckily, it was installed by two very thoughtful council workers who played their part in helping this couple to adjust to the change: they would not now be without their rail. This example shows that unless we attend to emotional issues – in this example, the importance and meaning that this couple gave to their capacity to be independent – our efforts can be sabotaged.

In relation to the wider picture within social work, a further pitfall in relation to caring for others is that, in some professional and personal contexts, caring can be used as a means of control, to engender guilt, obligation and compliance and to take away an individual's right to self-determination and autonomy. In its blatant form, this kind of 'social control' can be challenged. However, it can be quite subtle and, therefore, difficult to detect and to confront, particularly in relation to vulnerable groups, such as people with learning disabilities (Clark 2000: 21–2). The development of 'service user movements', such as those in relation to people with a disability and people in receipt of psychiatric services, challenges the way that services are controlled and highlights instead the importance of 'user-led' policies and provision (Croft and Beresford 2002: 389–90). Similarly, concepts such as 'normalization' and 'the social role of valorization' (Wolfensberger 1984) attempt to address the way that certain groups of people are devalued by society, stressing, in the area of disability, that disabled people have the right to lead a 'valued ordinary life', based on a belief in their equality as citizens and as human beings (Ramon 1991). In relation to social work skills, we need to take account of the wider context within which our work is located because the realities of practice may require great flexibility; we may walk in the door offering one skill and leave having offered another. At one time I found myself being asked to 'sort out' the 'problem behaviour' at a particular school, only to find myself acting in the role of advocate for young people's rights. My experience is not unique.

Modelling and social skills training

Modelling

According to Feltham and Dryden, modelling is 'the behavioural/social learning method of demonstrating procedures which the service user wishes or needs to adopt' (1993: 115). These behaviours or new responses can be acquired through various processes, including 'observational learning, vicarious learning, modelling, or imitation' (Sheldon 1995: 81), and can be broadly divided into two categories: inadvertent and deliberate modelling.

Inadvertent modelling refers to behaviour that the service user has learned through watching others. Most behaviour is learned in this way, both good and bad, particularly from parents and, in recent years, through the mass media:

> Modelling accounts for the acquisition of a vast range of very different behaviours: skills simple and complex, from washing dishes to brain surgery, from social good manners to conducting philosophical debate; and also those kinds of behaviours we do not designate as skills, such as reacting with anxiety to thunderstorms or being brave in the face of danger. Numerous experiments have shown that skills, attitudes and emotional responses can all be acquired through modelling.
>
> (Hudson and MacDonald 1986: 41)

In the social learning approach developed by Bandura (1977), modelling is more likely to be attractive and successful where the model is seen to have some standing and where the respect given to a model is linked to a particular behaviour. Also, it is important for there to be a similarity or shared sense of identity between subject and the model, an opportunity to practise the behaviour soon after it has been modelled and a climate where the newly acquired behaviour is reinforced by others (Hudson and MacDonald 1986: 45).

Deliberate modelling is generally employed in order to address behavioural problems, to reduce anxiety and to help re-establish or reinforce lost or suppressed behaviours (Sheldon 1995: 87). This may involve the live enactment of certain behaviours by the practitioner and, in formal modelling, include the following steps:

1 Specify the behaviour to be demonstrated and ask the observer to attend to it
2 Arrange demonstration
3 Ask the observer to imitate the behaviour immediately after the demonstration
4 Give feedback to imitate the behaviour immediately after the demonstration
5 Give further practice, and so on.

(Hudson and MacDonald 1986: 141)

Modelling is particularly useful where individuals have encountered worrying situations that they feel ill equipped to manage. In relation to service users, this intervention can be important in helping to tackle daunting situations such as court appearances, social security tribunals and school exclusion procedures, with the practitioner running through the various stages likely to be encountered.

Social skills training

Social skills training is based on the same social learning principles used in modelling. It is most often employed in helping service users to overcome behaviours that render them vulnerable to being isolated or socially excluded, or to develop and extend certain skills, such as how to respect another person's sense of space and privacy or how to be more assertive. Again, this may involve direct instruction or modelling by a practitioner, video demonstrations, role-plays and homework. A danger in relation to both modelling and social skills training is that social and cultural influences and differences may be ignored in favour of the norms of the dominant culture.

Reframing

This intervention is described little in social work texts yet it is one of the most important skills that a practitioner can have. It is a major technique of neurolinguistic programming (Feltham and Dryden 1993: 158) and family therapy (Watzlawick *et al*. 1974; Burnham 1986). Reframing also has much in common with cognitive-behavioural approaches where the aim is to change thought processes and behaviour. Its main advantage is that it provides an opportunity to describe a situation or behaviour from a different, more hopeful and optimistic perspective. This allows service users and practitioners to revisit decisions or opinions made previously, often by people in positions of authority, and to pose a different view of 'how situations are to be understood and what knowledge is to count as relevant' (Howe 1994: 526). As a result, factors located within the 'frame' can be viewed differently. For example, people described as having 'no motivation' can, within the same 'frame', be described as not wanting what is on offer, for very good reasons: 'For many stigmatized and oppressed groups "help" has come to equal control because that has been their experience' (Sheldon 1995: 241). To counter the stigmatizing experiences attached to labels such as 'alcoholic' or 'drug addict', reframing is used in motivational interviewing to help people to reframe the labels they have been given (Miller and Rollnick 2002: 61–2).

Reframing involves taking the same 'facts' but placing them in a different context or 'frame'. As a result, the 'entire meaning' is changed (Watzlawick 1974: 95). Its purpose is to 'change the meaning that an individual or family attaches to certain behaviours or interactions in such a way as to render the situation more amenable to behavioural and/or emotional change' (Burnham 1986: 147). These redefinitions can help to lift some of the 'sting' – the guilt or shame – and help to bring the behaviour within the grasp of the individual, perhaps through normalizing it. For example, reframing can be used to view a negative behaviour in a positive light or allow a less judgemental and more compassionate understanding of events. This is particularly valuable when working with people who have little confidence or low self-esteem, or who are racked with self-blame or guilt, such as parents experiencing difficulties with their children. Often the messages that service users give to themselves can be deeply critical, harsh and self-punishing. Reframing offers a way to replace these painful, negative *internal conversations* with words that are more understanding, optimistic and caring. It is important to stress that for reframing to be successful it must use the same concrete facts, and the alternative 'frame' should be believable and communicated in words that can be easily understood.

Reframing can sometimes be confused with making excuses but it is not the same. Making excuses involves justifying actions, thoughts and feelings or unacceptable behaviour, sometimes because we cannot deal with the conflict this arouses in us or because we feel scared to stand our ground. However, it is important to see the 'gentle art of reframing' (Watzlawick *et al.* 1974: 92–109) in its own right as an intervention that can be enormously valuable in helping people to feel less stuck and as a way of enabling people to move forward.

Examples

Service user: I'm too lazy to get out of bed.

Practitioner: Perhaps what you describe as being lazy is a feeling that there is nothing to get up for?

Service user: I think I'm a horrible mother. I'm really tired and bad-tempered and shout at my kids all the time ...

Practitioner: The fact that you felt able to tell me about how you are with your children shows that you want to have a better relationship with them – that you care about them. It takes courage for a parent to admit that things are going wrong – as you just did. It gives us the chance to build on the fact that you want to do something about these difficulties.

Service user: I decided yesterday not to come to see you today because I felt you would criticize me.

Practitioner: Then you were very brave to come.

Offering interpretations

Interpretations offer a new frame of reference, based on information provided by the individual but extended to include inferences derived from that information and from the practitioner's own perceptions and intuition. Three types of interpretation are common. First, in the field of therapy, particularly in psychoanalytic psychotherapy, interpretations are used to bring unconscious conflicts and motives into the conscious in order to facilitate integration through acquiring insight (Rycroft 1968: 76). This 'helps clients to understand the origins of their problems, and thereby gain more control over them and more freedom to behave differently' (McLeod 2003: 86). This kind of interpretation involves psychotherapeutic training and is, therefore, beyond the practice remit of social workers. Second, in relation to cognitive approaches, the emphasis is on understanding how service users interpret and misinterpret events, rather than the worker formulating interpretations (Feltham and Dryden 1993: 96). Third, interpretations are used to link and to connect the significance of certain thoughts, feelings or behaviours in order to draw the service user's attention to something that they appear to be unaware of (Feltham and Dryden 1993: 96). This is the form of interpretation most used in social work and the one emphasized in this section.

As social work practitioners, there is an ongoing and understandable tendency to want to 'interpret' a service user's behaviour, that is, to link one event with another. However, this presents problems because the connections we are making may be inaccurate and difficult to evidence (in terms of 'hard facts'). It is always difficult to know with any certainty whether our awareness is accurate unless the situation or relationship is uncomplicated. If it is accurate, however, it can place us in the difficult position of knowing more about an aspect of a service user's behaviour – or life – than they themselves are aware of. It can be hard to know how we can use this 'interpretation' in ways that enable service users to gain this awareness for themselves, thereby gaining advantage from this knowledge.

One of the most common examples of this dilemma relates to child sexual abuse, where it is quite common to hear disturbed or distress behaviour being 'interpreted' as a manifestation of early experiences of abuse, particularly sexual abuse. For some children, this interpretation may be true, but for others it may not. In fact, in my experience it is unlikely that severe disturbed behaviour can be linked to any one cause. This makes it important to analyse and question the assumptions that guide decision-making about when and how to offer an interpretation and to review critically evidence used to support a particular proposition. For example, it may be that not all abused children are traumatized by sexual abuse in ways that continue to have an impact on their behaviour or to limit their outlook on life (Bagley and King 1990: 220). However, it is also possible that children can be traumatized by the manner in which professionals react and attempt to address their experiences of abuse. To communicate a healthy sense of outrage at the suffering children experience is appropriate and understandable but needs to be kept within professional boundaries through the process of self-reflection, in order to ensure 'that our responses arise from the client's situation rather than our past or needs' (Lishman 2002: 100).

Well-timed and carefully worded interpretations have particular value in helping children and adults to understand themselves better, but this process can neither be rushed nor imposed from outside. For truth to have meaning in ways that can be integrated, it has to be explored and discovered by the person in question. This can be a difficult undertaking, particularly if the truth is locked within painful memories. For this reason, it is important that careful thought is given to the possible consequences of offering information or interpretations in situations where it is unclear whether the service user is ready to 'take in' this information. One way through these dilemmas is to frame our awareness and understanding as tentative hypotheses (Feltham and Dryden 1993: 96) and to present them in a low-key way that leaves service users free to take them up or not, depending on how they are feeling at the time. This emphasis places less importance on the content of the interpretation than on the process of trying to ensure that service users are aware of our commitment and our willingness to get alongside them in ways that facilitate greater under-standing and the possibility of moving their lives forward.

Adaptations

Most practitioners have met service users who communicate a need for help but who cannot make use of the services or resources on offer and frustrate our best efforts to get help to them. Such individuals are sometimes wrongly described as 'unmotivated'. Sheldon takes issue with this, stating that: 'Psychologically speaking, there is no such thing as an "unmotivated person"'. Instead, he suggests that the poor take-up of services may be an indication 'that they have not learned to want what we would like them to want' (Sheldon 1995: 126). This may be true. However, generalizations of this kind can fail to address all that is subtle and complex about human behaviour and motivation (Coulshed and Orme 1998: 134). A different way to understand behaviour which is frustrating or 'unmotivated' would be to emphasize that some service users may want what is on offer but lack what it takes emotionally to allow their needs to be met. This may be because their history of giving and receiving does not allow this freedom.

This difficulty in accessing or utilizing services on offer frequently indicates 'failures' experienced in early childhood. Such failures are, I believe, best understood in terms of an individual's attachment history and other 'relationship based theories' (Howe *et al.* 1999: 30), such as those put forward by Bowlby (1979), Winnicott (1958, 1965) and later writers in this field. This difficulty is often manifest in service users being unable to adapt their behaviour or needs in ways that facilitate the helping process. For example, service users may try to control events or the relationship, perhaps by refusing to see us unless we are prepared to visit them at home. This may mean that they miss out on being able to access other services available from our agency or within their local community. However, the need to control what is happening is so powerful that some service users would rather do without than accept services that are not presented on their terms.

Sometimes this need to control is understood in terms of service users being manipulative or uninterested and this may be the case. But, in other situations, it may be a need to ensure that predictability is preserved and uncertainty kept to a minimum. Another way to analyse this behaviour would be to see it as a manifestation of service users being wounded in the area of give and take or giving and receiving. People who have been given to in ways that were cruel or humiliating, or where the 'pay back' was too great, can find it hard to take from others; it can feel like losing control or exposing themselves to danger and further pain. Giving to others may be an easier undertaking but only if fear of rejection is not paramount.

These difficulties can be compounded in adulthood when service users have been 'abandoned by other sources of potential help' (Sheldon 1995: 118) or 'let down' in their significant attachments in other important ways. Whatever the reason, to be offered something – even something good and desired – can give rise to conflicts that result in people failing to take up what is on offer, or needing to transform it in such a way that they lose some of their original benefits. For example, they may attempt to control what can or cannot be discussed to a point where the value and benefits inherent in the practitioner–service user relationship are lost.

One way to enable service users to take up the services on offer is through *adaptation to need*, which involves setting up situations where we attempt to meet the unique needs of each individual. Many social work interventions personalize services in this way but, in the adaptation to need I am describing, this personalization is more detailed, focused and purposeful. It is based on Winnicott's work, described briefly in Chapter 3, on the importance of adaptation in early childhood development, relating to the journey from almost total dependence, to relative dependence, and independence towards interdependence (1965: 83–92). In this theory, healthy emotional development is based on the child being adapted to by his or her carers in ways that facilitate growth and the capacity to relate to self, others and their social environment. Failures in adaptation can result in infants developing a sense of self that is fragmented and unintegrated (Winnicott 1965: 58), which can lead to a premature and isolating self-sufficiency. To use Winnicott's words, the adaptation need not be perfect but only 'good-enough'.

In terms of our work, we regularly come into contact with men, women and children who have been neglected and uncared for in childhood, whose capacity, therefore, to see their environment and other people as a resource is severely limited (Howe *et al.* 1999: 30). In this context, adaptation to need can help to make resources and services more accessible for people who struggle in this way. Examples include tasks commonly undertaken by social workers, such as providing practical help (taxis, childcare, bus fares, adjusting our work patterns). The emphasis is on our adapting to the individual, rather than expecting service users to adapt to us or to 'fit in' (Trevithick 1993, 1995, 1998). Adaptation to need is consistent with user-led perspective approaches and is particularly valuable when working with minority groups, people with low self-esteem or those who feel marginalized and excluded. However, it may be a difficult intervention to implement in terms of agency policy and practice.

Counselling skills

The British Association for Counselling (BAC), the main accreditation body for counselling in the UK, describes counselling as:

> the skilled and principled use of relationships to develop self knowledge, emotional acceptance and growth, and personal resources. The overall aim is to live more fully and satisfyingly. Counselling may be concerned with addressing and resolving specific problems, making decisions, coping with crisis, working through feelings or inner conflict or improving relationships with others. The counsellor's role is to facilitate the client's work in ways that respect the client's values, personal resources and capacity for self determination.
>
> (BAC 1992)

Of the different 'schools of counselling', five are particularly influential within social work. These are:

- client-centred counselling (sometimes called person-centred or humanist counselling)
- feminist counselling
- cognitive-behavioural counselling
- psychodynamic counselling
- eclectic and integrative counselling (adhering to no one single 'school' but instead combining different approaches).

Within social work, humanist approaches have been particularly influential, specifically the work of Egan (1990), Rogers (1961) and Truax and Carkhuff (1967), mainly because they promote personal freedom and are consistent with anti-discriminatory and anti-oppressive perspectives. Brown summarizes Egan's model as having four components: 'exploration, understanding, action and evaluation' (2002: 146).

Rogers's 'core conditions' include congruence, unconditional positive regard and empathy, which Carkhuff and others adapted and developed to emphasize honesty and genuineness, warmth, respect, acceptance and empathetic understanding (Payne 1997: 178).

However, the place of counselling within social work is more confused than it first appears because a differentiation is not always made between the use of counselling skills, counselling or therapy (e.g. cognitive-behavioural therapy). Epstein illustrates this point: 'the practice of enhancing clients' knowledge and skill is referred to as counselling, or it may be called therapy or casework, depending on the language habits and preferences of a particular branch of the delivery system' (1980: 26). Or again, in the past, 'counselling' has been used interchangeably with 'casework' (Pinker 1990: 18), or any form of one-to-one work. Indeed, Parton argues that: 'In effect, casework has been reconstituted as counselling and a new, diverse and fast-growing occupation has developed' (1996: 12). This shift has been aided by the development of care managers.

For England, a social worker's role becomes that of a counsellor when he [sic] 'is concerned with improving his client's capacity' (1986: 14). However, social work 'usually exceeds counselling' because it emphasizes problem-solving and help that is 'concrete, specific and focused' (England 1986: 26). This distinction is important because it differentiates between counselling skills focused on addressing the emotional life of an individual and counselling skills focused on more problem-solving and practical aspects. Although counselling and social work practice may draw on the same concepts and skills, as this book confirms, and qualified social workers 'should be equipped to undertake at least the basics of counselling' (Thompson 2002b: 303), their purposes may be different. For this reason, it is essential to be clear in terms of our purpose, professional boundaries and the implications of our work in relation to confidentiality (Seden 1999: 15). This is particularly important when we find we have been drawn to explore emotional issues where this is not our primary role or purpose. Where we find ourselves having to deal with emotional issues on a regular basis, it may be advisable to seek additional training in counselling.

Aims of counselling

Depending on the needs of the 'client' and the different practice orientation adopted, McLeod identifies the following aims of counselling:

1   *Insight*. The acquisition of an understanding of the origins and development of emotional difficulties, leading to an increased capacity to take rational control over feelings and actions.
2   *Self-awareness*. Becoming more aware of thoughts and feelings

which had been blocked off or denied, or developing a more accurate sense of how self is perceived by others.

3 *Self-acceptance*. The development of a positive attitude towards self, marked by an ability to acknowledge areas of experience which had been the subject of self-criticism and rejection.

4 *Self actualization or individuation*. Moving in the direction of fulfilling potential or achieving an integration of previously conflicting parts of self.

5 *Enlightenment*. Assisting the client to arrive at a higher state of spiritual awakening.

6 *Problem-solving*. Finding a solution to a specific problem which the client had not been able to resolve alone. Acquiring a general competence in problem-solving.

7 *Psychological education*. Enabling the client to acquire ideas and techniques with which to understand and control behaviour.

8 *Acquisition of social skills*. Learning and mastering social and interpersonal skills such as maintenance of eye contact, turn-taking in conversations, assertiveness or anger control.

9 *Cognitive change*. The modification or replacement of irrational beliefs or maladaptive thought patterns associated with self-destructive behaviour.

10 *Behaviour change*. The modification or replacement of mala-daptive or self-destructive patterns of behaviour.

11 *Systemic change*. Introducing change into the way in which social systems (e.g. families) operate.

12 *Empowerment*. Working on skills, awareness and knowledge which will enable the client to confront social inequalities.

13 *Restitution*. Helping the client to make amends for previous destructive behaviour.

(McLeod 2003: 12–13)

These aims are illuminating because they cover many areas of interest to social workers. Research also indicates that counselling and casework approaches are highly rated by service users (Hardiker and Barker 1994: 34). However, although counselling is likely to flourish in the voluntary sector, its future in relation to statutory services remains unclear.

Containing anxiety

'Anxiety ... is a constant feature of our work with clients' (Sheldon 1995: 108), and many of the practice approaches used within social work acknowledge this fact and the distorting and debilitating impact that anxiety can have. The causes of anxiety are unique to each individual and dependent on different past and present experiences. However, one of the primary causes of anxiety is conflict, both internal and external (Howe 1987: 71). It is helpful to differentiate between fear and anxiety because they are different on two accounts and require different interventions. Fear is used to describe a reaction to present dangers, specific objects or events, where the object of the fear is known and, therefore, can be identified and talked about. Anxiety is used to describe a more generalized emotional state, where the sense of threat or danger does not have an object and, therefore, cannot be identified but is instead anticipated or imagined (Reber and Reber 2001: 270).

Common fears that service users describe include feeling ashamed about having to seek help, frightened that their children will be removed and worried that they will be criticized (Lishman 1994: 8). Often, offering reassurance can help to allay fears, but the skill is not to minimize the pain or confusion being experienced nor to be overly reassuring unless we are confident about what we are saying. Being patient, kind, caring, understanding, non-judgemental and non-intrusive are important attributes.

Anxieties, on the other hand, are more likely to be experienced as states of agitation, nervousness and panic, where service users find themselves forgetting things that they would normally remember, including the reason for their anxiety. Often what happens is that fear and anxiety accompany one another. For example, a person may be frightened to go to the housing department because they remember previous visits that were unpleasant (fear) yet also find themselves being unable to get out of the house, losing their house keys, unable to find a relevant letter, unable to remember the reason for their visit once they arrive and so on. This kind of amnesia is very common in anxiety states and something that militates against people being able to see things through and to effect change.

In these situations, containing anxiety involves being open and receptive to the thoughts and feelings of others – becoming a 'container' – so that these can be transformed into something more manageable. This is often achieved through the process of talking to someone who has the ability to listen, to empathize, to take in and to bear the worries being expressed, as well as the ability to come alongside the individual in ways that communicate an understanding and give the sense that the person is not alone. The final stage of this process involves offering back the concerns to the anxious person but in a modified form, where the major anguish is acknowledged but also altered so that it no longer carries the same 'sting' or sense of agitation or anguish.

In situations of mild anxiety, helping a service user to contain these feelings may not be a time-consuming activity. Often our openness, communicated by a few well thought-out words or gestures, can be sufficient to help people cope with mildly difficult emotions. In more intractable anxiety states, anxieties can feel like an unbuffered oil slick that keeps on spreading, contaminating almost everything we see and do. In these situations, greater resilience is called for on our part if we are to help service users to bear these difficult feelings. One way to do this may be to 'meet' the concerns by asking service users to describe in detail the thoughts, feelings and worries that they have. In doing so, our purpose is to try to break the hold that these anxieties are having on the individual concerned.

Conclusion

As human beings we gain great relief from the knowledge that others are prepared to help bear the weight we are carrying. The above skills demonstrate the importance of being able to embrace a range of different interventions, depending on the dilemmas being presented. However, the use of these interventions also involves building on the strengths and abilities that service users bring to an encounter. These may take different forms; for example, they may involve our acknowledging the courageous and honest way that service users explore what empowerment means to them, or the way they square up to the part they played in a particular dilemma. The ability to tell ourselves that truth can be a painful experience but one that can be deeply healing and reparative. For these reasons, it is important to remember that none of the interventions described in this and other chapters can be successfully undertaken without the active cooperation of the individuals involved, because this is central to the reciprocal relationship that lies at the heart of effective and reflective practice. In the past, we have not always created this participative and collaborative framework and, as a result, this has limited our effectiveness (Everitt and Hardiker 1996; Shaw and Shaw 1997).

7 EMPOWERMENT, NEGOTIATION AND PARTNERSHIP SKILLS

Many of the skills I describe in this section relate to working with a third party. I take as my starting point the importance of acknowledging and respecting other people's points of view and the need to establish a common purpose in relation to our work. This requires a degree of 'give and take' and stresses that the ability to compromise and the capacity to be flexible are essential qualities when attempting to work alongside others. The following skills are described:

- empowerment and enabling skills
- negotiating skills
- contracting skills
- networking skills
- working in partnership
- mediation skills
- advocacy skills
- assertiveness skills
- being challenging and confrontative
- dealing with hostility, aggression and violence.

Some skills belong to the same 'family' of negotiation skills but all carry important differences. Some skills are built on other skills. For example, advocacy carries with it the ability to negotiate. Most are finely balanced between the conflicting responsibilities of care and control, yet their overall purpose is to address the concerns of those individuals who seek, or are required to have, a social work service.

Empowerment and enabling skills

Considerable controversy surrounds the concept of empowerment: what is meant by the term; whether it is possible for us to empower others and, if so, how this is achieved in terms of the skills and resources required; and whether this falls with our role and agency expectations. For some writers, to 'empower' involves practitioners having to 'reinvent their practice and their perceptions of particular problems and solutions' (Smale *et al.* 1993: 42). Other writers are more cautious. Stevenson and Parsloe use the term to denote both 'process and goal' (1993: 6), but empowerment is more commonly used to describe service users being given 'meaningful choice' and 'valuable options' (Clark 2000: 57) in order to 'gain greater control over their lives and their circumstances' (Thompson 2002a: 91). For some, this process involves addressing the impact of inequalities, oppression and discrimination (O'Sullivan 1999: 27).

In most social work texts enabling is not referred to as a specific skill and, when it is, the reference tends to be quite general (Fawcett and Lewis 1996: 40; Payne 1997: 146; Seden 1999: 107). One reason for this may be that enabling is not seen to embody distinct characteristics nor, more importantly, to address the issue of power and power imbalances in ways embraced by concepts such as empowerment (Braye and Preston-Shoot 1995: 102), 'normalization' (Ramon 1991) or 'user-led' initiatives or movements (Croft and Beresford 2002). Instead, enabling could be thought of as emphasizing the importance of making something 'possible or easy' (Hanks 1979) and, like 'promoting', may be best thought of as forming a part of the empowerment process.

Braye and Preston-Shoot, drawing on user-led literature, write in detail about 'the key characteristics and qualities required' in relation to empowerment. These include:

- clarity about what involvement is being offered, and what its limits are;
- involvement from the beginning in ways which are central to agency structures and processes but which are also flexible;
- tangible goals for involvement;
- involvement by choice, not compulsion;
- involvement of black and minority perspectives;
- individual and collective perspectives;
- provision of time, information, resources and training;
- openness to advocacy;
- clear channels of representation and complaint;
- involvement of key participants, not just some;
- open agendas;
- facilitation of attendance;
- emphasis on channels, particularly when rights are at risk and the agency's perspective is backed by the statutory power to impose it.

(Braye and Preston-Shoot 1995: 118)

This account highlights important organizational and practical issues and attitudes. The use of advocacy, self-advocacy, users' rights and the development of user-led services and agendas is obviously important to this process (Braye and Preston-Shoot 1995: 102–18), but how effective these interventions are in practice – in relation to clients' capacity to direct the course of their lives and to improve their lives and situation – is not always clear. This has led to the criticism that empowerment has limited application in practice and that it is a term that 'is often invoked without being explained' (Wise 1995: 108). Part of the difficulty that the term empowerment causes relates to the context within which social work is located. As practitioners, we do not have unlimited choices. We are bound by the law and agency expectations, as well as the needs of service users. Social work agencies are also constrained by legal requirements, financial limitations and the expectations of government, other professions and the public at large.

Yet despite these constraints, the concept of empowerment is important because it attempts to identify particular purposes and how these might be achieved, namely how to help service users to take their lives forward. One account of this process is described in the work of Lorraine Gutiérrez, an African-American feminist, who identifies the changes sought through the process of empowerment as occurring 'on the individual, interpersonal, and institutional levels, where the person develops a sense of personal power, an ability to affect others, and an ability to work with others to change social institutions' (1990: 150). For Gutiérrez, empowerment provides a way to describe the transition from apathy and despair towards a sense of personal power. This involves four psychological changes:

1 Increasing self-efficacy (moving from reacting to events to taking action)
2 Developing group consciousness
3 Reducing self-blame
4 Assuming personal responsibility for change.

In this framework, to achieve this transition or change, practitioners need to be able to embrace five 'techniques' or interventions, which include providing practical assistance:

1 Accepting the client's definition of the problem
2 Identifying and building upon existing strengths
3 Engaging in a power analysis of the client's situation
4 Teaching specific skills
5 Mobilizing resources and advocating for clients.

(Gutiérrez 1990: 151–2)

This account is helpful because it identifies in greater detail the specific skills involved in empowerment. However, some writers in this field would be uncomfortable with this account because of its emphasis on the individual and on looking at psychological processes (Dominelli and McLeod 1989). It is these differences of opinion that make concepts like empowerment and partnership 'a minefield of ethical issues and dilemmas' (Stevenson and Parsloe 1993: 15). These dilemmas are not confined to direct work with service users because the concept of empowerment can be extended to include the empowerment of social workers, groups of people, organizations and agencies (Clark 2000: 29).

Internalized oppression

It is important to recognize that it takes time to help people to empower themselves, and to find ways to move their lives forward, not least because the very nature of oppression means that, for some, the confidence and courage to explore new areas and to take risks feels beyond their reach. When we encounter this sense of impossibility, hopelessness and defeat, the notion of 'internalized oppression' can be useful. It can give us a way to help people to understand and to talk about how they have come to believe negative statements about themselves to the point where they believe that these negative personal characteristics are fixed and part of their personality. Negative beliefs of this kind can sometimes be shifted by tracking their origins. Many stem from hurtful comments made by parents, but in my experience an alarming number can be traced back to teachers. For some years I ran workshops for working-class women at the London Women's Therapy Centre (Trevithick 1988). Much of our work involved helping women put words to negative beliefs that they had about themselves, locating the painful experiences that surrounded this process of internalization and helping them to see how untrue, unfair and unkind many of these comments were. They served to keep these women 'in their place' and to hold them hostage to these untruths.

People who come to believe, through the process of internalized oppression, that they are worthless, 'stupid', 'no good' or that they 'don't count' find it very difficult to stand up to others, to protect themselves or their loved ones from further oppression or to take risks without help. The way that help is offered is important: compassion, concern and the fact that we 'care' are important value perspectives we bring to our work but, in my experience, we are more likely to be successful and resilient in our efforts if our approach has a theoretical underpinning. In addition to Gutiérrez's work, quoted above, I have gained a great deal from the writings of Jean Baker Miller, particularly her concept of 'temporary inequality' (1976: 4–5). This describes how we can use the inequality that exists between workers and service users to name, analyse and address differences, including difficult feelings located in the present, as well as painful memories from the past. These difficulties are always present yet are rarely acknowledged when people of unequal status, authority and power encounter one another. (See Chapter 3 for a further account of Miller's work and that of the Stone Center, Boston, USA.)

Negotiating skills

Negotiating skills tend to be well covered in social work texts (Coulshed and Orme 1998: 49–51; Lishman 1994: 100; O'Sullivan 1999: 48), some concentrating on specific areas, such as negotiating the focus of the work (Trower *et al.* 1988: 34–6) or setting up contracts (Sheldon 1995: 185–7). The following is a summary of the main considerations and skills involved in negotiating.

Negotiation is primarily directed at achieving some form of agreement or understanding. Its importance can be seen in two ways. First, in relation to direct work with service users, negotiation skills are the tools that establish the climate of shared decision-making and collaboration, which lies at the heart of the concept of partnership. It is through negotiation that we arrive at a common agreement across different parties in terms of how problems are understood and how these might be overcome. Negotiation skills are also important in situations of disagreement. There may be no obvious way to overcome underlying differences but, where a degree of flexibility and compromise exists, this can be a foundation on which to negotiate. One way to achieve this would be to explore with service users – and other parties involved – their perception of events, particularly how they arrived at the particular position, or belief, they are holding and what their starting point was (Lishman 1994: 100). Entering into a dialogue about how an individual arrived at a particular view or position can reveal how painful certain experiences have been and how much their stance is designed to protect them from further pain. Part of our task may involve negotiating a shift in the balance, based on an understanding, respect and acceptance of people's perception of events but not necessarily our agreement. Since our position and starting point is likely to be different, it may be essential to point this out in a sensitive way as part of the negotiation.

For example, I once worked with a family where one of their five children, Tim, was constantly being scapegoated and marginalized within the family. A common phrase his parents used was 'He's always been like that, ever since a baby. When he's being like that, we ignore him.' 'Like that' was the shorthand way the parents communicated and justified their lack of empathy and tolerance for this child. As a result, Tim was neglected within the family and was showing his distress through stealing. The work we contracted to do involved helping Tim's parents to identify at what point they joined forces in the view that Tim was a difficult child and that the best course of action was to ignore him. This work took several months but eventually it transpired that his mother had had an affair and both parents believed Tim to be the child of a different father. A DNA test proved their 'belief' to be wrong, which meant we were then in a position to work on his mother's guilt and his father's rage about the affair and to negotiate a different place for Tim within the family. This took the form of revising the original contract, unpacking the 'beliefs' that Tim's parents had, some of which Tim had internalized, and carefully negotiating a new place for him in his family.

The second arena where negotiation skills are important is in relation to services. It is estimated that about one-third of our work involves face-to-face contact with service users (Coulshed and Orme 1998: 50). The remaining time is spent on indirect service provision, such as negotiating with our own agency and other organizations, or other parties who hold key resources or positions. This figure is likely to be higher where resources are scarce and/or the demands for professional accountability excessive, or for practitioners employed in certain settings, such as community work.

For example, as a field worker arguing for resources, I have spent many hours trying to negotiate residential placements, both for children and for older people. It took me some time to realize that I was more likely to be successful in my negotiations if I made sure there was a correct 'fit' between the resources being sought and the needs of the service user. This is very important. Where resources seemed to be withheld for no apparent reason, it sometimes helped to address the reservations of those individuals responsible for resource allocation. For example, many managers worry that once a place has been allocated, the social worker will 'disappear' from the life of the child, young person or older person and fail to maintain links with their family and other significant contacts (Millham *et al.* 1986). Although residential care is now a less favoured option in relation to children and young people, these concerns about maintaining links remain (Aldgate 2002: 23–4) and can require us to have sound negotiating skills.

The time and effort involved in mobilizing resources is considerable and can require our having to use collaborative, competitive or combative tactics depending on the situation and our response (Coulshed 1991: 62–4). In recent years mobilizing resources has been oriented to 'commissioning services for care management or negotiating packages of care' (Coulshed and Orme 1998: 50). Combative skills may be particularly important when we are dealing with injustice or inequalities in resource provision, and one way to see campaigning is as a form of political negotiation. However, our success in these and other endeavours is more likely to depend on how well we prepare and present our case, particularly factual information, and how carefully we have thought through where key figures in the negotiation are coming from. It may also be important to know where to enlist further support or leverage so that the same negotiation is being played from several sides.

In addition, it is essential to be in a position to highlight the advantages that a negotiated decision could bring to those who would normally be uninterested. One way to achieve this may involve appealing to a person's sense of fairness. According to Jordan, social work is 'crucially concerned with fairness, both in redistributing resources to people in need ... and in negotiations over problems in relationships in families, neighbourhoods and communities' (1990: 178). To enlist people's sympathy or sense of fairness – perhaps by asking them to imagine how they might feel in the same situation – can come across as manipulative, and the lines between being strategic, determined and manipulative can be difficult to draw. Honesty is an important safeguard. So too is the ability to acknowledge a respect for the other person's point of view, at the same time believing that we can 'change their mind', and do so in ways that retain a sense of personal integrity for all parties concerned.

Finally, it can be easy to give up in our efforts to negotiate if we are immediately unsuccessful, yet our success may depend on our being able to withstand rejection and failure. Resilience, determination and the skills of persuasion are the hallmarks of a successful negotiator.

Contracting skills

Drawing up contracts provides an opportunity to formalize and structure the nature of the contact between ourselves and service users in relation to the purpose of the work and the roles, responsibilities and expectations of those concerned. The process involved in arriving at this working agreement is as important as the task itself and acts as 'a tangible manifestation of working in partnership' (Aldgate 2002: 24). The contract must be based on the needs of service users and, for this reason, may be agreed verbally or in writing, sometimes in the form of a letter. Failing to keep a written record of agreements reached is dangerous; reliance on memory alone can be highly problematic, not least because we all hear through our histories and, as the game Chinese Whispers reveals, we can hear the same information quite differently. In some situations, however, perhaps where literacy is a problem, written agreements or contracts may not be appropriate.

Whatever the format, care should be taken to ensure that a shared understanding has been reached, and in a language that is clear, explicit and accessible, with sufficient information for the task at hand. Confusion and anxiety act as barriers to effective action. For example, contracts may specify the time and length of sessions, location, duration, ground rules, confidentiality and recording procedures. They can also state who is invited to attend, a summary of the major concerns, the purpose of the work in terms of objectives and the approaches to be used, emergency cover arrangements and how any breakdown of the agreement might be dealt with. It helps to build in some flexibility so that the contract can be revised if required.

Drawing up an action plan is an example of how a contract or working agreement might be used in practice (Payne 1994: 17–20). Action plans can take different forms. For example, I once ran a group for severely depressed women where suicidal thoughts and intentions were very much in evidence. In order to address the anxieties that this threat posed both to the workers and other women in the group, we drafted a plan of action in the event of accident or crisis, whether self-inflicted or not. When drafting individual plans, everyone in the group was asked to lay down in detail what steps we had to take, and in what order, should a crisis occur. We even included details of the next-of-kin. Fortunately, these plans never needed to be put into action.

Contracts provide the opportunity to formalize the relationship and the purpose of the work in ways that can bring people together to work in partnership. This structured approach towards a common purpose enables sensitive issues to be addressed at the outset, such as differences in status, authority, knowledge and experience that we, and service users, bring to the partnership and how these will be worked with. This can demystify the helping process, ensuring that as practitioners we are open about how much power service users and others have, and where our accountability lies (Preston-Shoot 1994: 185). It also provides an opportunity to build on service users' strengths and to provide help when needed.

On the other hand, some writers believe that drawing up contracts or written agreements can be oppressive because they assume a freedom of choice that has little bearing on service users' everyday experiences of social inequalities and injustices (Rojek and Collins 1988: 205). Are they contracts or 'con tricks' (Corden and Preston-Shoot 1987)? Similarly, our choices as practitioners are limited by agency policy, our legal responsibilities and scarcity in terms of resources and services. To enable 'mutuality and exchange' (Smale et al. 1993) between service users and practitioners, with 'users as equal partners in problem definition and negotiation about solutions' (Braye and Preston-Shoot 1995: 116), a fundamental shift is needed in the extent to which service users' views are allowed to determine problem definition and the solutions sought. Certainly at present, and probably in the foreseeable future, 'social workers and clients do not have equal power in their professional contact' (Lishman 1994: 91).

Finally, the term 'contract culture' describes the introduction of internal markets into health and social services in the 1990s and the commissioning of services by a purchaser from a provider. This approach to service delivery has been severely criticized, particularly for failing to increase user choice and involvement (Braye and Preston-Shoot 1995: 22), and for its emphasis on individualism, which is 'antithetical to mutual help, collaboration and co-operation' (Adams 2002b: 252).

Networking skills

According to Seed, a network is a 'system or pattern of links ... which have particular meaning' (1990: 19). These can be divided into:

- formal networks – such as planned formal support groups; and
- informal or natural networks – such as those made up of 'natural' carers who help others: family members, friends and neighbours.

In its recommendation for decentralized community based services, the Barclay Report recognized the importance of 'local networks of formal and informal relationships' and their 'capacity to mobilize individual and collective responses to adversity' (1982: xiii). Also, the importance of informal networks and caring resources was acknowledged in the Griffiths Report (1988) and built into the NHS and Community Care Act 1990, but in ways that were felt by many to be an appropriation by government of 'natural' support systems (Reigate 1997: 216). Whereas it is appropriate for statutory services to support existing 'natural' networks, 'attempting to replace formal provision with informal care or to change the existing patterns of informal care is likely to be unsuccessful' (Payne 1997: 152).

According to Coulshed and Orme (1998: 224) networking can involve three 'strategies':

- *network therapy* uses groupwork skills to help families in crisis by bringing together their network to act as the 'change agents' (e.g. Family Group Conferences used in child protection work);
- *problem-solving network meetings* bring together formal and informal carers, often to unravel who is doing what; and
- *network construction* is how to build new networks and sustain or change existing networks.

All of these involve mediating, advocating and organizing skills (Coulshed and Orme 1998: 149) and also the ability to assess the capabilities of the individual in question and of the social networks that are in existence and what these can sustain. Again, assessment skills are used when attempting to establish a 'personalized support network', perhaps for someone leaving residential care, where the work involves identifying key figures, described as 'central figures' (Collins and Pancoast 1976) or 'competent others' (Atkinson 1986: 84), to form part of a personalized support network, where this needs to be created.

The importance of networking in social work is to strengthen the links and connections that exist for people within a particular community or geographical area. This support is particularly important when there is the danger of people becoming isolated. For example, research indicates that people discharged from psychiatric hospital who have social support are less likely to be re-admitted (Huxley 2002: 68; Sheppard 1997: 214). The debilitating impact of isolation also exists for people with learning disabilities (Booth 2002: 74) and for elderly people (Phillipson 2002: 60–1). However, it is important to see social support networks as complementing other services, and not replacing the obligations of the state and social services to provide key services. Other forms of support, such as a 'close personal working relationship ... in order to sustain community living' (Huxley 2002: 69), are also crucial for individuals who have difficulty relating or those whose situation leaves them vulnerable to stigma and social exclusion.

Within this work, our knowledge of black networks may not be built on a 'proper understanding' of black people's experience and, as a result, we may fail to help black people to link to the networks that exist (Shah 1989: 179). The dangers here are many. For example, our failure to understand the complex nature of African-Caribbean and Asian cultures can mean that we focus on the problems or 'defects' rather than their resilient and supportive characteristics (Ahmed 1986: 141; Robinson 1995: 12). Although it is always important to locate people within their cultural context, there can be a pull to rely on cultural explanations at the expense of exploring other relevant factors, particularly structural influences and limitations (Ahmed 1986: 140). What is described as 'normal' and, therefore, acceptable for any culture, including aspects of working-class culture, needs to be analysed carefully. For example, it can be thought of as 'normal' and acceptable for working-class people to use physical force, or the threat of violence, to restrain and control their children. These assumptions need to be challenged and so-called 'normal' behaviour carefully scrutinized.

Working in partnership

Partnership, and the principles of participation and 'user involvement', inform current legislation in relation to health and social care, having found favour with both the political left and right, but for different reasons. 'Where the left saw empowerment of the poor and disadvantaged, the right saw growth in personal responsibility, independence and individual choice' (Howe 1996: 84). Similarly, it is possible for both left and right to share a commitment to empowerment and its emphasis on 'people taking control of their own lives and having the power to shape their own future' (Shardlow 2002: 38). This joint ownership might help to explain why partnership is considered to be 'very misleading without qualification' (Stevenson and Parsloe 1993: 6) and 'used to describe anything from token consultation to a total devolution of power and control' (Braye and Preston-Shoot 1995: 102).

The point to be stressed is that positive practice must involve service users if it is to achieve agreed objectives (empowerment and personal responsibility) and that within this process, service users must be seen not only in terms of the 'problems' they bring, but also as 'whole people' and 'full citizens' (Dalrymple and Burke 1995: 64) who have an important contribution to make in terms of their knowledge and perception of the situation, personal qualities and problem-solving capabilities. This differs from those approaches where there is a 'topdown hierarchical bureaucracy' (Braye and Preston-Shoot 1995: 116), dominated by agency policies and procedures, or an approach where the practitioner is seen to be the expert who diagnoses the problem and prescribes a cure.

One of the most helpful accounts of the principles and skills involved in working in partnership can be found in *The Challenge of Partnership in Child Protection: Practice Guide* (DoH 1995). Under four headings, this publication identifies the reasons for working in partnership with parents. These headings have been adapted to include other service user groups:

- *Effectiveness* More is likely to be achieved through an approach that is co-operative and collaborative (Howe 1987: 7; Sheldon 1995: 126; Thoburn *et al.* 1995; Roberts and Taylor 1996).
- *Clients as a source of information* It is important to build on the detailed knowledge and understanding that service users have of their situation and the problems they face (Sheldon 1995: 125), and to take as our starting point the priorities that they consider most urgent (Lishman 1994: 100).
- *Citizens' rights* Service users should have the right to know what is being said about them and to contribute to decisions that affect their lives.
- *Empowering parents* Involving service users in decision making helps to build self-esteem and confidence, and to enable clients to feel more in control of their lives.

(DoH 1995: 9–10)

The knowledge, values and skills required for working in partnership are summarized in this publication under the heading, 'Fifteen essential principles for working in partnership' (1995: 14). Many of the values and skills included in that list are described in this text, such as the importance of good communication, listening skills and observation skills; being respectful, caring, competent in our approach; being clear in our purpose and intentions, our professional boundaries and responsibilities including the language we use; being sensitive to the issue of power and power imbalances; being mindful of the importance of the strengths and potential that service users possess, as well as addressing 'weaknesses, problems and limitations'; being aware of our own 'personal feelings, values, prejudices and beliefs'; and being able to acknowledge our mistakes and to use supervision to ensure the quality of our work and its effectiveness (DoH 1995: 14).

This summary serves as a reminder that we have still much to learn about how to work in partnership in ways that enhance service users' capacity to consolidate and extend their self-knowledge, decision-making and problem-solving abilities. This work is much more complex than is sometimes described, particularly where this involves working across differences (Smale *et al.* 2000) and trying to understand the power differentials that exist between practitioners and service users from different cultural, ethnic and racial groups (DoH 1995: 24). For example, the contribution that service users feel they can give – and the knowledge they can actually access and communicate – may, in fact, be quite limited. Some may feel too depleted or have too little confidence to take on the responsibilities implied within the concept of partnership. This can result in an imbalance that must be worked through if service users are to continue to feel engaged and their contribution valued, no matter how limited this might be.

I recall working with a family where the children, aged two, three and five, were severely neglected. Both parents had been diagnosed as having learning difficulties, although what part this played in their ability to parent their children was never clear because both were known to have had impoverished childhoods, moving in and out of care. Their deep sense of mistrust and fear of social workers made any attempt to find a common purpose a seemingly impossible task. For a long time a stultifying silence and apparent lack of interest dominated the communication. In desperation, I took the issue to supervision and set about the task of analysing the blocks to communication and to establishing a rapport. One of the problems identified by my supervisor was that my agenda – the protection of the children – was getting in the way of establishing a rapport. I had failed to ask these parents what help they felt they most needed from social services and, in particular, from me. When I did ask this question, I found they wanted my help to press the housing department to mend their leaking roof. The other mistake I had made was that I had failed to reframe their actions and behaviour in positive terms. For example, they were always in when I visited and always allowed me to have contact with the children. They were also committed parents, determined not to see their children 'dumped into care' as they themselves had been. I had not seen their commitment; only their mistrust and lack of cooperation.

By reframing their actions in this way, new possibilities emerged (Watzlawick *et al.* 1974: 115; see also the section on 'reframing' earlier in this text). We were able to find 'mutual agreement' (Lishman 1994: 92): a common purpose. Together, our purpose was to ensure that they did not lose custody of their children. With this aim in mind, we negotiated different tasks, where control of the decision-making process was more equitable (O'Sullivan 1999: 49). I agreed to address the problem about the housing repairs, thereby hoping to bring about some improvement in the quality of their lives and, in this process, to gain some trust, but on condition that both parents attended parenting classes at the local health centre. In other words, I attended to their primary concern and, in return, they attended to mine.

This example highlights the fact that the partnerships created can take many forms. It can be helpful to stress this at the beginning of the contact. Also the fact that partnership does 'not imply an equality of power, or an equality of work' (Marsh 2002: 111). Addressing issues of this kind is a complex activity, requiring sophisticated communication skills. This is particularly true in the area of child protection where research findings indicate that greater parental involvement has been linked to better outcomes (Thoburn *et al.* 1995; Waterhouse and McGhee 2002: 278). The ability to create a climate of inclusion and collaboration, based on a recognition of the importance of everyone's contribution to the partnership process, is a key skill within this process.

The main concern that critics highlight in relation to the notion of partnership centres around the inequalities that exist in terms of power and control. This has been described as 'conflicting imperatives' with regard to 'rights versus risks, care versus control, needs versus resources, professionalism versus partnership with users, professional versus agency agendas' (Braye and Preston-Shoot 1995: 63). Where these conflicts and tensions are not addressed honestly and openly, the partnership or the experience of user involvement can feel hollow. As a result, service users can feel their involvement as 'stressful, diversionary and unproductive' (Croft and Beresford 2002: 387–8). This is particularly the case where service users are invited to 'participate in decisions over which they have no control' (Langan 2002: 215), thereby being rendered powerless. Equally, unless adequate resources are made available for the objectives being pursued, partnerships can become strained and vulnerable to being overtaken by events and the unwelcome intrusion of greater problems and desperate solutions (Howe 1996: 96). A final concern relates to where our professional responsibilities lie as practitioners in relation to working in partnership. If we are to act as gatekeepers to resources (Phillips 1996: 141), our power and authority need to be made explicit. But if our role is, as Jordan suggests, to exercise 'moral reasoning' and to use our 'judgement, discretion and skill' to highlight choice and resource inequalities (1990: 4), then this too needs to be made clear, as does the fact that little progress may be possible without this kind of agitation. How much service users feel able to become involved in this form of political negotiation should be discussed as part of the partnership agreement.

Despite these concerns, partnership can provide an important framework for us to work closely with service users. This is likely to involve the skills of working across differences, including cultural and racial differences:

> In order to achieve successful partnerships with families in child protection work, professionals must give special consideration to the different cultural, ethnic and racial origins of families and their different religious beliefs and languages. The many different ethnic and cultural variations in our society require all professionals to develop a personal and organisational commitment to equality and to meeting the needs of families and children as well as understanding the effects of racial discrimination, and cultural misunderstanding or misinterpretation.
>
> (DoH 1995: 24)

From this place, we can learn a great deal about the hardships experienced by service users and encounter first-hand the barriers and obstacles that block the way forward. This may require extending the remit of our role, and the objectives of the partnership, to include working with social or environmental factors that hinder progress, drawing on skills described in this and other chapters, such as negotiating skills, advocacy and so forth.

Mediation skills

Ensuring that different parties communicate with one another is an important skill within social work. Within this process, mediation skills have a particular part to play 'in disputes between parties to help them reconcile differences, find compromises, or reach mutually satisfactory agreements' (Barker 2003: 266). Although often grouped with advocacy skills, where our role is to represent, defend or speak for another person, mediation involves taking up 'a neutral role between two opposing parties (members of families, for example) rather than taking up the case of one party against another' (Thompson 2002b: 302). Common situations where mediation skills may be called for are disputes between neighbours in conflict or between divorcing parents. One approach to mediation would be to try to find some common ground. In the case of neighbours at 'war', they might share the desire to live in peace. For parents in dispute, the common ground may be their children's future: to want the best for them and to protect them from harm. To be a successful 'go-between' involves being able to gain a degree of trust from both or all parties to represent their point of view. This may or may not involve bringing people together in one setting. Mediation, conciliation and arbitration skills all belong to the same negotiating skills 'family'. To define these terms may be important if it helps to identify the focus of our work. For example, conciliation skills can involve attempting to pacify, whereas in some situations to act as a mediator may look more like being a referee.

The neutrality required of a mediator can be difficult to sustain in situations where one party is more articulate and powerful than the other. It can feel as if we are condoning the browbeating or bullying of another person. However, to be drawn outside the role, most commonly into the role of advocate, can have disastrous consequences because, once lost, neutrality may never be regained. One way to avoid this danger is to stay active. For example, we may ask both parties to direct their comments to one another through us, perhaps in the first instance suggesting or insisting they discuss issues likely to be less contentious and more amenable to agreement. Our role is then to address the comments of one party to the other and to feed replies back in the same way, doing so until it seems possible for both parties to speak directly. Within this process it may be helpful to reframe some comments, to keep the same 'frame' but to take some of the 'sting' out of what is being said. This is only possible where people feel comfortable about having the sense of what they are saying reframed in this way. If these efforts fail and we still feel we are being drawn out of role, it is wise to call the session to a halt so that we can reflect on events, seek help if necessary and review what other steps we (or others) need to take to move the situation forward to a satisfactory resolution. As these examples indicate, mediation is a 'highly skilled activity' (Smith 2002: 325).

'Mediation' is a term used in other situations. For example, mediators play an important role within cognitive-behavioural approaches as 'people in the client's surroundings who can record, prompt and reinforce appropriate behaviour' (Hudson and MacDonald 1986: 69; Sheldon 1995: 127). In this context, mediators may be family members, friends or volunteers. Mediation can also be found in divorce court welfare services, where its role is to reduce conflict and to work with parents to agree the arrangements for the upbringing of their children (James 2002: 217). Whereas conciliation was once the term used in divorce court proceedings, mediation is now the preferred term (Home Office 1994). The fact that these terms are sometimes used interchangeably highlights the importance of being clear ourselves in relation to our purpose and role in different situations.

Advocacy skills

Advocacy is a central skill within social work and one that links to other human and civil rights issues such as citizen's charters, empowerment, partnership, collaboration and participation. Advocacy involves representing the interests of others when they are unable to do so themselves (Thompson 2002b: 301–2). Central to this work is an acknowledgement of differences in power that disadvantage certain groups of people, denying access to certain resources or opportunities, including the right to participate as full members of society (Townsend 1993: 36). Advocacy aims to ensure that the voices and interests of service users are heard and responded to in ways that affect attitudes, policy, practice and service delivery. The mandate for this undertaking can be found in the objectives of the NHS and Community Care Act 1990, which is 'to give people a greater say in how they live their lives and the services they need to help them to do so' (DoH 1989).

A key concept within advocacy is that of representation, which can involve:

- supporting clients to represent themselves;
- arguing clients' views and needs;
- interpreting or representing the views, needs, concerns and interests of clients to others; and
- developing appropriate skills for undertaking these different tasks, such as listening and negotiating skills, empathy, assertiveness skills, being clear and focused, and so on.

Advocacy can involve speaking, writing, acting or arguing on behalf of others. According to Payne (1997: 269), this representation can take different forms:

- *Case advocacy* Advocating on behalf of another person for resources, services or opportunities. This may be undertaken by a professional, volunteer or peer.
- *Cause advocacy* Arguing for changes in policies or procedures and other forms of reform (e.g. entitlement to health services or welfare benefits).
- *Self-advocacy* People finding ways to speak for themselves in order to protect their rights and to advance their own interests. This links to self-help, group and peer advocacy. This type of advocacy is used by 'mental health system survivors' and people with learning disabilities.
- *Peer advocacy* This describes people working together to represent each other's needs. Many self-help groups undertake this kind of advocacy and some are also actively involved in campaigning to influence public opinion and government policies.
- *Citizen advocacy* This 'involves volunteers in developing relationships with potentially isolated clients, understanding and representing their needs'.

For advocacy to be seen as a legitimate element of the social work role, it is essential that adequate training, supervision and support are provided. To act as an advocate for another person requires considerable professional confidence and standing on the part of practitioners, particularly when confronted with officialdom and authority figures

(Kadushin 1990: 388–90). Some practitioners have neither the confidence nor the body of knowledge needed to be an effective advocate. This knowledge includes how to use the law, government guidance and regulations, agency policy and practices to act as an advocate for the rights and needs of service users (Braye and Preston-Shoot 1995: 65).

For example, many years ago I was involved in advocating on the behalf of a service user and her two children who were homeless and 'squatting' and had been threatened with eviction by the local authority. A telephone call to a squatter's rights organization in London revealed that the local authority had failed to provide three days' notice, which was then required for an eviction order. I passed this information on to the barrister representing this family, who duly presented this information to the judge. The case was adjourned, with the judge chastising the local authority for failing to prepare their case properly and requiring them to offer alternative accommodation before the next hearing. There was no legal requirement on the part of the local authority to adhere to the judge's requirement. This example highlights the fact that we are more likely to be successful in our role as advocate where we have gathered accurate, detailed and relevant facts, including those relating to the law or legal expectations.

As a final point, an important concept within advocacy work relates to the concept of normalization. This is often used to describe a commitment to provide an environment that gives people with disabilities the kind of social roles and lifestyle that other citizens enjoy. It is also sometimes used in relation to the rights and needs of people in residential care (Payne 1997: 271). Another way to see the concept of normalization would be as a description of what all human beings need: 'It contains, in prototype, a framework of minimum requirements for the good life' (Clark 2000: 130). We may be called to act as an advocate in relation to any of the five interdependent needs identified by Clark (2000: 130–1), which are similar to those identified by Maslow (1954), described in Chapter 3. They are:

- safety and psychological security (physical care, security and safety)
- means of life (basic needs such as food, shelter)
- opportunity for creativity (rewarding work, personal growth)
- social participation and status (recognition and respect)
- power and choice (to participate in society, to make choices).

Describing the different forms of advocacy is relatively straightforward. However, advocacy is a subject that remains bound by qualification and, sometimes, a mistrust about the intentions of practitioners and their skills to undertake this task well. Some writers express the danger of professionals taking over in such a way that service users' ability to represent themselves – or to learn to represent themselves – is undermined or disempowered through 'pressurizing or persuading' (Dalrymple and Burke 1995: 69). Others state that focusing solely on equalizing power imbalances between service users and others more powerful is not enough, and that practitioners should also 'challenge those inequalities within the system which contribute to or which cause difficulties' (Phillipson 1993: 183). However, it is not clear how this can be achieved and whether this form of advocacy is likely to be a priority for social work agencies constrained by other imperatives. Certainly, there is a need for some form of advocacy in areas where our involvement is both sanctioned and greatly needed, namely in relation to welfare rights, but this is an area increasingly neglected by social workers, partly due to the development of specialist welfare rights agencies (Burgess 1992: 175) and partly because addressing the issue is not considered a priority for some social workers (Walker and Walker 2002: 52).

Assertiveness skills

Ongoing experiences of defeat, oppression and exploitation can leave people feeling powerless and unable to protect themselves properly. This inability can include being unable to protect others in their care. Social workers, as well as service users, can find it difficult to be assertive, particularly when dealing with higher status professionals, such as psychiatrists, solicitors or higher management. One way to understand the lack of assertiveness is to analyse the issue of powerlessness, defined as 'the inability to manage emotions, skills, knowledge and/or material resources in a way that effective performance of valued social roles will lead to personal gratification' (Solomon 1976: 16), and to link this to concepts such as learned helplessness (Seligman 1975) and locus of control (Lefcourt 1976; Cigno and Bourn 1998: 102–5). These concepts help us to map the degree to which people feel in charge of their lives and feel able to influence their circumstances and future.

Passivity is seen to be the opposite of assertiveness or self-efficacy (Egan 1990: 99) and can lead to worrying consequences: 'Failure to act assertively often results in submission, exploitation and resentment or in aggression, misunderstanding and negative consequences' (Feltham and Dryden 1993: 12). Yet it can be very difficult for people to risk exploring other options, mainly because their view of themselves – their sense of worth as a human being – has taken too many blows and they cannot sustain the confidence or self-belief necessary to begin to effect change. Assertiveness skills can be an important starting point and are recognized as crucial in relation to concepts of empowerment, partnership and participation. Where service users lack necessary skills and confidence, it is assumed that practitioners should help them to acquire these skills (Croft and Beresford 2002), so that 'the possibilities for effective collaboration can be maximized' (Thompson 2002b: 304).

This transition can be difficult to achieve. Central to the task is encouraging service users to challenge self-defeating statements and helping them to substitute these with more positive and hopeful viewpoints. These self-defeating statements can be in the form of attitudes or beliefs, both about themselves or other people, or future possibilities and opportunities likely to improve their situation. It also involves helping to address and contain the fears and anxieties that are holding service users back, and encouraging and supporting them to risk taking small steps forward (Egan 1990: 99). This focus on the importance of assertiveness skills has been used a great deal in the USA, particularly in relation to women (Gilligan 1993) but also as a key empowerment strategy for other oppressed groups (Gitterman 1991).

Assertiveness training

There may be times when a more formal teaching approach to assertiveness skills is required. Assertiveness training involves teaching people how to stand up for themselves without being aggressive, threatening, punishing, manipulative or over-controlling, and without demeaning other people. Drawing on learning theory and other cognitive-behaviourist approaches, including modelling, rehearsal and operant reinforcement (Sheldon 1995: 202), assertiveness training is designed to identify and replace submissive and self-denying messages with statements that more accurately reflect what the individual feels, needs or wants for themselves. Assertiveness training encourages people to learn to say 'no', to defend themselves and to complain in ways that are likely to be beneficial and successful in terms of outcomes. Sheldon (1995: 203) identifies a range of skills and tasks associated with assertiveness training:

- *assessment* to gain an understanding of the extent of the problem;
- *discrimination training procedures* to help clients to learn the difference between assertiveness, false or compulsive compliance and aggression;
- *a modelling and rehearsal component* to show the client, step-by-step, the degree of assertiveness appropriate in different circumstances and to encourage the skills to be rehearsed, offering encouragement and validation;
- *a desensitization component* to help to remove the fears by exposing clients to frightening situations; and
- *generalization* to ensure that the skills learned can be generalized to everyday experiences and problems by relating them to real situations.

The importance of people being able to assert their thoughts, feelings, choices or needs openly and directly cannot be overstated, but its importance is not confined to service users. As practitioners, we too need to be able to assert and represent the needs and rights of others, as well as our own views and perspectives, and personal and professional needs.

Being challenging and confrontative

There are times when it is important to challenge or confront certain kinds of behaviour. This includes being able to manage conflict and bear confrontations (O'Sullivan 1999: 78). It also includes the right to be allowed to challenge our own agency policies and practices without the fear of reprisal (Mitchell 1996). The skill is to know when and how to do this in ways that help to move the situation forward. Some authors view 'challenging' as virtually synonymous with 'confrontation' (Feltham and Dryden 1993: 26; Lishman 1994: 121), whereas Egan associates confrontation with 'unpleasant experiences' (1990: 184), and close to bullying and coercion. It is for this reason that the terms are included together here.

Challenging

Within this text, 'challenging' describes a low-level, gentle yet firm invitation to face service users with 'contradictions, distortions, inconsistencies or discrepancies and inviting or stimulating them to reconsider and resolve the contradictions' (Lishman 1994: 121), where they may otherwise be reluctant to do so. The timing of challenges, and how they are undertaken, can be as important as what is actually said. This is because challenges should come at a point where it is clear that the service user is unlikely to pick up on the 'lack of fit' and needs us to intervene in order to move the situation forward. For example, some service users do not understand how they come across; the extent to which some of their behaviours are off-putting or set people against them. A well-timed challenge should strengthen our relationship, whereas one that is premature or inopportune, perhaps because it is too forceful, persistent or moves too far ahead of a service user, could damage the relationship and threaten progress, sometimes irreparably. Millar *et al.* see challenging as a form of feedback and stress the tentative nature of the communication as a means of aiding further self-reflection and understanding: 'What interviewees need is a chance to consider what behaviours they display, how they "come across". What appear to be less helpful are attempts to present analyses of underlying meanings, interpretations or evaluative statements' (1992: 97).

Confronting

Egan identifies a range of different behaviours that may warrant challenging:

- Failure to own problems.
- Failure to define problems in solvable terms.

- Faulty interpretations of critical experiences, behaviours, and feelings.
- Evasion, distortions, and game playing.
- Failure to identify or understand the consequences of behaviour.
- Hesitancy or unwillingness to act on new perspectives.

(Egan 1990: 187)

Similarly, Kadushin and Kadushin write of confrontation as 'pulling the interviewee up short ... By acting contrary to the usual social expectation that they will ignore inconsistencies, interviewers set up a new situation that requires resolution' (1997: 183). For Egan, it is 'all too common for clients to refuse to take responsibility for their problems and lost opportunities' (1990: 186). Service users must own their part in whatever problems they have because, without this ownership, they cannot own the solutions. Defining problems in terms of the past means that they cannot be solved because the past cannot be changed. For Egan, confronting clients is not to strip them of their defences, which could be dangerous because these are needed for survival, 'but to help them to overcome blind spots and develop new strategies' (1990: 194).

The ability to confront people without making them more defensive and guarded is a skilled activity, involving the qualities of tolerance, patience and acceptance, remembering that the ultimate goal 'is action and change' (Lishman 1994: 121). Nelson-Jones offers the following practice guidelines:

- start with reflective responding
- where possible, help speakers to confront themselves
- do not talk down
- use the minimum amount of 'muscle'
- avoid threatening voice and body language
- leave the ultimate responsibility with the speaker
- do not overdo it.

(Nelson-Jones 1990: 135–6)

It is important that we think beforehand about the kind of reaction that our challenge is likely to produce and what our response might be. Reactions can range from anger, rage and pain to a sense of relief. Also, challenging others can be a stressful undertaking, which may call for additional peer and supervision support.

As a final point, a word of warning is needed in relation to being challenging or confrontational. People who have experienced too many 'put-downs' or too much humiliation in their lives can be extremely sensitive to challenges of any kind and, where this is the case, can find the mildest rebuke quite devastating. Sometimes merely asking a particular kind of question can be construed as a form of criticism. This can be expressed in different ways. Some may become more withdrawn and silent, while others may become agitated or even aggressive. It is often hard to guess the kind of reaction criticism will elicit and even if it does bring about some kind of positive outcome, the ends never justify the means. It is possible that the same outcome could have been achieved by adopting a more caring and sensitive intervention. Also, some people can easily turn criticism against themselves or against others. In my experience, bullying and self-harm among young people can be triggered by criticism, or other 'put-downs', as can aggressive behaviour (Howe *et al*. 1999: 138).

This is not to ignore the importance of being able to challenge the difficult and sometimes abusive behaviour that some people demonstrate, particularly when we or others are being targeted. It is not possible to avoid feeling critical of some kinds of behaviour: it is part of being human. Some people justify unacceptable behaviour as being natural to a particular culture or group. This may be true and leave us feeling unable to challenge certain behaviours. In relation to child abuse, this can have serious consequences (Modi *et al*. 1995: 99; Trowell and Bower 1995). Some behaviour may still fall outside the realms of acceptability and need to be challenged. Where the unacceptable behaviour is extreme, the law should be our 'defining mandate' (Blom-Cooper 1985). Before these extremes are reached, it is important to use our interpersonal skills to help people to find appropriate ways to give vent to feelings of upset, anger and frustration that are not harmful to themselves or others.

Dealing with hostility, aggression and violence

Violence against social workers is increasing (Kemshall and Pritchard 1999; Pringle and Thompson 1999: 135–44; Littlechild 1996). For example, research indicates that 25 to 30 per cent of social workers have been physically assaulted at some point in their careers (Rey 1996). Clearly, it is important that we avoid hostile situations as much as possible and minimize the likelihood of being the victims of violence. This section explores the skills involved in dealing with aggressive and violent behaviour.

Sound organizational arrangements can help to keep our fears in check and avoid violent confrontations. The ideal location should be a room that cannot be locked from inside, which has an alarm/panic button, is within easy reach of others and has a window for colleagues to keep an unobtrusive yet watchful eye. The seating should be arranged so that it is easy for us or the service user to get to the door and leave. If a service user is known to be violent, it is important to work out a contingency plan beforehand. Our attempts to minimize the risk of violence need to be undertaken in ways that do not exacerbate the situation. Some practitioners easily fall into a 'siege mentality'. Visible protection devices, such as closed-circuit television, buzzers and combination locks, are important but it is essential to remember that most service users are not violent (Lishman 1994: 17) and that excessive preoccupation with self-protection among practitioners can interfere with our being able to establish a trusting rapport with service users. Clearly, we must protect ourselves, but our best protection is our skill and capacity to avoid or deal with aggressive and potentially violent encounters because, once we have acquired these skills, they travel with us into all situations.

For example, situations that involve depriving people of their liberty are the most likely to produce aggressive and violent reactions (Nathan 2002: 188–9). Given this fact, we need to reflect beforehand on whether our intervention is justified in a situation where the person may be a danger to themselves (suicide or deliberate self-harm) or to others (child abuse, domestic violence or attacks on others). We then need to consider what the person's reaction might be and to prepare our response (Lishman 1994: 59). For example, we might decide not to undertake a home visit or, if this is essential, take a colleague with us (although to outnumber the service user may be counterproductive).

We may also need to be clear how we intend to deal with actual violent attacks perpetrated against us or others. In my opinion, all violent attacks have to involve the police because, despite convincing justifications, violence goes beyond the realms of acceptable behaviour. If it is known that all attacks will be reported to the police, then this boundary is clear. People who choose violence know the consequences and that it will lead to police involvement. We may feel we played some part in provoking the attack. This too needs to be brought out into the open and our actions need to be seen in context. Some people are very frightening and this can affect our capacity to read situations accurately and our skills become lost because much of our thinking is taken up working out how to protect ourselves. If the threat is this serious, we need to find ways to leave or, if that is not possible, to ensure that the person in question can leave. Barring the door is unwise.

One of the best ways to defuse the situation is to try to engage the person in a dialogue. This cannot be forced but most people want to be understood. Many have serious grievances about the unfair way they have been treated, and their current behaviour may be some form of retaliation. It is important to listen to their story and to allow ourselves to be influenced by this, but not to the point where we make inappropriate promises. It also helps to remember that most people who are threatening or violent are frightened of themselves and of their own reactions. Many have suffered terrible experiences of violence and know what it is like to be terrified. To reveal how frightened we feel – and the fact that we mean them no harm – can sometimes help to establish a point of contact and help to defuse the situation (Jordan 1990: 185). We may also need to offer a gentle reminder that their current behaviour is unlikely to bring about the outcome they most desire and, indeed, can lead to negative consequences – but caution is needed. To stress negative consequences too much can be experienced as a threat and escalate the situation. To find a way for an individual to back down, but with honour and self-respect, is essential.

8 PROFESSIONAL COMPETENCE AND ACCOUNTABILITY

It is important to understand professional accountability in context and to attempt to differentiate between professionalism, professionalization and 'technicist' solutions. 'Professionalism' is defined by Barker as: 'The degree to which an individual possesses and uses the knowledge, skills, and qualification of a profession and adheres to its values and ethics when serving the client' (2003: 342). On the other hand, 'professionalization' involves the 'control of knowledge' (Payne 1997: 30), thereby excluding service users. Similarly, 'technicist' solutions fail service users by applying techniques 'regardless of wider debates about values and underlying social relations' (Mayo 1994: 70). Anti-oppressive practice calls for 'a redefinition of professionalism, with expertise being rooted in more power-sharing egalitarian directions and making explicit the value system to which the profession subscribes' (Dominelli 2002b: 7).

What this means in practice, in terms of the day-to-day experiences of practitioners and service users, is not clear. Most service users do not come to social services asking for 'power-sharing' or to be informed of the 'value system' of the agency, but they regularly request quality services, delivered in ways that are respectful and caring. Our value base and our desire to create more equitable relationships need to be linked more directly to practice and the context within which social work currently exists in terms of 'managerial categories of cost, efficiency and risk' (Clarke 1996: 58). They also need to be linked to the requirements of government, which for Social Services departments too involves meeting specific targets, such as those laid down in *Quality Assurance* and *Best Value*, and for practice to be based on 'the best evidence of what works' (DoH 1998b: 93). Linking our value base to an analysis of effectiveness is part of the challenge we face and, to some extent, this is already happening. For example, research findings indicate that our chances of success are likely to be enhanced if our skills include 'accurate empathy, warmth and genuineness which have long been known to be associated with effective practice' (Thoburn 2002: 205).

However, as social workers, our accountability to service users is only one of 'multiple accountabilities':

> Social workers are engaged in complex webs of social and institutional relationships, embracing multiple accountabilities: to the state; to their employers who provide social work services; to colleagues; to professional values; and not least towards the client and the wider community.
>
> (Adams 2002b: 263)

This can lead to conflicting demands as we attempt to balance the best interests of one group against those of another. For example, in children's services this can lead to tensions as we attempt to balance children's needs with the requirement to protect parents' rights (Hollis and Howe 1990: 549). Yet these themes are linked because the central task of social work involves problem-solving across these conflicting interests and competing needs. In this work, it is probably true to say that social work is 'crucially concerned with fairness' (Jordan 1990: 178), but the extent to which the pursuit of 'fairness' or, more particularly, redressing injustices is considered to be a legitimate part of our social work role is a controversial issue. Again, we are caught in a double-bind: we are being asked to be 'empowering' yet not political. It may not always be possible, or effective, to separate the two.

Practitioners who see their professional competence and accountability primarily in terms of their accountability to service users are likely to view their work and priorities differently from those who place agency accountability at the forefront. Some authors are clear that addressing underlying causes, such as poverty and discrimination, is not the main priority of social work. Other demands dominate: 'Social workers and their agencies are already very over-pressed with current commitments, many of them statutory, and cannot afford the resources for excursions into areas outside social work proper' (Clark 2000: 198). Other authors would take issue with this view and argue that the way social work is organized and managed is itself problematic and potentially oppressive (Mullender and Perrott 2002: 74). If professional competence means the ability to 'do the job', this raises the question, what is the 'job'? What is the role or task of social work and social workers, and how can effectiveness be measured? Whatever our views, most writers, practitioners, managers, policy-makers and politicians are clear that social work accountability, competence and effectiveness are centre stage.

These different views of practice are likely to be mirrored in the practice orientations, approaches and perspectives we use within our work, and to influence how we view professional competence and accountability (Clark 2000b: 273). For more detailed coverage on competence and competencies, see Chapter 2. These differences need to be borne in mind in the following account, which analyses in general terms the following skills:

- providing protection and control
- managing professional boundaries
- record keeping skills
- reflective and effective practice
- using supervision creatively.

Providing protection and control

One of the tasks of social work is to provide appropriate levels of *protection and control*. This can be seen as a manifestation of our dual role as carers and as 'agents of social control' (Coulshed and Orme 1998: 93). It is difficult to generalize about how these protection and control powers are used. Much depends on the situation, on our practice orientation and on the fact that there is a degree of discretion about the extent to which practitioners or agencies exercise the power that statute gives (Dalrymple and Burke 1995: 32). It has been argued, however, that this discretion is becoming increasingly bound in 'managerial imperatives', as well as 'statutory or legal framings' (Clarke 1996: 58).

This discussion links back to the nature and task of social work. For example, Blom-Cooper (1985) stated in the Beckford Report that the law should be social work's defining mandate, while others have challenged this narrow view and insisted that the defining mandate is our ethical duty to care, within which the law is centrally important but only one component (Stevenson 1988). The decision to adopt a more 'holistic' approach, which avoids the dangers of 'a narrow procedural legalistic approach' (O'Sullivan 1999: 170), is important, but so too is the need to have an in-depth knowledge of the law and legal procedures, including agency policy and procedures. This is our statutory responsibility. However, a knowledge of the law – or how to use the law – is also important because local authorities have a duty to provide certain services (see Chapter 2, Johns and Sedgwick 1999). Social workers can also use the law to protect children 'likely to suffer significant harm' (Children Act 1989, s47) and, under the Mental Health Act 1983, to safeguard the 'interests of the patient's health and safety, or the safety of others'; not, as frequently misquoted, to protect patients from being a danger to themselves or others (Pringle and Thompson 1999: 141).

In relation to our direct work with service users, concepts such as protection and control are important because they define a framework within which the relationship between service user and social worker, the individual and the state, is located. To cross over an invisible line into the realms of 'dangerous' behaviour brings into play certain 'safeguards'. Although these safeguards are designed to protect the individual or others from harm, it is not always clear – nor the case – that the protection given is warranted (as in the case of the compulsory sectioning under the Mental Health Act 1983 of people from ethnic minorities), nor that the type of protection offered is in any sense appropriate to that individual, empowering or enabling. This can lead to a moral dilemma because to fail to act can increase risk and threaten our professional credibility, yet to use our powers of protection and control could result in our being 'an active accessory to that exploitation and domination ... those constraints, exclusions and coercions which entrap and disempower clients' (Jordan 1990: 58). For these reasons, notions of protection and control have been scrutinized in recent years with the introduction of anti-discriminatory/ anti-oppressive perspectives within social work where the emphasis is on ensuring that people's rights are not violated (Dalrymple and Burke 1995: 30). An important focus has been to question who decides what protection and control are required and what part service users play in this decision-making process. This relates to earlier accounts in this text on empowerment and partnership.

The most common use of the term 'protection' relates to the concepts of 'risk' and 'vulnerability' to exploitation, neglect and/or abuse. Child protection services are the best known examples, but the concept of protection also extends to other vulnerable groups, such as some people with learning disabilities or emotional problems and older people. The concept of vulnerability is important. At present there is no law relating to vulnerable adults, but there is for children under the Children Act 1989. The Law Commission defined a 'vulnerable adult' as a person over 18 years of age who 'is or may be in need of community care services by reason of mental or other disability, age or illness and who is or may be unable to take care of himself or herself, or unable to protect himself or herself against significant harm or serious exploitation' (1995: 207).

Although the Law Commission 'urged the government to provide extra powers for assessment and removal of a vulnerable adult to a place of safety where these were significant concerns' (Brown 2000: 368), this recommendation has not been enacted. The concept of vulnerability is close to that of 'incapacity', which is a legal term that refers to people who are unable to 'make a valid decision (as opposed to a correct or right decision) or unable to give or withhold valid consent to medical or other treatment' (Munby 2000: 37).

Where children, or 'vulnerable' adults, are unable to articulate their needs, it can be difficult to gauge the necessary level of protection. This can lead to too much or too little protection, or to protection of the wrong kind, all of which could lead to negative outcomes. A different tension exists where people present a threat or danger to themselves and/or to others, such as the threat of suicide. Here we have a professional obligation to protect and control. If persuasion does not work, and if the person's life is to be saved and a breathing space provided from which other, better solutions can be sought, then an external control – sectioning under the Mental Health Act 1983 – may be the only alternative available.

Managing professional boundaries

Boundaries are important in social work, as in all other areas of professional activity, because they are a way of marking the responsibilities that lie within a particular role or task and of differentiating these from other activities or aspects of social work. The notion of boundaries can include work with individuals, groups, families, communities and organizations:

> This concept helps us to look at ways of marking off and establishing the identity of something, by differentiating it from other entities and from its surroundings. It is also concerned with setting limits, as we do in everyday life, for example whenever we delineate what is acceptable from what is not. Boundary definition gives enhanced understanding of the types of relationship and interchange that occur between one entity and another.
>
> (Brearley 1995: 49)

For example, an interview kept within clear boundaries will start and end on time. This clarity allows us to measure whether the service user is late or not. Similarly, we can learn a great deal about a service user's capacity to let go – to leave one experience and move on to another – if we set a time for the appointment or session to end and they try to extend this on a regular basis, perhaps with 'doorknob revelations'. Without these boundaries, which act as markers, we can fail to pick up on a range of behaviours that may be relevant. Service users who are trying to find employment but are always late for appointments with us may be at risk of losing any job they find due to poor timekeeping. To be able to help them, we have to know what they find difficult.

If we were to meet this same service user away from our agency, say at the local shops, our conversation would not need to be bound by time or other constraints because we are in a different role. It is important to strike the right balance. Too loose a boundary can result in insecurity and a loss of identity, whereas too rigid a boundary can feel too controlling or unnecessarily withholding.

This highlights that within any discussion of boundaries, there are areas of overlap. For this reason, Brearley suggests that it is better to think in terms of boundary regions rather than boundary lines. This helps to avoid taking up rigid inflexible positions but instead allows us to explore this overlap based on an acknowledgement of 'common ground and shared territory and concerns between one group or activity and another' (1995: 49).

There are several advantages for establishing and working within clear boundaries:

- Boundaries ensure that we keep to the task and roles designated and agreed, thereby ensuring that we are not drawn into other areas or issues. For example, some service users may like to become our friends (or we may want to become their friend). In work settings, this may actually contravene agency policy, as well as blurring professional boundaries.
- Boundaries ensure the economic use of time and resources. For example, if an interviewing room has been booked for an hour, it can disrupt and frustrate other practitioners if the session is allowed to extend beyond the allocated time so that it encroaches on their work.
- Practical arrangements can be formalized and the contact put on a professional footing. Some practical negotiations are similar to ground rules and can include: identifying the purpose of the work or the nature of the task and contract (written or otherwise); the frequency and location of the sessions; who is eligible to attend; agreement about record keeping; transport/childcare arrangements; expectations about punctuality; smoking prohibitions; how crises or emergencies will be dealt with; behaviour expectations (no alcohol, drug-taking, spitting or violence); and communication rules (no swearing or interrupting).

The above categories are sometimes summarized as the three 'Ts': time, territory and task. It is usual for practitioners to ensure that these three elements or other boundary issues are adhered to.

Limits of confidentiality

One of the most problematic boundary problems in social work is the issue of confidentiality. Confidentiality is essential to create a climate of trust and to protect service users' rights. The general rule is that no information will be disclosed without the service users' consent. Barker differentiates between absolute confidentiality, where no information is disclosed regardless of circumstances without consent (2003: 2), and relative confidentiality, indicating the circumstances where it is our ethical or professional responsibility to disclose information (2003: 365). Some situations may warrant absolute confidentiality. However, in addition to the needs of service users, our role is dictated by agency and legal requirements, as well as ethical and moral considerations. Although the 'precept of professional ethics [is] that the professional should not divulge the content of the client's communication unless the client clearly authorize otherwise' (Clark 2000: 184), in some circumstances this is not possible. Two suggestions have been put forward to help clarify our professional boundaries in relation to confidentiality. These are:

- for agencies to make their confidentiality policy available, in written form, as a guide for practitioners and service users, including the recording policy of each agency; and
- for the confidentiality policy to be translated, individualized and negotiated with every service user, thereby making it 'appropriate to the client's understanding, ability and emotional capacity to deal with them' (Clark 2000: 192).

It is important to remember the record keeping policy of the agency, particularly in relation to inter-agency collaboration or multiprofessional work. This may include service users' rights to see and contribute to their records, stipulating who has access to these records and under what circumstances (typists, supervisors, line managers, colleagues, other outside agencies or professional contacts) and security arrangements. It may also include service users being informed of information that is being passed between one agency and another.

One area where a boundary tension exists in relation to confidentiality is in the boundary between counselling and other social work tasks, particularly the use of interviewing skills. For a helpful account of this tension, see Seden (1999) and Brearley (1995).

Record keeping skills

Record keeping is an essential skill within social work and can be an intervention in its own right. However, record keeping is an area most criticized in the findings of the 45 public inquiries into child deaths held in Britain between 1973 and 1994. According to Munro, who analysed these findings, the main criticism centred on the lack of information:

Lack of information was particularly demonstrated by the poverty of social work records. Twenty-six reports (fifty-five per cent) criticize the standard of record keeping and conclude that it adversely affected the way the case was handled. Sometimes, records were inaccurate. Heidi Koseda's records contained falsely reassuring information that she had been seen in good health by the health visitor in September, even though, by this time, she would already have been showing signs of starvation.

(Munro 1998a: 94)

Other criticisms included: a lack of baseline details, making it difficult to assess improvement or deterioration; records failing to state who had been seen during visits or to note a child's absence; and a failure to collate and to link information. Evidence suggests that there has been no marked improvement. A Social Services Inspectorate report of all six local authorities noted that 'recording was below standard ... the content of the records was inadequate, making it difficult to understand what had been achieved through the investigation and post-case conference work' (Social Services Inspectorate 1993: 34).

Had sound record keeping formed a central part of the work mentioned above, it is likely that some errors of judgement could have been avoided. Given these findings, it is important to restate why record keeping is essential to the social work task. Its primary purpose is to enhance service delivery in relation to effectiveness, accountability and confidentiality. However, it is also a crucial learning tool because record keeping provides an opportunity for analytical reflection and evaluation, particularly in relation to decision-making, to formulating hypotheses and evolving collaborative ways of working. It provides an opportunity to step back and to think things through. The following is a helpful summary of the multipurpose nature of record keeping, which can be used:

- as learning and teaching material
- for supervision purposes
- for administrative purposes, e.g. budgeting
- to ensure accountability
- for research and evaluation
- to illustrate shortfalls or absence of services
- to 'cover' the worker for work done
- to provide continuity when workers change
- to aid planning and decision making
- to monitor progress
- as an *aide mémoire*
- to facilitate client participation, as indicated.

(Coulshed 1991: 41–2)

One of the greatest tensions within record keeping is how much information to record and how best to do this in ways that are accurate, objectively critical and sufficiently detailed yet also succinct. Much depends on how the records might be used. For example, as already implied, records in relation to legal proceedings need to be detailed. The four main methods used within social work include:

- process recording (sometimes called verbatim recording)
- diagnostic recording (often used in therapy)
- problem-centred (sometimes called task-centred) recording
- proforma (often computerized) recording.

All have advantages and disadvantages, but in recent years more structured, systematized forms of recording have been encouraged as a way of ordering information, checking its validity, drawing up and testing hypotheses, ensuring that facts can be differentiated from opinion or hearsay, relating information to a knowledge base and using this to inform future practice. For Coulshed and Orme, records should register 'significant facts, evidence, feelings, decisions, action taken and planned, monitoring, review, evaluation and costing information' (1998: 42). Sheldon recommends summarizing statements to represent 'the best-informed judgements' but that these should be tentative and open to refutation as new information emerges (1995: 123). However, structuring information does not in itself ensure good practice nor effectiveness. This is more likely to be achieved when service users have open access to their records and play an active part in the recording process as an integral part of the work. One way to symbolize this participative effort would be for service users to countersign their records (Neville and Beak 1990).

Data Protection Act 1998 and Freedom of Information Act 2000

In relation to personal information that is held by other bodies, the Data Protection Act 1998 applies. This act came into force on 1st March 2000 and applies to all bodies within the UK that hold personal information, whether held manually or electronically. Its intention is to protect people's privacy, to encourage good practice in the handling of personal information and to give individuals the right of access to information recorded about them, such as information kept by credit reference agencies. Notice must be given to the relevant organization, which is allowed 40 days to respond: a fee may be charged. However, care is taken 'not to release personal data that may relate to another individual, and in some circumstances the request may be refused if a disclosure would cause damage or distress to the data subject' (Brammer 2003: 115). Access to other sorts of information held by public authorities are dealt with according to the rules laid down in the Freedom of Information Act 2000, which came into force on the 1st January 2005. This act, which applies to England, Wales and Northern Ireland, gives people the right of access to information held by, or on behalf of, public authorities (Scotland has its own regulations). Its intention is to promote a culture of openness and accountability within the public sector by giving the public greater access to information about how decisions are taken in government and how public services are developed and delivered. It is now a criminal offence to tamper with or destroy records that have been requested (further information is available on www.foi.gov.uk).

Reflective and effective practice

According to Shaw, 'social work works' (1996: 166). Similarly, Cheetham *et al.* state that in some areas 'social work can now claim to be cost effective' (1992: 4). However, these statements call us to define what effectiveness means and how we measure success. One answer could be to say that 'social work is effective in so far as it achieves intended aims' (Cheetham *et al.* 1992: 10). However, we then must question whether these aims are too high, too low or appropriate to the situation, given the existence of other constraints and variables operating at the time. These variables over which we may have little or no control, together with the fact that we often encounter problems that are complex, multidimensional and intractable, make the task of evaluating effectiveness fraught. This difficulty is made worse by the fact that we know very little about what actually happens in practice in terms of the impact of particular interventions or services. Evidence of positive or beneficial outcomes is not enough to tell us what factors did or did not play a part in bringing about a particular outcome.

Yet despite these difficulties, it is important that we provide quality services and find ways to evidence effectiveness (Macdonald and Macdonald 1995). This is demanded of us in a climate, in terms of government policy, of 'what works is what counts'. 'Professionals must seek to ensure that their interventions are not only carried out with due competence and in good faith, but are effective in the sense that they lead to the desired outcomes' (Clark 2000: 56). It is also essential because mistakes can be very costly in terms of human lives, as the errors in child abuse cases and public inquiries reveal. Reflective practice provides an opportunity to review our decisions and decision-making processes, and to learn from the lessons of the past. An analysis of 45 inquiry reports into the deaths of children known to social services shows that in 42 per cent of reports social workers were not criticized, but other concerns prevail:

> The analysis however also reveals one persistent error: social workers are slow to revise their judgements. Psychology research indicates that this error is widespread and by no means peculiar to social workers but it means that misjudgements about clients that may have been unavoidable on the limited knowledge available when they were made continue to be accepted despite a growing body of evidence against them. Social workers need a greater acceptance of their fallibility and a willingness to consider that their judgements and decisions are wrong. To change your mind in the light of new information is a sign of good practice, a sign of strength not weakness.
>
> (Munro 1996: 793)

As well as arriving at decisions based on 'best evidence', reflective practice provides a vital link between theory and practice. This is particularly important for complex situations where, as a result of conflicting values and purposes, there is no guarantee that agreed tasks and objectives can be effectively implemented on the basis of theories, 'technical rationality'

(Schön 1991: 338) or undertaking. Reflection involves more than thinking things out carefully. It allows us to acknowledge that we are experiencing the situation we seek to understand and are a part of the interventions we are involved in providing. This creates a crucial link between task and process, and makes it important to 'look underneath the surface relationships and events which are presented to us' (Payne 2002: 126) in order to locate ourselves, and others, within the overall picture.

Reflective practice involves developing the capacity for flexible and creative thinking. Schön describes this as the 'unprecedented requirement for adaptability' (1991: 15), where we constantly need to engage in drawing up working hypotheses and testing these out by acting temporarily as if they were true. This means being involved in a process where thinking itself, and its attendant activities, are subject to critical scrutiny so that we are always open to looking again and to observing carefully the factors that influence the direction and content of our actions and those of others.

Although reflective practice of this kind may fit uneasily with more rationalist approaches encouraged with social work, Schön's concepts of *reflection-in-action* and *reflective conversation with the situation* provide a way of building on our knowledge base so that we can observe and attend to the uniqueness of every situation and human experience in order to link 'understanding, action and effect' (England 1986: 154). In terms of practice, Schön's concepts can help us to formulate a more rigorous approach to our judgements in deciding what practice orientation, approach, perspective and interventions should be used in relation to certain kinds of problems. These can then be tested, using different evaluative approaches. These can be broadly divided into an analysis of service user based or service based outcomes (O'Sullivan 1999: 163). For an account of different approaches to evaluation – managerialist, academic and participative – see Marsden *et al.* (1994).

Using supervision creatively

The purpose of supervision within social work is to facilitate the professional development of practitioners to ensure that our work is effective, efficient, accountable and undertaken in ways that sensitively address the needs of service users (Pritchard 1995). For this reason, regular supervision is recognized as an essential feature of social work practice. In general terms, supervision consists of three main components (Hawkins and Shohet 2000: 50–2):

- a management or an accountability component
- an educational component
- a supportive component.

The weight given to certain functions over others depends on a range of different factors, such as the nature of the work, agency requirements, the practice orientation of the supervisor and practitioner, and the particular features of the work at hand. For example, for some agencies the purpose of supervision is to establish the accountability of the worker to the organization. Lishman disagrees that this should be its main purpose, seeing supervision as 'different from management control and account-ability' because it is built on a 'professional-to-professional relationship rather than a superior-to-subordinate one' (1994: 39). Others endorse the importance of providing support but within a framework which 'offers challenges, professional in character, to an apparently fixed view of risk or fixed ideas about the appropriateness of therapeutic practitioners' decisions' (Sheldon 1995: 120). This emphasis is on how judgements are formed, and particularly on how to reduce worker bias (Coulshed and Orme 1998: 35) and to review decisions made (Munro 1996: 973; Milner and O'Byrne 2002: 177; O'Sullivan 1999: 167–70). For example, Hollis and Howe remind us that 'good intentions and keeping to the procedures' are not enough and that 'well judged risks sometimes lead to bad outcomes' (1990: 548–9). Where practitioners encounter this degree of uncertainty, one of the major functions of supervision can involve containing or managing anxiety and helping to cope with the demands that the work entails (Brearley 1995: 93). Given the lack of uniformity, it is essential that the purpose of the supervision relationship between practitioners and supervisors is clarified in the early stages of the relationship.

Most supervision takes place on a regular one-to-one basis with a line manager, although other forms can exist alongside, or instead of, individual supervision, such as peer, group and team supervision and also inter-agency supervision structures. 'Live' supervision, which may involve inviting a manager or colleague to sit in on a session in order to give their observations, can be particularly valuable, adding another dimension to our appraisal. Similarly, the range of information made available for supervision can vary and include written case notes or reports, tape or video recordings, and feedback from colleagues, service users and others who have direct experience of the work at hand and/or the practitioner's particular strengths and weaknesses. The range of issues that can form a part of the supervision session can also vary and include:

- an opportunity to reflect on the content of a particular session or details of an encounter;
- an analysis of the different practice choices adopted – that is, the method of intervention (work with individuals, families, groups and communities), theories, practice approaches, perspectives, interven-tions and skills, and their impact and overall effectiveness in terms of achieved and desired outcomes;
- exploring the service user–practitioner relationship, its strengths and

weaknesses, and how any of the feelings we or others have might enhance/detract from the work;

- looking at the supervision session and what is happening in the here and now, particularly with a view to seeing if issues in relation to the service user are being replayed in the supervision session (Mattinson 1975); and
- looking at practitioners' professional development, such as training and conference opportunities, and how these can be used to enhance practitioners' knowledge base and practice effectiveness (Lishman 2002: 105).

Supervision sessions that are carefully planned beforehand by all parties tend to be more supportive, informative and creative. Responsibility for establishing a rapport based on shared learning and exploration lies with both parties. However, to be able to use supervision creatively is a real skill (Brearley 1995: 92–8). For some practitioners, supervision is not a creative or comfortable experience, perhaps due to personality clashes or because exposing our work to scrutiny in this way feels threatening. If the supervision is to be effective and a support, it is important that these 'blocks' are addressed (Hawkins and Shohet 2000: 23–35). Where workload pressures are an inhibiting factor, these tensions need to be fed back into the agency or organizational structure so that accountability is not seen as a one-way process (Macdonald 1990: 542).

CONCLUSION

In this final chapter I want to return to a theme that I have looked at briefly in earlier chapters, namely the contribution that social work provides with regard to the more general health and social welfare picture within the UK. On this theme, England has argued that: 'Social work will ... never have any genuinely exclusive knowledge, nor its practitioners any exclusive competence' (1986: 33). Whilst I agree in part with this view, I think it is the context within which social work practitioners work – and the knowledge that we generate and use – that makes our contribution distinct. There is no other profession whose work is almost exclusively located in areas of urban decay and neglect, or whose efforts are almost solely targeted on working with people from deprived and disadvantaged sectors of the population, many of whom experience discrimination and social exclusion on a daily basis. This means that as a profession we have acquired considerable knowledge and understanding about the nature and impact of deprivation, disadvantage and discrimination and have also developed a range of skills and interventions that enable us to act on that knowledge and understanding. It is the extent to which we can *reliably* communicate and apply these attributes, in ways that are transferable across different settings and situations, that confirms the unique nature of our contribution (England 1986: 34).

In the past, our distinct contribution has not always been acknowledged. This is partly because we have made mistakes – but so too have other professions. The difference here is that other professions have not – and are not – subjected to the same public scrutiny that social work has experienced over the years. Nor are other professions required to meet the same range of expectations in a working environment that is poorly resourced and inadequately funded. Some commentators have argued that social workers are treated unfairly, or placed at the bottom of the professional hierarchy, because we are assigned the same status as the people we work with – that is, where service users' status is viewed as inferior, we too are considered to be inferior. If this is the case, it makes it all the more important for us to work on our own behalf – and in partnership with service users and others – to radically change this picture.

I have argued in this text that we work with some of the most vulnerable people in society, often dealing with intractable, complex, severe and enduring problems, and for this reason, social work is – and has to be – a highly skilled activity. These skills, and the interventions we choose, are often focused on the individual, but it is important to use our skills to address social, environmental and policy restraints that inhibit progress and the opportunity for effective action. Here, the role of groupwork can be important. So too is family work and community work. Whatever social work method we use, we need to be able to work creatively with people who are powerless, hopeless, helpless and despairing, and who lack the energy or resilience to sort out and work through the problems they face. This calls for the ability to motivate others: that we learn creative ways of helping people to get up, to move on and to keep going (Miller and Rollnick 2002). This skill is also valuable in relation to the demoralization that our colleagues sometimes feel.

As well as linking people to services, I believe we have an important part to play in helping service users to deal with the impact of trauma, deprivation and discrimination so that they can begin the work of reparation – to 'mend' themselves and to shape their lives in ways that meet their hopes for the future and the hopes that they share with others that they care for and love. Social work is well positioned to do this because of our history of working with people who are disadvantaged, and also because of our longstanding commitment to social justice. People at the edge of life rarely have a voice, but I believe it is important for us to speak up for this group and to reveal those 'social ills' that limit people's choices and life chances.

Here I am reminded of Peter Marris's (1996a) work, *The Politics of Uncertainty*. Marris argues that one of the consequences of living in an uncertain world is that those of us who have a degree of privilege – money or status – can choose a range of options to protect ourselves against future uncertainty. Having acquired these options, we can then protect ourselves further through our ability to buy a degree of certainty and predictability and a degree of control over an uncertain landscape. For example, we can buy insurance to protect us from the impact of events that might cause disruption or loss. People who are at the bottom of this hierarchy, whose choices and freedom are already narrowed, find their actions and options constrained even further by the way we use our power to protect against uncertainty. As a result, 'we often thrust a greater burden of uncertainty on to those who are weaker than ourselves' (Marris 1996b: 195). This leads Marris to conclude:

> For the most disadvantaged, everything is unstable – employment, family, shelter, neighbourhood, the intervention of social services –

and this, as I want to show, is a consequence of the way others, more fortunate, have been able to manoeuvre, displacing a cumulative burden of uncertainty onto the weakest. Conversely, great equality of power involves not only a redistribution of assets but greater reciprocity in relationships, articulating collaborative strategies of choice within a framework of mutual commitments.

(Marris 1996a: 88)

Sometimes the mending that is required involves working creatively with the impact of unwantedness, a task that might be described as therapeutic social work, or simply as 'cure' (Howe 1994). Children and adults who are unwanted are some of the most vulnerable individuals in society. They risk being abused in a range of different ways, often living in harsh worlds, with no one to protect them. Adults who have grown up in an environment where they were not wanted often carry with them a deep sense of 'not counting'. This can seriously inhibit their ability to create the life that they want to live and to embrace the opportunities that they deserve to have. I hope that the direction that social work takes with the development of the new degree allows this creative work to happen. As an example of the kind of work we can engage in with appropriate training, support and supervision, I would like to end this book by describing my experiences of working with Michael.

Michael

In telling this story, my aim is to describe how we might work more creatively with the suffering and anguish that is brought to us for 'mending'. I once worked with a 13-year-old, Michael, whose behaviour was so negative and self-destructive that it was almost impossible not to feel rejected by this individual. We were 'forced together' in a residential setting, and whenever we had to meet, he refused to speak, preferring to use his body language to communicate. He would arrive late and then need to go to the toilet, where he would linger until I came to find him. Once inside the room, he would refuse to sit down, but instead spent the time shuffling from one foot to the other, with his arms crossed and his eyes cast to the ceiling. His two consistent comments beyond ignoring me could be summarized as 'don't know' and 'can I go now?' One regular point of contact was police stations, as we waited for hours while his latest episode of damaging and dangerous behaviour was recorded and processed.

Over a period of months, Michael gradually began to reveal why his behaviour was so dismissive. It came from a profound belief in the pointlessness and futility of his life. He appeared not to care whether he lived or died: life had no meaning for him. The immediate causes for this terrible despair were many, but for Michael they stemmed from the fact that throughout his young life he felt that he had never been wanted. Michael had spent most of his life in care, having been rejected and abandoned by his parents. He managed to deal with this rejection by blaming social services for 'taking him away' from his parents, thereby protecting himself from his sense of unwantedness. Then one day, the story bubble burst when his mother, in a heated argument, said she had tried to abort him when she was pregnant and that she wished he had never been born. From that time, the meaning he ascribed to his experience was not only that he was not wanted but also that he would never be wanted. From this place, he felt there was no point in living. No one could replace the mother he wanted to love him, and his clearest message to those who came into his life was that he did not want them. I believe that not being wanted is one of the most devastating experiences that any human being can be asked to endure and one that is very difficult to overcome (Jacobs 1995). This was certainly the case for Michael.

My approach to this terrible dilemma was to add another element to the story of his conception and creation. I added the fact that providence wanted him. I did this by reminding Michael that a baby is not always made every time two people make love. Therefore, for conception to occur, there have to be three elements present: the mother and father, and that third element – providence (had Michael been religious, I may have described God as the third element). Even if his parents did not want him, the fact that he was conceived and born meant that providence wanted him; that providence had set aside a place for him on this earth and that he had a right to take up this place.

Fortunately, I had the opportunity to work with Michael over a long period. This allowed us to address, slowly and carefully, his feelings of unwantedness. In time, we worked together to create a new and different meaning about his conception based on the idea of a 'providence parent', whom he nicknamed 'PP' to protect himself from outside intrusion or ridicule. In the story he created, he made himself an only child and described different imaginary exchanges with his PP. He imagined doing things and saying things to his PP. Sometimes his PP was his companion, someone to talk to when he felt lonely and uncared for. Other times his PP acted as a source of encouragement or chastisement. He regularly switched the gender of his PP, depending on what role he wanted them to play. Interestingly, his imaginary parents were quite stereotypical in terms of the gendered roles he gave them.

I do not think that it would have been possible for this young man to embrace this imaginary realm had he not had some hope and trust that we could build on. This suggests that he had experienced some degree of stability and security in his early life (Winnicott 1971: 1–25; Winnicott 1986: 150–66; Dockar-Drysdale 1990). It always felt that he was building on some positive experiences. Maybe some hardship or adversity interfered with his parents' ability to care for him: it was never clear why the family break-up occurred. Whichever way, he managed to create an imaginary parent who wanted him and who gave his life a sense of meaning and purpose. I think that life will always be a struggle for Michael but I hope he continues to feel less alone in that struggle.

APPENDIX 1

Behaviourist approaches

Description/definition

Based on the work of Pavlov (1927), Skinner (1938) and Watson (1970), behaviourism focuses on behaviour itself, as opposed to analysing the underlying conflicts or causes. Thus feelings of distress or neurosis come about through *faulty conditioning*; what needs to be changed, therefore, is this *maladaptive behaviour*. Later writers such as Bandura (1977) stressed the importance of *social learning theory*: that behaviours are learned and, therefore, can be unlearned. There are different types of behaviourism, such as *radical behaviourism,* which 'is the philosophy related to applied behaviour analysis', the latter involving 'the application of findings from the experimental analysis of behaviour to concerns of social importance' (Gambrill 1995: 48).

This approach stresses the importance of observable, testable, measurable, reproducible and objective responses and behaviours: 'we are as we behave'. As a therapy, it is considered to be particularly effective in relation to fears and phobias, as well as for obsessional states or compulsive behaviours. However, 'behaviour therapists vary tremendously in both theory and practice ... that denies reduction to a few techniques' (Prochaska and Norcross 2003: 280). In relation to social work, many of the influential writers in this field originally focused on the importance of behavioural approaches within social work (Gambrill 1985, 1995; Hudson and Macdonald 1986; Sheldon 1982). Some now promote cognitive-behavioural approaches (Sheldon 2000: 65–83) but continue to emphasize a more behavioural than cognitive orientation, hence their inclusion in this section. Gambrill (1995) highlights the clarity of a behaviourist approach, as follows.

Gambrill's 'indicators of behavioral practice'

A   What will be found
1   A focus on altering complaints of concern to clients and significant others
2   Translation of complaints into specific behaviors (including thoughts and feelings) that if altered would remove complaints
3   Reliance on basic behavioral principles and related learning theory to guide assessment and intervention
4   Descriptive analysis of problems and related circumstances based on

observation (i.e. clear description of problem-related behaviors and related setting events, antecedents, and consequences)

5 Functional analysis: identification of factors that influence problem-related behaviors by rearranging environmental factors and observing the effects

6 Identification of client assets that can be put to good use in attaining desired outcomes

7 Involvement of significant others

8 Selection of intervention programs based on what research suggests is effective and what clients find acceptable

9 Ongoing evaluation of progress using both subjective and objective measures; comparison of data gathered during intervention with baseline data when feasible

10 Clear description of assessment, intervention, and evaluation methods

11 A concern for social validity: (i.e. outcomes attained are valued by clients and significant others; procedures used are acceptable to clients)

12 Inclusion of procedures designed to enhance generalization and maintenance of positive gains.

B What will not be found

1 Appeals to thoughts or feelings as sole causes of behavior

2 Appeals to personality dispositions as sole causes of behavior

3 Use of uninformative diagnostic labels (they provide neither information about problem-related causes nor guidelines for selecting intervention plans)

4 Reliance on self-report alone for assessment, evaluation, or both

5 Vague statements of outcome, problems, or progress indicators

6 Claims of success based on questionable criteria such as testimonials, and anecdotal experience.

(Gambrill 1995: 462)

Key terms

Behaviourist approaches primarily involve *behaviour modification techniques,* that is, a method of assessing and altering behaviour based on the methods of applied behaviour analysis. Many techniques are used in this process, although used differently by therapists. For example, the importance assigned to the therapeutic relationship can vary widely. Some of the key terms used in behavioural approaches/therapy include: classical conditioning, operant conditioning (OC), conditioned stimulus (CS), conditioned response (CR), unconditioned stimulus (US), unconditional response (UR). Some of the main behavioural techniques used include: assertiveness training, aversion therapy/conditioning, extinction, modelling, reinforcement, social skills training, and systematic desensitization (SD). For a fuller account of the meaning and use of these terms, see Sheldon (1995).

Advantages

• Behavioural techniques are relatively easy to understand, to learn and to use effectively and can be used alongside other interventions and practice approaches.

• Some techniques can be enormously successful, such as social skills or assertiveness training, and highly adaptable across different service user/carer groups and different social work settings.

- The scientific foundation of this approach and the use of techniques in a systematic way, plus the importance given to baseline data focusing on target behaviours, means that the effectiveness of this approach can be demonstrated empirically.
- Behaviourist techniques and approaches are widely used in multidisciplinary contexts, such as health and education, making access to additional training comparatively easy.

Limitations

- The terminology used in behavioural approaches can be experienced as mechanistic and uncaring, and unappealing as a therapy and as a practice approach.
- It is a directive approach with relatively high expectations of service users and their commitment to the treatment programme.
- Its focus on modifying certain behaviours, and not underlying causes, can mean that more complex and intractable problems are not addressed.
- The addition of new behavioural techniques, and different orientations among therapists, can make it difficult for service users and carers ('patients'), and practitioners as 'purchasers of care', to distinguish which therapist to choose and to assess practice competence.

REFERENCES

Bandura, A. (1977) *Social Learning Theory*. Englewood Cliffs, NJ: Prentice-Hall.

Gambrill, E. D. (1985) Behavioral approach, in J. B. Turner (ed.) *Encyclopedia of Social Work*, 18th edn. Vol. 1. Washington, DC: National Association of Social Workers.

Gambrill, E. D. (1995) Behavioural theory, in R. L. Edwards (ed.) *Encyclopedia of Social Work*, 19th edn. Vol. 1. pp. 323–34. Washington, DC: National Association of Social Workers.

Hudson, B. L. and MacDonald, G. (1986) *Behavioural Social Work: An Introduction*. London: Macmillan.

Pavlov, I. P. (1927) *Conditional Reflexes*. London: Oxford University Press.

Prochaska, J. O. and Norcross, J. C. (2003) *Systems of Psychotherapy: A Transtheoretical Analysis*. Pacific Grove, CA: Brooks/Cole.

Sheldon, B. (1982) *Behaviour Modification: Theory, Practice and Philosophy*. London: Tavistock.

Skinner, B. F. (1938) *The Behavior of Organisms: An Experimental Analysis*. New York: Appleton-Century-Crofts.

Skinner, B. F. (1974) *About Behaviourism*. London: Jonathan Cape.

Watson, J. B. (1970) *Behaviourism*. New York: Norton.

APPENDIX 2

Cognitive approaches

Description/definition

Alfred Adler is said to have been the major influence in the development of cognitive therapeutic approaches. These include different therapies, such as reality therapy, existential social work, cognitive analytic therapy (CAT), Beck's 'Cognitive Therapy' and Ellis's Rational Emotive Behaviour Therapy (REBT). 'Whereas behaviour therapy assumes that faulty learning is at the core of problem behaviours and emotions, cognitive therapies assume that the culprit is *faulty thinking*' (Hockenbury and Hockenbury 2002: 636). Cognitive therapies argue that human emotions and behaviours are largely formed on the basis of what people think, imagine or believe – by their cognitive processes. What people think or believe about these specific events can lead to difficulties: cognitive approaches work to help people to change their cognitive thought processes.

It is important to note that 'the lines separating cognitive, cognitive-behavioural, and some behaviour therapies are blurring ... contemporary behaviour therapy is progressively becoming more cognitive, and practically every cognitive therapy incorporates elements of behaviour therapy' (Prochaska and Norcross 2003: 334). In 1993, Ellis added the word 'behaviour' to Rational Emotive Therapy because he believed that behaviour was receiving too little focus.

Key terms and techniques of cognitive approaches

Cognitions describe the 'mental activities involved in acquiring, retaining, and using knowledge' (Hockenbury and Hockenbury 2002: 280). Thus cognitive therapies attempt to identify and challenge specific instances and general patterns of distorted thinking or unrealistic beliefs (Payne 1997: 115). In this task, different terms are used to describe irrational thoughts, feelings and beliefs, such as cognitive dissonance, cognitive dysfunction and cognitive map, and a range of techniques are adopted, such as cognitive restructuring, where the focus is to encourage individuals to think differently about situations they find troubling. Albert Ellis (1977, 1997) and Aaron Beck (1976) are profoundly influential in this field. The similarities and differences in their approaches are as follows:

Ellis

Source of Problems (REBT)	Treatment Techniques	Goals of Therapy
Irrational beliefs	Very distinctive: identify, dispute, and challenge irrational beliefs	Surrender of logically irrational beliefs and absolute demands

Beck

Source of problems (Cognitive Therapy)		
Unrealistic, distorted perceptions and interpretations of events due to cognitive biases	Directive collaboration: teach client to monitor automatic thoughts; test accuracy of conclusions; correct distorted thinking and perception	Accurate and realistic perceptions of self, others, and external events

(Hockenbury and Hockenbury 2002: 640)

Ellis's ABCDE theory of emotions

A 'cornerstone' (Dryden 1999: 7) of REBT, and an intervention that is accessible to both service users/carers and practitioners, is the ABCDE theory of emotions. Some writers tend to focus on the ABC section only (Dryden 1999), but Ellis considers all stages to be important to avoid 'backsliding' or the possibility of relapse (Ellis *et al.* 1997: 67):

A **Activating event or situation**
(Case example: Mr Radley's wife died suddenly)

B **Beliefs (self-defeating beliefs)**
iB – irrational belief *(Had I called the doctor earlier, my wife would not have died. It's all my fault)*

C **Consequences (the emotional/behavioural consequences of these thoughts, feelings, beliefs)**
iC – irrational emotional/behavioural consequence *(I deserve to suffer for what I have done. I don't deserve to be helped)*

D **Disputation**
Through exploring the implicit thoughts and dysfunctional emotions and/or behaviours with the guidance of the practitioner, the service user or carer is taught to replace irrational beliefs (iB) with rational beliefs (rB)
rB – rational belief *(I don't have the power to give life to another human being, or to take life away)*

E **Evaluation (new effective approach to the problem)**
The process of disputation (D) should produce an evaluation of the activating (A) event or situation and the emotional/behavioural consequences (C) that this event produced

Full sequence   A → B → C → D → E

Advantages

- Cognitive approaches are time-limited (1–20 weeks), relatively low in cost and applicable across a range of different emotional problems.
- The directive, active, focused and 'no-nonsense' nature of the approach makes it possible to address distorted perceptions or unrealistic beliefs within a short

time-span. The use of homework places the 'client' at the centre of the recovery process.

- Beck's work has been shown to be particularly effective in the field of depression. His instruments, such as the Beck Depression Inventory (Beck and Steer 1987) and Beck Anxiety Inventory are widely used in health contexts.
- The ABCDE theory of emotions is an intervention that can be taught and learned easily. The challenging yet collaborative feature of this approach can be important in situations where people's thoughts, feelings and beliefs are hindering the opportunity to move forward.

Limitations

- This highly individualized approach is not appropriate for some people or situations. Some emotions may not be irrational but an appropriate and natural response to events such as bereavement, violent attacks or the hardships of discrimination and oppression.
- The language used within cognitive therapies, such as distorted cognitions, dysfunctional, irrational and immature behaviour, can be off-putting both to service users/carers and to practitioners.
- Individuals who are more articulate and in touch with their thoughts, feelings and beliefs are likely to be able to use this approach more effectively. More complex or enduring emotional problems, such as those associated with severe depression or schizophrenia, are found to be less successful.
- Although Ellis is said to have published hundred of articles, there is very little data on outcome studies (Prochaska and Norcross 2003: 364). Beck's approach has more data but limited analysis on how people develop 'distorted cognitions'.

REFERENCES

Barker, R. L. (2003) *The Social Work Dictionary*, 5th edn. Washington, DC: NASW Press.
Beck, A. (1976) *Cognitive Therapy and the Emotional Disorders*. New York: International University Press.
Beck, A. and Steer, R. (1987) *Beck Depression Inventory: Manual*. San Antonia: Psychological Corporation.
Dryden, W. (1999) *Rational Emotive Behavioural Counselling in Action*, 2nd edn. London: Sage.
Ellis, A. (1977) The basic clinical theory of rational-emotive therapy, in A. A. Ellis and R. Greiger (eds) *Handbook of Rational-Emotive Therapy*, Vol. 1. New York: Springer.
Ellis, A., Gordon, J., Neenan, M. and Palmer, S. (1997) *Stress Counselling: A Rational Emotive Behaviour Approach*. London: Cassell.
Hockenbury, D. H. and Hockenbury, S. E. (2002) *Psychology*, 3rd edn. New York: Worth Publication.
Payne, M. (1997) *Modern Social Work Theory: A Critical Introduction*, 2nd edn. Basingstoke: Macmillan.
Prochaska, J. O. and Norcross, J. C. (2003) *Systems of Psychotherapy: A Transtheoretical Analysis*. Pacific Grove, CA: Brooks/Cole.
Trower, P., Casey, A. and Dryden, W. (1988) *Cognitive-Behavioural Counselling in Action*. London: Sage.

APPENDIX 3

Crisis intervention

Description/definition

For understandable reasons, crisis intervention is often confused with crisis work. As a result, its distinct theoretical and practice framework has tended to become obscured, and it is rarely used in UK social work today because of its heavy resource and cost implications. However, similar, intense forms of support continue to be developed, such as assertive outreach used in the field of mental health (McCulloch 2000: 18–19). In the USA, crisis intervention is used with older people with dementia, people who are bereaved, terminally ill or suicidal, in the aftermath of a disaster and in cases involving domestic violence (Chui and Ford 2000: 41). Also, as a time-limited approach, it shares some similarities with brief therapy and other types of focused approaches. However, these do not share the same theoretical framework, a feature that distinguishes crisis intervention as a practice approach (Payne 1997: 95–104; Roberts 1990).

In different cultures, *crisis* can be seen as:

- a hazardous event (UK)
- decision-making (Greek)
- danger and opportunity (Chinese), represented in two Chinese characters, *Wei* and *Chi* (Chui and Ford 2000: 42).

Crisis can be conceptualized in a range of different ways and is sometimes linked to the concept of stress. In western culture, the term is often used to suggest a negative or fraught experience. In the USA, the development of crisis intervention as an approach was led by Caplan (1964), Lindemann (1965), Parad (1965) and Rapoport (1967). Crisis is defined as a 'breakdown of *homeostasis* or psychological equilibrium' (O'Hagan 2000: 79), meaning that for a time an individual is thrown into 'an upset in a steady state' (Rapoport 1967). As a result, people can find themselves unable to benefit from their normal methods of coping. 'What happens in a crisis is that our habitual strengths and ways of coping do not work; we fail to adjust either because the situation is new to us, or it has not been anticipated, or a series of events become too overwhelming' (Coulshed and Orme 1998: 96). Crises do not have to be urgent situations: an admission to hospital could lead to a crisis. Hence the importance of individual reactions to external events.

Key concepts

Caplan (1964) described a three-stage model, based on the view that people act as self-regulating systems to try to maintain an internal state of equilibrium. These phases of a crisis are:

- *impact* – recognizing a threat to the equilibrium;
- *recoil* – attempting to restore the equilibrium but being unable to do so, leaving the individual physically or psychologically exhausted, defeated and showing signs of stress or crisis; and
- *adjustment/adaptation* or *breakdown* – where the individual begins to move through to a higher level of functioning or to a lower level.

The approach is based on the perspective that crises are time-limited and usually last no longer than six weeks. It draws from psychoanalytic theory, particularly ego psychology, and emphasizes that people's capacity to deal with problems – to be able to return to a steady state from an upset in the steady state – is based on three factors:

- people's internal psychological strengths and weaknesses (ego strength)
- the nature of the problem faced
- the quality of help provided.

Advantages

- As a time-limited (1–6 weeks) and focused approach, it can be considered highly effective in terms of effort and resources.
- It can be adapted to practice in a number of different contexts. People who are helped and supported to develop new adaptive ways of coping can sometimes function at a higher level, such as people who work through bereavement.
- Its sound theoretical and practice framework provides an analysis of both internal and external factors, providing a way to understand the link between internal crises and external changes.
- It is relevant and useful across a range of short-term crises, particularly experiences of bereavement and loss, depression, traumatic experiences such as accidents and other situations where people feel 'thrown' and unable to cope.

Limitations

- The term 'crisis intervention' is confusing because the words crisis and intervention are regularly used in social work but in different ways. As a result, crisis intervention is often used by practitioners to describe general emergencies or immediate responses, or to describe work that focuses on people living in a chronic state of crisis.
- Specific training is required for this approach to be used effectively. Such training is not easily available in the UK.
- It may not be possible, because of limited resources, funding or time, to assemble all the elements necessary for positive change to occur. As a result, unless fundamental changes are introduced, it is unlikely that this approach will be seen as a viable option, particularly under funded statutory social work contexts.

- It can involve workers being highly intrusive and directive, which can raise important ethical issues, particularly in terms of the notion of empowerment and service users' rights to be at the centre of the decision-making process.

REFERENCES

Caplan, G. (1964) *Principles of Preventative Psychiatry*. New York: Basic Books.

Chui, W. H. and Ford, D. (2000) Crisis intervention as common practice, in P. Stepney and D. Ford (eds) *Social Work Models, Methods and Theories*. Lyme Regis: Russell House.

Coulshed, V. and Orme, J. (1998) *Social Work Practice: An Introduction*, 3rd edn. Basingstoke: Macmillan/BASW.

Lindemann, E. (1965) Symptomatology and management of acute grief, in H. J. Parad (ed.) *Crisis Intervention: Selected Readings*. New York: Family Service Association of America.

McCulloch, A. (2000) Assertive outreach, in M. Davies (ed.) *Blackwell Encyclopaedia of Social Work*. Oxford: Oxford University Press.

O'Hagan, K. (2000) Crisis intervention, in M. Davies (ed.) *Blackwell Encyclopaedia of Social Work*. Oxford: Oxford University Press.

Parad, H. J. (1965) *Crisis Intervention: Selected Readings*. New York: Family Service Association of America.

Payne, M. (1997) *Modern Social Work Theory*, 2nd edn. Basingstoke: Macmillan.

Rapoport, L. (1967) Crisis-orientated short term casework, *Social Services Review*, 41: 31–44.

Roberts, A. R. (1990) *Crisis Intervention Handbook: Assessment, Treatment and Research*. Belmont, CA: Wadsworth.

APPENDIX 4

Person/client-centred approaches

Description/definition

A person/client-centred approach is usually attributed to the work of Carl Rogers. It is mainly associated with counselling rather than social work and is best used in this context (Thorne 2002: 175). Rogers based his work on the humanist belief that human beings have an innate motivation to grow, develop and change, i.e. to self-actualize (see Maslow's Triangle in Chapter 3):

> One of the most revolutionary concepts to grow out of our clinical experience is the growing recognition that the innermost core of a man's [*sic*] nature, the deepest layers of his personality, the base of his 'animal nature' is positive in nature – is basically socialized, forward-moving, rational and realistic.
>
> (Rogers 1961: 90–1)

Key concepts

In order for people to move forward, Rogers argued that they need a non-directive stance, where their thoughts, feelings and actions are not subject to advice, interpretation, criticism, confrontation or challenge beyond encouraging people to clarify what they see to be happening. To steer the counselling session or discussion in a particular direction would be seen to contravene a person's innate ability to be his/her own change agent. This non-directive, non-judgemental, accepting, warm and caring stance forms part of the 'facilitative conditions', which Rogers summarized as involving empathy, unconditional positive regard and congruence:

- *empathy* – caring, warmth. 'It means entering the private perceptual world of the other and becoming thoroughly at home in it' (Rogers 1975: 2);
- *unconditional positive regard* – respect, non-possessive warmth, acceptance and non-judgementality even if the social worker personally does not approve of or condone the person's actions;
- *congruence* – genuineness, authenticity, acting in a human way as a real person and not someone hiding behind a mask or professional role.

This is one of the most popular approaches among practitioners (Marsh and

Triseliotis 1996: 52) because of its hopefulness, accessibility and flexibility. It has also given rise to other developments and research (Truax and Carkhuff 1967). However, the distinct features of this approach can be misunderstood or denied. For example, treating people with warmth, respect and dignity – or 'centring' our focus on service users and their concerns – is sometimes incorrectly described as adopting a person/client-centred approach. This denies the distinct features of this approach, which was designed for counselling. Other difficulties also emerge for practitioners, such as the difference between acceptance and approval. It can be difficult to reconcile cruel behaviour with 'unconditional positive regard'.

Rogers's 'seven stages of progress'

Rogers provides a framework for understanding personal change in terms of seven 'stages of progress' (Rogers 1961: 132–59). Within this, his 'necessary and sufficient conditions of therapeutic personality change' (1957) are located in the therapeutic relationship between the client and therapist, with the process of change leading not only to changes in behaviour but also to a fundamental shift in the way individuals relate to themselves. The changes identified involve moving away from the past and blaming external causes (parents, employers, school, life's adversity) to a more balanced perspective, embracing greater personal responsibility. McLeod summarizes these seven stages:

1 *Communication is about external events.* Feelings and personal meanings are not 'owned'. Close relationships are construed as dangerous. Rigidity in thinking. Impersonal, detached. Does not use first-person pronouns.
2 *Expression begins to flow more freely in respect of non-self topics.* Feelings may be described but not owned. Intellectualization. Describes behaviour rather than inner feelings. May show more interest and participation in therapy.
3 *Describes personal reactions to external events.* Limited amount of self-description. Communication about past feelings. Beginning to recognize contradictions in experience.
4 *Descriptions of feelings and personal experiences.* Beginning to experience current feelings, but fear and distrust of this when it happens. The 'inner life' is presented and listed or described, but not purposefully explored.
5 *Present feelings are expressed.* Increasing ownership of feelings. More exactness in the differentiation of feelings and meanings. Intentional exploration of problems in a personal way, based on processing of feelings rather than reasoning.
6 *Sense of an 'inner referent, or flow of feeling which has a life of its own.* 'Physiological loosening', such as moistness in the eyes, tears, sighs or muscular relaxation, accompanies the open expression of feelings. Speaks in present tense or offers vivid representation of past.
7 *A series of felt senses connecting the different aspects of an issue.* Basic trust in own inner processes. Feelings experienced with immediacy and richness of detail. Speaks fluently in present tense.

(McLeod 2003: 178)

Advantages

- It is an accessible approach that is easy to understand (but not always easy to achieve).
- All forms of experience are valued. People are encouraged to find their own way in their own time.
- It resists the temptation to criticize or to see events in a negative light.
- It encourages the development of an equal, non-authoritarian relationship where both service user and social worker work together to establish a significant and meaningful relationship.

Limitations

- It is difficult for practitioners to demonstrate empathy, unconditional positive regard and congruence in their everyday work, unless in a counselling role. This means this approach has to be adapted: this may be inconsistent with its philosophy.
- This approach involves considerable motivation and cooperation on the part of service users, making it difficult to use when working with people who are resistant, 'involuntary', destructive or dangerous.
- Its focus on individual change tends to ignore the importance of changing external constraints, including social structures that are discriminatory or oppressive.
- There are doubts whether this approach can be used with problems that are severe or where the individual does not have the capacity for reflection (McLeod 2003: 90).

REFERENCES

Marsh, P. and Triseliotis, J. (1996) *Ready to Practise? Social Workers and Probation Officers: Their Training and First Year at Work*. Aldershot: Avebury.

McLeod, J. (2003) *An Introduction to Counselling*, 3rd edn. Buckingham: Open University.

Mearns, D. and Thorne, D. (2000) *Person-centred Therapy Today: New Frontiers in Theory and Practice*. London: Sage.

Rogers, C. R. (1951) *Client-Centred Therapy*. Boston: Houghton Mifflin.

Rogers, C. R. (1957) The necessary and sufficient conditions of therapeutic personality change, *Journal of Consulting Psychology*, 21: 95–103.

Rogers, C. R. (1961) *On Becoming a Person*. Boston: Houghton Mifflin.

Rogers, C. R. (1975) Empathic: an unappreciated way of being, *Counseling Psychologist*, 5: 2–10.

Thorne, B. (2002) Person-centred counselling, in M. Davies (ed.) *The Blackwell Companion to Social Work*, 2nd edn. Oxford: Blackwell.

Truax, C. B. and Carkhuff, R. R. (1967) *Towards Effective Counselling and Psychotherapy*. Chicago: Aldine.

APPENDIX 5

Psychosocial approaches

Description/definition

Psychosocial approaches within social work draw on psychoanalytic theory and practice derived from the work of Freud and his followers. Florence Hollis, an important writer in this field, summarizes the main elements of the psychosocial approach as follows:

> It is ... an attempt to mobilize the strengths of the personality and the resources of the environment at strategic points to improve the opportunities available to the individual and to develop more effective personal and interpersonal functioning.
>
> (Hollis 1977: 1308)

This definition stresses the importance of both internal and external factors in relation to people's capacity to cope with the everyday stresses of modern living. As such, it contradicts the myth that psychosocial approaches are only concerned with people's inner, emotional life: the external world is also an important area of analysis and concern. It is important to note that psychoanalysis has been influential in the development of a range of different theories and therapeutic approaches that are relevant to social work, such as: ego psychology; crisis intervention; attachment theory; Erikson's conceptualization of the 'eight stages of man'; group therapy, particularly group analysis; and psychoanalytic perspectives developed in relation to systems theory, ecological perspectives, and family therapy. In the past, a psychosocial approach has been linked to the term casework or 'social casework' (Howe 2002b: 171). At the heart of casework – and a psychosocial approach – lies the relationship created between the service user/carer and social worker. 'The social worker shows human concern for clients but disciplines his or her use of the relationship in keeping with the assessment of the client's needs and interventive goals' (Goldstein 1995: 1950).

Key concepts

What differentiates psychoanalytic perspectives from other schools of thought is the concept of the unconscious. Other concepts are also central, the most relevant for social work being the defences (or defence mechanism), resistance, repression, regression, splitting, transference and countertransference (Brearley 1991: 50–5), some of which are defined below:

The unconscious

Central to the concepts of transference and resistance is the notion of the unconscious that is 'mental processes of which the subject is not aware'.

(Rycroft 1968: 172)

Defence mechanism

Defences are strategies which a person employs either knowingly or unknowingly, in order to avoid facing aspects of the self which are felt to be threatening.

(Jacobs 1999: 98)

Transference

Transference is a description of the way that people transfer 'past emotions to the present situation. Hence, understanding what is happening in the relationship between the worker and ... client is of the utmost importance. Transference may not only distort the therapeutic relationship, but it may also cause the client to confuse other relationships as older feelings are transferred to new, unconnected situations. ... Transference is said to be taking place when there is a repetition of the past which is inappropriate to the present. To the extent that a person continues to react to the new relationship as if it was an old experience, he [sic] is dealing with the real situation inappropriately'.

(Howe 1987: 75–6)

Transference occurs in every human relationship in that it involves passing on or 'transferring' an emotion or pattern of relating from one person to another person or object. Feelings of mistrust, dislike, love and care can be in response to the practitioner's particular qualities but can also be a reflection of earlier feelings, fears and anxieties being activated. In this situation, it is important not to collude or to allow ourselves to be manipulated by these positive and negative feelings, but instead to help the individual to understand what these feelings represent and what we have become for them. For example, a female pupil who is refusing to attend school may experience her social worker as blaming her, or as judging her critically, when the social worker has neither felt nor indicated such unsympathetic reactions. The practitioner might pick up these feelings through her recognition of countertransference reactions.

Advantages

- Concepts such as the unconscious, transference, countertransference, attachment and emotional development are important in helping us to understand human behaviour – it is 'the "bread and butter" of our job' (Coulshed and Orme 1998: 141).
- It is a theory that can explain all human behaviour, including complex, difficult behaviour and what meaning individuals place on events.

- Its recognition of good and bad elements within human nature and neutrality about emotions encourages understanding and avoids the danger of judging people.
- It has inspired the development of many other theories and practices and continues to do so, including transactional analysis, crisis intervention and approaches based on ego psychology.

Limitations

- Because of its links with psychoanalysis, a psychosocial approach can be seen as elitist, potentially oppressive and lacking clear time boundaries. As a theory, its concepts can be difficult to grasp.
- It can create an unhealthy dependency and power imbalance in the therapist–patient relationship.
- External factors, such as social causes and cultural influences, can sometimes be neglected. Also, a political perspective is often lacking, leading to the criticism that practitioners working from psychosocial approach are out of touch with 'bread and butter' issues.
- The benefits and outcomes of a psychosocial approach can be hard to evaluate in terms of effectiveness because of the emphasis placed on quality of life issues, such as the capacity to cope and to relate to oneself and to others in ways that feel more personally satisfying.

REFERENCES

Barker, R. L. (2003) *The Social Work Dictionary*, 5th edn. Washington, DC: National Association of Social Work Press.

Brearley, J. (1991) A Psychoanalytic approach to social work, in J. Lishman (ed.) *Handbook of Theory for Practice Teachers*. London: Jessica Kingsley.

Coulshed, V. and Orme, J. (1998) *Social Work Practice: An Introduction*, 3rd edn. Basingstoke: Macmillan/BASW.

Goldstein, E. G. (1995) Psychosocial approach, in R. L. Edwards (ed.) *Encyclopedia of Social Work*, 1948–1954. Washington: National Association of Social Workers.

Hollis, F. (1977) Social casework: the psychosocial approach, *Encyclopedia of Social Work*, 17th edn, pp. 1300–07. Washington: National Association of Social Workers.

Howe, D. (1987) *An Introduction to Social Work Theory*. Aldershot: Gower.

Howe, D. (2002b) Psychosocial work, in R. Adams, L. Dominelli and M. Payne (eds) *Social Work: Themes, Issues and Critical Debates*, 2nd edn. Basingstoke: Macmillan.

Jacobs, M. (1999) *Psychodynamic Counselling in Action, 2nd edn.* London: Sage.

Kenny, L. and Kenny, B. (2000) Psychodynamic theory in social work: a view from practice, in P. Stepney and D. Ford (eds) *Social Work Models, Methods and Theories*. Lyme Regis: Russell House.

Nathan, J. (2002) Psychoanalytic theory, in M. Davies (ed.) *The Blackwell Companion to Social Work*, 2nd edn. Oxford: Blackwell.

Rycroft, C. (1968) *A Critical Dictionary of Psychoanalysis*. Harmondsworth: Penguin.

APPENDIX 6

Task-centred approaches

Description/definition

Task-centred practice is a technology for alleviating specific target problems perceived by clients, that is, particular problems clients recognize, understand, acknowledge, and want to attend to.... Task-centred practice has a particular way of unfolding. It consists of a start-up and four sequential but overlapping steps. The regularity of the steps is important because orderly, systematic processes are most likely to result in good outcomes. Under the pressure of problem-solving, these steps tend to occur out of sequence; nonetheless, the practitioner should return to the normal procedure as soon as possible.

(Epstein and Brown 2002: 93)

Basic map in task-centred work

Start up: Client referred by an agency

or   Client applies independently and voluntarily

↓

Step 1:   Client target problems identified (three maximum)

↓

Step 2:   Contract: plans, target problem priorities, goals,
practitioner tasks, duration, schedule and
participants

↓

Step 3:   Problem-solving

↓

Step 4:   Termination

(Epstein and Brown 2002: 93)

All approaches involve undertaking a range of activities, or tasks, but it is argued that unlike other practice approaches, task-centred practice does not have a distinct theoretical base (Marsh 2002: 106) and, therefore, should not be referred to as an 'approach', but task-centred work or practice. However, according to Doel, it does have a knowledge base: 'Task-centred practice is a member of the family of problem-solving methods and its knowledge base derives largely from a combination of systems and learning theory' (2000: 344). Also, unlike other practice approaches, task-centred practice was 'developed within and for social work, originating from research into social work practice' (Ford and Postle 2000: 52). Its roots derive from the research undertaken by Reid and Shyne (1969) and Reid and Epstein (1972) who found that short-term interventions were as effective as long-term work (Doel 2002: 191). These findings challenged the ideas dominant at that time, particularly the principles that underpinned long-term work. 'In doing this, it recognized that the person with the problems also had the means to resolve them, and that social work intervention should become more of a partnership. In this way, task-centred casework can be seen to be at the beginning of attempts to empower users of social work services' (Coulshed and Orme 1998: 115).

This strategy involves working in close collaboration with service users, and others, in order to agree specific goals or outcomes and to identify what steps, task or 'building blocks' need to be undertaken to achieve those goals. Focusing on tasks in this way is one of the best ways we have of identifying whether an individual is motivated and whether s/he has the necessary skills, knowledge, confidence and resources to undertake and complete a particular task or to achieve a specific goal or outcome (Marsh and Doel 2005). This helps us to see what role we might need to play in this collaborative endeavour. This may involve teaching specific skills, such as how to make a telephone call, or providing vital information, such as where to go for help. It may also involve our taking responsibility for specific tasks appropriate to our professional role, such as liaising with agencies. At the heart of task-centred work lies the importance of utilizing, extending and consolidating service users' strengths and abilities to address key issues in ways that 'reflect the actual reality of the users' relationships and lives' (Marsh 2002: 110).

Advantages

- Tasks and goals are discreet and chosen because they are achievable. This enhances the likelihood of success and builds confidence because its focus is on enhancing people's capacities and strengths.
- Task-centred work is time-limited, usually spanning three months. Its outcomes and effectiveness are easy to evaluate and to research (Epstein and Brown 2002: 92; Ford and Postle 2000: 52).
- It is based on a person-centred approach and works on close collaboration between the practitioner and service user. The importance of service user self-determination is central to the decision-making process.
- Practitioners can learn this strategy relatively easily. It is also adaptable. For example, identifying target problems and specific tasks in this systematic way can be used as part of other practice approaches.

Limitations

- Despite claims to the contrary, this may be a difficult strategy to use when working with reluctant or 'involuntary' service users who may not be prepared to collaborate.
- More difficult, underlying problems may never be identified to be worked on. Also, the work can result in despondency and loss of confidence if tasks are not achieved.
- Some people are overwhelmed by the problems they face and may not have the energy to work on the tasks they have agreed to take on.
- There may be too much focus on service users adjusting to difficult situations: 'At worst – when a genuinely necessary resource is unavailable and no satisfactory substitute is possible – the practitioner should help the client relinquish the expectations that the resource can be obtained' (Epstein 1995: 321).

REFERENCES

Coulshed, V. and Orme, J. (1998) *Social Work Practice: An Introduction,* 3rd edn. Basingstoke: Macmillan/BASW.

Doel, M. and Marsh, P. (1992) *Task-Centred Social Work.* Aldershot: Ashgate.

Doel, M. (2002) Task-centred work, in R. Adams, L. Dominelli and M. Payne (eds) *Social Work: Themes, Issues and Critical Debates,* 2nd edn. Basingstoke: Macmillan.

Epstein, L. (1995) Brief Task-Centred Social Work, in R. L. Edwards (ed.) *Encyclopedia of Social Work,* 19th edn. Vol. 1. pp. 313–23. Washington: National Association of Social Workers.

Epstein, L. and Brown, L. B. (2002) *Brief Treatment and a New Look at the Task-Centred Approach.* London: Allyn and Bacon.

Ford, P. and Postle, K. (2000) Task-centred practice and care management, in P. Stepney and D. Ford (eds) *Social Work Models, Methods and Theories.* Lyme Regis: Russell House.

Marsh, P. (2002) Task-centred work, in M. Davies (ed.) *The Blackwell Companion to Social Work,* 2nd edn. Oxford: Blackwell.

Marsh, P. and Doel, M. (2005) *The Task-Centred Book.* London: Routledge/ Community Care.

Reid, W. J. and Epstein, L. (1972) *Task-Centred Casework.* New York: Columbia University Press.

Reid, W. J. and Shyne, A. (1969) *Brief and Extended Casework.* New York: Columbia University Press.

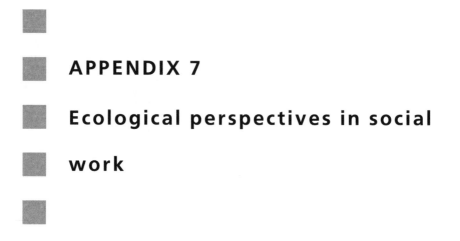

APPENDIX 7

Ecological perspectives in social work

Description/definition

An individual must be located within the context of the family and the groups/networks to which they belong, and of the wider communities in which they live. A wide range of environmental factors can affect people's functioning, such as the wider family, belonging to specific groups, network and communities, housing, employment, income, the family's/group's/community's integration and access to services. The importance of the interface between environmental considerations, and the influence of environmental factors on people's capacity to respond to social work intervention must be recognized and incorporated into any assessment and care plan.

(NOS 2002: 14 [Working Copy])

Key points

An ecological perspective draws heavily on systems theory – a framework that analyses the complex reciprocal connections and interrelationship that exists between elements that make up the whole *system*, and other mutually influencing factors in the social setting and wider environment, known as the *subsystems* (Preston-Shoot and Aqass 1990: 43). Changes in one system impact on other parts of the system, and vice versa. Systems theory has been particularly influential in family therapy, as well as ecological theory.

This perspective takes into account wider social support networks, analysing both formal and informal sources of support that may be available to the individual, family, group or community. Its appeal can be seen in several important documents, such as the *Framework for the Assessment of Children in Need and their Families* (Department of Health 2000: 11) and National Occupational Standards, and it is promoted in the area of health promotion (McLeroy *et al.* 1988). It is also influential in the USA in the field of human development (Bronfenbrenner 1979) and in the area of child abuse, where social support networks indicate a protective factor (Garbarino and Kostelny 1992). In the UK, it is being studied by the Labour government for its potential to promote behaviour change and greater personal responsibility (Halpern and Bates 2004). When applied to social work, different features are stressed. For example, Germain and Gitterman state: 'Ecological thinking is less concerned with cause and more concerned with the consequences of exchanges between A and B, and how to help modify maladaptive exchanges' (1995: 817). Ecological concepts are central to a 'life model' of social work practice, which focuses on:

1 people's strengths, their innate push toward health, continued growth, and release of potential;
2 modification of the environment, as needed, so that they sustain and promote well-being to the maximum degree possible; and
3 raising the level of person:environment [*sic*] fit for individuals, families, groups and communities.

(Germain and Gitterman 1995: 817)

Other writers in this field emphasize the radical potential of this perspective and the links that can be made between structural disadvantage and life chances (Jack and Jack 2000: 93). This is a focus that is consistent with practice perspectives and interventions that embrace an anti-oppressive and empowerment perspective.

Key concepts

- *micro-systems* – the context that individual's create around them
- *meso-system* – interactions between micro-systems, where interactions take place that influence individual development
- *exo-systems* – settings that do not directly influence individual development yet play a part, such as parental income
- *macro-system* – all other systems, such as the cultural and societal context or environment
- *social support* – range and quality of social support networks or systems that have important emotional and physical health benefits
- *social capital* – includes the relationships and exchanges between all members of a neighbourhood or a society. The level of social capital in a community has a significant impact on individual health and behaviour' (Jack and Jack 2000: 96)
- *collective efficacy* – seen as a measure of social capital. High levels of unemployment and poverty can undermine collective efficacy.

Advantages

- It is built on systems theory and, therefore, locates individuals in their wider context and provides the opportunity to incorporate a sociological perspective into an assessment.
- Its broader social and cultural analysis enables us to see the impact of government policy on everyday life – an important perspective for people living in poverty.
- It resists the temptation to individualize problems and solutions, or to see the complex way that different factors interweave.

- It encourages the development of an equal, non-authoritarian relationship where both service user and social worker work together to establish a significant and meaningful relationship.

Limitations

- Complex familial, social, cultural and environmental factors, and their interconnections, can be difficult to identify and to unravel, making it difficult to know where to intervene – if at all.
- Different perspectives adopted, which can range from support for radical change to those designed to reinforce the status quo, can lead to uncertainty.
- Most social workers have not had the training required to apply this perspective.
- Unless additional resources are made available, social workers attempting to apply this perspective can be set up to fail (Jack and Gill 2003).

REFERENCES

Bronfenbrenner, U. (1979) *The Ecology of Human Development.* Cambridge, MA: Harvard University Press.

Department of Health (2000) *Framework for the Assessment of Children in Need and their Families.* London: Department of Health.

Garbarino, J. and Kostelny, K. (1992) Child maltreatment as a community problem, *Child Abuse and Neglect,* 16: 455–64.

Germain, C. B. and Gitterman, A. (1995) Ecological Perspective, in R. L. Edwards (ed.) *Encyclopedia of Social Work,* 19th edn. Vol. 1. Washington, DC: National Association of Social Workers.

Halpern, D. and Bates, C. (2004) with Beales, G. and Heathfield, A. *Personal Responsibility and Changing Behaviour: The state of knowledge and its implications for public policy.* London: Cabinet Office: Prime Minister's Strategy Unit.

Jack, G. (2000) Ecological approach to social work, in M. Davies (ed.) *Blackwell Encyclopaedia of Social Work.* Oxford: Oxford University Press.

Jack, G. and Gill, O. (2003) *The Missing Side of the Triangle: Assessing the Importance of Family and Environmental Factors in the Lives of Children.* Ilford: Barnardo's.

Jack, G. and Jack, D. (2000) Ecological social work: the application of a systems model of development in context, in P. Stepney and D. Ford (eds) *Social Work Models, Methods and Theories.* London: Russell House.

McLeroy, K. R., Bibeau, D., Steckler, A. and Glanz, K. (1988) An Ecological Perspective on Health Promotion Programs, *Health Education Quarterly,* 14(4): 351–77.

APPENDIX 8

Feminist perspectives in social work

Description/definition

Dominelli defines feminist social work as follows:

> feminist social work (is) a form of social work practice which takes gendered inequality and its elimination as the starting point for working with women, whether as individuals, in groups or within organisations, and seeks to promote women's well-being as women define it.
>
> (Dominelli 2002a: 97)

Focus of feminist social work

Social work is very much a women's issue: 'Most social work is undertaken by women and with women, either as clients in their own right or as part of an infrastructure on which agencies depend to support services' (Orme 2002: 218). Feminist analysis attempts to define – and to redefine – women's roles and responsibilities and how oppression and disadvantage impact on women as service users, carers and practitioners. This is sometimes called a *woman-centred perspective,* where the 'commonalities' that women share as women are incorporated 'as visible parts of our practice' (Hamner and Statham 1999: 21). This perspective suggests that because men lack the experience of being a woman, they can develop a 'gender perspective' but not a 'woman-centred perspective' (Hamner and Statham 1999: 21). This is an important, complex and controversial issue.

The feminist phrase, 'the personal and the political', has been enormously influential worldwide and has enabled women to analyse, through the process of *consciousness raising,* their experiences of inequality and oppression and to politicize these experiences in campaigns designed to challenge government policy and patriarchal ideology (Hartman 1981). It was feminists who first threw light on sexual abuse, domestic violence, rape and other important issues once thought to belong to the private sphere of the family and be beyond public scrutiny (Hester and Pearson 1998). Different 'schools of feminist thought' exist

(Dominelli 1997: 29), but a feminist perspective usually embraces certain principles:

1 A recognition of the inequalities that exist between men and women and a belief that patriarchal assumptions inhibit women's opportunities and life chances.
2 A commitment to explore ways to circumvent – or overcome – sexist barriers that assail women's sense of confidence, self-esteem and status. These barriers may be kept in place by *internalized oppression*, that is, by the way that women have come to accept negative beliefs about themselves and other women.
3 An emphasis on women putting themselves, and their interests, needs and concern, at the centre of their thinking and decision-making. This may involve redefining the roles they have been ascribed, or adopted, and supporting women in ways that enable them to find their voice, personal power and autonomy.
4 A way of working that acknowledges power and status differences (Wise 1995: 113) yet works to establish egalitarian, honest and open relationships between female social workers and service users/carers.
5 A perspective that links 'personal' and 'political' issues in ways that enhance awareness and that seek collective solutions to individual problems, based on a recognition of women's contribution and the diversity of women's experience, knowledge and strengths.

Advantages

- Feminism draws on a rich theoretical framework that is capable of providing in-depth analyses of women's experiences, both within and outside social work. It can also analyse the impact of sexism on men and boys and apply feminist principles in relation to work with men (Dominelli 2002c: 163).
- Feminism has had a profound impact on social work, seen most clearly in areas such as sexual abuse, domestic violence, childcare provision and so forth (Featherstone 2000: 136–7). It can also be seen where gender inequalities exist in relation to income (equal pay), housing provision, employment, educational opportunities and so on.
- Linking 'the personal and the political' is an accessible perspective, and one that speaks to the experiences of women from different disadvantaged groups. Feminism has shown that oppressed people, in this case women, can change the course of history through collective action.
- A feminist analysis can mean that areas of women's lives, that may have been previously ignored, can be brought into the frame and included as a focus of the work to be undertaken.

Limitations

- Most women experience additional oppressions, such as discrimination in relation to class, race, age, disabilities, sexual orientation, culture and religious beliefs. These additional oppressions are not always given sufficient weight.
- Applying a feminist perspective is not easy (Trevithick 1998; Wise 1990). Many of the same inequalities and barriers that exist for women as service users and

carers also exist for feminist practitioners. Like other organizations, the hierarchy of social work is male dominated and located within patriarchal assumptions (Dominelli 2002c: 43).

• There is no clear or agreed position among feminists about the negative impact of sexism on men and male children. Some argue that feminism should embrace the whole of humanity.

• Some women (and men) see feminism as divisive and do not want to explore differences between men and women, or issues of inequality and discrimination.

REFERENCES

Dominelli, L. (1997) *Sociology of Social Work*. Basingstoke: Macmillan.

Dominelli, L. (2002a) Feminist theory, in M. Davis (ed.) *The Blackwell Companion to Social Work*, 2nd edn. Oxford: Blackwell.

Dominelli, L. (2002c) *Feminist Social Work Theory and Practice*. Basingstoke: Palgrave.

Featherstone, B. (2000) Feminist theory and practice, in M. Davies (ed.) *Blackwell Encyclopaedia of Social Work*. Oxford: Oxford University Press.

Hamner, J. and Statham, D. (1999) *Women and Social Work: Towards a Woman-Centred Practice*, 2nd edn. Basingstoke: Macmillan/BASW.

Hartman, H. (1981) The unhappy marriage of Marxism and feminism: towards a more progressive union, in L. Sargent (ed.) *Women and Revolution*. Boston MA: South End.

Orme, J. (2002) Feminist social work, in R. Adams, L. Dominelli and M. Payne (eds) *Social Work: Themes, Issues and Critical Debates*, 2nd edn. Basingstoke: Palgrave.

Trevithick, P. (1998) Psychotherapy and working class women, in I. B. Seu and M. Colleen Heenan (eds) *Feminism and Psychotherapy: Reflections on Contemporary Theories and Practices*. London: Sage.

Wise, S. (1990) Becoming a feminist social worker, in L. Stanley (ed.) *Feminist Praxis: Research, Theory and Epistemology in Feminist Sociology*. London: Routledge.

Wise, S. (1995) Feminist ethics in practice, in R. Hugman and D. Smith (eds) *Ethical Issues in Social Work*. London: Routledge.

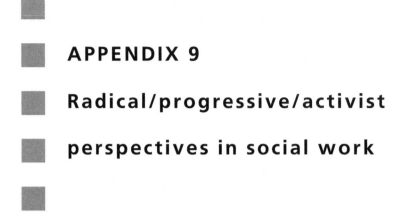

APPENDIX 9

Radical/progressive/activist

perspectives in social work

Description/definition

Aspects of radical/progressive/activist social work are described in different ways: as 'progressive' (Bombyk 1995), 'activist' (Healy 2000), 'political' social work, 'critical social work practice' (Fook 2002) and as an 'emancipatory approach' (Dominelli 2002b: 4). Some address the same issues as anti-oppressive/feminist perspectives. All these perspectives stress the connection between 'personal troubles' and 'public issues' (Mills 1959: 130), taking as their starting point the view that social inequalities are built into the fabric of most western capitalist societies, and that 'the injustices in institutions, systems, beliefs, and social practices ... cause the poorest and most vulnerable groups to suffer' (Bombyk 1995: 1933). Where problems – their causes and solutions – are individualized, people can become divided and isolated from those who share similar experiences.

Radical social work was most prominent in Great Britain in the 1970s, in the wake of the civil rights/black movement, feminist and anti-war movements. Social workers interested in radical reform drew their inspiration from *Case Con* – a 'revolutionary magazine for social workers', published from 1970 to 1977 – and other important texts (Bailey and Brake 1975; Corrigan and Leonard 1978; Langan and Lee 1989). Similar developments occurred in the USA, Canada and Australia, but with the political shift away from progressive politics in the 1980s, the voice of radical/progressive/activist social work became less directly influential.

Focus of radical social work

In the past and today, practitioners who work from a radical/progressive/activist perspective are involved in a range of issues relevant to social justice and the 'rights of clients'. The following gives a picture of the kind of issues considered relevant.

Social, economic and political solutions

This emphasizes the importance of social, economic and political solutions to 'social problems', thereby shifting the onus of blame from the individual, without denying the importance of individual responsibility. This involves pressing for 'economic, political, and social alternatives that prevent or mitigate poverty, violence, unemployment, illness, crime, and the host of other social problems affecting our society more seriously with each passing year' (Bombyk 1995: 1933).

Collective action

A radical/progressive/activist social work perspective stresses the importance of bringing people together to ensure, through collective action, that the voice of disadvantaged people can be heard. Groupwork skills are particularly important in this regard. So too is consciousness raising, which involves becoming aware – and helping others to become aware – of the way that issues of power and domination, and social and economic inequalities, impact on the lives of people who are disadvantaged.

Another aspect of collective action is bringing practitioners together. For example, in the mid-1970s, myself and other 'members' of *Case Con* initiated a meeting where we challenged psychiatrists about the way patients were treated, particularly the use of electric shock treatment. We were involved in similar actions in relation to homelessness, the 'cohabitation rule' and so forth.

Influencing social work practice

Concerns were voiced in the 1970s about the allocation of resources, and how inequalities and discriminatory practices impacted on the availability and quality of service provided. These concerns continue today in the way that social work services are fragmented, 'bureaucratized', restricted and under-resourced – a situation that has led to the call for collective action (Jones *et al.* 2003).

Advantages

- Practitioners who work from a radical/progressive/activist perspective are passionately committed to the issue of social justice and to working alongside people from disadvantaged groups in order to initiate change.
- In the past, radical social work included direct action, such as probation officers protesting outside 'short-sharp shock' centres for young people. This also involved bringing social workers together so that their collective voice could be heard.
- This perspective has the potential to form alliances with other progressive groups or organizations, such as those involved with social justice and anti-poverty, both at home and abroad.
- The influence of radical/progressive/activist perspectives has been far reaching and has been embodied in the development of anti-oppressive and anti-racist social work practice (Jones *et al.* 2003). Its influence can also be seen in the way that the concept of empowerment and user/carer/consumer representation has been embodied within social work (Langan 2002: 209) and other areas of health and welfare policy.

Limitations

- Radical/progressive perspectives can be ambivalent or unclear about the issue of personal responsibility and the point at which people need to be held to account for their actions and behaviour.
- Encouraging people to come together can be a difficult task. Some people may not be able to see the benefits of collective action or may be reluctant to share their personal experiences with others.
- This work is more likely to be successful where practitioners have a good knowledge base about key issues – on poverty, take up of benefits, housing, transport, education and employment policy – and how these issues impact on specific communities. Acquiring this level of information takes time and skill.
- Agitating for policy change takes courage, as well as time and effort. It can be difficult to keep going, and to keep issues alive, when progress is slow and other pressures mount.

REFERENCES

Bailey, R. and Brake, M. (1975) *Radical Social Work*. London: Edward Arnold.
Bombyk, M. (1995) Progressive social work, in R. L. Edwards (ed.) *Encyclopedia of Social Work*, 19th edn. Vol. 1. pp. 323–34. Washington, DC: National Association of Social Workers.
Corrigan, P. and Leonard, P. (1978) *Social Work Practice under Capitalism: A Marxist Approach*. Basingstoke: Macmillan.
Dominelli, L. (2002b) Anti-oppressive practice in context, in R. Adams, L. Dominelli and M. Payne (eds) *Social Work: Themes, Issues and Critical Debates*, 2nd edn. Basingstoke: Palgrave.
Fook, J. (2002) *Social Work: Critical Theory and Practice*. London: Sage.
Healy, K. (2000) *Social Work Practices: Contemporary Perspectives on Change*. London: Sage.
Jones, C., Ferguson, I., Lavalette, M. and Penketh, L. (2003) *Social Work and Social Justice: A Manifesto for a New Engaged Practice*. Available at www.liverpool.ac.uk/sspsw/manifesto
Langan, M. (2002) The legacy of radical social work, in R. Adams, L. Dominelli and M. Payne (eds) *Social Work: Themes, Issues and Critical Debates*, 2nd edn. Basingstoke: Macmillan.
Langan, M. and Lee, P. (eds) (1989) *Radical Social Work Today*. London: Unwin Hyman.
Mills, C. W. (1959) *The Sociological Imagination*. Oxford: Oxford University Press.

APPENDIX 10

Stages of Change (or *Cycle of Change*)

Description/definition

The *Stages of Change*, also known as the *Cycle of Change* is a central concept within the 'transtheoretical model of psychotherapy'. This approach is committed to integrating different models of psychotherapy and behaviour change, thereby drawing 'from the entire spectrum of the major theories – hence the name *transtheoretical*' (Prochaska and Norcross 2003: 516). The model covers three dimensions: the processes, stages, and levels of change. This summary focuses on five *stages of change*, namely precontemplation, contemplation, preparation, action and maintenance, which describe the stages that people go through during the change process. Change is not conceptualized as a linear process but as a spiral, where individuals progress through the stages haphazardly, although no stage can be skipped. Relapse can happen at any stage and, at this point, the individual regresses to an earlier stage. Since people who are not ready for change set themselves up (or are set up) for failure, it is important to know at what stage an individual is located, so that problem-solving efforts can be maximized (Prochaska *et al.* 1994: 39). The five stages are described below.

Precontemplation

People at this stage cannot see the problem, although this may be clearly visible to others, such as their family, friends, doctor or social worker. Therefore, 'there is no intention to change behaviour now or in the future' (Prochaska and Norcross 2003: 519). Some may make the right noises, complain that they are being coerced or locate the problem in others. The reality is that they may be too well defended, or too hopeless or demoralized, to try to effect change.

Contemplation

People at this stage have acknowledged that there is a problem but are 'not quite ready to go yet' (Prochaska *et al.* 1994: 42). 'Readiness for change' is an important issue in this approach (DiClemente *et al.* 2004). People can remain stuck in 'chronic contemplations' for long periods, where the attempt to understand the problem, its cause and possible solutions is at the expense of moving forward. As a result, thinking can become a substitute for action (Prochaska and Norcross 2003: 520).

Preparation

'Individuals in this stage are intending to take action immediately and report some small behavioural changes' (Prochaska and Norcross 2003: 520). However, although they appear committed and ready for action, some ambivalence may be evident about the prospect of change, perhaps expressed in an undue concern about the best course of action, a desire to move too quickly, an inability to set clear targets or 'a clear criterion for success' (Barber 2002: 26).

Action

'In this stage, individuals modify their behaviour, experiences, and/or environment in order to overcome their problems' (Prochaska and Norcross 2003: 521). This stage involves energy and commitment and changes initiated are likely to be quite visible and given the greatest recognition by others. This last point is important. The danger at this stage is that people, including professionals, may confuse action with change. This may eventually lead to failure because the changes effected have become estranged from the preceding stages.

Maintenance

'In this final stage, people work to prevent relapse and consolidate the gains attained during action. Traditionally, maintenance has been viewed as a static stage. However, maintenance is a continuation, not an absence, of change' (Prochaska and Norcross 2003: 522). Maintaining the changes achieved can take more than initiating new changes, mainly because maintenance is spread over a longer period and often not marked with the same sense of recognition or achievement. 'Quickfix' approaches, offering easy solutions, often fail at this stage.

Termination is a feature of this framework but is not cited as one of the stages by Prochaska and Norcross (2003). However, some publications cite relapse/recycle as a final stage (Lancaster 2000: 80; Velasquez *et al.* 2001). Termination occurs when temptation has abated and the individual does not have to struggle to avoid relapse. In relation to serious addictions, people may take three, four or more attempts before lasting behaviour change is achieved. Some workers in the field of addiction, such as those involved with Alcoholics Anonymous programmes, believe that some maintenance will always be required. A great deal depends on the individual and, more importantly, the external support for change.

The stages of change can be represented as shown on p. 294:

Advantages

- This approach has been adopted in a wide range of different health and welfare contexts – for drug addiction, smoking cessation, eating disorders, etc. (Halpern and Bates 2004: 21).

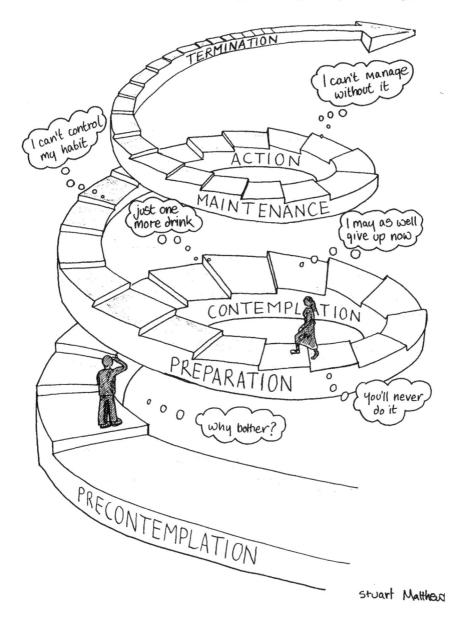

- It provides an accessible framework from which to analyse change, and the change process, making it possible to identify appropriate strategies (Barber 2002: 29).
- This approach is compatible with other approaches, such as motivational interviewing (DiClemente and Velasquez 2002), cognitive interventions in the early stages and behavioural/task-centred approaches in the later stages.
- Considerable research evidence supports the view that people pass through the stages identified (Prochaska and Norcross 2003: 536).

Limitations

- This approach does not provide a coherent theory/practice about how to bring about change. It is 'more successful as a description *of* change than as a prescription *for* change' (Barber 2002: 33).
- Its individualistic focus, dominant in the USA, places too much weight on individual effort and not enough on environmental causation and support structures.
- A sociological analysis is largely absent. Thus the link between the causes of addictive behaviour and social disadvantage are not addressed.
- Treatment methods used at different stages tend to be vague and largely untested. Some authors question the research findings (Barber 2002: 33).

REFERENCES

Barber, J. G. (2002) *Social Work with Addictions*, 2nd edn. Basingstoke: Palgrave Macmillan.

DiClemente, C. C. (2003) *Addiction and Change*. London: Routledge.

DiClemente, C. C. and Velasquez, M. M. (2002) Motivational Interviewing and the Stages of Change, in W. R. Miller and S. Rollnick (eds) *Motivational Interviewing: Preparing People for Change*, 2nd edn. London: Guilford Press.

DiClemente, C. C., Schlund, D. and Gemmell, L. (2004) Readiness and stages of change in addiction treatment, *America Journal on Addictions*, 13(2): 103–19.

Halpern, D and Bates, C. (2004) (with Greg Beales and Adam Heathfield) *Personal Responsibility and Changing Behaviour: The State of Knowledge and its Implications for Public Policy* (Discussion paper). Cabinet Office: Prime Minister's Strategy Unit.

Lancaster, E. (2000) Cycle of change, in M. Davies (ed.) *Blackwell Encyclopaedia of Social Work*. Oxford: Oxford University Press.

Miller, W. R. and Rollnick, S. (2002) *Motivational Interviewing: Preparing People for Change*, 2nd edn. London: Guilford Press.

Prochaska, J. O. and Norcross, J. C. (2003) *Systems of Psychotherapy: A Transtheoretical Analysis*. Pacific Grove, CA: Brooks/Cole.

Prochaska, J. O., Norcross, J. C. and DiClemente, C. C. (1994) *Changing for Good*. New York: Avon.

Velasquez, M. M., Maurer, G. G., Crouch, C. and DiClemente, C. C. (2001) *Group Treatment for Substance Abuse: A Stages-of-Change Therapy Manual*. New York: Guilford.

APPENDIX 11

National Occupational Standards

Unit 1: Indicative Knowledge Base

The following is an account of the knowledge base required of social workers, taken from the National Occupational Standards. It states that 'in your specific area of practice you must understand, critically analyse, evaluate, and apply the following knowledge' (TOPSS 2004: 21):

1 The legal, social, economic and ecological context of social work practice

a Country, UK, EU legislation, statutory codes, standards, frameworks and guidance relevant to social work practice and related fields, including multi-disciplinary and multi-organisational practice, data protection and confidentiality of information
b Social policy, including policy on social care, criminal justice, education, health, housing, income support
c Demographic and social trends
d Theories of poverty, unemployment, health, impairment and other sources of discrimination and disadvantage and their impact on social exclusion
e Policies on diversity, discrimination and promoting independence/autonomy of adults, children, families, groups and communities, and research on their effectiveness

2 The context of social work practice for this area of work

a Historical perspectives of social work and social welfare
b International law and social policy, in broad terms, for the purpose of comparison
c Contemporary issues and trends in social work
d Understanding of why people use social work and social care services
e Psychological and sociological explanations of:
- human growth and development and the factors that impact on it
- mental health and well being
- social interactions and relationships
- discrimination and oppression
- human behaviour

f   Knowledge of the range of local resources and services
g   Theories about how systems work
h   Organisational structures, policies and procedures for referral
i   Policies, procedures and legal requirements for the security and confidentiality of information
j   How to access and use information and communications technology (ICT) and other electronic systems that may help in the collection of information

3   Values and ethics

a   Awareness of your own values, prejudices, ethical dilemmas and conflicts of interest and their implications on your practice
b   Respect for, and the promotion of:
   • each person as an individual
   • independence and quality of life for individuals, whilst protecting them from harm
   • dignity and privacy of individuals, families, carers, groups and communities
c   Recognise and facilitate each person's use of language and form of communication of their choice
d   Value, recognise and respect the diversity, expertise and experience of individuals, families, carers, groups and communities
e   Maintain the trust and confidence of individuals, families, carers, groups and communities by communicating in an open, accurate and understandable way
f   Understand and make use of strategies to challenge discrimination, disadvantage and other forms of inequality and injustice

4   Social work theories, models and methods for working with individuals, families, carers, groups and communities

a   Principles, theories and methods of social work practice
b   Theories about the impact of authority and power in the social work role
c   Theories about the impact of discrimination, and methods of working with diversity
d   Theories and methods about working with the main groups of people using services. These include childcare, mental health, learning difficulties, older people, minority and ethnic groups, drug and alcohol use, disability and impairment
e   Principles about balancing the rights of individuals, families, carers, groups and communities with the interests of society and the requirements of practice
f   Lessons learned from both serious failure of service and practice, and from successful interventions
g   Approaches to evidence and knowledge based practice
h   Theories of organizations, group behaviour and organisational change
i   Theories and methods of promoting personal, social and emotional well being
(NOS 2004: 20)

REFERENCES

Abercrombie, N., Hill, S. and Turner, B. S. (2000) *Penguin Dictionary of Sociology*, 4th edn. London: Penguin Books.

Adams, R. (1998) *Quality Social Work*. Basingstoke: Macmillan.

Adams, R. (2002a) Quality assurance, in R. Adams, L. Dominelli and M. Payne (eds) *Critical Practice in Social Work*. Basingstoke: Palgrave.

Adams, R. (2002b) Social work process, in R. Adams, L. Dominelli and M. Payne (eds) *Social Work: Themes, Issues and Critical Debates*, 2nd edn. Basingstoke: Macmillan.

Adams, R., Dominelli, L. and Payne, M. (eds) 2002a) *Critical Practice in Social Work*. Basingstoke: Palgrave.

Adams, R., Dominelli, L. and Payne, M. (2002b) *Social Work: Themes, Issues and Critical Debates*, 2nd edn. Basingstoke: Palgrave.

Ahmed, S. (1986) Cultural racism in work with Asian women and girls, in S. Ahmed, J. Cheetham and J. Small (eds) *Social Work with Black Children and their Families*. London: Batsford.

Ainsworth, M. D. S., Blehar, M., Walters, E. and Wall, S. (1978) *Patterns of Attachment: A Psychological Study of the Strange Situation*. Hillsdale, NJ: Lawrence Erlbaum.

Aldgate, J. (2002) Family breakdown, in M. Davies (ed.) *The Blackwell Companion to Social Work*, 2nd edn. Oxford: Blackwell.

Aldgate, J., Tunstill, J. and McBeth, G. (1994) *Implementing Section 17 of the Children Act – the First 18 Months*. University of Leicester (see Annual Reports of Children Act for Summaries).

Allan, G. (2000) Sociology, in M. Davies (ed.) *Blackwell Encyclopaedia of Social Work*. Oxford: Oxford University Press.

Angelou, M. (1994) *Wouldn't Take Nothing for my Journey Now*. London: Virago.

Applegate, J. S. and Bonovitz, J. M. (1995) *The Facilitating Partnership: A Winnicottian Approach for Social Workers and other Helping Professionals*. Northvale, NJ: Jason Aronson.

Atkinson, D. (1986) Engaging competent others: a study of the support network of people with mental handicap, *British Journal of Social Work*, supplement, 16: 33–101.

Audit Commission (1992) *Community Care: Managing the Cascade of Change*. London: HMSO.

Aymer, C. and Okitikpi, T. (2000) Epistemology, ontology and methodology: what's that got to do with social work?, *Social Work Education*, 19(1), 67–75.

Bagley, C. and King, K. (1990) *Child Sexual Abuse*. London: Tavistock/Routledge.

Bailey, D. (2002) Mental health, in R. Adams, L. Dominelli and M. Payne (eds) *Critical Practice in Social Work*. Basingstoke: Palgrave.

Bailey, R. and Brake, M. (1975) *Radical Social Work*. London: Edward Arnold.

Ball, C. (1997) The Law, in M. Davies (ed.) *The Blackwell Companion to Social Work*, 1st edn. Oxford: Blackwell.

Bandura, A. (1969) *Principles of Behavior Modification*. New York: Holt, Rinehart and Winston.

Bandura, A. (1977) *Social Learning Theory*. Englewood Cliffs, NJ: Prentice-Hall.

Bannock, G., Baxter, R. E. and Davis, E. (1998) *The Penguin Dictionary of Economics*. London: Penguin.

Barber, J. G. (2002) *Social Work with Addictions*, 2nd edn. Basingstoke: Palgrave Macmillan.

Barclay Report (1982) *Social Workers: Their Roles and Task*. London: Bedford Square Press.

Barker, R. L. (1995) *The Social Work Dictionary*, 3rd edn. Washington, DC: NASW Press.

Barker, R. L. (1999) *The Social Work Dictionary*, 4th edn. Washington, DC: NASW Press.

Barker, R. L. (2003) *The Social Work Dictionary*, 5th edn. Washington, DC: NASW Press.

Barton, R. (2000) Carer, in M. Davies (ed.) *Blackwell Encyclopaedia of Social Work*. Oxford: Oxford University Press.

Barton, R. (2002) The carer's perspective, in M. Davies (ed.) *The Blackwell Companion to Social Work*, 2nd edn. Oxford: Blackwell.

Bateman, N. (2000) *Advocacy Skills for Health and Social Care Professionals*. London: Jessica Kingsley.

Beck, A. (1976) *Cognitive Therapy and the Emotional Disorders*. New York: International University Press.

Beck, A. and Steer, R. (1987) *Beck Depression Inventory: Manual*. San Antonia: Psychological Corporation.

Benjamin, J. (1990) *The Bonds of Love*. London: Virago.

Benjamin, J. (1995) *Like Subjects, Like Objects*. London: Yale University Press.

Beresford, P. and Croft, S. (2000) User participation, in M. Davies (ed.) *Blackwell Encyclopaedia of Social Work*. Oxford: Oxford University Press.

Biestek, F. P. (1961) *The Casework Relationship*. London: Allen & Unwin.

Bion, W. R. (1967) A theory of thinking, in W. R. Bion (1984) *Second Thoughts: Selected Papers in Psychoanalysis*. London: Karnac Books.

Birdwhistell, R. (1970) *Kinesics and Context*. Philadelphia, PA: University of Pennsylvania.

Blom-Cooper, L. (1985) *A Child in Trust: A Report of the Panel of Inquiry into Circumstances Surrounding the Death of Jasmine Beckford*. London: London Borough of Brent.

Bombyk, M. (1995) Progressive social work, in *Encyclopedia of Social Work*, 19th edn. Vol. 1, 323–34, Washington, DC: National Association of Social Workers.

Booth, T. (2002) Learning difficulties, in M. Davies (ed.) *The Blackwell Companion to Social Work*, 2nd edn. Oxford: Blackwell.

Boseley, S. (2004) Big rise in the number of children given mind-altering drugs, *Guardian,* 18 November 2004.

Boushel, M. (1994) The protective environment of children: towards a framework of anti-oppressive, cross-cultural and cross-national understanding, *British Journal of Social Work,* 24: 173–90.

Bowlby, J. (1979) *The Making and Breaking of Affectional Bonds.* London: Tavistock.

Bowlby, J. (1980) *Attachment and Loss, Vol. III: Loss, Sadness, and Depression.* London: Hogarth.

Bowlby, J. (1988) *A Secure Base: Clinical Applications of Attachment Theory.* London: Routledge.

Brammer, A. (2003) *Social Work Law.* Harlow: Pearson Education.

Brand, D. (2000) The regulation of professional social work practice, in M. Davies (ed.) *The Blackwell Encyclopaedia of Social Work,* 2nd edn. Oxford: Blackwell.

Brandon, M., Schofield, G. and Trinder, L. (1998) *Social Work with Children.* Basingstoke: Macmillan.

Braye, S. and Preston-Shoot, M. (1995) *Empowering Practice in Social Care.* Buckingham: Open University Press.

Brearley, J. (1991) A psychodynamic approach to social work, in J. Lishman (ed.) *Handbook of Theory for Accredited Practice Teachers in Social Work.* London: Jessica Kingsley.

Brearley, J. (1991) A psychoanalytic approach to social work, in J. Lishman (ed.) *Handbook of Theory for Practice Teachers.* London: Jessica Kingsley.

Brearley, J. (1995) *Counselling and Social Work.* Buckingham: Open University Press.

British Association for Counselling (1992) *16th Annual Report 1991/92.* Rugby: BAC.

Bronfenbrenner, U. (1979) *The Ecology of Human Development.* Cambridge, MA: Harvard University Press. **Check ref**

Broverman, I., Broverman, D., Clarkson, F., Rosenkrantz, P. and Vogal, S. (1970) Sex-role stereotypes and clinical judgements of mental health, *Journal of Consulting and Clinical Psychology,* 34: 1–7.

Brown, G. and Atkins, M. (1997) Explaining, in O. Hargie (ed.) *A Handbook of Communication Skills,* 2nd edn. London: Routledge.

Brown, G. W. and Harris, T. (1978) *Social Origins of Depression.* London: Tavistock.

Brown, H. (2000) Vulnerable adults, in M. Davies (ed.) *Blackwell Encyclopaedia of Social Work.* Oxford: Oxford University Press.

Brown, H. C. (2002) Counselling, in R. Adams, L. Dominelli and M. Payne (eds) *Social Work: Themes, Issues and Debates,* 2nd edn. Basingstoke: Macmillan.

Brown, M. (ed.) (1983) *The Structure of Disadvantage.* London: Heinemann.

Buckland, S. and Gorin, S. (2001) *Involving consumers? An exploration of consumer involvement in NHS Research & Development managed by Department of Health Regional Offices.* Consumers in NHS Research Support Unit.

Bullock, A. and Trombley, S. (eds) (2000) *The New Fontana Dictionary of Modern Thought,* 3rd edn. Hammersmith: HarperCollins.

Burgess, P. (1992) Welfare rights, in C. Hanvey and T. Philpot (eds) *Practising Social Work.* London: Routledge.

Burnham, J. B. (1986) *Family Therapy*. London: Routledge.

Bywaters, P. (1986) Social work and the medical profession – arguments against unconditional collaboration, *British Journal of Social Work*, **16**: 661–7.

Bywaters, P. (1999) Social work and health inequalities, *British Journal of Social Work*, 29: 811–16.

Cabinet Office/Office of Public Service and Science/Office of Science and Technology (1993) *Realising our Potential: A Strategy for Science, Engineering and Technology*. Cm 2250. London: HMSO.

Cabinet Office (1999) *Modernising Government*. London: The Stationery Office.

Camilleri, P. (1999) Social work and its search for meaning: theories, narrative and practices, in J. Pease and J. Fook (eds) *Social Work Practice: Postmodern Critical Perspectives*. London: Routledge.

Caplan, G. (1964) *Principles of Preventative Psychiatry*. New York: Basic Books.

Care Council for Wales (2003) *Rules for the Approval of Courses in Social Work*. Cardiff: NAW.

Central Council for Education and Training in Social Work (CCETSW) (1989) *Requirements and Regulations for the Diploma in Social Work – Paper 30*. London: CCETSW.

Central Council for Education and Training in Social Work (CCETSW) (1996) *Assuring Quality in the Diploma in Social Work – 1: Rules and Requirements for the DipSW*. 2nd revision. London: CCETSW.

Cheetham, J. (2002) The research perspective, in M. Davies (ed.) *The Blackwell Companion to Social Work*, 2nd edn. Oxford: Blackwell.

Cheetham, J., Fuller, R., McIvor, G. and Petch, A. (1992) *Evaluating Social Work Effectiveness*. Buckingham: Open University Press.

Chodorow, N. J. (1978) *The Reproduction of Mothering: Psychoanalysis and the Sociology of Gender*. Berkeley, CA: University of California Press.

Chodorow, N. J. (1989) *Feminism and Psychoanalytic Theory*. London: Yale University Press.

Chodorow, N. J. (1994) *Femininities Masculinities Sexualities: Freud and Beyond*. London: Free Association.

Chodorow, N. J. (1999) *The Power of Feelings: Personal Meaning in Psycho-analysis, Gender and Culture*. London: Yale University Press.

Chui, W. H. and Ford, D. (2000) Crisis intervention as common practice, in P. Stepney and D. Ford (eds) *Social Work Models, Methods and Theories*. Lyme Regis: Russell House.

Cigno, K. (2002) Cognitive behavioural practice, in R. Adams, L. Dominelli and M. Payne (eds) *Social Work: Themes, Issues and Critical Debates*, 2nd edn. Basingstoke: Palgrave.

Cigno, K. and Bourn, D. (1998) *Cognitive-behavioural Social Work in Practice*. Aldershot: Arena.

Clandinin, D. and Connelly, F. (1994) Personal experience methods, in N. Denzin and Y. Lincoln (eds) *Handbook of Qualitative Research*. London: Sage.

Clark, C. (1998) Self-determination and paternalism in community care: practice and prospects, *British Journal of Social Work*, 28: 387–402.

Clark, C. (2000a) The use of language, in M. Davies (ed.) *Blackwell Encyclopaedia of Social Work*. Oxford: Oxford University Press.

Clark, C. (2000b) Professional ethics, in M. Davies (ed.) *Blackwell Encyclopaedia of Social Work*. Oxford: Blackwell.

Clark, C. (2000c) Values in social work, in M. Davies (ed.) *Blackwell Encyclopaedia of Social Work*. Oxford: Blackwell.

Clark, C. L. (2000) *Social Work Ethics. Politics, Principles and Practice*. Basingstoke: Macmillan.

Clarke, J. (ed.) (1993) *A Crisis in Care: Challenges to Social Work*. London: Sage.

Clarke, J. (1996) After social work, in N. Parton (ed.) *Social Theory, Social Change and Social Work*. London: Routledge.

Cochrane Collaboration (2001) *Reviewers' Handbook Glossary* (Cochrane RHG), version 4.1.4. Available at http://www.cochrane.dk/cochrane/handbook/hbook.htm

Colebatch, H. K. (2002) *Policy*. Buckingham: Open University Press.

Coleman, J., Lyon, J. and Piper, R. (1995) *Teenage Suicide and Self-harm*. London: Trust for the Study of Adolescence.

Collins, A. H. and Pancoast, D. L. (1976) *Natural Helping Networks*. Washington, DC: NASW.

Conant, J. and Haugeland, J. (2000) *Thomas S. Kuhn. The Road Since Structure: Philosophical Essays, 1970–1993*. With an autobiographical interview with Thomas S. Kuhn. London: University of Chicago Press.

Copley, B. and Forryan, B. (1997) *Therapeutic Work with Children and Young People*. London: Cassell.

Corby, B. (1993) *Child Abuse: Towards a Knowledge Base*. Buckingham: Open University Press.

Corden, J. and Preston-Shoot, M. (1987) Contract or con trick? A reply to Rojek and Collins, *British Journal of Social Work*, 17: 535–43.

Corney, R. (ed.) (1991) *Developing Communication and Counselling Skills*. London: Routledge.

Corrigan, P. and Leonard, P. (1978) *Social Work Practice under Capitalism: A Marxist Approach*. Basingstoke: Macmillan.

Coulshed, V. (1990) *Management in Social Work*. Basingstoke: Macmillan/BASW.

Coulshed, V. (1991) *Social Work Practice: An Introduction*, 2nd edn. Basingstoke: Macmillan/BASW.

Coulshed, V. and Mullender, A. (2001) *Management in Social Work*, 2nd edn. Basingstoke: Palgrave.

Coulshed, V. and Orme, J. (1998) *Social Work Practice: An Introduction*, 3rd edn. Basingstoke: Macmillan/BASW.

Cournoyer, B. (2000) *The Social Work Skills Workbook*, 3rd edn. Belmont, CA: Brooks/Cole Publishing.

Cowger, C. D. (1992) Assessment of client strengths, in D. Saleebey (ed.) *The Strengths Perspective in Social Work Practice*. London: Longman.

Craib, I. (1989) *Psychoanalysis and Social Theory: The Limits of Sociology*. Hemel Hempstead: Harvester Wheatsheaf.

Cree, E. C. (2002) The changing nature of social work, in R. Adams, L. Dominelli and M. Payne (eds) *Social Work: Themes, Issues and Critical Debates*, 2nd edn. Basingstoke: Macmillan.

Crisp, B. R., Anderson, M. R., Orme, J. and Lister, P. L. (2003) *Learning and Teaching in Social Work Education: Assessment*. Bristol: Policy Press.

Croft, S. and Beresford, P. (2002) Service users' perspectives, in M. Davies (ed.) *The Blackwell Companion to Social Work*, 2nd edn. Oxford: Blackwell.

Dalrymple, J. and Burke, B. (1995) *Anti-oppressive Practice: Social Care and the Law*. Buckingham: Open University Press.

Dalrymple, J. and Burke, B. (2002) Intervention and empowerment, in R. Adams, L. Dominelli and M. Payne (eds) *Critical Practice in Social Work*. Basingstoke: Palgrave.

Daniel, B. (2002) Psychology and social work, in M. Davies (ed.) *The Blackwell Companion to Social Work*, 2nd edn. Oxford: Blackwell.

Daniel, B. and Simpson, M. (2000) User-led policy, in M. Davies (ed.) *Blackwell Encyclopaedia of Social Work*. Oxford: Oxford University Press.

Darlington, Y. and Scott, D. (2002) *Qualitative Research in Practice: Stories from the Field*. Buckingham: Open University Press.

Dartington Social Research Unit (1995) *Child Protection and Child Abuse: Messages from Research*. London: HMSO.

Davies, M. (1981) *The Essential Social Worker: A Guide to Positive Practice*. Aldershot: Arena.

Davies, M. (1994) *The Essential Social Worker: a Guide to Positive Practice*, 3rd edn. Aldershot: Arena.

Davies, M. (ed.) (2000) *Blackwell Encyclopaedia of Social Work*. Oxford: Oxford University Press.

Davies, M. (ed.) (2002) *The Blackwell Companion to Social Work*, 2nd edn. Oxford: Blackwell.

Davis, A. and Ellis, K. (1995) Enforced altruism in community care, in R. Hugman and D. Smith (eds) *Ethical Issues in Social Work*. London: Routledge.

Department for Education and Skills (2003) *Every Child Matters*. Nottingham: DfES. Available at http://www.rcu.gov.uk/articles/news/everychildmatters.pdf; http://www.everychildmatters.gov.uk/

Department for Education and Skills (2004) *Every Child Matters: Change for Children* (Nottingham: DfES). (See 'Useful websites' at the end of References).

Department of Health (1989) *The Care of Children: Principles and Practice in Regulations and Guidance*. London: HMSO.

Department of Health (1995) *The Challenge of Partnership in Child Protection*. London: HMSO.

Department of Health (1998a) *Quality Protects Circular: Transforming Children's Services*. London: The Stationery Office.

Department of Health (1998b) *Modernising Social Services: Promoting Independence, Improving Protection, Raising Standards* (London: The Stationery Office).

Department of Health (2000a) *Framework for the Assessment of Children in Need and their Families*. London: Department of Health.

Department of Health (2000b) *A Quality Strategy for Social Care*. London: Department of Health.

Department of Health (2001) *Valuing People*. London: The Stationery Office.

Department of Health (2002) *Requirements for Social Work Training*. London: HMSO.

Department of Health (2003) *The Victoria Climbié Inquiry*. London: Department of Health.

Department of Health (2005) *Adult Social Care*. London: Department of Health. (See 'Useful websites').

Department of Health and Social Security (1982) *Child Abuse: A Study of Inquiry Reports*, 1973–81. London: HMSO.

Dickson, D. and Bamford, D. (1995) Improving the Inter-personal Skills of Social Work Students – the Problem of Transfer of Learning and What to Do About It, *British Journal of Social Work*, 25: 85–105.

DiClemente, C. C. (2003) *Addiction and Change*. London: Routledge.

DiClemente, C. C. and Velasquez, M. M. (2002) Motivational Interviewing and the Stages of Change, in W. R. Miller and S. Rollnick (eds) *Motivational Interviewing: Preparing People for Change*, 2nd edn. London: Guilford Press.

DiClemente, C. C., Schlund, D. and Gemmell, L. (2004) Readiness and stages of change in addiction treatment, *America Journal on Addictions*, 13(2): 103–119.

Dockar-Drysdale, B. (1990) *The Provision of Primary Experience: Winnicottian Work with Children*. London: Free Association Books.

Doel, M. (1994) Task-centred work, in C. Hanvey and T. Philpot (eds) *Practising Social Work*. London: Routledge.

Doel, M. (2000) Task-centred social work, in M. Davies (ed.) *Blackwell Encyclopaedia of Social Work*. Oxford: Blackwell.

Doel, M. (2002) Task-centred social work, in R. Adams, L. Dominelli and M. Payne (eds) *Social Work: Themes, Issues and Critical Debates*, 2nd edn. Basingstoke: Macmillan.

Doel, M. (2005) *Using Groupwork*. London: Routledge/Community Care.

Doel, M. and Marsh, P. (1992) *Task-Centred Social Work*. Aldershot: Ashgate.

Doel, M and Shardlow, S.M. (2005) *Modern Social Work Practice*. Aldershot: Ashgate.

Dominelli, L. (1997) *Sociology of Social Work*. Basingstoke: Macmillan.

Dominelli, L. (2000) Empowerment: help or hindrance in professional relationships, in P. Stepney and D. Ford (eds) *Social Work Models, Methods and Theories*. Lyme Regis: Russell House.

Dominelli, L. (2002a) Feminist theory, in M. Davis (ed.) *The Blackwell Companion to Social Work*, 2nd edn. Oxford: Blackwell.

Dominelli, L. (2002b) Anti-oppressive practice in context, in R. Adams, L. Dominelli and M. Payne (eds) *Social Work: Themes, Issues and Critical Debates*, 2nd edn. Basingstoke: Palgrave.

Dominelli, L. (2002c) *Feminist Social Work Theory and Practice*. Basingstoke: Palgrave.

Dominelli, L. and McLeod, E. (1989) *Feminist Social Work*. Basingstoke: Macmillan.

Dorling, D. and Thomas, B. (2004) *People and Places: A 2001 Census Atlas of the UK*. Bristol: Policy Press.

Doyle, C. (1997) *Working with Abused Children*. Basingstoke: Macmillan/BASW.

Drakeford, M. (2002) Social work and politics, in M. Davies (ed.) *The Blackwell Companion to Social Work*, 2nd edn. Oxford: Blackwell.

Dryden, W. (1999) *Rational Emotive Behavioural Counselling in Action*, 2nd edn. London: Sage.

Edwards, J. B. and Richards, A. (2002) Relational teaching: a view of relational teaching in social work education, *Journal of Teaching in Social Work*, 22(1/2): 33–48.

Egan, G. (1990) *The Skilled Helper: A Systematic Approach to Effective Helping*. California: Brooks/Cole.

Egan, G. (2002) *The Skilled Helper: A Systematic Approach to Effective Helping*, 7th edn. Pacific Grove, CA: Brooks/Cole.

Egan, G. and McGourty, R. (eds) (2002) *Exercises in Helping Skills: A Training Manual to Accompany The Skilled Helper*. Pacific Grove, CA: Brooks/Cole.

Eichenbaum, L. and Orbach, S. (1982) *Outside In: Inside Out. Women's Psychology: A Feminist Psychoanalytic Approach*. Harmondsworth: Penguin.

Eichenbaum, L. and Orbach, S. (1984) *What do Women Want?* London: Fontana.

Ellis, A. (1977) The basic clinical theory of rational-emotive therapy, in A. A. Ellis and R. Greiger (eds) *Handbook of Rational-Emotive Therapy*, Vol. 1. New York: Springer.

Ellis, A., Gordon, J., Neenan, M. and Palmer, S. (1997) *Stress Counselling: A Rational Emotive Behaviour Approach*. London: Cassell.

England, H. (1986) *Social Work as Art: Making Sense of Good Practice*. London: Allen & Unwin.

Ennis, E. (2000) Practical help, in M. Davies (ed.) *Blackwell Encyclopaedia of Social Work*. Oxford: Oxford University Press.

Ennis, J. (2000) Survivors, in M. Davies (ed.) *Blackwell Encyclopaedia of Social Work*. Oxford: Oxford University Press.

Epstein, L. (1980) *Helping People: The Task-centered Approach*. St. Louis, Missouri: Mosby.

Epstein, L. (1995) Brief Task-Centred Social Work, in R. L. Edwards (ed.) *Encyclopedia of Social Work*, 19th edn. Vol. 1. pp. 313–23. Washington, DC: National Association of Social Workers.

Epstein, L. and Brown, L. B. (2002) *Brief Treatment and a New Look at the Task-Centred Approach*, 4th edn. Boston: Allyn and Bacon.

Erikson, E. (1965) *Childhood and Society*. 2nd edn. Harmondsworth: Penguin.

Ernst, S. and Maguire, M. (eds) (1987) *Living With the Sphinx: Papers from the London Women's Therapy Centre*. London: Women's Press.

Evans, D. R., Hearn, M. T., Uhlemann, M. R. and Ivey, A. E. (1989) *Essential Interviewing: A Programmed Approach to Effective Communication*. Belmont, CA: Brooks/Cole.

Everitt, A. (2002) Research and development in social work, in R. Adams, L. Dominelli and M. Payne (eds) *Social Work: Themes, Issues and Critical Debates*, 2nd edn. Basingstoke: Macmillan.

Everitt, A. and Hardiker, P. (1996) *Evaluating Good Practice*. Basingstoke: Macmillan/BASW.

Fahlberg, V. (1991) *A Child's Journey Through Placement*. London: BAAF.

Fanger, M. T. (1995) Brief therapies, in R. L. Edwards (ed.) *Encyclopedia of Social Work*, 19th edn. Vol. 1. pp. 323–34. Washington, DC: National Association of Social Workers.

Fawcett, M. and Lewis, K. (1996) Competence in conciliation work, in K. O'Hagan (ed.) *Competence in Social Work Practice: A Practical Guide for Professionals*. London: Jessica Kingsley.

Featherstone, B. (2000) Feminist theory and practice, in M. Davies (ed.) *Blackwell Encyclopaedia of Social Work*. Oxford: Oxford University Press.

Feltham, C. and Dryden, W. (1993) *Dictionary of Counselling*. London: Whurr.

Ferguson, H. (2003) Outline of a critical best practice perspective on social work and social care, *British Journal of Social Work*, 33: 1005–24.

Finkelhor, D. (1990) Early and long-term effects of child sexual abuse, *Professional Psychology: Research and Practice*, 21: 325–30.

Fischer, J. (1973) Is casework effective? A review, *Social Work*, 1: 107–10.

Fischer, J. (1978) *Effective Casework Practice: An Eclectic Approach*. New York: McGraw-Hill.

Fisher, M. (ed.) (1983) *Speaking of Clients*. Sheffield: Social Services Research.

Fisher, M. (1998) Research, knowledge and practice in community care, *Issues in Social Work Education,* 17(2): 1–14.

Fisher, M. (2002) The Social Care Institute for Excellence: the role of a national institute in developing knowledge and practice in social care, *Social Work and Social Sciences Review*, 10(1): 36–64.

Fisher, M. (2003) Preface to Pawson, R., Boaz, A., Grayson, L., Long, A. and Barnes, C. *Types and Quality of Knowledge in Social Care*, SCIE Knowledge Review 7. Bristol: Policy Press.

Flax, J. (1981) The conflict between nurturance and autonomy in mother–daughter relationships and within feminism, in E. Howell and M. Bayes (eds) *Women and Mental Health*. New York: Basic Books.

Flax, J. (1991) *Thinking Fragments: Psychoanalysis, Feminism and Postmodernism in the Contemporary West*. Berkeley, CA: University of California Press.

Flax, J. (1993) *Disputed Subjects: Essays on Psychoanalysis, Politics and Philosophy*. London: Routledge.

Fook, J. (2002) *Social Work: Critical Theory and Practice*. London: Sage.

Foot, H. C. (1997) Humour and laughter, in O. D. W. Hargie (ed.) *The Handbook of Communication Skills*, 2nd edn. London: Routledge.

Ford, D. and Hayes, P. (1996) *Educating for Social Work: Arguments for Optimism*. Aldershot: Avebury.

Ford, P. and Postle, K. (2000) Task-centred practice and care management, in P. Stepney and D. Ford (eds) *Social Work Models, Methods and Theories*. Lyme Regis: Russell House.

French, R. (1999) The importance of capacities in psychoanalysis and the language of human development, *International Journal of Psychoanalysis*, 80: 1215–25.

French, R. and Vince, R. (eds) (1999) *Group Relations, Management and Organizations*. Oxford: Oxford University Press.

French, S. and Swain, J. (2002) The perspective of the disabled people's movement, in M. Davies (ed.) *The Blackwell Companion to Social Work*, 2nd edn. Oxford: Blackwell.

Freud, S. (1924) *Collected Papers* (Vol. 11). London: Hogarth.

Froggett, L. (2002) *Love, Hate and Welfare: Psychosocial Approaches to Policy and Practice*. Bristol: Policy Press.

Frost, N. (2002) Evaluating practice, in R. Adams, L. Dominelli and M. Payne (eds) *Critical Practice in Social Work*. Basingstoke: Palgrave.

Fuller, R. and Petch, A. (1995) *Practitioner Research: the Reflective Social Worker*. Buckingham: Open University Press.

Fuller, S. (2000) Social capital, in A. Bullock and S. Trombley (eds) *The New Fontana Dictionary of Modern Thought*, 3rd edn. Hammersmith: HarperCollins.

Gabbay, J. and le May, A. (2004) Evidence based guidelines or collectively conducted 'mindlines?' Ethnographic study of knowledge management in primary care, *British Medical Journal*, 329: 1013–16.

Gambrill, E. D. (1985) Behavioural approach, in J. B. Turner (ed.) *Encyclopedia of Social Work*, 18th edn. Vol. 1. Washington, DC: National Association of Social Workers.

Gambrill, E. D. (1995) Behavioural theory, in R. L. Edwards (ed.) *Encyclopedia of Social Work*, 19th edn. Vol. 1. pp. 323–34. Washington, DC: National Association of Social Workers.

Gambrill, E. (1997) *Social Work Practice: A Critical Thinker's Guide*. Oxford: Oxford University Press.

Garbarino, J. and Kostelny, K. (1992) Child maltreatment as a community problem, *Child Abuse and Neglect,* 16: 455–64.

Garbarino, J., Stott, F. M. and Faculty of the Erikson Institute (1992) *What Children can Tell Us? Eliciting and Evaluating Critical Information from Children*. San Francisco, CA: Jossey-Bass.

Germain, C. (1983) *Handbook of Clinical Social Work*. San Francisco: Jossey-Bass.

Germain, C. B. and Gitterman, A. (1995) Ecological Perspective, in R. L. Edwards (ed.) *Encyclopedia of Social Work*, 19th edn. Vol. 1. pp. 816–24. Washington, DC: National Association of Social Workers.

Gibbs, L. and Gambrill, E. (1996) *Critical Thinking for Social Workers: Exercises for the Helping Profession*. Thousand Oaks, CA: Pine Forge Press.

Giddens, A. (2001) *Sociology*, 4th edn. Cambridge: Polity Press.

Gilligan, C. (1993) *In a Different Voice: Psychological Theory and Women's Development*, 2nd edn. Cambridge, MA: Harvard University Press.

Gitterman, A. (ed.) (1991) *Handbook of Social Work Practice with Vulnerable Groups*. New York: Columbia University Press.

Godfrey, M. (2004) *Depression and Older People: Towards Securing Well-Being in Later Life*, with Tracy Denby. Bristol: Polity Press.

Goldstein, B. P. (2002) Black perspectives, in M. Davies (ed.) *The Blackwell Companion to Social Work*, 2nd edn. Oxford: Blackwell.

Goldstein, E. G. (1995) Psychosocial approach, in R. L. Edwards (ed.) *Encyclopedia of Social Work,* 1948–1954. Washington, DC: National Association of Social Workers.

Gordon, D., Adelman, L., Ashworth, K., Bradshaw, J., Levitas, R., Middleton, S., Pantazis, C., Patsios, D., Payne, S., Townsend, P. and Williams, J. (2000) *Poverty and Social Exclusion in Britain*. York: Joseph Rowntree Foundation.

Gordon, D. and Spicker, P. (eds) (1999) *The International Glossary on Poverty*. New York: Zed Books.

Goring, D. and Thomas, B. (2004) *People and Places: A 2001 Census Atlas of the UK*. Bristol: Polity Press.

Gough, D. (1993) *Child Abuse Investigations: A Review of the Research Literature*. London: HMSO.

Gould, L. J. (1999) A political visionary in mid-life: notes on leadership and the life cycle, in R. French and R. Vince (eds) *Group Relations, Management and Organization*. Oxford: Oxford University Press.

Griffiths, R. (1988) *Community Care: Agenda for Action*. London: HMSO.

Guntrip, H. (1977) *Psychoanalytic Theory, Therapy and the Self*. London: Hogarth.

Gut, E. (1989) *Productive and Unproductive Depression: Success or Failure of a Vital Process*. London: Tavistock/Routledge.

Gutiérrez, L. M. (1990) Working with women of color: an empowerment perspective, *Social Work*, 35(2): 149–53.

Hadot, P. (1995) *Philosophy as a Way of Life: Spiritual Exercises from Socrates to Foucault*. Oxford: Blackwell.

Hague, G. and Malos, E. (eds) (2005) *Domestic Violence: Action for Change*, 3rd edn. Cheltenham: New Clarion Press.

Halpern, D. and Bates, C. (2004) (with Greg Beales and Adam Heathfield) *Personal Responsibility and Changing Behaviour: The State of Knowledge and its Implications for Public Policy* (Discussion paper). Cabinet Office: Prime Minister's Strategy Unit.

Hamner, J. and Statham, D. (1999) *Women and Social Work: Towards a Woman-Centred Practice*, 2nd edn. Basingstoke: Macmillan/BASW.

Hanks, P. (ed.) (1979) *Collins Dictionary of the English Language*. London: Collins.

Hanvey, C. and Philpot, T. (eds) (1994) *Practising Social Work*. London: Routledge.

Hardiker, P. and Barker, M. (eds) (1981) *Theories of Practice in Social Work*. London: Academic Press.

Hardiker, P. and Barker, M. (1994) *The 1989 Children Act – Significant Harm. The Experience of Social Workers Implementing New Legislation*. Leicester: University of Leicester School of Social Work.

Hargie, O. D. W. (ed.) (1997) *The Handbook of Communication Skills*, 2nd edn. London: Routledge.

Hart, J. T. (2004) Inverse and positive care laws, *British Journal of General Practice*, December.

Harris, J. (2003) Let's talk business, *Community Care*, 21st August: 36–7.

Hartman, A. (1992) In search of subjugated knowledge, *Social Work*, 37, Nov, 483–4.

Hartman, H. (1981) The unhappy marriage of Marxism and feminism: towards a more progressive union, in L. Sargent (ed.) *Women and Revolution*. Boston MA: South End.

Hartmann, F. (1958) *Ego Psychology and the Problem of Adaptation*. New York: International Universities Press.

Harwin, N., Hague, G. and Malos, E. (eds) (1999) *The Multi-Agency Approach to Domestic Violence: New Opportunities, Old Challenges?* London: Whiting & Birch.

Hawkins, P. and Shohet, R. (2000) *Supervision in the Helping Professions*, 2nd edn. Buckingham: Open University Press.

Hawton, K., Fagg, J. and Simkin, S. (1996) Deliberate self-poisoning and self-injury in adolescents: a study of characteristics and trends in Oxford. 1976–1993, *British Journal of Psychiatry*, 169: 741–7.

Hayes, N. (1994) *Foundations of Psychology*. London: Routledge.

Hayman, V. (1993) Re-writing the job: a sceptical look at competences, *Probation Journal*, 40(4): 180–3.

Healy, K. (2000) *Social Work Practices: Contemporary Perspectives on Change*. London: Sage.

Hepworth, D. H., Rooney, R. H. and Larsen, J. A. (2002) *Direct Social Work Practice: Theory and Skills*, 6th edn. Pacific Grove, CA: Brooks/Cole Publishing.

Herbert, M. (2002) The human life cycle: adolescence, in M. Davies (ed.) *The Blackwell Companion to Social Work*, 2nd edn. Oxford: Blackwell.

Herbert, M. (2002) The human life cycle: adolescence, in M. Davies (ed.) *The Blackwell Companion to Social Work*, 2nd edn. Oxford: Blackwell.

Hester, M. and Pearson, C. (1998) *From Periphery to Centre: Domestic Violence in Work with Abused Children*. Bristol: Policy Press.

Hester, M., Kelly, L. and Radford, J. (eds) (1996) *Women, Violence and Male Power*. Buckingham: Open University Press.

Hibbert, J. and van Heeswyk, D. (1988) Black Women's Workshop, in S. Krzowski and P. Land (eds) *In Our Experience: Workshops at the Women's Therapy Centre*. London: Women's Press.

Hill, M. (1990) The manifest and latent lessons of child abuse inquiries, *British Journal of Social Work*, 20: 197–312.

Hockenbury, D. H. and Hockenbury, S. E. (2002) *Psychology*, 3rd edn. New York: Worth Publication.

Hoggett, P. (2000) *Emotional Life and the Politics of Welfare*. Basingstoke: MacMillan.

Hollis, F. (1964) *Casework: A Psychosocial Therapy*. New York: Random House.

Hollis, F. (1977) Social casework: the psychosocial approach, in *Encyclopedia of Social Work*, 17th edn. pp. 1300–7. Washington DC: NISW Press.

Hollis, M. and Howe, D. (1990) Moral risks in the social work role: a response to Macdonald, *British Journal of Social Work*, 20: 547–52.

Holman, R. (1993) *A New Deal for Social Welfare*. Oxford: Lion.

Home Office (1994) *National Standards for Probation Service Family Court Welfare Work*. London: Home Office.

Horder, W. (2002) Care management, in M. Davies (ed.) *The Blackwell Companion to Social Work*, 2nd edn. Oxford: Blackwell.

Horton, R. (2002) What the UK government is (not) doing about health inequalities, *Lancet*, 360, 20 July.

Howe, D. (1987) *An Introduction to Social Work Theory*. Aldershot: Gower.

Howe, D. (1993) *On Being a Client: Understanding the Process of Counselling and Psychotherapy*. London: Sage.

Howe, D. (1994) Modernity, post modernity and social work, *British Journal of Social Work*, 24: 513–32.

Howe, D. (1996) Surface and depth in social-work practice, in N. Parton (ed.) *Social Theory, Social Change and Social Work*. London: Routledge.

Howe, D. (1998) Relationship-based thinking and practice in social work, *Journal of Social Work Practice,* (16)2, 45–56.

Howe, D. (2002a) Relating theory to practice, in M. Davies (ed.) *The Blackwell Companion to Social Work*, 2nd edn. Oxford: Blackwell.

Howe, D. (2002b) Psychosocial work, in R. Adams, L. Dominelli and M. Payne (eds) *Social Work: Themes, Issues and Critical Debates*, 2nd edn. Basingstoke: Macmillan.

Howe, D., Brandon, M., Hinings, D. and Schofield, G. (1999) *Attachment Theory, Child Maltreatment and Family Support*. Basingstoke: Macmillan.

Howell, E. and Bayes, M. (eds) (1981) *Women and Mental Health*. New York: Basic Books.

Huber, N. (1999) Milburn demands 'excellence not excuses' from local authorities, *Community Care*, 4–10 November.

Hudson, B. L. and MacDonald, G. (1986) *Behavioural Social Work: An Introduction*. London: Macmillan.

Hudson, B. L. and Sheldon, B. (2000) The cognitive-behavioural approach, in M. Davies (ed.) *Encyclopaedia of Social Work*. Oxford: Oxford University Press.

Humphreys, K. and Thiara, R. (2002) *Routes to Safety: Protection Issues Facing Abused Women and Children and the Role of Outreach Services*. Bristol: Women's Aid Federation of England.

Huxley, P. (2002) Mental illness, in M. Davies (ed.) *The Blackwell Companion to Social Work*, 2nd edn. Oxford: Blackwell.

Illich, I. D. (1976) *Limits to Medicine*. Harmondsworth: Penguin.

Irvine, J. (2000) Vision-impairment, in M. Davies (ed.) *The Blackwell Encyclopaedia of Social Work*, 2nd edn. Oxford: Blackwell.

Jack, G. (2000) Ecological approach to social work, in M. Davies (ed.) *Blackwell Encyclopaedia of Social Work*. Oxford: Oxford University Press.

Jack, G. and Gill, O. (2003) *The Missing Side of the Triangle: Assessing the Importance of Family and Environmental Factors in the Lives of Children*. Ilford: Barnardo's.

Jack, G. and Jack, D. (2000) Ecological social work: the application of a systems model of development in context, in P. Stepney and D. Ford (eds) *Social Work Models, Methods and Theories*. Lyme Regis: Russell House.

Jackson, S. (2000) Children's rights, in M. Davies (ed.) *Blackwell Encyclopaedia of Social Work*. Oxford: Blackwell.

Jacobs, M. (1999) *Psychodynamic Counselling in Action*, 2nd edn. London: Sage.

Jacobs, M. (ed.) (1995) *Charlie: an Unwanted Child?* Buckingham: Open University Press.

James, A. L. (2002) The community child care team, in M. Davies (ed.) *The Blackwell Companion to Social Work*, 2nd edn. Oxford: Blackwell.

Jewett, C. (1997) *Helping Children Cope with Separation and Loss*. London: Free Association Books.

Johns, R. and Sedgwick, A. (1999) *Law for Social Work Practice: Working with Vulnerable Adults*. Basingstoke: Macmillan.

Jones, C. (1996) Anti-intellectualism and the peculiarities of British social work, in N. Parton (ed.) *Social Theory, Social Change and Social Work*. London: Routledge.

Jones, C. (2002a) Poverty and social injustice, in M. Davies (ed.) *The Blackwell Companion to Social Work*, 2nd edn. Oxford: Blackwell.

Jones, C. (2002b) Social work and society, in R. Adams, L. Dominelli and M. Payne (eds) *Social Work: Themes, Issues and Critical Debates*, 2nd edn. Basingstoke: Macmillan.

Jones, C., Ferguson, I., Lavalette, M. and Penketh, L. (2003) *Social Work and Social Justice: A Manifesto for a New Engaged Practice*. Available at www.liverpool.ac.uk/sspsw/manifesto

Jordan, B. (1990) *Social Work in an Unjust Society*. London: Harvester Wheatsheaf.

Jordan, B. and Parton, N. (2000) Politics and social work, in M. Davies (ed.) *Blackwell Encyclopaedia of Social Work*. Oxford: Oxford University Press.

Jordan, B. (2004) Emanicipatory social work? Opportunity or Oxymoron, *British Journal of Social Work*, **34**: 5–19.

Jordan, J. V. (1991) Empathy, mutuality, and therapeutic change: clinical implications of a relational model, in J. V. Jordan, A. G. Kaplan, J. B. Miller,

I. P. Stiver and J. L. Surrey (eds) *Women's Growth and Connection: Writings from the Stone Center*. New York: Guilford Press.

Jordan, J. V. (ed.) (1997) *More Writings from the Stone Center*. New York: Guilford Press.

Jordan, J. V., Kaplan, A. G., Miller, J. B., Stiver, I. P. and Surrey, J. L. (eds) (1991) *Women's Growth and Connection: Writings from the Stone Center*. New York: Guilford Press.

Kadushin, A. (1990) *The Social Work Interview*, 3rd edn. New York: Columbia University Press.

Kadushin, A. and Kadushin, G. (1997) *The Social Work Interview*, 4th edn. New York: Columbia University Press.

Karpman, S. (1968) Fairy tales and script drama analysis, *Transactional Analysis Bulletin*, 7: 39–48.

Kemshall, H. and Pritchard, J. (1999) *Good Practice in Working with Violence*. London: Jessica Kingsley.

Kennard, D., Roberts, J. and Winter, D. A. (1993) *A Work Book of Group-Analytic Interventions*. London: Routledge.

Kenny, L. and Kenny, B. (2000) Psychodynamic theory in social work: a view from practice, in P. Stepney and D. Ford (eds) *Social Work Models, Methods and Theories*. Lyme Regis: Russell House.

Kernberg, O. F. (1969) *Object Relations Theory and Clinical Psychoanalysis*. New York: Jason Aronson.

Kernberg, O. F. (1984) *Severe Personality Disorders: Psychotherapeutic Strategies*. New Haven, CT: Yale University Press.

Kisthardt, W. E. (1992) A strengths model of case management: the principles and functions of a helping partnership with persons with persistent mental illness, in D. Saleebey (ed.) *The Strengths Perspective in Social Work Practice*. London: Longman.

Klein, M. (1975) *Envy and Gratitude*. London: Hogarth Press.

Kohlberg, L. (1969) *Stages in the Development of Moral Thought and Action*. New York: Holt, Rinehart and Harcourt Brace.

Kohon, G. (1988) *The British School of Psychoanalysis: The Independent Tradition*. London: Free Association Books.

Kohut, H. (1971) *The Analysis of Self*. London: Hogarth Press.

Kohut, H. (1977) *The Restoration of Self*. Madison, CT: International University Press.

Kroger, J. (1996) *Identity in Adolescence: The Balance between Self and Other*. London: Routledge.

Kuhn, T. S. (1970) *The Structure of Scientific Revolutions*. Chicago: Chicago University Press. (First published in 1962.)

Laming, H. (2003) *The Victoria Climbie Inquiry: Report of an Inquiry*. London: HMSO.

Lancaster, E. (2000) Cycle of change, in M. Davies (ed.) *Blackwell Encyclopaedia of Social Work*. Oxford: Oxford University Press.

Lancet (2003) Investing in children for a better future, *Lancet*, 362, 1 November.

Land, H. and Rose, H. (1985) Compulsory altruism for some or an altruistic society for all, in P. Bean, J. Ferris and D. Whynes (eds) *In Defence of Welfare*. London: Tavistock.

Langan, M. and Lee, P. (eds) (1989) *Radical Social Work Today*. London: Unwin Hyman.

Langan, M. (2002) The legacy of radical social work, in R. Adams, L. Dominelli and M. Payne (eds) *Social Work: Themes, Issues and Critical Debates*, 2nd edn. Basingstoke: Macmillan.

Law Commission (1995): *Who Decides? Making Decisions on behalf of Mentally Incapacitated Adults*. Report 231. London: Lord Chancellor's Department.

Lefcourt, H. M. (1976) *Locus of Control: Current Trends in Theory and Research*. Hillsborough, NJ: Lawrence Erlbaum.

Legge, D. (1970) *Skills*. Harmondsworth: Penguin.

Levinson, D. J. (1978) *The Seasons of a Man's Life*. New York: Alfred A. Knopf.

Levinson, D. J. (1996) *The Seasons of a Woman's Life*. New York: Alfred A. Knopf.

Light, K. (2003) The Cochrane Library. *Self Training Guide and Notes*, Issue 4. Centre for Reviews and Dissemination, University of York.

Lindemann, E. (1965) Symptomatology and management of acute grief, in H. J. Parad (ed.) *Crisis Intervention: Selected Readings*. New York: Family Service Association of America.

Lishman, J. (1994) *Communication in Social Work*. Basingstoke: Macmillan/BASW.

Lishman, J. (2002) Personal and professional development, in R. Adams, L. Dominelli and M. Payne (eds) *Social Work: Themes, Issues and Critical Debates*, 2nd edn. Basingstoke: Palgrave.

Little, M. (2000) Family support, in M. Davies (ed.) *The Blackwell Encyclopaedia of Social Work*, 2nd edn. Oxford: Blackwell.

Littlechild, R. (1996) Risk and older people, in H. Kempshall and J. Pritchard (eds) *Good Practice in Risk Assessment and Risk Management*. London: Jessica Kingsley.

Lloyd, M. and Taylor, C. (1995) From Hollis to the Orange Book: developing a holistic model of assessment in the 1990s, *British Journal of Social Work*, 25: 691–710.

London Borough of Brent (1985) *A Child in Trust: the Report of the Panel of Inquiry into the Circumstances Surrounding the Death of Jasmine Beckford*. London: London Borough of Brent.

Lupton, C. (2000) Interdisciplinary practice, in M. Davies (ed.) *The Blackwell Encyclopaedia of Social Work*, 2nd edn. Oxford: Blackwell.

Macdonald, G. (1990) Allocating blame in social work, *British Journal of Social Work*, 20: 525–46.

Macdonald, G. (2002) The evidence-based perspective, in M. Davies (ed.) *The Blackwell Companion to Social Work*, 2nd edn. Oxford: Blackwell.

Macdonald, G. and Macdonald, K. (1995) Ethical issues in social work research, in R. Hugman and D. Smith (eds) *Ethical Issues in Social Work*. London: Routledge.

Macdonald, G., Sheldon, B. and Gillespie, J. (1992) Contemporary studies of the effectiveness of social work, *British Journal of Social Work*, 22: 615–43.

Mahler, M. S., Pine, F. and Bergman, A. (1975) *The Psychological Birth of the Human Infant*. New York: Basic Books.

Main, M. (1995) Recent studies in attachment: overview, with selected implications for clinical work, in S. Goldberg, R. Muir and J. Kerr (eds)

Attachment Theory: Social, Developmental and Clinical Perspectives. Hillside, NJ: Analytic Press.

Marris, P. (1996a) *The Politics of Uncertainty: Attachment in Private and Public Life.* London: Routledge.

Marris, P. (1996b) *The management of uncertainty,* in S. Kraemer and J. Roberts (eds) *The Politics of Attachment: Towards a Secure Society.* London: Free Association Books.

Marsden, D., Oakley, P. and Pratt, B. (1994) *Measuring the Process: Guidelines for Evaluating Social Development.* Oxford: Intrac Publications.

Marsh, P. (2002) Task-centred work, in M. Davies (ed.) *The Blackwell Companion to Social Work,* 2nd edn. Oxford: Blackwell.

Marsh, P. and Doel, M. (2005) *The Task-Centred Book.* London: Routledge/ Community Care.

Marsh, P. and Triseliotis, J. (1996) *Ready to Practise? Social Workers and Probation Officers: Their Training and First Year at Work.* Aldershot: Avebury.

Marziali, E. (1988) The first session: an interpersonal encounter, *Social Casework,* 69(1): 23–7.

Maslow, A. H. (1954) *Motivation and Personality.* New York: Harper and Row.

Matthews, S., Harvey, A. and Trevithick, P. (2003) Surviving the swamp: using cognitive-behavioural therapy in a social work setting, *Journal of Social Work Practice,* 17(2), November.

Mattinson, J. (1975) *The Reflection Process in Casework Supervision.* London: Institute of Marital Studies.

Mayer, J. E. and Timms, N. (1970) *The Client Speaks.* London: Routledge and Kegan Paul.

Mayo, M. (1994) Community Work, in C. Hanvey and T. Philpot (eds) *Practising Social Work.* London: Routledge.

Mayo, M. (2002) Community work, in R. Adams, L. Dominelli and M. Payne (eds) *Social Work: Themes, Issues and Critical Debates,* 2nd edn. Basingstoke: Macmillan.

McCulloch, A. (2000) Assertive outreach, in M. Davies (ed.) *Blackwell Encyclopaedia of Social Work.* Oxford: Oxford University Press.

McLeod, E. and Bywaters, P. (2000) *Social Work, Health and Equality.* London: Routledge.

McLeod, J. (2003) *An Introduction to Counselling,* 3rd edn. Buckingham: Open University Press.

McLeroy, K. R., Bibeau, D., Steckler, A. and Glanz, K. (1988) An Ecological Perspective on Health Promotion Programs, *Health Education Quarterly,* 14(4): 351–77.

Means, R., Richards, S. and Smith, R. (2003) *Community Care: Policy and Practice,* 3rd edn. Basingstoke: Palgrave Macmillan.

Mearns, D. and Thorne, D. (2000) *Person-centred Therapy Today: New Frontiers in Theory and Practice.* London: Sage.

Mehrabian, A. (1972) *Nonverbal Communication.* Chicago, IL: Aldine.

Mercer, S. W. and Reynolds, W. J. (2002) Empathy and quality of care, in *British Journal of General Practice,* Quality Supplement, October.

Millar, R., Crute, V. and Hargie, O. (1992) *Professional Interviewing.* London: Routledge.

Miller, J. B. (ed.) (1976) *Toward a New Psychology of Women*. Harmondsworth: Penguin.

Miller, J. B. (1986) *What do we mean by relationships?* Work in Progress 22. Wellesley, MA: Stone Center Publication.

Miller, J. B and Stiver, I. P. (1997) *The Healing Connection: How Women Form Relationships in Therapy and in Life*. Boston: Beacon Press.

Miller, W. R. and Rollnick, S. (2002) *Motivational Interviewing: Preparing People for Change*, 2nd edn. London: Guilford Press.

Millham, S., Bullock, R., Hosie, K. and Haak, M. (1986) *Lost in Care*. Aldershot: Gower.

Mills, C. W. (1959) *The Sociological Imagination*. Oxford: Oxford University Press.

Milner, J. (2000) Solution focused therapy, in M. Davies (ed.) *Blackwell Encyclopaedia of Social Work*. Oxford: Oxford University Press.

Milner, J. and O'Byrne, P. (2002) *Assessment in Social Work*, 2nd edn. Basingstoke: Macmillan.

Mitchell, D. (1996) Fear rules, *Community Care*, 14–20 March: 18–19.

Mitchell, J. (1974) *Psychoanalysis and Feminism*. Harmondsworth: Penguin.

Mitchell, J. (1984) *Women: the Longest Revolution: Essays in Feminism, Literature and Psychoanalysis*. London: Virago.

Modi, P., Marks, C. and Watley, R. (1995) From the margin to the centre: empowering the child, in C. Cloke and M. Davies (eds) *Participation and Empowerment in Child Protection*. London: Pitman.

Montgomery, M. (1995) *An Introduction to Language and Society*, 2nd edn. London: Routledge.

Mruk, C. J. (1999) *Self-Esteem: Research, Theory and Practice*, 2nd edn. London: Free Association Books.

Mullender, A. and Perrott, S. (2002) Social work and organisations, in R. Adams, L. Dominelli and M. Payne (eds) *Social Work: Themes, Issues and Critical Debates*, 2nd edn. Basingstoke: Palgrave.

Munby, T. (2000) Capacity/incapacity, in M. Davies (ed.) *Blackwell Encyclopaedia of Social Work*. Oxford: Oxford University Press.

Munby, T. (2002) The legal perspective, in M. Davies (ed.) *The Blackwell Companion to Social Work*, 2nd edn. Oxford: Blackwell.

Munro, E. (1996) Avoidable and unavoidable mistakes in child protection work, *British Journal of Social Work*, **26**: 793–808.

Munro, E. (1998a) Improving social workers' knowledge base in child protection work, *British Journal of Social Work*, **28**: 89–105.

Munro, E. (1998b) *Understanding Social Work: An Empirical Approach*. London: Athlone Press.

Myers, L. L. and Thyer, B. A. (1997) Should social work clients have the right to effective treatment? *Social Work*, 42(3): 288–98.

Nathan, J. (2002) Psychoanalytic theory, in M. Davies (ed.) *The Blackwell Companion to Social Work*, 2nd edn. Oxford: Blackwell.

National Occupational Standards – see TOPSS.

Nelson-Jones, R. (1990) *Human Relationship Skills*. London: Cassell.

Nelson-Jones, R. (2000) *Introduction to Counselling Skills: Text and Activities*. London: Sage.

Nettleton, S. (1995) *The Sociology of Health and Illness*. Cambridge: Polity Press.

Neville, D. (2004) *Putting Empowerment into Practice: Turning Rhetoric into Reality*. London: Whiting and Birch.

Neville, D. and Beak, D. (1990) Solving the case history mystery, *Social Work Today*, 28 June.

NICE (see National Institute of Clinical Excellence)

O'Hagan, K. (1996) *Competence in Social Work Practice: A Practical Guide for Professionals*. London: Jessica Kingsley.

O'Hagan, K. (2000) Crisis intervention, in M. Davies (ed.) *Blackwell Encyclopaedia of Social Work*. Oxford: Oxford University Press.

O'Hare, T. (1991) Integrating research and practice: a framework for implementation, *Social Work*, 36(3): 220–3.

O'Sullivan, T. (1999) *Decision-making in Social Work*. Basingstoke: Macmillan.

O'Sullivan, T. (2000) Decision making in social work, in M. Davies (ed.) *Blackwell Encyclopaedia of Social Work*. Oxford: Oxford University Press.

Oliver, M. (1996) *Understanding Disability: From Theory to Practice*. London: Macmillan.

Onyett, S. (2000) Mental illness, in M. Davies (ed.) *Blackwell Encyclopaedia of Social Work*. Oxford: Oxford University Press.

Orme, J. (2001) Regulation or fragmentation? Directions for social work under New Labour, *British Journal of Social Work*, 31: 611–24.

Orme, J. (2002) Feminist social work, in R. Adams, L. Dominelli and M. Payne (eds) *Social Work: Themes, Issues and Critical Debates*, 2nd edn. Basingstoke: Palgrave.

Palmer, G., Carr, J. and Kenway, P. (2004) *Findings: Monitoring Poverty and Social Exclusion 2004*. York: Joseph Rowntree Foundation.

Parad, H. J. (1958) *Ego Psychology and Dynamic Casework*. New York: Family Service Association of America.

Parad, H. J. (1965) *Crisis Intervention: Selected Readings*. New York: Family Service Association of America.

Parad, H. J. and Parad, L. G. (1990) Crisis intervention: an introductory overview, in H. J. Parad and L. G. Parad (eds) *Crisis Intervention Book 2: The Practitioner's Sourcebook for Brief Therapy*. Milwaukee, WI: Family Service Association of America.

Parsloe, P. (1988) Developing interviewing skills, *Social Work Education*, 8(1): 3–9.

Parsloe, P. (2000) Generic and specialist practice, in M. Davies (ed.) *Blackwell Encyclopaedia of Social Work*. Oxford: Oxford University Press, p. 145.

Parton, N. (ed.) (1996) *Social Theory, Social Change and Social Work*. London: Routledge.

Parton, N. (2000) Some thoughts on the relationship between theory and practice in and for social work, *British Journal of Social Work*, 30: 449–63.

Paterson, C. (2002) *The context, experience and outcome of acupuncture treatment: users' perspectives and outcome questionnaire performance*. Unpublished PhD dissertation. University of London.

Pavlov, I. P. (1927) *Conditional Reflexes*. London: Oxford University Press.

Pawson, R., Boaz, A., Grayson, L., Long, A. and Barnes, C. (2003) *Types and Quality of Knowledge in Social Care*, SCIE Knowledge Review 7. Bristol: Policy Press.

Payne, C. (1994) The systems approach, in C. Hanvey and T. Philpot (eds) *Practising Social Work*. London: Routledge.

Payne, M. (1996) *What is Professional Social Work?* Birmingham: Venture.

Payne, M. (1997) *Modern Social Work Theory*, 2nd edn. Basingstoke: Macmillan.

Payne, M. (2000) Social work theory, in M. Davies (ed.) *Blackwell Encyclopaedia of Social Work*. Oxford: Oxford University Press.

Payne, M. (2002) Social work theories and reflective practice, in R. Adams, L. Dominelli and M. Payne (eds) *Social Work: Themes, Issues and Critical Debates*, 2nd edn. Basingstoke: Palgrave.

Payne, M., Adams, R. and Dominelli, L. (2002) On being critical in social work, in R. Adams, L. Dominelli and M. Payne (eds) *Critical Practice in Social Work*. Basingstoke: Palgrave.

Penna, S. (2000) Modernity, in M. Davies (ed.) *Blackwell Encyclopaedia of Social Work*. Oxford: Oxford University Press.

Perlman, H. H. (1986) The problem-solving model, in F. J. Turner (ed.) *Social Work Treatment: Interlocking Theoretical Approaches*, 3rd edn. New York: Free Press.

Petch, A. (2000) Work with adult service users, in M. Davies (ed.) *The Blackwell Encylopaedia of Social Work*, 2nd edn. Oxford: Blackwell.

Petch, A. (2002) Needs-led policies, in M. Davies (ed.) *The Blackwell Companion to Social Work*, 2nd edn. Oxford: Blackwell.

Phillips, A. (1988) *Winnicott*. London: Fontana.

Phillips, J. (1996) The future of social work with older people in a changing world, in N. Parton (ed.) *Social Theory, Social Change and Social Work*. London: Routledge.

Phillipson, C. (1993) Approaches to advocacy, in R. Adams, L. Dominelli and M. Payne (eds) *Social Work: Themes, Issues and Critical Debates*. Basingstoke: Macmillan.

Phillipson, C. (2002) The frailty of old age, in M. Davies (ed.) *The Blackwell Encyclopaedia of Social Work*, 2nd edn. Oxford: Blackwell.

Piaget, J. (1932) *The Moral Judgement of the Child*. London: Routledge and Kegan Paul.

Piaget, J. (1959) *The Language and Thought of the Child*. London: Routledge and Kegan Paul.

Pierson, J. (1994) The behavioural approach to social work, in C. Hanvey and T. Philpot (eds) *Practising Social Work*. London: Routledge.

Pierson, J. and Thomas, M. (2002) *Collins Dictionary of Social Work*, 2nd edn. London: Collins.

Pinker, R. (1990) *Social Work in an Enterprise Society*. London: Routledge.

Popper, K. L. (1994a) *Knowledge and the Body-mind Problem: In Defence of Interaction*. Edited by M. A. Notturno. London: Routledge.

Popper, K. L. (1994b) *The Myth of the Framework: In Defence of Science and Rationality*. Edited by M. A. Notturno. London: Routledge.

Popper, K. L. (1999) *All Life is Problem Solving*. London: Routledge.

Portnoy, D. (1999) Relatedness: Where humanistic and psychoanalytic psychotherapy converge, *Journal of Humanistic Psychology*, 39(1): 19–34.

Preston-Shoot, M. (1994) Written agreements: a contractual approach to social work, in C. Hanvey and T. Philpot (eds) *Practising Social Work*. London: Routledge.

Preston-Shoot, M. and Agass, D. (1990) *Making Sense of Social Work*. Basingstoke: Macmillan.

Preston-Shoot, M. (2004) Evidence: the final frontier? Star Trek, groupwork and the mission of change, *Groupwork*. 14(3): 18–43.

Prideaux, D. (2002) Researching the outcomes of educational interventions: a matter of design, *British Medical Journal*, 324: 126–7.

Pringle, N. N. and Thompson, P. J. (1999) *Social Work, Psychiatry and the Law*. Aldershot: Arena.

Pritchard, C. (2000a) Self-harm, in M. Davies (ed.) *The Blackwell Encylopaedia of Social Work*, 2nd edn. Oxford: Blackwell.

Pritchard, C. (2000b) Suicide, in M. Davies (ed.) *The Blackwell Encylopaedia of Social Work*, 2nd edn. Oxford: Blackwell.

Pritchard, J. (ed.) (1995) *Good Practice in Supervision*. London: Jessica Kingsley.

Prochaska, J. O. and DiClemente, C. C. (1984) *The Transtheoretical Approach*. Homewood, IL: Dow Jones-Irwin.

Prochaska, J. O. and Norcross, J. C. (2003) *Systems of Psychotherapy: A Transtheoretical Analysis*. Pacific Grove, CA: Brooks/Cole.

Prochaska, J. O., Norcross, J. C. and DiClemente, C. C. (1994) *Changing for Good*. New York: Avon Books.

Ramon, S. (1991) *Beyond Community Care: Normalization and Integration Work*. London: Macmillan.

Rapoport, L. (1967) Crisis-orientated short term casework, *Social Services Review*, 41: 31–44.

Reber, A. S. and Reber, E. (2001) *Dictionary of Psychology,* 3rd edn. London: Penguin.

Reid, W. J. (1978) *The Task-centred System*. New York: Columbia University Press.

Reid, W. J. and Epstein, L. (1972) *Task-Centred Casework*. New York: Columbia University Press.

Reid, W. J. and Shyne, A. (1969) *Brief and Extended Casework*. New York: Columbia University Press.

Reigate, N. (1997) Networking, in R. Adams, L. Dominelli and M. Payne (eds) *Social Work: Themes, Issues and Critical Debates*. Basingstoke: Macmillan.

Rey, L. D. (1996) What social workers need to know about client violence, *Families in Society*, 77(1): 33–9.

Richards, S. (2000) Bridging the divide: elders and the assessment process, *British Journal of Social Work*, 30: 37–49.

Richards, S., Ruch, G. and Trevithick, P (2005) Communication skills training for practice: the ethical dilemma for social work education, *Social Work Education* (awaiting publication).

Roberts, A. R. (1990) *Crisis Intervention Handbook: Assessment, Treatment and Research*. Belmont, CA: Wadsworth.

Roberts, G. and Preston-Shoot, M. (2000) Law and social work, in M. Davies (ed.) *Blackwell Encyclopaedia of Social Work*. Oxford: Oxford University Press.

Roberts, J. and Taylor, C. (1996) Sexually abused children and young people speak out, in L. Waterstone (ed.) *Child Abuse and Child Abusers: Protection and Prevention*. London: Jessica Kingsley.

Robinson, L. (1995) *Psychology for Social Workers: Black Perspective*. London: Routledge.

Robinson, L. (1998) *Race: Communication and the Caring Professions*. Buckingham: Open University Press.

Robinson, L. (2000) Social work practice in a multi-cultural society, in M. Davies (ed.) *The Blackwell Encyclopaedia of Social Work*, 2nd edn. Oxford: Blackwell.

Rogers, C. R. (1951) *Client-Centred Therapy*. Boston, MA: Houghton Mifflin.

Rogers, C. R. (1957) The necessary and sufficient conditions of therapeutic personality change, *Journal of Consulting Psychology*, 21: 95–103.

Rogers, C. R. (1961) *On Becoming a Person*. Boston: Houghton Mifflin.

Rogers, C. R. (1975) Empathic: an unappreciated way of being, *Counseling Psychologist*, 5: 2–10.

Rojek, C. and Collins, S. (1988) Contact or con trick?, *British Journal of Social Work*, 18: 11–22.

Rowe, D. (1994) *Breaking the Bonds: Understanding Depression, Finding Freedom*. London: HarperCollins.

Roy, A. Wattam, C. and Young, F. (2002) Looking after children and young people, in R. Adams, L. Dominelli and M. Payne (eds) *Critical Practice in Social Work*. Basingstoke: Palgrave.

Rutter, M. and Rutter, M. (1993) *Developing Minds: Challenge and Continuity Across the Life Span*. Harmondsworth: Penguin.

Rycroft, C. (1968) *A Critical Dictionary of Psychoanalysis*. Harmondsworth: Penguin.

Sackett, D. L., Rosenberg, W. M., Jray, J., Haynes, R. B. and Richardson, W. S. (1996) Evidence-based practice: what it is and what it isn't, *British Medical Journal*, 312 7023): 71–2.

Sainsbury, E. (1987) Client studies: their contribution and limitations in influencing social work practice, *British Journal of Social Work*, 17: 635–44.

Sainsbury, E., Nixon, S. and Phillips, D. (1982) *Social Work in Focus; Clients' and Social Workers' Perceptions of Long Term Social Work*. London: Routledge and Kegan Paul.

Saleebey, D. (ed.) (1992) *The Strengths Perspective in Social Work Practice*. London: Longman.

Saleebey, D. (2003) Strengths-based practice, in R. A. English (ed.) *Encyclopedia of Social Work*, 19th edn, 2003 Supplement, pp. 150–62. Washington, DC: National Association of Social Workers.

Salzberger-Wittenberg, I. (1970) *Psycho-analytic Insight, and Relationships*. London: Routledge.

Scambler, G. (ed.) (2003) *Sociology as Applied to Medicine*, 5th edn. London: Saunders.

Schmidt, R. A. (1975) *Motor Skills*. London: Harper and Row.

Schön, D. (1991) *The Reflective Practitioner: How Professionals Think in Action*. Aldershot: Arena.

Seden, J. (1999) *Counselling Skills in Social Work*. Buckingham: Open University Press.

Seed, P. (1990) *Introducing Network Analysis in Social Work*. London: Jessica Kingsley.

Seligman, M. E. P. (1975) *Helplessness*. San Francisco, CA: Freeman.

Seu, I. B. and Heenan, M. C. (eds) (1998) *Feminism and Psychotherapy: Reflections on Contemporary Theories and Practices*. London: Sage.

Shah, N. (1989) It's up to you sisters: black women and radical social work, in M. Langan and P. Lee (eds) *Radical Social Work Today*. London: Unwin Hyman.

Shardlow, S. (2002) Values, ethics and social work, in R. Adams, L. Dominelli and M. Payne (eds) *Social Work: Themes, Issues and Critical Debates*, 2nd edn. Basingstoke: Palgrave.

Shaw, I. (1996) *Evaluating in Practice*. Aldershot: Arena.

Shaw, I. and Shaw, A. (1997) Keeping social work honest; evaluating as profession and practice, *British Journal of Social Work*, 27: 847–69.

Shaw, I. (2000) Research in social work, in M. Davies (ed.) *Blackwell Encyclopaedia of Social Work*. Oxford: Oxford University Press.

Shaw, I. F. (2003) Cutting edge issues in social work research, *British Journal of Social Work*, 33, 107–16.

Shaw, M. and Dorling, D. (2004) Who cares in England and Wales? The positive care law: cross-sectional study, *British Journal of General Practice,* December 2004.

Sheldon, B. (1982) *Behaviour Modification: Theory, Practice and Philosophy*. London: Tavistock.

Sheldon, B. (1995) *Cognitive-behavioural Therapy: Research, Practice and Philosophy*. London: Routledge.

Sheldon, B. (2000) Cognitive behavioural methods in social care: a look at the evidence, in P. Stepney and D. Ford (eds) *Social Work Models, Methods and Theories*. Lyme Regis: Russell House.

Sheldon, B. and Macdonald, G. (1999) *Research and Practice: Mind the Gap*. Exeter: Centre for Evidence Based Social Services.

Sheppard, M. (1994) Maternal depression, child care and the social work role, *British Journal of Social Work*, 24: 33–51.

Sheppard, M. (1995) Primary health care and the social organisation of interprofessional collaboration in mental health: lessons from general practice and social work, in C. Duggan, A. Williamson, S. Ritter and M. Watkins (eds) *Multiprofessional Co-operation in Community Mental Health*. Sevenoaks: Hodder and Stoughton.

Sheppard, M. (1997) The psychiatric unit, in M. Davies (ed.) *The Blackwell Companion to Social Work*. Oxford: Blackwell.

Sheppard, M. (1998) Practice validity, reflexivity and knowledge for social work, *British Journal of Social Work*, 28: 763–81.

Sheppard, M. (2002) Mental health and social justice: gender, race and psychological consequences of fairness, *British Journal of Social Work*, 32: 779–97.

Sheppard, M., Newstead, S., DiCaccavo, A. and Ryan, K. (2000) Reflexivity and the development of process knowledge in social work: a classification and empirical study, *British Journal of Social Work,* 30: 465–88.

Sheppard, M., Newstead, S., DiCaccavo, A. and Ryan, K. (2001) Comparative Hypothesis Assessment and Quasi Triangulation as Process Knowledge Assessment Strategies in Social Work Practice, *British Journal of Social Work,* 31: 863–85.

Sheppard, M. and Ryan, K. (2003) Practitioners as Rule Using Analysts: A Further Development of Process Knowledge in Social Work, *British Journal of Social Work,* 33: 157–76.

Shulman, L. (1984) *The Skills of Helping*: *Individuals and Groups*, 2nd edn. Itasca, IL: Peacock.

Shulman, L. (1999) *The Skills of Helping Individuals, Families, Groups and Communities*, 4th edn. Itasca, IL: Peacock.

Sinason, V. (1988) Smiling, swallowing, sickening and stupefying: the effect of sexual abuse on the child, *Psychoanalytic Psychotherapy*, 3(2): 97–111.

Sinclair, I. (2002) A quality-control perspective, in M. Davies (ed.) *The Blackwell Companion to Social Work*, 2nd edn. Oxford: Blackwell.

Skinner, B. F. (1938) *The Behavior of Organisms. An Experimental Analysis*. New York: Appleton-Century-Crofts.

Skinner, B. F. (1974) *About Behaviourism*. London: Jonathan Cape.

Smale, G. and Tuson, G. with Biehal, N. and Marsh, P. (1993) *Empowerment, Assessment, Care Management and the Skilled Worker*. London: HMSO.

Smale, G. and Tuson, G. with Biehal, N. and Statham, D. (2000) *Social Work and Social Problems*. Basingstoke: Macmillan.

Smith, D. (2002) Social work with offenders, in R. Adams, L. Dominelli and M. Payne (eds) *Social Work: Themes, Issues and Critical Debates*, 2nd edn. Basingstoke: Macmillan.

Smith, J. (2004) A speech by Rt. Hon. Jacqui Smith MP, Minister of State for Industry and the Regions and Deputy Minister for Women and Equality to the 'Social Work Steps Forward' National Conference, 12th May 2004. Available online at http://www.dh.gov.uk/PolicyAndGuidance/HumanResourcesAnd-Training/SocialCareTraining/NewSocialWorkDegree/NewSocialWorkDe-greeBackground/fs/en?CONTENT_ID = 4080766&chk = Fc/9T0

Smith, V. (1986) Listening, in O. Hargie (ed.) *A Handbook of Communication Skills*. London: Routledge.

Social Services Inspectorate (1991) *Getting the Message Across: A Guide to Developing and Communicating Policies, Principles and Procedures on Assessment*. London: HMSO.

Social Services Inspectorate (1993) *Evaluating Child Protection Services: Findings and Issues*. London: Department of Health.

Social Trends (2004) No. 34. London: HMSO. Available online at http://www.statistics.gov.uk/statbase/Product.asp?vlnk = 57488&More = N

Solomon, B. B. (1976) *Black Empowerment: Social Work with Oppressed Communities*. New York: Columbia University Press.

Stepney, P. (2000a) An overview of the wider policy context, in P. Stepney and D. Ford (eds) *Social Work Models, Methods and Theories*. Lyme Regis: Russell House.

Stepney, P. (2000b) The theory to practice debate revisited, in P. Stepney and D. Ford (eds) *Social Work Models, Methods and Theories*. Lyme Regis: Russell House.

Stepney, P. and Ford, D. (2000) *Social Work Models, Methods and Theories*. Lyme Regis: Russell House.

Stern, D. N. (1987) *The Interpersonal World of the Infant: A View for Psychoanalysis and Developmental Psychology*. New York: Basic Books.

Stevenson, O. (1988) Law and social work education: a commentary on the 'Law Report', *Issues in Social Work Education*, 8(1): 37–45.

Stevenson, O. (1989) *Age and Vulnerability. A Guide to Better Care*. London: Edward Arnold.

Stevenson, O. and Parsloe, P. (1993) *Community Care and Empowerment*. York: Joseph Rowntree Foundation.

Stewart, J. (2000a) Poverty, in M. Davies (ed.) *Blackwell Encyclopaedia of Social Work*. Oxford: Blackwell.

Stewart, J. (2000b) Social policy, in M. Davies (ed.) *Blackwell Encyclopaedia of Social Work*. Oxford: Oxford University Press.

Sugarman, L. (1986) *Life-Span Development: Concepts, Theories and Interventions*. London: Methuen.

Surrey, J. L. (1991) Relationships and empowerment, in J. V. Jordan, A. G. Kaplan, J. B. Stiver, I. P. and J. L. Surrey (eds) *Women's Growth and Connection: Writings from the Stone Center*. New York: Guilford Press.

Susser, M. (1968) *Community Psychiatry: Epidemiologic and Social Themes*. New York: Random House.

Thoburn, J., Lewis, A. and Shemmings, D. (1995) *Paternalism or Partnership? Family Involvement in the Child Protection Process*. London: HMSO.

Thoburn, J. (2002) The community child care team, in M. Davies (ed.) *The Blackwell Companion to Social Work*, 2nd edn. Oxford: Blackwell.

Thompson, N. (1995) *Theory and Practice in Health and Social Welfare*. Buckingham: Open University Press.

Thompson, N. (2000a) Reflective practice, in M. Davies (ed.) *The Blackwell Encyclopaedia of Social Work*, 2nd edn. Oxford: Blackwell.

Thompson, N. (2000b) *Understanding Social Work: Preparing for Practice*. Basingstoke: Palgrave.

Thompson, N. (2002a) Anti-discriminatory practice, in M. Davies (ed.) *The Blackwell Companion to Social Work*, 2nd edn. Oxford: Blackwell.

Thompson, N. (2002b) Social work with adults, in R. Adams, L. Dominelli and M. Payne (eds) *Social Work: Themes, Issues and Critical Debates*, 2nd edn. Basingstoke: Macmillan.

Thompson, N. (2002c) *People Skills*, 2nd edn. Basingstoke: Palgrave Macmillan.

Thompson, N. (2003) *Communication and Language: A Handbook of Theory and Practice*. Basingstoke: Palgrave Macmillan.

Thorne, B. (1992) *Carl Rogers*. London: Sage.

Thorne, B. (2002) Person-centred counselling, in M. Davies (ed.) *The Blackwell Companion to Social Work*, 2nd edn. Oxford: Blackwell.

TOPSS UK (2002) *The National Occupational Standards for Social Work*. Working Copy. Available online at http://www.topss.org.uk/uk_eng/standards/cdrom/England/Main.htm

TOPSS UK (2004) *The National Occupational Standards for Social Work*. April 2004.

Townsend, P. (1993) *The International Analysis of Poverty*. Hemel Hempstead: Harvester Wheatsheaf.

Trevithick, P. (1988) Unconsciousness raising with working class women, in S. Krzowski and P. Land (eds) *In Our Experience: Workshops at the Women's Therapy Centre*. London: Women's Press.

Trevithick, P. (1993) Surviving childhood sexual and physical abuse: the experience of two women of Irish-English parentage, in H. Ferguson, R. Gilligan and R. Torode (eds) *Surviving Childhood Adversity: Issues for Policy and Practice*. Dublin: Social Studies Press.

Trevithick, P. (1995) 'Cycling over Everest': groupwork with depressed women, *Groupwork*, 8(1): 5–33.

Trevithick, P. (1998) Psychotherapy and working class women, in I. B. Seu and M. Colleen Heenan (eds) *Feminism and Psychotherapy: Reflections on Contemporary Theories and Practices*. London: Sage.

Trevithick, P. (2003) Effective relationship-based practice: a theoretical exploration, *Journal of Social Work Practice*, 17(2), November.

Trevithick, P., Richards, S., Ruch, G. and Moss, B. (2004) *Knowledge Review: Teaching and Learning Communication Skills in Social Work Education*. Bristol: Policy Press.

Trotter, C. (1999) *Working with Involuntary Clients: A Guide to Practice*. London: Sage.

Trowell, J. and Bower, M. (1995) *The Emotional Needs of Young Children and their Families*. London: Routledge.

Trower, P., Casey, A. and Dryden, W. (1988) *Cognitive-Behavioural Counselling in Action*. London: Sage.

Truax, C. B. and Carkhuff, R. R. (1967) *Towards Effective Counselling and Psychotherapy*. Chicago, IL: Aldine.

Ussher, J. (1991) *Women's Madness: Misogyny or Mental Illness*. Hemel Hempstead: Harvester Wheatsheaf.

Velasquez, M. M., Maurer, G. G., Crouch, C. and DiClemente, C. C. (2001) *Group Treatment for Substance Abuse: A Stages-of-Change Therapy Manual*. New York: Guilford.

Wade, D. T. and Halligan, P. W. (2004) Do biomedical models of illness make for good healthcare systems, *British Medical Journal*, 329, 1398–401.

Walker, C. and Walker, A. (2002) Social policy and social work, in R. Adams, L. Dominelli and M. Payne (eds) *Social Work: Themes, Issues and Critical Debates*, 2nd edn. Basingstoke: Palgrave.

Walker, S. (2003) *Social Work and Child and Adolescent Mental Health*. Lyme Regis: Russell House.

Walter, I., Nutley, S., Percy-Smith, J., McNeish, D. and Frost, S. (2004) *Improving the Use of Research in Social Care Practice*, SCIE Knowledge Review 3. Bristol: Polity Press.

Waterhouse, L. and McGhee, J. (2002) Social work with children and families, in R. Adams, L. Dominelli and M. Payne (eds) *Social Work: Themes, Issues and Critical Debates*, 2nd edn. Basingstoke: Palgrave.

Watson, J. B. (1970) *Behaviourism*. New York: Norton.

Watt, G. (2001) Policies to tackle social exclusion, *British Medical Journal*, 323, 28 July.

Watzlawick, P., Weakland, J. and Risch, R. (1974) *Change: Principles of Problem Formation and Problem Resolution*. London: Norton.

Webb, D. (1996) Regulation for radicals: The state, CCETSW and the academy, in N. Parton (ed.) *Social Theory, Social Change and Social Work*. London: Routledge.

Webb, S. A. (2001) Some considerations on the validity of evidence-based practice in social work, *British Journal of Social Work*, **31**, 57–79.

Weick, A. (1983) A growth-task model of human development, *Social Casework*, 64(3): 131–7.

Welford, A. T. (1958) *Ageing and Human Skill*. London: Oxford University Press.

Whittington, C. (2000) Education and training for social work, in M. Davies (ed.) *Blackwell Encyclopaedia of Social Work*. Oxford: Oxford University Press.

Williams, J. (2001) 1998 Human Rights Act: social work's new benchmark, *British Journal of Social Work*, 31, 831–44.

Williams, J. (2004) Social work, liberty and the law, *British Journal of Social Work*, 34: 37–52.

Wilson, K. (2000) Therapeutic intervention, in M. Davies (ed.) *Encyclopaedia of Social Work*. Oxford: Oxford University Press, p. 350.

Winnicott, D. W. (1958) *Through Paediatrics to Psycho-Analysis*. London: Hogarth Press.

Winnicott, D. W. (1965) *The Maturational Process and the Facilitating Environment: Studies in the Theory of Emotional Development*. London: Hogarth (also published in 1990 by Karnac Books).

Winnicott, D. W. (1971) *Playing and Reality*. London: Routledge.

Winnicott, D. W. (1986) *Home Is Where We Start From*. Harmondsworth: Penguin.

Wise, S. (1990) Becoming a feminist social worker, in L. Stanley (ed.) *Feminist Praxis: Research, Theory and Epistemology in Feminist Sociology*. London: Routledge.

Wise, S. (1995) Feminist ethics in practice, in R. Hugman and D. Smith (eds) *Ethical Issues in Social Work*. London: Routledge.

Wolfensberger, W. (1984) A reconceptualization of normalization as social role valorization, *Mental Retardation*, 34: 22–5.

Worden, W. J. (2000) *Grief Counselling and Grief Therapy*, 3rd edn. Hove: Brunner-Routledge.

Yates, J. (2004) Evidence, effectiveness and groupwork developments in youth justice. *Groupwork*, 14(3): 81–100.

Yelloly, M. (1980) *Social Work Theory and Psychoanalysis*. New York: Van Nostrand.

Zubrzycki, J. (2003) *The construction of personal and professional boundaries in Australian social work: a qualitative exploration of the self in practice*. Unpublished PhD dissertation. School of Social Work and Social Policy, Curtin University of Technology, Australia.

Useful websites

British National Formulary – http://www.bnf.org

Centre for Reviews and Dissemination (CRD), University of York – http://www.york.ac.uk/inst/crd/clibsec1/pdf

Cochrane Library's consumer-friendly website – http://www.informedhealthonline.org

Cochrane Library's official site – http://www.cochrane.org

Department for Education and Skills (2004) *Every Child Matters: Change for Children* (Nottingham: DfES) http://www.everychildmatters.gov.uk

Department of Health (2005) *Adult Social Care* (http://www.dh.gov.uk/PolicyAndGuidance/HealthAndSocialCareTopics/SocialCare/fs/en).

For depression, NHS Direct website – http://www.nhsdirect.nhs.uk/en.asp?TopicID = 154

General Social Care Council – http://www.gscc.org.uk.

International Association of Schools of Social Work (IASSW) website - http://www.iassw.soton.ac.uk

International Federation of Social Work (IFSW) website - http://www.ifsw.org

Mental Health Act 1983 – http://www.dh.gov.uk/PolicyAndGuidance/HealthAndSocialCareTopics/MentalHealth

National Electronic Library for Health – http://wwe.nelh.nhs.uk

National Institute of Clinical Excellence (NICE) – http://www.nice.org.uk/page.aspx?o = cat.diseaseareas

NHS Direct – http://www.nhsdirect.nhs.uk

Quality Assurance Agency for Higher Education – www.qaa.ac.uk/crntwork/benchmark/socialwork.pdf

Social Policy and Social Work subject centre (SWAP) – http://www.swap.ac.uk

INDEX

abuse, of children/young people, 137, 141, 145, 152, 159, 159, 169, 210, 239, 240, 245, 251, 257, 278, 281, 282
  working with abused children and adults, 107, 108, 122, 137, 141, 152, 159, 169, 178, 210, 239, 257, 278–9, 280
abuse of women, 281, 282
abusing/unacceptable behaviour, 96, 134, 159, 169, 178, 209, 239
  see also drug/alcohol abuse
academic curriculum, 16, 24, 27, 29, 38, 56, 60, 62, 109, 252
academics, 4, 19, 30, 51, 52, 56, 58, 60, 61, 68, 127
acceptance, 10, 93, 150, 156, 187, 205, 213, 214, 215, 220, 222, 238, 251, 269
access to files, 43, 173, 248, 250
access to resources/services, 15, 43, 52, 132, 162, 173, 195, 212, 229, 277, 278
  rationing/difficulties accessing resources, 12, 111, 115, 116, 129, 130, 202, 203, 233
accountability, professional, 12, 18, 55, 170, 190, 194, 223, 225, 242, 243, 249, 250, 252, 253, 254
  see also social workers
achievement/achievable, 34, 74, 75, 88, 91, 93, 105, 138, 148, 170, 200, 276, 288
action plan, 137, 225
action, see effective action
actualizing tendency/self-actualizing, 91, 92, 93, 94, 215, 269
Adams, R., 6, 46, 52, 61, 73, 75, 170, 192, 226, 243, 274

adapting/adaptation, importance of, 31, 83, 103, 190, 211, 213, 267
addiction, 50, 114, 117, 187, 208, 288, 290
adolescents/young people, 35, 42, 82, 86, 121, 130, 165, 168, 192, 206, 233, 239, 285
administration and organization skills, 1, 8, 16, 30, 137, 138, 249
adoption, 131, 141, 147
Adult Social Care, 17
adversity, 32, 90, 94, 105, 106, 109, 112, 117, 132, 226, 248, 258, 270
  hardship/suffering, 11, 116, 117, 144, 156, 178, 180, 210, 231, 240, 244, 257, 258, 265, 284
  see also poverty and disadvantage
advice, 66, 82, 116, 167, 193–4, 196, 197, 202, 269
advocacy, 53, 69, 74, 75, 83, 119, 202, 206, 218, 219, 220, 226, 231, 232–5
agency
  constraints/under-resourcing, 3, 9, 43, 49, 74, 89, 134, 135, 138, 146, 220, 243, 245, 251, 267, 285
  inter-agency collaboration, 43, 109, 123, 131, 248, 253
  policy/practice, 17, 47, 51, 66, 67, 83, 146, 160, 213, 225, 234, 243, 244, 247, 253
  voluntary, 31, 119, 151, 196
  see also multi-disciplinary/ interdisciplinary work
  see also social services
aggression, 72, 76, 83, 235, 236, 239–41
agreements/working agreements, 19, 158, 180, 185, 186, 222, 224, 225, 229, 230, 231, 232, 247
  see also contracts

alcohol addiction/abuse, 36, 96, 114, 117, 187, 208, 247, 288, 292
    see also drug abuse; addiction; *Stages of Change*
Aldgate, J., 146, 170, 223, 224
anti-discriminatory perspectives/practice, 80, 133, 162, 171, 192, 213, 245
anti-oppressive perspectives/practice, 61, 80, 82, 133, 157, 162, 192, 213, 242, 245, 279, 285
anti-racist perspectives/practice, 58, 80, 82, 285
analytical skills/critical analysis, 7, 9, 40, 45–48, 291
    see also critical thinking and analysis, critical reflection, reflexivity
anxiety/containing anxiety, 6, 190, 194, 195, 200, 207, 215–7, 224, 225, 236, 253
approaches, *see* practice approaches
    see also skills
approval, 93, 199, 269, 270
assertiveness, 83, 208, 215, 218, 237, 235–6, 266
    training, 236, 261, 262
assessment
    baseline data, importance of 53, 57, 71, 88, 96, 248, 261, 262
    'best evidence', 55, 135, 137, 242, 251
    common purpose, identifying a 119, 163, 218, 225, 229
    decision-making, 1, 19, 31, 38, 43, 49, 55, 113, 131, 135–7, 138, 140, 194, 201, 229, 249, 251, 266
        service user involvement in, 52, 67, 94, 116, 127, 135–7, 222, 230, 245, 268, 276, 282,
    definition, 127
    differences in emphasis, 132
    environmental/social factors, 127, 129, 130, 132, 133
    evidence based, 4, 23, 27, 39, 43, 48, 49, 54–7
    groupthink, 131
    information gathering skills, 51, 52, 53, 86, 87, 140
    involvement of service users, 133, 134, 136, 138, 139
    judgements, 10, 43, 49, 73, 80, 126, 136–7, 157, 159, 200, 230, 249, 250, 251, 253
    needs-led versus resource-led, 72, 130–2

observation, 1, 19, 26, 27, 53, 54, 71, 75, 86, 87, 96, 113, 120, 121–2, 129, 134, 138, 164, 207, 228, 253, 261
outcomes, 1, 12, 19, 56, 65, 96, 129, 133–5, 142, 171, 230, 236, 245, 251, 252, 253, 261, 274, 275, 276
past on present, impact of, 91, 102, 104, 127–8, 145, 151, 159, 163, 169, 179, 180, 198, 221, 238, 270, 273
problem-solving skills, 113, 135–6, 275, 276
    practitioners', 1, 3, 39, 42, 49, 52, 113, 116, 135–6, 138, 214, 228, 229, 243, 275
    service users', 52, 133, 135–6, 141, 194, 215, 275, 289
risk, 10, 29, 35, 52, 66, 70, 74, 86, 87, 91, 111, 115, 126, 130, 174, 219, 230, 239, 242, 245, 253, 257
variables, 39, 56, 57, 76, 120, 134, 251
    see also critical thinking and analysis
    see also evidencing effectiveness/ evaluation of effectiveness,
    see also reflective practice,
assistance, *see* practical and material assistance
assumptions, 24, 30, 32, 34, 45, 46, 68, 107, 108, 116, 131, 133, 166, 175, 210, 227, 282
    about others, 29, 31, 47, 109, 110, 119, 120, 122, 124, 129, 166, 175, 210, 227, 282
attachment/attachment theory
    affectional bonds, 100
    Bowlby, J., 91, 100–2, 211
    different attachment classifications, 102
    importance of, 102
    separation reactions, 102
    'strange situation' test, 102
attribute, 6, 61, 64, 68, 111, 120, 143, 150, 154, 157, 216, 255
Audit Commission, 13, 15, 205
authentic, 150, 269
authority, 6, 17, 68, 159, 197, 201, 202, 208, 222, 225, 230, 233
    see also local authorities
    see also boundaries; role
autonomy, 101, 131, 191, 193, 206, 282, 291
aversion therapy, 96, 261

Bandura, A., 96, 207, 260
Barber, J. G., 50, 187, 188, 288, 290
Barker, R. L., 26, 47, 56, 65, 66, 78, 95, 116, 140, 147, 231, 242, 247
baseline data, importance of, 53, 57, 71, 88, 96, 248, 261, 262
Beck, A., 53, 263, 264, 265
behaviour
    behaviour as clues, 104, 117
    behaviour change, 1, 29, 96, 215, 273, 279, 287, 288
    personal responsibility for, 3, 9, 220, 227, 228, 238, 270, 279, 286
    see also Chapter Three: Understand Human Beings, 90–112
behaviourism, 7, 19, 34, 91, 92, 95–8, 260
    behaviourist approaches, 67, 76, 92, 260, 261, 262
    cognitive-behavioural approaches, 19, 92, 97, 98, 132, 135, 199, 202, 208, 213, 214, 232, 263
    rule based behaviour, 39
beliefs
    defined, 24
    irrational/negative beliefs, 181, 187, 215, 221, 222, 223, 229, 231, 236, 257, 263, 264, 265, 282, 284
benefits, see welfare rights/benefits
Benjamin, J., 107
bereavement/loss, 65, 104, 105, 111, 185, 191, 265, 277
'best evidence', 55, 135, 137, 242, 251
    see also evidencing effectiveness
    see also research
Best Value, 12, 242
bias, 80, 107, 124, 199, 253, 264
Biestek, F. P., 193
black/ethnic minority groups, 4, 40, 80, 82, 90, 108, 109–110, 128, 151, 165, 192, 219, 227, 228, 229, 231, 245, 282, 292
Blom Cooper, L., 16
body language/non-verbal communication, 113, 119–21, 124, 138, 142, 155, 156, 158, 238, 257
bonds/bonding/affectional bonds, 100
boundaries, 144, 145, 171, 182, 240, 246, 247, 248, 274
    professional role, 9, 83, 131, 147, 157, 214, 228, 244, 246–7, 248, 276
Bowlby, J., 91, 100–2, 211
Braye, S., 9, 18, 146, 219, 220, 225, 226,
228, 230, 234
Brearley, J., 107, 246, 248, 253, 254, 273
brief therapy/time-limited work, 67, 83, 104, 163, 264, 266, 267, 276
British Association for Counselling (BAC), 213
building blocks, 276
    see task-centred approaches
bullying, 232, 237, 239
bureaucracy/'bureaucratized', 146, 285

Carkhuff, R. R., 7, 213, 214, 270
capacity/ies
    capacity building and social work, 2, 4–6, 23
    capacity to grow and change, 90, 95, 103,
    coping capacity, 5, 53, 98, 104, 132, 139, 203, 204, 272, 274
    defined, 4
    'incapacity', 245
    practitioners' capacities, 2, 4–6, 8, 9, 23, 43, 61, 73–4, 85, 89, 117, 118, 132, 135, 156, 171, 179, 180, 192, 205, 240, 247, 252, 278
    service users'/carers' capacities, 2, 4–6, 8, 10, 23, 71, 72–3, 87, 89, 94, 95, 98, 102, 106, 111, 132, 135, 144, 172, 195, 205, 211–2, 214, 220, 229, 246, 247, 271, 272, 276, 278
    social/environmental capacities, 1, 2, 4–6, 9, 53, 71, 74–5, 103, 212, 226, 247, 278
care and control, 204, 218, 230
care/caring, 10, 31, 34, 35–6, 42, 44, 54, 61, 68, 101, 102, 115, 121, 129, 133, 140, 145, 153, 154, 163, 173, 191, 193, 202, 204–6, 226, 230, 234, 239, 244, 273, 278, 291
    pitfalls in caring, 205–6
    quality of care, 11, 12, 13, 35–6, 61, 106, 147, 153, 191, 202, 204–6
    self care, 9, 10, 34, 35–6, 226, 245, 256
    social care, 11, 12, 13, 14, 15, 16, 17, 24, 34, 52, 62, 129, 130, 223, 226, 233, 244, 278, 291
    in care/'looked after', 141, 155, 168, 170, 181, 198, 258, 259
carers, 4, 5, 6, 9, 23, 32, 45, 52, 61, 71, 73, 74, 103, 116, 127, 129, 130, 136, 146, 153, 154, 180, 204, 205, 212, 226

Carers (Recognition and Services) Act (1995), 17, 129, 130
foster carers/foster care, 102, 120, 131, 146, 147, 168, 172
Carers and Disabled Children's Act (2000), 129
case conferences, 130, 131, 249
casework, 7, 107, 215, 272
Central Council for Education and Training in Social Work (CCETSW), 14, 58, 61, 62
challenge/challenging, 35, 74, 83, 107, 169, 181, 206, 218, 227, 235, 236, 237, 238, 239, 242, 253, 263, 264, 265, 281, 285, 292
change, 1, 2, 3, 4, 9, 23, 28, 33–6, 53, 61, 68, 69, 72, 74, 89, 90, 91, 96, 97, 106, 127, 133, 142, 231, 255, 272, 280–2, 283–5, 288
behaviour change, 1, 3, 29, 96, 215, 273, 279, 287, 288
first-order/second-order change, 127
human growth and development, 90, 91, 93, 94, 95, 98, 103, 105, 149, 212, 227, 291
personal change, 33–6, 68, 270
social change, 1, 3, 68, 69, 74–7
checklists, 62, 126, 145
Cheetham, J., 54, 56, 68, 71, 74, 115, 116, 122, 129, 133, 134, 149, 204, 205, 250, 251
child abuse, 137, 122, 141, 145, 152, 159, 159, 169, 210, 239, 240, 245, 251, 257, 278, 281, 282
working with abused children and adults, 107, 108, 122, 137, 141, 152, 159, 169, 178, 210, 239, 257, 278–9, 280
child deaths and inquiries, 16, 69, 126, 138, 145, 248, 251, 294, 307
child neglect, 104, 212, 222, 229, 245
child protection, 130, 131, 137, 140, 226, 228, 230, 231, 245
children and young people
child development, 102, 106, 115, 243
children's rights, 80, 88
children's services, 13, 16, 17, 115, 243
early provision, benefits of, 115, 258
in care/'looked after', 141, 155, 168, 170, 181, 198, 258, 259
legislation, see below
survival skills/resilience, 159

UN Convention on the Rights of the Child, 17
young people/adolescents, 35, 42, 82, 87, 88, 100, 101, 121, 130, 165, 168, 176, 192, 206, 223, 239, 285
Children Act, England (1989), 16, 146, 224, 245
Children Act (2004), 17
Chodorow, N. J., 107
clarifying/clarification, 48, 72, 157, 158, 164, 165–7
class, 41–3, 75, 90, 121
middle class, 110, 117
Registrar General's classification of socio-economic classes, 41
working class, 68, 108, 221, 227
inverse care law, 41
see also poverty
client, see service user
client-centred approaches (Rogerian), see person/client-centred approaches
closed questions, 64, 86, 143, 155, 160, 161–2
codes, 14, 17, 30, 39, 98, 291
policy, codes defined, 17
cognitive-behavioural approaches, 19, 92, 97, 98, 132, 135, 199, 202, 208, 213, 214, 232, 260
cognitive approaches, 19, 37, 66, 67, 79, 81, 97, 135, 260, 263–5
collaboration, 89, 101, 127, 132, 138, 217, 223, 226
inter-agency collaboration, 109, 123, 131, 248
collective action, 49, 68, 69, 75, 226, 279, 282, 285, 286
Commission for Healthcare Audit and Inspection (CHAI), 13
Commission for Social Care Inspection (CSCI), 13
common purpose, establishing a, 19, 119, 163, 218, 225, 229
common sense, 45, 47
communication
Braille, 119
British Sign Language (BAL), 119
defined, 116
dress as communication, 121
importance within social work, 8–10, 116–122
importance of listening skills, 123–5

interpersonal skills, 46, 61, 113, 117, 118, 215, 220, 239, 272
  jargon, 164, 119
  body language/non-verbal communication, importance of, 113, 119–21, 124, 138, 142, 155, 156, 158, 238, 257
  Makaton, 119
  non-verbal, 119–121
  tone and timing, importance of, 162, 163, 172, 173, 198
  see interviewing skills
  see language/choice of words
communities, 34, 74, 116, 140, 146, 163, 194, 212, 224, 226, 227, 243, 246, 278, 279, 286, 292
  community care, 16, 131, 147, 204, 245
  community work, 3, 5, 34, 55, 66, 67, 69, 78, 106, 116, 223, 256, 278
Community Care (Direct Payments) Act (1996), 130
competence, 61–3
  competency-based approaches, 61, 63
  see also skills
complaints, 17, 170, 219, 260
conciliation skills, 231, 232
confidentiality, 134, 150, 153, 214, 224, 247, 248, 291, 292
  Data Protection Act (1998), 52, 250
  limits of confidentiality, 247
conflict, 6, 65, 95, 98, 99, 113, 209, 210, 212, 213, 216, 230, 231, 237, 292
confrontation, 72, 76, 99, 100, 122, 206, 215, 233, 237–9, 269
congruence, 86, 87, 95, 214, 269, 271
conscious, 91, 99, 156, 158, 210, 281
containing anxiety, 6, 190, 194, 195, 200, 207, 215–7, 224, 225, 236, 253
contract, 12, 83, 174, 218, 222, 223, 224–5, 247, 275
  see also written agreement/s,
coping skills, service users', 5, 6, 35, 53, 98, 104, 132, 135, 139, 180, 203, 204, 213, 216, 253, 266, 267, 272, 274
Coulshed, V., 1, 28, 48, 58, 61, 66, 114, 127, 132, 136, 148, 157, 202, 211, 222, 223, 226, 244, 249, 250, 253, 266, 273, 276
counselling, 29, 34, 67, 77, 78, 84, 85, 86, 87, 88, 94, 95, 116, 117, 167, 187, 191, 197, 203, 213–4, 248, 269

aims of counseling, 214
counter transference, 99, 273
crime
  Crime and Disorder Act (1998), 16
  Criminal Justice Act (1991), 16, 91
  criminal justice system, 16, 32, 35, 96, 126, 291
  work with offenders, 32, 35, 96, 291
Crisis Intervention, 37, 79, 81, 107, 266–8, 272, 274
critical thinking, 22, 42, 43, 44, 45, 46–7, 50, 58, 89, 137
Cylcle of Change, see Stages of Change

Data Protection Act (1998), 52, 250
Davies, M., 35, 52, 59, 115, 146, 147, 194
decision-making, 1, 19, 31, 38, 43, 49, 55, 113, 131, 135–7, 138, 140, 194, 201, 229, 249, 251, 266
  service user involvement in, 52, 67, 94, 116, 127, 135–7, 222, 230, 245, 268, 276, 282
  see also judgements
defences, 99, 105, 149, 171, 128, 272
  defence mechanism defined 173
Department of Health (DoH), 11, 12, 13, 14, 15, 16, 17, 69, 72, 102, 126, 228, 229, 231, 233, 242, 278
dependence/dependency, 9, 32, 33, 35, 44, 47, 103–4, 108, 116, 117, 129, 135, 137, 154, 184, 191, 193, 212, 274
  independence, 36, 91, 94, 103, 104, 117, 129, 137, 149, 168, 191, 200, 206, 212, 227, 275, 291, 292
  interdependence, 103, 104, 212, 234
  unhealthy dependency, 135, 184, 193, 274
depression, 33, 51, 52, 53, 59, 117, 150, 179, 193, 225, 265, 267
deprivation, 1, 2, 3, 10, 21, 47, 74, 110, 111, 112, 225, 226
  see also; poverty and disadvantage
despair, 10, 99, 101, 102, 138, 220, 256, 258
developmental process, 91, 104, 105
  see human growth and development; psychology
developmental psychology, 90, 91
  see also psychology
DiClemente, C.C., 36, 287, 290
Diploma in Social Work, 61

directive interventions, 66, 67, 76, 82, 188, 190, 201, 202, 262, 264, 268
disability, 4, 9, 17, 42, 79, 80, 90, 111, 119, 129, 130, 195, 196, 206, 245, 292
access, 153
Chronically Sick and Disabled Persons Act (1971), 130
Disabled Children's Act (2000), 129
Disabled Persons Act (1986), 196
Disability Discrimination Act (1995), 17
disadvantage, 3, 32, 34, 40, 42, 47, 69, 74, 111, 112, 128, 225, 227, 233, 255, 256, 279, 281, 282, 285, 290, 291, 292
defined, 111
discrimination, 17, 20, 21, 42, 69, 74, 80, 118, 133, 219, 231, 243, 255, 256, 265, 271, 282, 285, 291, 292
see also anti discriminatory/anti-oppressive perspectives
diversity, cultural 73, 111, 112, 291, 292
Dole, M., 69, 70, 78, 116, 133, 140, 276
doctors, 3, 32, 41, 117, 161
see also medicine
domestic violence, 17, 240, 266, 281, 282
Dominally, L., 20, 29, 33, 34, 35, 44, 61, 80, 113, 115, 133, 144, 154, 157, 221, 142, 274, 277, 281, 282, 284
'doorknob revelations', 182, 183, 246
drug addiction/abuse, 21, 33, 36, 50, 52, 114, 117, 208, 247, 288, 292
see alcohol abuse; addiction; Stages of Change
Dryden, W., 92, 123, 148, 164, 193, 203, 206, 208, 210, 211, 235, 237, 264
duty, 30, 69, 129, 196, 244
policy, duty defined, 17

eclectic approaches, 65, 77, 213
ecological theory/perspectives, 5, 37, 40, 75, 80, 81, 126, 272, 278–80, 291
economics, relevance to social work, 3, 30–1, 40, 41–2, 55, 62, 69, 111, 112
education, 30, 74, 75, 111, 131, 134, 170, 215, 252, 262, 282, 286, 291
see social work education
effective action, 42, 114, 115, 127, 163, 208, 209, 229, 224, 256,
intellectual and knowledge based, 18, 33, 39, 44, 46, 55, 58, 59, 60, 76, 77, 89, 270

personal responsibility, 3, 6, 9, 30, 46, 70,75, 97, 98, 120, 132, 135, 153, 161, 163, 171, 188, 205, 220, 224, 227, 228, 238, 254, 270, 279, 285, 286
professional responsibility, 69, 70, 72, 75, 132, 153, 157, 163, 171, 190, 194, 197, 205, 218, 223, 224, 230, 238, 242, 254, 276, 223, 247
effectiveness, 1, 5, 11, 22, 43, 54, 55, 56, 57, 58, 60, 62, 76, 89, 131, 139, 148, 217, 228, 242, 243, 249, 250, 251, 253, 260, 274, 276, 291
barriers/resource limitations, 12, 111, 115, 116, 129, 130, 202, 203, 233
baseline data, importance of 53, 57, 71, 88, 96, 248, 261, 262
'best evidence', 55, 135, 137, 242, 251
difficulty evaluating effectiveness, 134, 251
evaluation, 10, 23, 46, 73, 96, 124, 129, 133, 170, 191, 213, 249, 250, 252, 264
defined, 133–4
evidence, 3, 4, 10, 12, 15, 17, 22, 23, 24, 27, 37, 43, 46, 48, 49, 52, 53, 54, 55, 56, 57, 62, 71, 100, 116, 123, 134, 135, 137, 139, 143, 145, 151, 157, 158, 170, 187, 203, 210, 242, 250, 251, 290, 292
evidence based practice, 4, 23, 27, 39, 43, 48, 49, 54–7
influences on effectiveness, 71–5
outcomes, 1, 12, 19, 56, 65, 96, 129, 133–5, 142, 171, 230, 236, 245, 251, 252, 253, 261, 274, 275, 276
practitioners' effectiveness, 11, 19, 43, 47, 50, 54, 63, 64, 70, 71, 85, 89, 118, 133, 229, 254
task v process, 134–5
three 'Es' – effectiveness, economy and efficiency, 31
'what works', 11, 15, 47, 54, 56, 242, 251
see also research
Egan, G., 73, 117, 123, 125, 154, 156, 168, 169, 174, 213, 235, 236, 237
ego, 98, 99, 100
ego psychology, 107, 267, 272, 274
Erikson, E. H., 90, 91, 99–100, 101, 272
Erikson's Eight stages of development, 99–101

Ellis, A., 19, 205, 263–5
emancipatory practice/perspectives, 35,
    115, 284
emotional development, 90, 91, 98, 102,
    105, 107, 212, 273
emotional energy, 6, 94, 104, 105, 144,
    149, 180, 193, 195, 256, 277, 288
empathy, 7, 44, 64, 68, 87, 106, 108, 123,
    145, 149, 153–7
    and person/client-centred approach, 7,
        95, 269–71
    defined, 154
    and sympathy, 125, 154, 155, 156–7
empirical, 3, 50, 54, 89, 95, 96, 107
    defined, 54
empowerment skills, 1, 8, 9, 61, 69, 72, 74,
    80, 82, 83, 141, 149, 159, 215,
    218–221, 227, 228, 232, 236, 243,
    245, 268, 276, 279, 285
    features/benefits of empowerment, 219,
        220
enabling, 160, 164, 205, 209, 215, 245
    part of empowerment process, 219
encouragement, 96, 116, 136, 152, 156,
    170, 172, 173, 174, 185, 188, 192,
    196, 199, 203, 236, 258, 263, 269,
    271, 274, 286
    importance of validation, 200, 203
endings/disengagement/termination, 82,
    104, 138, 143, 181–6, 195, 288
    closing a case/ending the relationship,
        184–6
    ending an interview, 182–4
energy/emotional energy, 6, 94, 104, 105,
    144, 149, 180, 193, 195, 256, 277,
    288
engaging/engagement, 46, 123, 143, 144,
    201, 220
England, H., 5, 20, 26, 33, 44, 58, 60, 90,
    132, 137, 157, 191, 202, 203, 214,
    254, 255
environmental factors, 2, 5, 9, 63, 68, 74,
    74–7, 90, 96, 127, 133, 133, 231,
    261, 278, 280
    environmental capacities, 2, 5, 9
    social change, 1, 3, 68, 69, 74–7
epistemology, 31
equality, 118, 206, 230, 231, 257
    inequality/ies, 27, 31, 38, 41–2, 107,
        108, 111, 129, 144, 201, 205, 215,
        219, 221, 223, 225, 230, 235, 281,
        282, 283, 284, 285, 292

equal opportunities, 41
ethics/ethical ethical practice, 31, 32, 56,
    63, 96, 117, 199, 221, 224, 247,
    267, 292
ethnic/black minority groups, 4, 40, 80,
    82, 90, 108, 109–110, 128, 151,
    165, 192, 219, 227, 228, 229, 231,
    245, 282, 292
Eurocentric bias, 29, 110
evaluation, 10, 23, 46, 73, 96, 124, 129,
    133, 170, 191, 213, 249, 250, 252,
    264
    defined, 133–4
*Every Child Matters: Change for
    Children*, 17
evidence, *see* effectiveness
evidence based practice, 4, 23, 27, 39, 43,
    48, 49, 54–7
eye contact, 123, 215
excluded/exclusion, 4, 9, 10, 40, 42, 47,
    130, 150, 208, 213, 227, 242, 245,
    255, 291
    see also poverty and disadvantage
experiences, new, 6, 43, 103, 205
    difficult, 95, 121, 180
    negative, 5, 6, 10
    positive, 5, 10, 106, 144, 188–9, 258
'experts', service users as, 23, 39, 58, 89,
    193, 242, 292
explanations
    as an intervention, 50, 61, 79, 82, 86,
        121, 182, 190, 194, 196–9, 291
    as theorizing, 26–7, 28, 30, 36, 38, 48,
        50, 61, 78, 79, 94, 112, 291

facilitate/facilitative, 23, 34, 58, 65, 160,
    170, 187, 210, 211, 212, 213, 219,
    249, 252, 269, 292
    see also empowerment
Fair Access to Care, 12
Family Law Act (1996), 17
family therapy, 78, 135, 163, 208, 272, 278
family/domestic violence, 17, 240, 266,
    281, 282
family work/support, 70, 78, 81, 115, 135,
    163, 208, 272, 278, 291, 292
family/ies, 2, 3, 10, 17, 20, 40, 42, 66, 74,
    75, 84, 85, 101, 110, 111, 114, 126,
    131, 140, 141, 146, 203, 215, 223,
    224, 226, 231, 232, 279, 280, 291,
    292,
fathers, 141

fear/s, 95, 96, 97, 138, 145, 158, 159, 160,
    182, 195, 216, 236, 239, 260, 270
    differentiated from anxiety, 216
feedback, 64, 82, 122, 124, 129, 134, 137,
    138, 143, 164, 169–70, 196, 199,
    200, 207, 237, 253
Feltham, C., 92, 123, 148, 164, 193, 203,
    206, 208, 210, 211, 235, 237
feminism/feminist perspectives, 37, 51,
    58, 80, 81, 141, 280–3
feminist therapy, 107–8
    Stone Center (Boston, USA), 108, 149,
        150, 222
    Women's Therapy Centre, 87, 108, 221
files, access to, 43, 173, 248, 250
financial problems/hardships, 167
    see poverty
Fisher, M., 24, 42, 56, 202
Fook, J., 26, 27, 28, 31, 32, 35, 38, 39, 46,
    47, 50, 68, 78, 284
Ford, D., 36, 52, 61, 117, 266, 276
foster carers/foster care, 102, 120, 131,
    146, 147, 168, 172
fragmentation, 11, 12, 24, 28, 58, 106,
    212, 285
Freedom of Information Act (2000), 52, 250
Freud, S., 90, 91, 98, 99, 107
    psychoanalysis, 5, 27, 36, 91, 98–105,
        108, 210, 267, 272, 274
    psychosocial, 7, 23, 34, 37, 67, 79, 81,
        100, 101, 102, 128, 272–4

Gambrill, E. D., 6, 26, 37, 38, 39, 43, 44,
    54, 55, 58, 67, 96, 97, 122, 260
Garbarino, J., 26, 279
gatekeeping, 115
gender, 4, 29, 88, 90, 107, 110
    feminism/feminist perspectives, 58,
        141, 280–2, 283
    sexism, 107, 282
General Social Care Council (GSCC), 2,
    7, 13, 14, 69, 76
    composition, majority service users/lay
        people, 14
generalist skills, 1, 53, 18, 19, 53, 65–68,
    72, 83, 86, 87
    see also skills
genuine/genuineness, 7, 133, 148, 150,
    156, 179, 214, 243, 269
    congruence, 86, 87, 95, 214, 269, 271
gesture/s, 118, 120, 121, 151, 153, 154, 216
'Gloucester Judgement', 130

goals/objectives, see outcomes
Gordon, D., 38, 111, 112
government, role in relation to social
    work, 7, 9, 11–3, 14, 15, 16, 17, 18,
    30, 32, 58, 62, 115, 116, 129
    modernization programme, 11–3, 16
    see also law/legislation
groupthink, 131
groupwork/working with groups, 21, 69,
    70, 78, 81, 226, 256, 285, 291, 292
growth, personal, 5, 6, 10, 32, 34, 36, 90,
    91, 93, 94, 95, 98, 103, 105, 149,
    212, 227, 291
guidance
    as an intervention, 28, 38, 64, 69, 77,
        126, 185, 193, 196, 197, 264,
    policy guidance, 16, 17, 22, 146, 234, 291
    policy, guidance defined, 17
    social work training guidance
        documents, 22, 75, 85, 126, 234, 291

hardship/suffering, 11, 116, 117, 144, 156,
    178, 180, 210, 231, 240, 244, 257,
    258, 265, 284
    see adversity; poverty and disadvantage
hate object, 44, 45
health, 4, 7, 13, 23, 30, 32, 36, 38, 40–2,
    47, 52, 59, 73, 74–5, 90, 101, 103,
    107, 109, 111, 129, 196, 225, 227,
    233, 244, 248, 250, 262, 265, 279,
    288, 291, 292
    illness/ill health, 30, 41, 47, 74–5, 187,
        195, 245, 226, 285
    inverse care law, 41
    mental health, 16, 17, 21, 52, 59, 107,
        130, 140, 203, 233, 244, 245, 246,
        266, 291, 292
Healy, K., 35, 38, 285
heirarchy of needs, 92–4
help/helping, 190–3
Hollis, F., 107, 243, 272
Holman, R., 205
honesty, 139, 214, 224, 282
hope, 10, 74, 135, 188, 258
hostility, 65, 83, 101, 141, 180, 239–240
housing, 30, 38, 42, 75, 111, 119, 216, 278,
    286, 291
Howe, D., 7, 8, 10, 24, 25, 26, 27, 34, 35,
    44, 61, 62, 76, 78, 90, 102, 106,
    132, 134, 135, 138, 192, 198, 208,
    211, 213, 216, 227, 228, 230, 239,
    243, 253, 257, 272, 273

human growth and development, 5, 6, 10,
    32, 34, 36, 90, 91, 93, 94, 95, 98,
    103, 105, 149, 212, 227, 291
Human Rights Act (1998), 18
humanism/humanist approaches, 27, 29,
    33, 34, 36, 91, 92–5, 106, 213, 269
  person/client-centred approaches, 7,
    29, 33, 34, 37, 67, 79, 81, 86, 87,
    94–5, 125, 128, 154, 171, 187, 188,
    201, 213, 269–71, 276
humour, 82, 143, 179–181
hunches, see intuition
hypotheses/hypothesis, 22, 24, 26, 38, 43,
    48, 70, 71, 78, 95, 121, 139, 145,
    157, 158, 174, 211, 249, 252

id, 98
identity, 44, 100, 101, 106, 207, 283
ideology, 9, 22, 24, 31–3, 58, 281
implementation, 16, 18, 30, 33, 35, 43, 48,
    59, 85–88, 89, 134, 138, 146, 169,
    188, 213, 251
individualism/individualizing problems,
    34, 35, 37, 69, 75, 106, 110, 111,
    248, 265, 279, 284
individuation, 215
  autonomy, 101, 131, 191, 193, 206, 282,
    291
independence, 36, 91, 94, 103, 104, 117,
    129, 137, 149, 168, 191, 200, 206,
    212, 227, 275, 291, 292
inequality/ies, 27, 31, 38, 41–2, 107, 108,
    111, 129, 144, 201, 205, 215, 219,
    221, 223, 225, 230, 235, 281, 282,
    283, 284, 285, 292
information
  information gathering skills, 51, 52, 53,
    86, 87, 140
  providing information, 52, 64, 66, 82,
    86, 116, 174, 190, 194–5, 204
  leaflets and written information, 195–6
injustice, 4, 112, 156, 223, 225, 243, 284,
    292
Inspectorate,
  Commission for Social Care Inspection
    (CSCI), 13
  Social Services Inspectorate, 13, 15, 18,
    119, 164, 249
inter-agency work, 43, 109, 123, 131, 248,
    253
  multi/interdisciplinary practice, 43, 52,
    53, 109, 131, 262, 291

interdependence, 103, 104, 212, 234
internalized oppression/internalization,
    31, 94, 97, 98, 101, 180, 221–2
interpersonal skills, 46, 61, 113, 117, 118,
    215, 220, 239, 272
interpretation, 23, 83, 99, 120, 122, 170,
    190, 197, 209–11, 231, 237, 238,
    264, 269,
interventions
  and empowerment, 220–1
  and social work skills, 60–89
  defined, 60
  directive interventions, 66, 67, 76, 82,
    188, 190, 201, 202, 262, 264, 268
  factors influencing intervention
    effectiveness, 71–5
  the focus of interventions, 68–9
  implementation, 16, 18, 30, 33, 35, 43,
    48, 59, 85–88, 89, 134, 138, 146,
    169, 188, 213, 251
  interconnection with skills, 64
  intellectual in character, 18, 59
  intervention research, lack of, 43, 55,
    57
  method of intervention, 70, 78, 81, 85,
    87, 253
  non-directive interventions, 66–7
  practice terminology, 76–81
  ten practice choices, 81–88
  time periods and levels of intensity,
    67–9
  transferability of skills, 21, 28, 59,
    75–7, 142–3
  when and how to intervene, 69–71
  see also skills
interviews/interviewing skills
  basic interviewing skills, 140–189
  body language/non-verbal
    communication, importance of,
    113, 119–21, 124, 138, 142, 155,
    156, 158, 238, 257
  creating a rapport and establishing a
    relationship, 147–50
  defined, 140
  interviews as positive experiences, 144,
    188–9
  language/verbal communication, 31,
    18–9
  motivational interviewing, 187–8, 208,
    290
  planning and preparation, 144–6
  interviews in different settings, 146–7

see also communication skills
see also language
intuition, 44, 48, 82, 99, 123, 143, 145,
    148, 151, 152, 156, 157–8, 159, 210
investigation/s, 53, 141
INVOLVE, 129
involvement of service users, 133, 134,
    136, 138, 139
isolation, dangers and impact of 103, 106,
    178, 204, 208, 212, 227, 233, 284

Jack, G., 279, 280
Jacobs, M., 99, 258, 273
Jones, C., 6, 33, 38, 39, 58, 68, 74, 109,
    202, 285
Jordan, B., 58, 224, 230, 240, 243, 245
judgements, 10, 43, 49, 73, 80, 126, 136–7,
    157, 159, 200, 230, 249, 250, 251,
    253
justice/social justice, 1, 3, 4, 32, 35, 118,
    256, 284, 285

Kadushin and Kadushin, 120, 121, 125,
    140, 145, 147, 149, 150, 154, 159,
    175, 176, 179, 181, 184, 199, 200,
    238
knowledge base of social work
    analysing the task and purpose of
        social work, 33–36
    ambivalent relationship between theory
        and practice, 58–9
    baseline data, importance of 53, 57, 71,
        88, 96, 248, 261, 262
    drawn/'borrowed' from other
        disciplines, 28–31
    different types of knowledge, 18, 25,
        51–3, 3
    evidence based practice, 4, 23, 24, 27,
        37, 39, 43, 48, 49, 51, 54–7
    factual knowledge, 18, 22, 25, 30,
        37–43, 51–2, 59, 72, 76
    ideology, role of, 9, 22, 24, 31–3, 58,
        281
    'indigenous' knowledge, 23
    informed by research, 53–9
    knowledge requirements (NOS), 40–3,
        291–2
    practice knowledge, 18, 25, 43–51, 52–3
    practice theories, 36–7
    practice wisdom 22, 43, 47, 50
    practitioner-generated knowledge, 43,
        50–1

subjugated knowledge, 23
science/empirical knowledge, 50, 54,
    89, 96
social sciences, importance of, 28, 29,
    30, 31, 33, 59
tacit knowledge, 44, 49, 158
theoretical knowledge, 18, 25–33, 51
theory, 26–8,
truth, 23, 24, 27, 54
see also belief
see also research
see also theory

labels/labelling, 31, 111, 124, 125, 208,
    261
stereotyping, 124, 125, 136, 145, 181,
    191
language
    avoiding jargon/keeping language
        accessible, 20, 86, 87, 118–9, 142,
        164, 195, 196
    body language/non-verbal
        communication, 113, 119–21, 124,
        138, 142, 155, 156, 158, 238, 257
    choice of words/tone and timing, 20,
        31, 118–9, 133, 162, 163, 165, 172,
        173, 198, 205
    effective communication, 8, 40
    terminology, absence of a common
        language, 7, 20, 36, 43, 50, 56, 60,
        76–7, 88
    see also communication
    see also interviewing skills
law/legislation/policy requirements
    Adult Social Care, 17
    Best Value, 12, 242
    Carers (Recognition and Services) Act
        (1995), 17, 129, 130
    Carers and Disabled Children's Act
        (2000), 129
    Children Act (2004), 17
    Children Act, England (1989), 16, 146,
        224, 245
    codes, 14, 17, 30, 39, 291
    codes, defined, 17
    Criminal Justice Act (1991), 16, 91
    Community Care (Direct Payments)
        Act (1996), 130
    Data Protection Act (1998), 52, 250
    Disability Discrimination Act (1995),
        17
    duty, 17, 30, 69, 129, 196, 244

duty, defined, 17
European Union (EU) legislation, 17,
    191
*Every Child Matters: Change for
    Children*, 17
Fair Access to Care, 12
Family Law Act (1996), 17
Freedom of Information Act (2000), 52,
    250
'Gloucester Judgement', 130
guidance, from government, 16, 17, 22,
    30, 291
guidance, defined, 17
Human Rights Act (1998/2000), 17, 18
Law Commission, 245
legal authority/mandate of social
    workers, 18
Local Authority Social Services Act
    (1970), 17
Long Term Care Charter, 12
Mental Health Act (1983), 16, 52, 59,
    244, 245, 246
Modernising Government, 11, 12
Modernising Social Services, 11
National Health Service (NHS) and
    Community Care Act (1990), 16,
    130, 226, 233
Ombudsman, 17
powers, 16, 17, 18, 29, 30, 38, 62, 115,
    130, 224, 245
powers, defined, 17
Quality Strategy for Social Care, 11, 15
regulation, 12, 13, 15, 16, 17, 30, 234,
    250
regulation, defined, 17
teaching, law, 38
United Nations Convention on the
    Rights of the Child, 17
Valuing People, 12
vulnerable adults, defined, 245
leaflets/written information, 195–6
learned helplessness, 97, 235
learning difficulties/disabilities, 65, 159,
    292
life span theory, 90, 91, 100
story-telling/narrative approaches, 128, 198
Lishman, J., 11, 44, 47, 67, 68, 69, 80, 120,
    121, 123, 129, 141, 143, 145, 146,
    153, 157, 159, 163, 166, 178, 191,
    193, 194, 196, 199, 200, 202, 211,
    216, 222, 225, 228, 229, 237, 238,
    240, 253, 254

listening skills
    active listening, 123
    credulous listening, 123
    hearing versus listening, 124
    importance of, 1, 86, 98, 116, 124, 138,
        139, 157, 161, 164, 165, 166, 187,
        195, 203, 216, 240
    non-selective, 123, 124
    pretend/limited/self-centred listeners,
        124
    20 basic skills, 123–4
local authorities, 12, 13, 17, 224, 249, 234
Local Authorities Social Services Act
    (1970), 17
locus of control, 97–8, 235
Long Term Care Charter, 12
loss/bereavement, 65, 104, 105, 111, 185,
    191, 265, 277

McLeod, J., 99, 117, 210, 214, 270, 271
managerialist, culture in social work, 11,
    31, 58, 252
    'beaucratized', 228, 285
    'marketization' of social work, 31
marginalized/marginalization, 9, 130,
    213, 240
Marsh, P., 2, 36, 37, 72, 133, 230, 269
Marris, P., 2, 256, 257
Maslow, A. H., 90, 91, 92–4, 234, 269
material assistance, 94, 191, 202–3
meaning, 10, 23, 26, 31, 34, 44, 73, 89, 92,
    100, 106, 112, 117, 118, 120, 121,
    124, 140, 142, 144, 154, 155, 196,
    202, 206, 211, 237, 258, 270, 273
medicine, 4, 30, 31, 32, 49, 51, 52, 54, 57,
    64, 79, 103, 105, 187, 201, 245
    medical model, 30, 31, 51, 79, 187
men, 31, 41, 51, 107, 108, 151, 281, 282,
    283
Mental Health Act (1983), 16, 52, 59, 244,
    245, 246
mental health/mental illness, 17, 21, 52,
    59, 130, 140, 203, 266, 285, 291,
    292, 233
    'survivors', 51, 80, 233
method, 78
    method of intervention, 70, 78, 81, 85,
        87, 253
methodology, defined, 78
middle class, 110, 117
Miller, J. B., 108, 149, 150, 221–2
Miller, W. R., 133, 187, 188, 208, 256

Mills, C. W., 8, 27, 284
Mitchell, J. 107
modelling/social skills training, 66, 82, 96, 190, 206–8, 236, 261
models, 36, 37, 78–9, 110
  social model of disability, 79
  medical model, 30, 31, 51, 79, 187
modernization agenda, 11–5, 16
Modernising Government, 11, 12
Modernising Social Services, 11
monitor/monitoring, 11, 12, 13, 15, 57, 71, 88, 127, 132, 134, 137, 249, 250, 264
  improving the organisation, delivery and monitoring of services, 12–3
moral issues, 31, 32, 68, 69, 98, 107, 136, 193, 245, 247
mothers, 100, 103, 258
motivate/motivation, 9, 29, 36, 70, 73, 91, 92, 93, 94, 98, 133, 139, 150, 169, 187, 188, 200, 205, 208, 211, 256, 269, 271, 276, 290
motivational interviewing, 187–8, 208, 290,
multi-cultural/cultural diversity, 29, 73, 110, 111, 112, 153, 291, 292
multi-disciplinary/interdisciplinary work, 29, 52, 53, 109, 131, 248, 262, 291
Munro, E., 54, 69, 137, 138, 142, 157, 248, 251, 253
mutual/mutuality, 95, 106, 108, 147, 149, 192, 205, 225, 226, 229, 231, 257
  see also self-help; reciprocity

Narrative approaches, 128, 198
National Care Standards Commission (NCSC), 13
National Health Service (NHS) and Community Care Act (1990), 16, 130, 226, 233
National Health Service (NHS), 33, 52, 59
National Occupational Standards (NOS), 11, 5, 7, 14, 19, 40, 62, 63, 78, 278, 291–2
needs-led versus resource-led, 72, 130–2
needs, 1, 8, 9, 34, 35, 67, 72, 73, 74, 90, 93, 94, 103, 128, 129, 136, 138, 142, 144, 146, 183, 190, 192, 195, 196, 198, 199, 211, 212, 230, 233, 272, 282
  children's needs, 106, 231, 243
  Maslow's *heirarchy of needs*, 92–4

service users' needs, 130, 131, 132, 214, 220, 223, 224, 234, 247, 252
negotiation skills, 202, 218, 222–4, 225, 230, 231, 233, 247
networking skills, 83, 218, 226–7
networks/social networks, 74, 88, 119, 126, 141, 194, 204, 278, 226, 227, 272
  communities, 34, 74, 116, 140, 146, 163, 194, 212, 224, 226, 227, 243, 246, 278, 279, 286, 292
non-verbal communication/body language, 113, 119–21, 124, 138, 142, 155, 156, 158, 238, 257
Norcross, J. C., 188, 260, 263, 265, 287, 288
normative/normalization, 109, 110, 111, 206, 209, 219, 234

observation, 1, 19, 26, 27, 53, 54, 71, 75, 86, 87, 96, 113, 120, 121–2, 129, 134, 138, 164, 207, 228, 253, 261
offenders/offending behaviour, 32, 35, 96, 291
  see also crime
older people, 32, 153, 223, 245, 266, 292
  abuse/neglect of older people, 32, 206, 227
open questions, 82, 143, 160–1, 162
operant conditioning, 96, 261
oppression/oppressed, 1, 20, 27, 34, 90, 91, 108, 109, 118, 144, 180, 208, 219, 236, 280, 281, 282, 291
  internalized oppression/internalization, 31, 94, 97, 98, 101, 180, 221–2
organization
  organization/s, 5, 7, 12, 15, 20, 66, 75, 81, 128, 132, 187, 220, 221, 223, 246, 250, 253, 283, 285
  organizational and administrative skills, 1, 113, 137–8, 239
  organizational structure, 6, 11, 13, 17, 18, 30, 58, 89, 195, 223, 253, 254, 283
  organizational theory, 7, 30, 31
  see also planning and preparation
Orme, J., 1, 48, 58, 61, 66, 114, 127, 136, 148, 157, 202, 211, 222, 223, 226, 244, 250, 253, 266, 273, 276
outcomes, 1, 12, 19, 56, 65, 96, 129, 133–5, 142, 171, 230, 236, 245, 251, 252, 253, 261, 274, 275, 276

paradigm, defined, 34

paraphrasing, 82, 143, 165, 166, 173

parents, 42, 45, 48, 99, 100, 102, 103, 106, 131, 141, 159, 168, 203, 207, 209, 221, 228, 230, 231, 232, 243, 270, 279

participation, 46, 73, 112, 116, 127, 128–9, 175, 217, 227, 230, 232, 233, 234, 235, 249, 250, 270

partnership in social work, 8, 58, 61, 73, 83, 89, 116, 136, 138, 141, 149, 192, 218, 221, 222, 224, 225, 227–31, 232, 235, 245, 246, 276

Parton, N., 30, 35, 56, 214

past on present, impact of, 91, 102, 104, 127–8, 145, 151, 159, 163, 169, 179, 180, 198, 221, 238, 270, 273

patriarchy/patriarchal ideology, 29, 281, 282, 283

patronizing, being, 172, 192, 193, 199, 200, 205

Payne, M., 34, 35, 36, 39, 46, 54, 61, 68, 77, 79, 80, 115, 138, 148, 181, 193, 214, 219, 225, 226, 233, 234, 252, 253, 263, 265, 266

peer contact/support, 49, 106, 149, 204, 233, 238, 253

permanence, lack of, 102

personal change and growth, 33–6, 68, 270

    human growth and development, 90, 91, 93, 94, 95, 98, 103, 105, 149, 212, 227, 291

    person/client-centred approaches, 7, 29, 33, 34, 37, 67, 79, 81, 86, 87, 94–5, 125, 128, 154, 171, 187, 188, 201, 213, 269–71, 276

perception, 28, 120, 121, 129, 134, 168, 170

persuasion, 24, 66, 82, 188, 190, 201–2, 224, 246

    being directive, 66, 67, 76, 82, 188, 190, 201, 202, 262, 264, 268

Phillipson, C., 80, 204, 227, 235

philosophy, relevance to social work 31, 33, 43, 155, 207, 260

phobia/s, 95, 260

physical contact/touching, 95, 151, 152, 260

    emotionally touched, 152, 200

Piaget, J., 90, 107

planning and preparation, 82, 127, 137, 138, 140, 143, 144–6, 181

points of failure/failure situations, 103, 104–5

police, and violent attacks, 240

policy/ies

    agency policy/practice, 17, 47, 51, 66, 67, 83, 146, 160, 213, 225, 234, 243, 244, 247, 253

    changes in social work education, 16

    government policy, 7, 11, 30, 62, 233, 251, 279, 281

    international, comparative law and social policy, 291

    law, changes in, 16–18

    managerialist, culture in social work, 11, 31, 58, 228, 252, 285

    social policy, 15, 30, 291

politics, and social work, *see* radical social work

poor people, *see* poverty

Popper, K. L., 23, 24, 26, 84, 114, 135

postmodernism, 27

poverty and disadvantage

    a central concern in social work, 4, 10, 37, 40, 41, 47, 68, 69, 74, 75, 112, 14, 202, 202, 227, 243, 248, 279, 285, 286, 291

    poverty defined, 112

    adversity, 32, 90, 94, 105, 106, 109, 112, 117, 132, 226, 248, 258, 270

    defined, 111

    deprivation, 1, 2, 3, 10, 21, 47, 74, 110, 111, 112, 225, 226

    poverty and disadvantage, 3, 32, 34, 40, 42, 47, 69, 74, 111, 112, 128, 225, 227, 233, 255, 256, 279, 281, 282, 285, 290, 291, 292

    discrimination, 17, 20, 21, 42, 69, 74, 80, 118, 133, 219, 231, 243, 255, 256, 265, 271, 282, 285, 291, 292

    excluded/social exclusion, 4, 9, 10, 40, 42, 47, 130, 150, 208, 213, 227, 242, 245, 255, 291

    justice/social justice, 1, 3, 4, 32, 35, 118, 256, 284, 285

    hardship/suffering, 11, 116, 117, 144, 156, 178, 180, 210, 231, 240, 244, 257, 258, 265, 284

    inequality/ies, 27, 31, 38, 41–2, 107, 108, 111, 129, 144, 201, 205, 215, 219, 221, 223, 225, 230, 235, 281, 282, 283, 284, 285, 292

marginalized/marginalization, 9, 130, 213, 240
stigma/sigmatized, 20, 208, 227
power, 4, 9, 13, 16, 29, 30, 31, 34, 56, 62, 68, 115, 130, 133, 149, 210, 219, 220, 222, 225, 227, 228, 229, 230, 233, 234, 242, 244, 245, 256, 257, 274, 282, 285, 292
policy, powers defined, 17
powerlessness, 97, 178, 230, 235, 256
   internalized oppression/internalization, 31, 94, 97, 98, 101, 180, 221–2
   learned helplessness, 97, 235
   locus of control, 97–8, 235
   see also empowerment and enabling skills
practical help/material assistance, 82, 94, 191, 194, 202–3, 213
practice approaches
   behaviourist approaches, 67, 76, 92, 260, 261, 262
   cognitive approaches, 19, 37, 66, 67, 79, 81, 97, 135, 260, 263–5
   cognitive-behavioural approaches, 19, 92, 97, 98, 132, 135, 199, 202, 208, 213, 214, 232, 263
   Crisis Intervention, 37, 79, 81, 107, 266–8, 272, 274
   person/client-centred approaches, 7, 29, 33, 34, 37, 67, 79, 81, 86, 87, 94–5, 125, 128, 154, 171, 187, 188, 201, 213, 269–71, 276
   psychosocial, 7, 23, 29, 34, 37, 67, 79, 81, 100, 101, 102, 128, 213, 272–4
   solution focused/strengths-based approaches, 5, 72, 73, 135
   task-centred approaches, 67, 72, 78, 79, 81, 132, 135, 249, 275–7, 276
   Stages of Change or Cycle of Change, 36, 37, 81, 287–900
   see also perspectives
practice perspectives, 2, 3, 4, 5, 18, 23, 27, 29, 32, 33, 35, 37, 51, 52, 54, 56, 59, 64, 66, 67, 71, 72, 73, 86, 88, 132, 163, 164, 168, 252, 253
   a partial 'view of the world', 80
   anti-discriminatory perspectives/ practice, 80, 133, 162, 171, 192, 213, 245
   anti-oppressive perspectives/practice, 61, 80, 82, 133, 157, 162, 192, 213, 242, 245, 279, 285

capacities perspectives, 73, 75
   ecological perspectives, 5, 37, 75, 80, 81, 126, 272, 278–80
   feminist perspectives, 37, 51, 58, 80, 81, 86, 141, 280–3
   practice perspectives, 19, 56, 77, 80–1, 86, 108, 133, 163, 279
   radical/progressive/activist perspectives, 35, 80, 81, 274, 284–6
   relationship perspective, 7–8
   strengths perspectives, 5, 72, 73
practice skills, see skills
practice theory, 36
practice wisdom, 22, 43, 47, 50
   practitioner-generated knowledge/ research, 43, 50–1
practitioners, see social workers
premature self-sufficiency, 103
Preston-Shoot, M., 9, 17, 18, 30, 50, 70, 146, 219, 220, 225, 226, 228, 230, 234, 278
prevention/early intervention, 114
primary health, 52
prison/s, 84, 130, 146, 173
probation, 2, 32, 36, 146, 151, 285
   see also crime
problem,
   as 'unsatisfied wants', 113–4
   differentiated from difficulties, 114
   social problems, 44, 50, 51, 114, 285
problem-solving skills, 113, 135–6, 275, 276
   practitioners', 1, 3, 39, 42, 49, 52, 113, 116, 135–6, 138, 214, 228, 229, 243, 275
   service users', 52, 133, 135–6, 141, 194, 215, 275, 289
process and task, 134–5
Prochaska, J. O., 36, 188, 260, 263, 265, 287, 288
professional development, 5, 47, 50, 76, 252, 254
professional role, 9, 83, 131, 147, 157, 214, 228, 244, 246–7, 248, 276
   see also social workers
prompting, 82, 143, 147, 172, 174, 232
protection
   and control, 204, 218, 230
   child protection, 130, 131, 137, 140, 226, 228, 230, 231, 245
   providing protection, 17, 35, 244, 246, 291

self-protection, 147, 239–40
protective factors, 91, 132, 147, 279
    see also resilience
psy complex,, 111
psychiatric services/settings, 51, 126, 146, 147, 203, 227, 235, 285
psychoanalysis, 5, 27, 36, 91, 98–105, 108, 210, 267, 272, 274
    Freud 90, 91, 98, 99, 107
psychosocial, 7, 23, 29, 34, 37, 67, 79, 81, 100, 101, 102, 128, 213, 272–4
psychology,
    and importance in social work, 29, 251
    behaviourism, 95–8
    cognitive theory, 19, 29, 44, 76, 90, 93, 132, 263, 264, 265
    Eurocentric bias, 29, 110–11
    feminist, 29, 51, 107–8
    human growth and development, 90, 91, 93, 94, 95, 98, 103, 105, 149, 212, 227, 291
    humanism, 92–5
    psychoanalytic, 98–105
'public issues', 8, 284
public inquiries into child deaths, 16, 69, 126, 138, 145, 248, 251, 294, 307
punctuality, 121, 143, 247
purchaser/providers, 225, 262

Quality Assurance, 170, 242
    see also Best Value, 12, 242
questions,
    closed, 64, 86, 143, 155, 160, 161–2
    open, 82, 143, 160–1, 162
    unhelpful, 162
    'what' questions, 162–3
    why, 162
quality control, 36
quality of life, 68, 115, 126, 204, 274, 292
Quality Strategy for Social Care, 11, 15

race and mental illness, 245
race and probation, 131
race 4, 90, 110, 151, 192, 282
    anti-racism, 58, 80, 82, 285
    black/ethnic minority groups, 4, 40, 80, 82, 90, 108, 109–110, 128, 151, 165, 192, 219, 227, 228, 229, 231, 245, 282, 292
radical/progressive/activist perspectives, 35, 80, 81, 274, 284–6

randomized control trials (RTCs), 55, 56, 57
rapport, creating a rapport and establishing a relationship, 118, 145, 147–8
rationing resources, 277
Realising our Potential, 129
reassurance, 152, 171, 200–1, 216
Reber, A. S. and Reber, E., 90, 99, 216
reciprocity, 9, 101, 103, 112, 149, 192, 205, 217, 257, 278
records/record keeping skills
    access to files, 173, 248, 250
    four main types, 249
    multi purpose nature of, 249
    skills, 248–50
referral, 48, 84, 114, 115, 132, 167, 194, 292
reflective practice, 45, 46, 49, 217, 250–2
    critical thinking, 22, 42, 43, 44, 45, 46–7, 50, 58, 89, 137
    critical reflection, 22, 43, 45–6, 47, 50, 87–8
    evidence based practice, 4, 23, 27, 39, 43, 48, 49, 54–7
    reflexivity, defined, 46
reframing, 83, 188, 208–9, 232
regulation, 12, 13, 15, 16, 17, 30, 234, 250
    policy, regulation defined, 17
Reid, W. J., 113–4, 276
relationships, importance in social work
    a relationship perspective, 7–8
    creating a rapport and establishing a relationship, 147–50
    ending the contact/relationship, 184–6
reliability and consistency, 45, 63, 104, 121, 143, 149, 154
reluctant/involuntary service users, 73, 134–5, 148, 277
Requirements for Social Work Training (DoH), 16
research and social work
    'best evidence', 55, 135, 137, 242, 251
    'multi-method research', 54
    'what works' approach, 11, 15, 47, 54, 56, 242, 251
    dissemination of research, 15
    empirical research, empirical, 3, 50, 54, 89, 95, 96, 107,262
    evidence based practice, 4, 23, 27, 39, 43, 48, 49, 54–7
    meta analysis, 56

methodology, 23, 55, 57, 78
N of 1 design/N = 1 design, 56
practice, difficulty applying research,
43, 58
practitioner-generated research, 43,
50–1
qualitative methods, 53, 54
quantitative methods, 53, 54, 56
randomized control trials (RTCs), 55,
56, 57
relevance of research originating
outside social work, 57
research and practice, 2, 3, 12, 13, 23,
27, 36, 37, 38, 39, 42, 43, 49, 50,
51, 56, 57, 58, 65, 89, 96, 129, 132,
142, 143, 157, 202, 203, 215, 227,
230, 239, 251
research defined, 53
research review, 15, 55
scientific methods, 24, 27, 48, 54, 55,
95, 100, 262
single case design/single subject design,
55, 56
Social Care Institute for Excellence
(SCIE), 15, 24, 126
social work practice, limited research
studies, 13, 15
systematic review, 43, 49, 50, 57, 142,
157
variables, 39, 56, 57, 76, 120, 134, 251
resources, access to, 277,
respect, 44, 68, 124, 141, 150, 153, 154,
180, 192,200, 208, 213, 218, 224,
228, 234, 242, 269, 292
residential care, 44, 84, 102, 116, 146, 223,
226, 234
resilience, 105
practitioner resilience, 72, 139, 143,
217, 221, 224, 256
service user resilience, 105, 109, 159,
227
review/revising/updating our knowledge,
38, 45, 50, 71, 137, 210, 232, 250,
251
Richards, S., 32
rights, 1, 17,18, 32, 52, 129, 160, 205, 219,
230, 232, 233, 234, 236, 268, 284,
292
'rights' linked to 'responsibilities', 9
welfare rights/benefits, 9, 32, 38, 40, 68,
134, 167, 174, 194, 203, 233, 286
risk, 10, 29, 35, 52, 66, 70, 74, 86, 87, 91,
111, 115, 126, 130, 174, 219, 230,
239, 242, 245, 253, 257
Robinson, L., 29, 109–10, 227
Rogers, C., 7, 34, 91, 94, 117, 154, 199,
213, 214, 269, 270
see also person/client-centred
approaches, 7, 29, 33, 34, 37, 67,
79, 81, 86, 87, 94–5, 125, 128, 154,
171, 187, 188, 201, 213, 269–71,
276
role/professional role, 9, 83, 131, 147,
157, 214, 228, 244, 246–7, 248, 276
Rollnick, S., 133, 187, 188, 208, 256
rule based behaviour, 39

Sackett, D. L., 54, 57
Schön, D., 39, 46, 48, 158, 252
SCIE (Social Care Institute for
Excellence), 15, 24, 126
scientific/empirical methods, 3, 27, 29, 50,
54, 55, 89, 95, 96, 107,262
secure base, 100
Seden, J., 157, 159, 160, 162, 164, 165,
214, 219, 248
Saleebey, D., 5, 72
self-actualization/actualizing tendency,
91, 92, 93, 94, 215, 269
self-advocacy, 200, 233
self-awareness/self-knowledge, 43–5, 72,
82, 143, 152, 155, 156–7, 171, 178,
192, 229
self-determination, 29, 144, 149, 150, 159,
171, 193, 206, 276
self-disclosure, 82, 143, 157, 178–9
self-esteem/self-worth, 5, 100, 101, 150,
199, 201, 209, 213, 228
self-harm, 87, 88
self-help, 9, 194, 233
self-sufficiency, 9, 94, 103, 193, 206, 212
sense of self, 106, 144, 212
see also self-esteem/self-worth
separation, reactions in children, 102
service provision, 12, 13, 116, 136, 223
service user/s
access to resources/services, 6, 12, 15,
43, 52, 111, 115, 116, 129, 130,
132, 162, 173, 195, 202, 203, 212,
233, 229, 277, 278
as 'experts', 23,39, 58, 89, 193, 242, 292
coping skills, 5, 6, 35, 53, 98, 104, 132,
135, 139, 180, 203, 204, 213, 216,
253, 266, 267, 272, 274

capacities, 2, 4–6, 8, 9, 10, 23, 53, 71, 72–3, 87, 89, 90, 94, 95, 98, 102, 106, 111, 132, 135, 144, 172, 195, 205, 211–2, 214, 220, 229, 246, 247, 271, 272, 276, 278
involvement in decision-making, 52, 67, 94, 116, 127, 135–7, 222, 230, 245, 268, 276, 282,
needs, 130, 131, 132, 214, 220, 223, 224, 234, 247, 252
needs-led versus resource-led services, 72, 130–2
problem-solving, 52, 133, 135–6, 141, 194, 215, 275, 289
user-led policies,
setting/practice setting, 20, 57, 65, 67, 76, 88, 102, 116, 121, 122, 124, 146–7
sexism, 107, 282
sexual abuse, 107, 159, 178, 210, 281, 288
see abuse of children and adolescents
see abuse/violence against women
sexual orientation/preference, 4, 90, 110, 282
shaking hands, 151
shame, 10, 101, 178, 179, 191, 209, 216
Shaw, I., 27, 41, 54, 55, 140, 198, 217, 250
Sheldon, B., 4, 7, 19, 20, 24, 26, 28, 54, 55, 56, 57, 65, 77, 78, 96, 97, 115, 122, 127, 128, 132, 199, 202, 207, 208, 211, 212, 215, 222, 228, 232, 236, 250, 253, 260
Sheppard, M., 38, 39, 43, 46, 47, 48, 51, 52, 55, 109, 112, 203, 227
Shulman, L., 154, 156
silences, 82, 122, 124, 143, 160, 175–8, 229
skills
    advanced skills, 64, 65, 66
    basic skills, 64, 66, 83, 123
    choices, ten practice choices, 18, 81–8, 253
    competences/competency-based practice, 61–3
    core skills, underpin other skills, 1
    directive interventions, 66, 67, 76, 82, 188, 190, 201, 202, 262, 264, 268
    duration, 83
    eclectic approaches, 65, 77, 213
    effectiveness, see evidencing effectiveness/evaluation of effectiveness

environment, importance of, 74–5
factors influencing effectiveness, 71–5
focus of interventions, 68, 69
generalist skills, 1, 53, 18, 19, 53, 65–68, 72, 83, 86, 87
implementation, 16, 18, 30, 33, 35, 43, 48, 59, 69–71 85–88, 89, 134, 138, 146, 169, 188, 213, 251
importance of communication and interviewing skills, 8–10, 117, 140–2, 144, 188–9
intensity, level of, 67, 84
intermediate skills, 65
interpersonal skills, 46, 61, 113, 117, 118, 215, 220, 239, 272
interventions, see interventions
level of skill, 64–5
methods, 77–8
method of intervention/five areas of practice, 70, 78, 81, 85, 87, 253
model, 78–9
non-directive interventions, 66–7
perspectives, see practice perspectives
practice approaches, see practice approaches
practice theories, defined, 79
skill, definition of, 63
specialist skills, 65
terminology, 56, 60, 76–81, 127, 262
training/skills development, 2, 64, 65, 67, 77, 85
transferability of skills, 21, 28, 59, 75–7, 142–3
see also knowledge base of social work
Skills for Care, 14–5
social action, 68, 69, 74
social beings, 91
social capital, 5, 74, 279
social care, 11, 12, 13, 14, 15, 16, 17, 24, 34, 52, 62, 129, 130, 223, 226, 233, 244, 278, 291
social care legislation/regulation/research, 11, 12, 13, 14, 15, 16, 17, 24, 34, 52, 62, 129, 130, 223, 226, 233, 244, 278, 291
Social Care Institute for Excellence (SCIE), 15, 24, 126
social class, see class
social control, 206, 244
social/cultural context, 29, 75, 100, 102, 123, 193, 227
see also environmental factors

social exclusion, 4, 9, 10, 40, 42, 47, 130, 150, 208, 213, 227, 242, 245, 255, 291
social justice, *see* justice
social learning theory, 91, 97, 236, 260, 276
social networks, *see* network
Social Policy and Social Work Subject Centre *(SWAP)*, 15
social problems, *see* problems
social psychology, *see* psychology
social services, 11, 12, 13, 14, 15, 16, 17, 18, 30, 31, 69, 75, 89, 114, 118, 126, 129, 134, 138, 140, 146, 151, 195, 204, 225, 227, 242, 249, 251, 256
under-funding/resourcing constraints, 3, 9, 43, 49, 74, 89, 134, 135, 138, 146, 220, 243, 245, 251, 267, 285
Social Services Inspectorate, 13, 15, 18, 119, 164, 249
social skills training, 66, 82, 206–8, 190, 261
social support, 74, 203, 204, 227, 278, 279
social work theory, *see* theory; knowledge base of social work
social work education and training, recent changes, 1, 11, 13, 14, 15, 16, 61, 62, 65, 77, 85, 109, 126
social work/social workers
accountability, 12, 18, 55, 170, 190, 194, 223, 225, 242, 243, 249, 250, 252, 253, 254
administration and organization skills, 1, 8, 16, 30, 137, 138, 249
as a skilled activity, 1, 72, 256
boundaries/professional role, 9, 83, 131, 144, 145, 147, 157, 171, 182, 211, 214, 228, 240, 244, 246–7, 248, 274
decision-making, 1, 19, 31, 38, 43, 49, 55, 113, 131, 135–7, 138, 140, 194, 201, 229, 249, 251, 266
judgements, 10, 43, 49, 73, 80, 126, 136–7, 157, 159, 200, 230, 249, 250, 251, 253
practice as an intellectual activity, 60, 76, 77
see assessment
see capacity/ies
see communication
see effectiveness
see interventions
see interviews/interviewing skills
see knowledge base of social work
see law/legislation/policy requirements/legal mandate
see poverty and disadvantage
see practice approaches
see practice perspectives
see research and social work
see service users
see skills
see theory
sociology, 18, 29–30, 37, 42, 72, 76, 111, 112, 279, 290, 291
solution focused/strengths-based approaches, 5, 72, 73, 135
specialist skills, 65
spiritual dimension, importance of, 4, 215
stage theory, 90–1
Stages of Change or *Cycle of Change,* 36, 37, 81, 287–900
statutory social work/responsibilities, 18, 29, 43, 47, 52, 56, 58, 70, 89, 115, 219, 226, 243, 244 267, 291
under-funding/resourcing constraints, 3, 9, 43, 49, 74, 89, 134, 135, 138, 146, 220, 243, 245, 251, 267, 285
Stepney, P., 28, 31, 34, 36, 45, 47, 52, 115
stereotyping, 124, 125, 136, 145, 181, 191
stigma/sigmatized, 20, 208, 227
Stone Center (Boston, USA), 108, 149, 150, 222
'strange situation' test, 102
strengths/solution-based approaches, 5, 72, 73
students, 11, 16, 19, 38, 60, 62, 64, 142
educators, 60, 77
suicide, 240, 246
summarizing, 82, 143, 168–70, 250
superego, 98
supervision, 47, 77, 83, 85, 87, 88, 99, 122, 141, 170, 184, 204, 229, 233, 244, 249, 252–4, 257
three components of supervision, 252
support, emotional/practical/social support, 94, 74, 148, 191, 203, 204, 226, 227, 278, 279
'survivors', 51, 80, 233
SWAP (Social Policy and Social Work Subject Centre), 15
symbolic communication, 121, 196
sympathy, 125, 154, 155, 156–7
see also empathy

systems theory/systemic change, 135, 215, 267, 272, 276, 278, 279, 292

tacit knowledge, 44, 49, 158
  defined, 49
task-centred approaches, 67, 72, 78, 79, 81, 132, 135, 249, 275–7, 276
task, time and territory, 247
team, 131, 153
technicist, 242
termination/endings/disengagement, 82, 104, 138, 143, 181–6, 195, 288
theoretical approaches, *see* practice approaches
theory/theoretical knowledge,
  ambivalence/tensions between theory and practice, 58–9
  anecdotal/common sense notions, 27
  as explanations, 26
  borrowed, from other disciplines, 28–31
  bottom-up theorizing, 26
  contested, 23
  defined, 26
  grand theory, 27
  ideology, role of, 31–3
  middle-range, 27
  practice theories, 36–7
  theories analyzing the task/purpose of social work, 33–6
  theories illuminate understanding, 27
  top-down, 27
  see also knowledge base of social work; factual knowledge; practice knowledge
  see also skills
therapeutic, 34, 108, 115, 148, 210, 253, 261, 263, 270, 272, 273
therapy, 73, 94, 95, 96, 97, 101, 106, 107, 108, 210, 214, 221, 226, 249, 260, 261, 262, 263, 264
  family therapy, 78, 135, 163, 208, 272, 278
Thoburn, J., 9, 129, 146, 202, 203, 228, 230, 243
Thompson, N., 27, 29, 31, 46, 67, 69, 77, 78, 116, 117, 118, 133, 192, 214, 219, 231, 232, 235, 239, 244
Thorne, B., 8, 29, 95, 269
TOPSS (Training Organisation for the Personal Social Services), 1, 5, 13, 14–5, 62, 74, 78, 85, 291

touching/physical contact, 95, 151, 152, 260
training, *see* social work education and training
transferability of skills, 21, 28, 59, 75–7, 142–3
transference, 79, 99, 273
transpersonal theory/analysis (*Stages of Change*) 36, 37, 81, 287–900
trauma, 4, 103, 105, 127, 161, 181, 210, 256, 267
Treseliotis, J., 2, 36, 37, 270
Trevithick, P., 5, 15, 32, 36, 51, 53, 108, 145, 213, 221, 282
Truax, C. B., 7, 213, 214, 270
truth, 149, 170, 200, 211, 217, 221
  and philosophy, 23, 24, 27, 54

unconscious, 92, 95, 98, 99, 105, 210, 272, 273
United Nations Convention on the Rights of the Child, 17
unwantedness, 257, 258
urban/rural neglect and decay, 42, 255
  inverse care law, 41
users, *see* service users

validation, 82, 95, 166, 199, 200, 203, 236
validity, 361–2
value for money, 16, 275, 282, 305, 306
values in social work, 3, 4, 6., 7, 31, 32, 34, 38, 44, 61, 62, 63, 65, 66, 71, 73, 85, 89, 110, 119, 144, 156, 193, 199, 213, 228, 229, 242, 243, 251, 292
  ethics/ethical ethical practice, 31, 32, 56, 63, 96, 117, 199, 221, 224, 247, 267, 292
Valuing People, 12
variables, 39, 56, 57, 76, 120, 134, 251
violence/violent attacks, 240
voluntary sector, 12, 31, 52, 119, 151, 196, 215
voluntary/involuntary service users, 21, 73, 134, 135, 271, 277
volunteers, 217, 293–4
vulnerable people, 105, 112, 115, 116, 191, 206, 208, 227, 230, 245, 256, 257, 284
vulnerable adults defined, 245

warmth, 7, 68, 124, 133, 154, 156, 204,
    214, 243, 269, 270
  see welcoming skills
Watzlawick, P., 114, 115, 127, 163, 208,
    209, 229
Weick, A., 5, 36, 73
welcoming skills, 147, 150, 151, 153
welfare rights/benefits, 9, 32, 38, 40, 68,
    134, 167, 174, 194, 203, 233, 286
welfare state, 3, 4, 7, 9, 11, 12, 23, 30, 32,
    35, 36, 38, 111, 116, 167, 194, 198,
    255, 285, 288, 291
  see also modernization agenda
what questions, 162–3
'what works', 11, 15, 47, 54, 56, 242, 251
  see also effectivevess
Winnicott, D. W., 5, 32, 35, 36, 44, 45, 91,
    103–5, 106, 108, 211, 212, 258
wisdom, defined 45, 47, 101, 182
  practice wisdom, 22, 43, 47, 50
Wise, S., 20, 220, 282
women, 31, 38, 42, 51, 110, 205, 225, 236,
    281–3
  black/ethnic minority, 4, 40, 80, 82, 90,
    108, 109–110, 128, 151, 165, 192,
    219, 227, 228, 229, 231, 245, 282,
    292
  domestic violence, 17, 240, 266, 281, 282

impact of inequality and
    discrimination, 21, 41–2, 166, 205,
    212, 236, 281–3
  impact of sexual abuse, 107, 108, 152,
    169, 178, 210, 257, 281, 282
  working class women, 41, 42, 221
women's psychology, 88, 107–8, 110,
    149–50
  feminist therapy, 87, 91, 107–8, 110,
    149–50
women's liberation movement, *see*
    feminism
working model, 101
working with abused children and adults,
    107, 108, 122, 137, 141, 152, 159,
    169, 178, 210, 239, 257, 278–9, 280
working-class, 4, 41–2, 68, 108, 221, 227
workload, 47, 138, 254
work with offenders, 32, 35, 96, 291
written agreement/s, 224, 229, 245
  see also contracts
writing skills, 4, 165, 202, 224, 233

young people/adolescents, 35, 42, 82, 87,
    88, 100, 101, 121, 130, 165, 168,
    176, 192, 206, 223, 239, 285
  and self-harm, 87, 88
youth offending, 32, 35, 285